PASTORAL

Mediaeval into Renaissance

Frontispiece

The Annunciation to the Shepherds
Hours of Charles of Angoulême, B.N. MS Lat. 1173 f. 20ᵛ
late fifteenth century (*Photo: Bibliothèque Nationale, Paris*)

PASTORAL

Mediaeval into Renaissance

HELEN COOPER

D. S. BREWER · ROWMAN AND LITTLEFIELD

© Helen Cooper 1977

Published by D. S. Brewer Ltd, PO Box 24, Ipswich IP1 1JJ
and Rowman & Littlefield, 81 Adams Drive, Totowa, NJ 07512

First published 1977
Reprinted 1978
ISBN 0 85991 022 9 UK
    0 87471 906 2 USA

Cooper, Helen
    Pastoral: Mediaeval into Renaissance.
    1. Pastoral literature, European – History and criticism
    I. Title
    809'.91   PN56.P3

ISBN 0 85991 022 9

Printed and bound in Great Britain by
REDWOOD BURN LIMITED
Trowbridge & Esher

PREFACE

I wish it were possible to write the definitive work on pastoral; but the resulting volumes would be of a size and weight to flatten the greatest enthusiasm. My hope for this book is that it may give some idea of the richness both of pastoral poetry and of the ideas that lie behind it. Almost every great poet of the Middle Ages and the Renaissance, from Dante to Shakespeare, as well as hundreds of lesser known or anonymous writers, wrote some pastorals; and so the selection of material for both the text and the bibliography of this book has had to be stringent to the point of brutality, especially as regards criticism. I have tried to cover the pastoral literature of the least known area – the Middle Ages – fairly comprehensively; for the rest, I have just tried to indicate the abundance of material to hand.

This book has been several years in the making, and I have contracted many debts in that time. I am especially grateful to the many people who have helped it on its way. Professor J. A. W. Bennett and Dr. Richard Axton watched over its earliest stages as a doctoral thesis and have continued to give help and encouragement. So many people have provided general stimulation, or produced a shepherd I might have missed, that it seems invidious to select a few; but it would be impossible not to mention Dr. John Stevens, who has provided me with criticism and information on everything from general layout to obscure musical instruments; Dr. Michael Lapidge, for helping to keep me on a straight course in matters of mediaeval Latin; and above all Dr. Ruth Morse, who has shown a constant interest in all aspects of the book and who has made many suggestions for improvement. I apologize to them all for the many places where I have fallen below the standards they set, and especially where that is due to ignoring their advice. In the last place – the place of the shepherd – I must thank my husband, for his unstinting support, his determined interest in all things pastoral, and his assistance in keeping the typewriter and the babies in good working order.

Many institutions have also helped me in my work, and I must express my thanks to them too: to the Cambridge University Library, the British Library, the Bodleian Library, the Bibliothèque Nationale and the Leningrad Publichnaya Biblioteka im. M. E. Saltykova-Shchedrina for access to books and manuscripts in their possession, and to their staff for unfailing helpfulness. New Hall, Cambridge, generously provided me with a Research Fellowship which enabled me to complete my work.

My gratitude also goes to the British Academy, for a subvention that speeded the final publication of this book.

AUTHOR'S NOTE

Translations are given of all quotations of more than a few words in all languages other than Modern French; passages in Middle English, or simple passages in Middle French, are glossed where they might provide difficulty. All the translations are my own, and I have occasionally translated *ad sensum* rather than *ad litteram*. I have retained the spelling of all printed sources and manuscripts, but contractions are silently expanded and typeface standardized.

The first reference to any work is given in full; later references are given by the catch-word for locating it in the bibliography. Reprints are indicated by a stroke (/) between the date of the first edition and the edition used.

CONTENTS

ABBREVIATIONS

B.M.	British Museum (British Library)
B.N.	Bibliothèque Nationale
CFMA	Classiques Français du Moyen Age
EETS	Early English Text Society
EH	*Englands Helicon*
ISG	Drayton's *Idea: The Shepheards Garland*
JWCI	*Journal of the Warburg and Courtauld Institutes*
MED	*Middle English Dictionary*
Mod. Phil.	*Modern Philology*
OED	*Oxford English Dictionary*
Pa.	Drayton's *Pastorals*
PL	*Patrologia Latina*
PLAC	*Poetae Latini Aevi Carolini*
RES	*Review of English Studies*
Rom. Forsch.	*Romanische Forschungen*
SATF	Société des Anciens Textes Français
SC	Spenser's *Shepheardes Calender*
SI	Scrittori d'Italia
STS	Scottish Text Society
TLF	Textes Littéraires Français

BIBLIOGRAPHICAL NOTE

All quotations of Spenser are from *The Poetical Works of Edmund Spenser* edited by J. C. Smith and E. de Selincourt (Oxford Standard Authors, 1912/1965); quotations of Virgil are from *Eclogues Georgics, Aeneid I-VI* edited by H. Rushton Fairclough (Loeb, revised edition 1935).

INTRODUCTION

This book is about the pastoral literature of the Middle Ages, and the part it played in creating the pastoral of Renaissance England. The idea of pastoral no longer needs any justification; a recognition of its remarkable symbolic richness has generally replaced the condemnations of it as artificial or escapist which prevented a proper appreciation of it for so long and which were in any case based on only a small part of the whole tradition. Mediaeval pastoral is in many ways more immediately attractive than its later developments. It is very seldom escapist – it is an art that is deeply concerned with social, moral or religious matters; but above all it is an art, so that its serious concerns are offset by the artist's imagination and by the quality of his poetry. There has been a tendency to omit the Middle Ages almost entirely from histories of pastoral, to jump from Virgil to Sannazaro or Spenser, with perhaps a passing reference to the eclogues of the ninth century or to Petrarch; [1] but it was in these centuries that pastoral poetry developed many of the ideas and themes that later writers were to take up. Elizabethan pastoral has been seen as a perversion of Classical; [2] but the change was not a Renaissance process. It was the conclusion of centuries of development, interpretation and accretion, the drawing together of many different pastoral traditions. Between Virgil's and Spenser's understanding of pastoral there is a gulf that is bridged by the works of dozens of other writers; and without passing over that bridge, it is not possible to make the link between the two. Pastoral, perhaps more than any other mode or form of literature, is a matter of tradition, of authority and model and influence, and no work can be understood in isolation. The foundations of Renaissance pastoral were laid in the centuries immediately preceding, not in ancient Rome; and although after the first decades of the Renaissance Italian and French poets became increasingly absorbed by ideas and concerns that owed comparatively little to the Middle ages, the Elizabethans continued to build on the original foundations. They used everything and forgot nothing – contemporary continental pastoral, the Classics, the mediaeval traditions; and this width of reference means that specific imitation is of little importance – much less so than in the more Classical French poetry, for instance. It is their participation in the whole mode of thought underlying the tradition that matters, the quality of the stimulation they received from it and not the quantity of lines they borrowed. It was only in England that the full potential of the European pastoral poetry of the Middle Ages was worked out with the new brilliance of the Renaissance.

Poets of the Middle Ages and Renaissance gave a very specific literary meaning to the word 'pastoral': the traditional image of the shepherd world. Ideas of the simple life in general, or even of other specific occupations such as the ploughman, have distinct literary histories of their own. This limitation of meaning did not make for narrowness in the literature itself. The basic idea of the function of pastoral has always been the same, 'the process of putting the complex into the simple', as William Empson described it.[3] This is the crucial point that makes poetry pastoral: the term has nothing to do with the modern tendency to make it almost a synonym for 'idyllic' – a glance at almost any pastoralist writing before the mid-seventeenth century, Virgil included, destroys that idea. It is in the metaphorical or ironic relationship between the world created by the poet and the real world that pastoral exists. Empson's interpretation of his definition of pastoral almost threatens to extend to include all literature, through the particular relationship of any work to mankind or society in general; but earlier ages limited the idea to the metaphor of the shepherd. The deliberate restriction of focus makes the idea in a master's hands all the more dynamic. The shepherd world is made the simple image of life, of a complex society, or occasionally of a complex idea. This is the only definition that can be applied with equal validity to works as different in intention and period as Sidney's *Arcadia* and that doctrinal schoolbook of the early Middle Ages, the eclogue of Theodulus; to the authoritative master-work of the pastoral tradition, Virgil's *Bucolics*, and pieces which have not even been recognized as part of the tradition such as the shepherd mystery plays of the Wakefield Master. All these authors set out to create a world that is the image of life but distinct from it, that has the freshness and sharp focus of metaphor whether it is explicitly allegorical or not. To take the simple life itself, as Wordsworth does, and to try to draw meanings out of it, is a different process. The shepherd world of pastoral may be realistic or not, as the poet chooses; but realism itself is used because it best serves the poet's artistic purpose. Pastoral is never the product of the particular section of society it claims to depict. It is the attempt of the court or city to find an image of life outside itself, and the simple life of the pastoral world is the opposite of the society that creates it. This could result in the eighteenth-century escape into an idyllic fairyland, but in the Middle Ages and the Renaissance it was more likely to take the form of some kind of social criticism. The pastoral of the Petit Trianon left society in order to forget it, the poets of the Middle Ages withdrew in order to comment on it.

First of all, therefore, pastoral is a mode of thought – a way of re-casting and projecting experience. It is not confined to the eclogue, the shepherd *ecloga*, or 'selected poem', on the Classical model; it may find widespread expression there, but different ages and cultures have found other genres more suitable for conveying their ideas of pastoral, in lyrics, plays, pageants, moral poems, tracts, or the great Renaissance invention of the pastoral romance.[4] Studies of the pastoral tradition always begin with Theocritus and Virgil; but pastoral as a way of thinking seems to be a recurrent characteristic of the European mind, so that further traditions appear, develop and finally attach themselves to the Classical tradition. That was, essentially, the Virgilian tradition, for Theocritus was known only by reputation throughout the Middle Ages, and his influence made itself felt only slowly in the course of the sixteenth and seventeenth centuries. Renaissance pastoral is made up of the merging of two main streams, which had intermingled occa-

sionally from as early as the thirteenth century but only now came together:
the Latin eclogue tradition; and the entirely independent tradition of vernacular pastoral, which ran in an increasingly strong course in the later
Middle Ages in Western Europe, in France, Flanders, England and Scotland.
The fusion of the two is seen at its most complete in the work of Spenser;
and his poetry appears, not as a Renaissance corruption of antiquity, but as
the high point of the two mediaeval traditions illuminated and transformed
by Renaissance humanism. For this reason, although Virgil was the acknowledged master of the formal eclogue in the Middle Ages and later, it is
misleading to take his *Bucolics* as the standard of criticism for later pastoral;
plenty of pastoral literature was written that bears no relation to that work.
Of the two periods when the pastoral tradition was at its height, Rome and
the Renaissance, it is the second that most illuminates the Middle Ages. The
mystery plays of the shepherds, even Petrarch's eclogues, bear little or no
resemblance to Virgil; set beside Spenser, their function as pastoral becomes
apparent. If a single work can be taken as the 'typical' pastoral of the years
before Pope and Johnson, it is not the *Bucolics* but the *Shepheardes Calender*.

None the less, Virgil is of crucial importance for the history of pastoral;
but the *Bucolics* appeared rather differently to the Elizabethans from the way
they appear to a modern reader. The work reached them after being filtered
through centuries of interpretation and gloss, and enlightened Renaissance
humanism did not succeed in stripping off all the accretions. The kind of
processing his eclogues underwent can be illustrated by a highly selective
account of the history of two of the best known of them: the first, the dialogue
of Tityrus and Meliboeus; and the fourth, *Pollio*, the 'Messianic' eclogue.

The interpretation almost universally given by the commentators to the
first, that it is a loose allegory of Virgil's own gratitude to Octavian for the
return of his confiscated farm, is almost certainly not in fact true;[5] but in
any case it encouraged the continual use of the eclogue for political panegyric. The identification of Virgil himself as Tityrus, the shepherd-poet,
which is unquestionable in the sixth eclogue whatever Virgil intended in the
first, was also of wide significance for the later history of pastoral. Less
strikingly obvious now, but of great importance earlier, is the portrayal in
the eclogue of the troubles of life by contrast with their opposite, as Tityrus
the fortunate is balanced by Meliboeus the exile; idyllic pastoral is the most
telling indictment of war with its hardships and miseries, the emphasis
falling as much on the misery as on the idyll. The theme was given an even
sharper expression in French vernacular pastoral in the Middle Ages, and
Virgil was eventually called in as an authoritative witness. The Elizabethans
were well acquainted with the idea, to the point where Sidney makes it the
central issue in his defence of pastoral in the *Apology for Poetry*:

> Is the poore pipe disdained, which somtimes out of Mælibeus mouth, can shewe
> the miserie of people, under hard Lords, and ravening souldiers? And again by
> Titerus, what blessednesse is derived, to them that lie lowest, from the goodnesse of
> them that sit highest? Sometimes under the prettie tales of Woolves and sheepe,
> can enclude the whole considerations of wrong doing and patience; sometimes shew
> that contentions for trifles, can get but a trifling victory.[6]

This is not a piece of special pleading on behalf of the genre he is trying to
justify, but a fair account of the central traditions of pastoral as they had
been handed down. Biblical parables, beast-fables, political criticism and
panegyric have as rightful a place in the mode as pure poetry. The

particular issue here – the potential of pastoral to present a Golden Age landscape, and so its use as an ironic medium for describing human suffering – is still current even in the eighteenth century, when a series of five English eclogues was written, perhaps by the young Thomas Warton, modelled closely on Virgil but describing the sufferings of the German peasants during the War of Austrian Succession.[7]

Virgil's fourth eclogue was interpreted from a very early date as being a prophecy of Christ. It was widely accepted as such by the Fathers (St. Jerome was a rare exception), and a sermon on the prophets attributed to St. Augustine was responsible for Virgil's being included in the appropriate section of the liturgy and in the dramatic *Ordo Prophetarum*. The eclogue appeared to give full authority to later poets to use pastoral for purposes that had even less to do with the countryside than usual: 'Paulo maiora canamus', 'Let us sing of somewhat greater things', Virgil had begun, and the ways were open for practically any subject whatsoever to be introduced. The themes Virgil himself appeared to be taking up were panegyric and religion – panegyric even more fulsome than in the first eclogue; religion, in the celebration of the birth of the child who would restore the Golden Age, and who, as all its Christian readers knew, was Himself to be called the Lamb of God or the Good Shepherd. The mythological background to this poem was most familiar to later readers from Ovid's account of the original Golden Age under Saturn in Book I of the *Metamorphoses*: it was the era when Astraea, the maiden Justice, lived on the earth, when the soil brought forth fruit of its own accord, when the seasons were in perfect balance, when there was no war or oppression or crime, before cities were built or men tempted the sea. Later writers saw a double potential in the Golden Age theme as applied to the contemporary political scene: it could lead either to elaborate compliment, with the assertion of its imminent or actual return, or else to devastating political or social criticism, in a contrast of what might have been with what actually was. The Christian interpretation given to the birth of the child led eventually to a series of Nativity eclogues, especially on the Annunciation to the Shepherds; and it makes a link too – not entirely coincidental as far as the pastoral tradition was concerned – between Classical and mediaeval English pastoral, as the shepherds of the first Wakefield play invoke Virgil's fourth eclogue among the other prophecies of Christ's birth.

Virgil was always seen as the supreme master of the eclogue tradition, but few later pastoralists imitated him alone. The *Bucolics* were supplemented by other seminal works from the great age of Classical literature, in particular by Ovid's account of the Golden Age and by Virgil's own lines in praise of the simple life at the end of Book II of the *Georgics*. Two additional series of eclogues were known in the early Middle Ages and rediscovered in their entirety only in the fourteenth century: those of Calpurnius, written in the course of Nero's rule in the first century A.D., and four poems by Nemesianus, of the third century. The two sets of poems were frequently confused until the Renaissance, and even then it was believed that the two poets were contemporaries. Calpurnius' most significant contribution to the genre was to emphasise the use Virgil had made of it for panegyric – to take pastoral further from the countryside and closer to the political centre of the age. Virgil had prophesied the return of the Golden Age; Calpurnius claimed that under Nero it had indeed dawned anew. The poets at the court of

Charlemagne took up the theme, and it became a commonplace of court
flattery in the Renaissance. Most later mediaeval scholars knew the works
of Calpurnius and Nemesianus only through a few lines preserved in florilegia;[8] one poet alone in the High Middle Ages, the man who calls himself
Martius Valerius, shows that he knew the complete eclogue cycles. He was
probably writing in the twelfth century; the next poet to show any acquaintance with their complete work is Boccaccio, and it was not until the fifteenth
century that they were generally known. It is the poets who did know their
work, however, who alone in the Middle Ages seem to have been able to
see Classical pastoral in something of a correct perspective. The *Bucolics*
could only be seen through a glass, darkly – the glass being the commentary
that enclosed the poems. Calpurnius, with his stress on panegyric, altered the
focus of the eclogue; but it was the commentators who brought about the
first major changes in the understanding of the mode. The most widely
known commentary was that of Servius, written in about 400 A.D. It is
apparent from his repeated refutation of allegorical readings that it was
already common practice not to take the *Bucolics* at face value – a tendency
that was taken to extraordinary lengths over the next thousand years. Servius himself does allow for the existence of some allegory; but paradoxically
a number of lines in later eclogues can be traced to interpretations he quotes
only in order to deny, and which indeed he is responsible for preserving. One
effect of the commentaries was that later poets imitated not just the original
text but the gloss as well, so that allegory became increasingly complex and
interpretation increasingly difficult; and the inevitable result was that the
Latin pastoral written in the millenium following the fall of Rome came to
have very little to do with the shepherd.

The mediaeval vernacular tradition of pastoral, which can first be traced
in the twelfth century, was a very different matter. The shepherd himself is
the key figure here; and he is presented in an entirely different way from in
the eclogue. Realism in this tradition is all-important; yet it is also in a sense
illusory. It seems to have been exceptionally difficult in the Middle Ages to
bring a shepherd, no matter how naturalistically described, into a work of
literature without having him begin to move on a multiplicity of levels of
meaning, to assume a new importance and new significances. The further
meanings that grow around the figure of the shepherd – the significance
that makes a work pastoral, as distinct from happening to be about shepherds – grow out of the realistic presentation, and transcend it. The Classical
or Renaissance or Restoration pastoral shepherd is obviously an 'artificial'
figure in the Elizabethan sense – created by art to serve the purposes of art.
The shepherd world, if it is used to comment on life at all, is set against the
real world in an artistic contrast. The typical mediaeval method is to take
a small part of the real world, that of the shepherd, and to make it a microcosm of the whole. What remains constant in both processes is the idea of
'putting the complex into the simple', reflecting the multifariousness of life
and society in the pastoral world. This procedure can be seen at work even
in the best known genre of mediaeval shepherd literature, the pastourelle.
In its simplest form, as the lyric where the first-person narrator, usually a
knight, asks a shepherdess for her love, either successfully or, perhaps more
characteristically, to his discomfiture, it scarcely counts as pastoral at all;
but the projection of more complex issues onto the genre is apparent from
the very earliest examples, so that it becomes a medium for criticizing

higher society, its attitudes, its morals and its politics. Sometimes these ideas are subordinated to the main narrative theme; sometimes they are the *raison d'être* of the poem, and the pastourelle becomes fully pastoral. This was by no means the only genre of vernacular pastoral in the Middle Ages. Realism expresses itself best in forms other than the lyric, and a criticism of society is usually more strikingly done on a larger scale. The principal non-vernacular literary influence in all this was not the Classical eclogue but the Bible. The herdsman's first duty, both there and in life, is to look after his flock – to be a Good Shepherd; and when pastoral life is represented as an ideal it is usually a social ideal based on the moral ground of responsibility.

It follows from this that the *kind* of significance attached to the shepherd in the Latin and vernacular traditions is basically different. In the eclogue tradition he will probably be allegorical; in the vernacular, he is characteristically figural – that is, whereas in allegory the poetry is of greater, more 'universal' significance than the original historically limited action or theme it describes, in figural literature the action presented is often only a symbol of a greater, often divine significance. Allegory presents a completed metaphor; figuralism provides an image for apprehending the ineffable. Not all mediaeval vernacular pastoral takes this form, of course, but there is a sense in which it all could: its concerns are general, with man and morals and society, and they easily go beyond the earthly to the heavenly. The eclogue is almost always concerned with the particular, and the imaginative richness of symbolism is generally beyond its scope. Fifteenth-century French pastoral, for instance, often took the good prince as its theme, seeing his land as a kind of image of Heaven; Petrarch, on the other hand, inveighs against the bad government of specific popes and rulers. The difference between the two traditions means that vernacular pastoral has a range that the bucolic lacks; and this is shown at its sharpest in their different ideals. The Classically-derived eclogue looks to the Golden Age – that perfect age in the history of the world that might yet be recovered under the wise rule of Charlemagne, or some Italian prince, or even Catherine de' Medici. The vernacular poets look to Paradise; backwards to Eden, which was equated with the Golden Age in the mediaeval attempts to square Classical mythology with Biblical, but which was far richer in connotation; forwards to the promise of Heaven itself. The poets speak not from a present that is the age of iron but as men living in a fallen world. The pastoral image, the life enjoyed by the first age of mankind, the image chosen by Christ as His own symbol, offered a way of expressing Christian man's highest aspirations and his keenest longings.

The richness of English Renaissance pastoral springs from the successful mingling of traditions that often seem to be contradictory: satirical allegory and idyllic romance, realism and high poetry. There is too one contradiction, a paradox central to pastoral in any form, that was never faced except by the Elizabethan poets: the problem of decorum, of suitability of treatment to subject. The ostensible material of pastoral is rustic, the inner significance and the poetry itself are usually far more elevated. The Latin tradition tended to solve the problem by ignoring the shepherd; the vernacular tradition could not rediscover the poetic significance of the mode because of their naturalistic conception of him. The eclogue abandoned nature, mediaeval vernacular avoided too much art. The Elizabethans created a new kind of pastoral that embraced all these disparate, even conflicting, elements and ideas, and they were able to conceive of the shepherd world as a unity (however much variety it might contain) and on a scale that had not been known before. The various forms of pastoral in existence by the mid-sixteenth century provided the Elizabethans with a unique opportunity for poetic development, and they exploited it to the full. The pastoral mode had come to provide a kind of dialectic framework in which to work out the tensions between court and city, culture and country simplicity, between Paradise and hardship, unfettered freedom and the responsibilities and limitations of normal life, between Nature and Art. The shepherd world was essentially the same to the Elizabethans as it had been to the Middle Ages: a world of peace and content, that could be upset by war or social abuse, but that offered an image of the stability of eternal life. It was free from care, but not free from responsibility, and so it could serve as a moral, political or ecclesiastical model. The essence of the pastoral mode is the search for an ideal; but not an escapist one. The shepherd must turn from his pipes to his flock; the golden Arcadian world is always broken, the perfection of art brought into conflict with natural mutability, through war or corruption, by winter and age and death. But the breaking only makes the value and appeal of pastoral more intense. Life does not conform to the patterns of art, but there must be a point of contact. The shepherd's voice is the voice of the poet in the brazen world trying to reach the golden, the voice of Man in the fallen world trying to regain Paradise.

It is the Elizabethans' consciousness of all this that gives their pastoral its quality; this is why they found the mode so fascinating, and so serious. But the delicate blend that proved so powerful in their hands soon broke up again. The debate about the nature of pastoral that raged in the early years of the eighteenth century shows how completely any sense of the mode as a dynamic idea had been lost. Augustan poetry polarized into the sharply witty parodies of John Gay and the saccharine idylls of the imitators of Pope; and Dr. Johnson gave pastoral its death-blow with his characterization of it as 'easy, vulgar, and therefore disgusting'. Pastoral had lost its focus: the sharp perspective it had given on society, its unique value as an optic on the nature of art, on art and nature, were forgotten. The history of the mode in the eighteenth century is an account of its decline. This book is about its growth and its blossoming.

I

THE ECLOGUE IN THE LATIN MIDDLE AGES

The changes in the approach of poets and scholars to the pastoral mode
from Classical Rome to the fourteenth century reflect in microcosm the
varying intellectual movements of the Middle Ages. The eclogue flourished
afresh with each new revival of Classical learning, in the ninth century, fit-
fully in the twelfth, and again in the fourteenth and late fifteenth centuries;
and the era of the schoolmen and Thomas Aquinas was also the era of the
theoretical study of the mode. There was effectively no contact between the
pastoral poetry of the early Middle Ages and the late, and so there is no
single mediaeval eclogue tradition; each poet, or group of poets, had to
re-create for themselves an idea of what pastoral should, or could, be. The
one line of contact common to them all was the *Bucolics*, but even they were
interpreted in widely differing ways and provided no single pattern of
authority. The eclogue was a fashionable poetic form among the Carolingians
and the early Italian humanists; but in the course of the intervening centuries
– almost four hundred years, from the fading out of the Carolingian intellectual spirit in the mid-tenth century to the end of Dante's life, around
1320 – only three poets turned their attention to the bucolic, each writing in
isolation. Yet it is in these years that the scholarly understanding of pastoral
seems to have undergone a complete change. Even if so few poets set out to
create new bucolics of their own, there were many more critical theorists who
adapted, developed and passed on ideas of what the eclogue was and how it
should be written, and who promulgated a whole new way of looking at the
shepherd world. Before this movement started, poets of the ninth century, the
first great age of mediaeval bucolic, were working in the true Classical
tradition, adapted to a new set of political and literary circumstances, but
none the less clearly based on Virgil; but by the time Petrarch was writing,
in the mid-fourteenth century, the 'perversion' of pastoral had been accomplished, and even the most cultured of Renaissance humanists were unable
to restore the eclogue as Virgil had left it. Petrarch's eclogues look at first like
a startling innovation in the understanding of the idea of pastoral; but in fact
he is taking to its conclusion the interpretation of the *Bucolics* started by its
earliest readers and developed throughout the Middle Ages, and he is putting
into practice in an extreme form some of the theory that had become the
critical orthodoxy of the age.

Little coherent idea of the whole pastoral mode, or even of the genre of the
bucolic alone, can be derived from a study of the eclogues written between
the fall of the Roman Empire and the Italian Renaissance. It was often
doubtful whether the eclogue would survive at all as a living poetic form

rather than as a historical curiosity to be commented upon; but the essential appeal of pastoral enabled it to stay alive, to become in the Renaissance a major literary form with an importance and a popularity it had never possessed before. There are three principal phases in the post-Classical history of the eclogue – phases that cannot be tied to precise periods: literary movements, like historical ones, are seldom a matter of fixed changes at fixed dates. The first phase is the most genuinely Classical in inspiration: the Carolingians' revival of the eclogue, brought about directly by their reading of Virgil, and later attempts to imitate or re-create the art of the Virgilian bucolic. This movement was fading by the tenth century, but it had a final late resurgence in the twelfth, reaching its culmination in the otherwise unknown Martius Valerius, and its nadir in Metellus, a monk of Tegernsee. The second phase consisted of the gradual emergence over many centuries of a new, distinctively mediaeval interpretation of the genre. The first signs of this occur as early as the late fourth century, in an isolated bucolic poem and in the late Classical commentaries; but the movement only really got under way in the tenth century. It gradually took over the field from the Virgilian tradition, invading poetic theory and practice alike, and it took a mind of the stature of Dante's to resist its force. This chapter is concerned with the development of each of these types of pastoral. The third phase, starting in the Renaissance itself, was marked by an attempt to return to pure Classical practice; but humanist poets, however unintentionally, always looked back to Virgil through the optic of their mediaeval predecessors, and the eclogue could never be quite the same again.

I. *The Classical Inheritance*

The scholars that Charlemagne collected around himself at Aachen were inspired by a common sense of purpose: to rescue Classical learning from its genuine danger of extinction, to preserve their great Latin inheritance, and to re-create as far as they could the cultural milieu of the age of Augustus at the court of their own Emperor. Their work has a double emphasis, in education, the preservation and teaching of what was known, and creativity, the expression of their own love of literature and of the Classical tradition. They were men who were thoroughly familiar with all the great Latin poets whose works were available to them, and their own poetry is full of reminiscences of their reading. The *Bucolics* themselves are among the works most frequently echoed or quoted, in poetry on any subject, pastoral or not; one gets the impression that many of the greatest Carolingian scholars knew them by heart. It was not surprising, therefore, that several poets should have experimented further with extended pastoral imagery or with actual eclogues: it was by this kind of re-creation of Classical forms that the Carolingian Empire could be celebrated as the rebirth of the Roman. The scholars formed themselves into a kind of academy, and gave themselves pseudonyms that evoke even more clearly their idea of themselves as descendants of the great poets of the past: Modoin of Autun was Naso (after Ovid), Alcuin Flaccus (Horace), Angilbert Homer; and others called themselves after Virgil's shepherd-poets, Melibeus, Dafnis or Coridon. Charlemagne himself was David, at once king, shepherd and poet. The particular interpretation of the eclogue made by these poets was governed by the fact that Calpurnius and Nemesianus were known to them as well as Virgil: it was easier to see what the Roman pastoralists had really been doing when Servius and a multitude of other scholars were not blocking the entire approach. Calpurnius' emphasis on panegyric also suited their purpose particularly well. All their literature is written with a self-confidence that accepts the past as their birthright and looks to great things for the future; and political eulogy is not mere flattery but a genuine expression of their hopes and beliefs. There is a sense in which they did not need to extend the range of the eclogue: it already provided a model for much of what they wanted to say. Panegyric is certainly not the only theme of their pastoral, but it is perhaps the most typical.

The Carolingian poem that comes closest to the heart of the bucolic genre, the two-part *Ecloga* of Modoin, who became bishop of Autun in 815, is the best example of this.[1] He draws particularly heavily on the first eclogue of Calpurnius, in which Virgil's prophecy of the approaching Golden Age becomes the hyperbolic declaration of the imminent return of Astraea under the rule of the young emperor Nero, when oppression will end and peace and justice reign supreme. 'The golden age is reborn in lasting peace,'

Aurea secura cum pace renascitur aetas,[2]

is part of a message found carved on a beech by Calpurnius' shepherds. The prophecy has been inscribed not by a shepherd or wayfarer but by Faunus himself: even at this early period, it would seem, the poet was at least aware of the problem of decorum, as if in spite of his choosing to write in the pastoral mode he recognized that a eulogy of the Emperor required someone more than a mere shepherd to utter it. Nero is honoured by the gods themselves. Modoin imitates this directly in the second part of his eclogue; in the first part he solves the problem by making his characters specifically shepherd-poets, emphasising the ideal qualities of the pastoral world he describes. At the time he was writing, between 804 and 814,[3] the omens seemed set fair for a renewal of the Empire, for an age of peace and prosperity. The 'First Book' of the eclogue is a dialogue between a youth and an old man, a 'senex vates'. The boy's very first lines set the tone for the whole poem: it is not only the world of the Classical pastoral, but the new world of peace in which age and learning are honoured, security is guaranteed and poetry flourishes.

Tu frondosa, senex vates, protectus opaca
Arbore, iam tandem victrici palma potitus,
Ludis habens nivea circumdata tempora lauro,
Arguto tenui modularis carmine musa.   (1–4)

You, venerable poet, lying in the tree's protective shade, now that you have at last achieved the victor's palm and have your white temples encircled with laurel, take your pleasure and sing in melodious verse with your pastoral muse.

The youth himself has not yet won recognition as a poet, and he is still outside the enchanted circle of the court, still subject to the shipwrecks of the world, 'naufraga mundi': one is reminded of the Classical concept of the Golden Age, past and future, as a time when men no longer tempt the storms of the sea. The Golden Age has become a truth for the old man, but the youth is excluded and envies him. The person who has made all this possible is David, Charlemagne himself. He is the peak of human endeavour, and Aachen is the new Rome, the place where the 'antiquos mores' of the Empire are preserved, the centre of growth of a new civilization: Calpurnius' line declaring the dawning of an age of peace becomes the promise of a Golden Age developing from here,

Aurea Roma iterum renovata renascitur orbi, (27)

Rome the golden, renewed in the course of the world's ages, is born again.

The old man discourages the boy's enthusiasm. His answer to this vision of limitless hope is a reminder of the youth's inexperience and poetic ineptitude:

Hic, audax iuvenis, qui te cupis esse poetam,
Rustica raucisonae meditaris carmina Musae? (28–9)

Bold young man, who are you to want to be a poet, playing the rustic songs of your harsh-voiced muse?

Modoin, like Virgil or Calpurnius, is manipulating the pastoral paradox: a panegyric such as the boy's is technically out of place in the pastoral setting, yet it is heightened by it, and the modest disclaimer of poetic merit here emphasises the contrast. Even this eulogy is boorish and harsh. The youth closes by repeating his hope for patronage, citing a series of *exempla* of other poets both Classical and modern who have been rewarded for their skill. The continuation of Latin cultural tradition at Charlemagne's court is again being stressed: the poets and scholars are presented as inhabiting the same pastoral landscape as Virgil himself.

The second part of Modoin's eclogue is effectively a separate poem, though the two were published together with a short dedicatory prologue and epilogue in elegiacs. This poem is again a dialogue between an old man, Micon, and a youth, Nectilus; the theme is the same as in the first section, the return of the Golden Age, but without the secondary concern with poetry and patronage; and the structural outline and many details are drawn once more from Calpurnius' first eclogue. Both open with a description of the summer landscape; the shepherds retreat to the shade, and find a message carved by a divine hand on a tree. But whereas in Calpurnius the message prophesies the imminent return of the Golden Age, Modoin declares it to be already present. Especially striking is the way in which Modoin unifies the structure and imagery of the poem. Micon describes a golden countryside:

Aurea rura, puer, ridentia flore videto, (7)

See, boy, the golden land smiling with blossom.

Birds are singing from the woods, the 'sol aureus' is bleaching the fields, the herds are seeking cool shade. The setting is soon given wider implications. Nectilus congratulates Micon on his peace of mind, his prosperity, his skill in singing; and he describes a world of pastoral harmony such as Virgil had dreamed of.

Tu recubas lenta felix securus in umbra.
Carmina rara canis, respondent cetera silvae.
Auribus erectis adstant pecudes feraeque,
Pascere desistunt, gaudent tua iubila tauri.
Descenduntque truces gelido de monte leones...
Agna lupo properans, ovibus saevissimus ursus
Occurrit cum pace pia. (35–41)

Happy man, to lie untroubled in the slowly-moving shade, singing occasional songs, and the woods reply with the rest. The herds and wild beasts stand close by with ears pricked, they cease grazing, the bulls rejoice in your shepherd's song. The fierce lions come down from the frozen mountains...the she-lamb hurrying with the wolf, the savage bear runs beside the sheep in hallowed peace.

This is the world in which the carved message of peace is appropriate. Micon goes on to describe the harmony of the whole world, of which the landscape is the microcosm. A cloudless sun is shining that makes all the nations of Europe rejoice, a sun that brings civilization, peace, law: the sun of Charlemagne himself. Wars are silent, and

> Aurea securis nascuntur regna Latinis, (92)
>
> *Golden eras are brought to birth for the Latin races at peace.*

As in *Pollio*, the earth brings forth fruit of its own accord, commerce and poverty are both at an end. The Old Testament vision of Isaiah, the nostalgia of Ovid and Virgil's prophecy are combined in a poetic declaration of a present Golden Age. Key words, *aureus, lux, sol*, are echoed from line to line of the poem. Micon concludes by praising Charlemagne directly, not as David but as Carolus.

Modoin ends the poem with a plea for his work to be presented to the Emperor, but again with a declaration of modesty, of his lack of pretension to high artistic status:

> Caesareas referet haec haec Melibeus ad aures,
> Rustica raucisonae cecini quae carmina Musae, (120–21)
>
> *May Melibeus bring to the Emperor's hearing these crude songs of my harsh muse that I have sung.*

This is even more of a palpable lie than usual. Apart from the quality of the writing itself and the skilful construction of the poem, Modoin has chosen the most elevated pastoral poetry available as his models: the idea that *Pollio* was well above the normal run of humble pastoral had been explicitly stated by Virgil and the point driven home by Servius, and Calpurnius also disclaims anything resembling even literary shepherd origins for his panegyric. The value of the pastoral mode for this kind of writing is none the less clear. The distance between theme and matter, the Golden Age of the Empire and the shepherd world, goes a long way in itself towards avoiding the risk of the poet's sounding either pretentious or presumptuous, and the limited mode helps to unify the subject on a single plane. The shepherd-poet, the pastoral landscape, are potent and easily comprehensible images for the complex interrelationships of learning, the spread of civilization, the unification of Europe and the hope that the dawning enlightenment may lead to an endless day, 'aeternam terris per secula pacem' (II.68). The reign of Charlemagne is seen as the fulfilment of Classical prophecies. The impersonal fictional cover also gives the poem the universal claim of allegory, removing it from the realm of either personal opinion or flattery – a useful characteristic of pastoral that was to be noted by Renaissance theorists: 'vnder this personnes, as it were in a cloake of simplicitie, they would...sette foorth the prayses of theyr freendes, without the note of flattery'.[4] The metaphor of the summer sun enables Modoin to write artistically acceptable hyperbole, to combine vision and hope with his confidence that a new age had come.

Few of the other eclogues written by scholars at Charlemagne's court are absorbed so completely into the pastoral mode. Many use pastoral machinery only incidentally, as a kind of background metaphor or style to be taken up or abandoned at will, rather than making the shepherd world the vehicle for their ideas; and they found in the *Bucolics* principally a model form for a short poem of panegyric or lament or meditation. Most critical discussion of Carolingian pastoral has in fact used form rather than content as the criterion of definition. Any poem designed as dialogue or dramatic monologue could be derived from the *Bucolics*; but this alone will not make it pastoral if the key image, the image of the shepherd world, is lacking. Angilbert's poem in praise of Charlemagne, for instance, is given the editorial title *Ecloga ad Carolum Regem*,[5] though neither the setting nor the characters belong to the shepherd world; the form of the poem, however, with a series of recurring refrains, is drawn from Virgil's eighth eclogue, and the refrain of the middle section presents the author as the shepherd-poet:

Surge, meis caris dulces fac, fistula, versus,

On, my pipe, make sweet poetry for those dear to me.

Alcuin too was thoroughly familiar with the *Bucolics*, but his use of pastoral imagery is again often casual. His *Versus de Cuculo*,[6] for instance, takes the form of a pastoral lament in which he calls on Dafnis and Menalcas to mourn for the cuckoo, a young scholar who has abandoned the intellectual life, but the pastoralism of the poem is never more than perfunctory. The points of most interest for the whole pastoral mode in these works are the persistent tendency to use the shepherd world as a disguise, as an underlying metaphor that enables the poet to focus on whatever aspects of the real world he chooses; and the equation of shepherd with poet – an equation taken for granted by a post-Renaissance reader, but which was lost for most of the Middle Ages. The image is never developed at this stage, however: there is none of the sense of the pastoral world as the artist's creation for exploring his art such as the Elizabethan poets were to delight in.

The matter of form versus content as the distinguishing feature of the eclogue becomes crucial in the much debated question of whether the debate poem, the *conflictus*, derives from the singing-match of Classical bucolic, of Virgil's third and seventh eclogues in particular. The first mediaeval debate poem, the *Conflictus Veris et Hiemis*,[7] takes the form of a pastoral eclogue, and the most famous eclogue of the Middle Ages, that of Theodulus, is also a debate; but while this would seem too good a coincidence to be purely accidental, it does not necessarily prove anything about the origins of the *conflictus*. The arguments in favour of the direct descent of the debate from the singing-match were first set out in detail – the assumption had been made for some time before – by J. H. Hanford;[8] more recently it has been argued that the debate has a Classical origin quite separate from the eclogue, and that the connection of the two in the Middle Ages was a matter of chance – they 'merge only when a poet occasionally combines them'.[9] As far as the mediaeval pastoral tradition is concerned, it is practice rather than theoretical origins that are important – that poets do occasionally combine them. Two points stand out in connection with this. One is that the fully dramatized eclogue – eclogue consisting of dialogue alone, with no narrative intrusions – becomes the standard form. The two debate eclogues themselves, the *Conflictus Veris et Hiemis* and the *Ecloga Theoduli*, have short narrative introductions with the substance of the poem in dialogue; Modoin's eclogue is in dialogue alone, and most of the Italian humanists, Petrarch and Boccaccio and their successors up to and including Mantuan, also use this pattern. The freedom of form that Virgil displays in the *Bucolics* was almost entirely lost by the fifteenth century. The second point, of more importance for this early period, is that the commentators themselves appear to have accepted the singing-match and the debate as being two sides of the same coin. Servius could be at the root of the identification, as he is of so much mediaeval stylistic theory. His introduction to Virgil's third eclogue, the singing-match, reads:

> He passes on to an eclogue full of quarrelling and pastoral invective...this poem truly contains a dispute and conflict.[10]

It was perhaps enough of a hint to be picked up by the Carolingians, though literary influence of this kind is generally too tenuous to leave any hard evidence; certainly the fact that they did associate the *conflictus* with the eclogue is an indication that they felt the debate to be appropriate for the shepherd world. The point is taken up again by later commentators. Conrad of Hirsau, writing in the early twelfth century, explains how fitting it is that the *Ecloga Theoduli* should be a pastoral debate:

> It is not without reason that shepherds are brought into this theme of disputation, because that kind of person is always quarrelsome, attacking an opposing viewpoint with a contradictory one and stirring up brawls because of the ill-will or deceit of either side.[11]

The strangest thing about this statement is not its empirical improbability (and in any case literal truth would be beside the point) but its irrelevance to the subject under discussion. Theodulus' shepherds are idealized in the Virgilian fashion as well as being allegorical. Conrad is trying to find a rational basis for the association of shepherd and *conflictus*. He is developing an idea he found in Bernard of Utrecht's commentary on Theodulus; and a commentary printed as late as 1492 is still repeating the point, that 'shepherds often quarrel among themselves, even more than others'.[12] Other writers emphasise the link between the Virgilian singing-match and the debate; John of Garland puts the two on an equal footing when he cites Theodulus and the *Bucolics* as examples of people's disputes and the matches of lovers, 'altercatione personarum et certamine amancium'.[13] *Certamen* is used by Virgil as the term for a singing-match, and by the author of the *Conflictus Veris et Hiemis* to describe the debate between the seasons. This poet – perhaps Alcuin, perhaps an anonymous Irishman at Charlemagne's court[14] – was a man too closely familiar with Classical poetry not to be aware of the differences between debate and singing-match; but equally he must have felt them to be sufficiently closely connected to make the *conflictus* suitable material for an eclogue.

Throughout the Middle Ages, the debate was an acceptable part of pastoral even if a poet were using Classical models, and it had a more obvious didactic use. The idea of art for art's sake that the singing-match implies was almost totally alien to the scholarly poetic theory of the Middle Ages, and scarcely any true singing-matches were written during the period; it only recovered its place in the artistic eclogue of the Renaissance. The exceptions tend to be more apparent than real. Metellus of Tegernsee produced one accidentally in the course of his slavish rewriting of the *Bucolics;* Boccaccio wrote two poems that are ostensibly singing-matches, but the nature of the opposing parties brings them closer to a debate. The shepherds in his thirteenth eclogue represent the poet and the merchant, and each sings in praise of his own way of life; and in the eclogue inserted into the *Ameto*, his vernacular semi-mythological *comedia*, the rival shepherds sing apparently in support of the worldly and ascetic lives, or perhaps the active and contemplative.[15] The only pastoral singing-matches of the Middle Ages that really take poetry as their subject are one by the twelfth-century Martius Valerius, in Latin, and one in French in the *Pastoralet*.

The *Conflictus Veris et Hiemis* is one of the most Classical in tone of the Carolingian eclogues in spite of its form. It is fully pastoral, with no interruptions from the real world of political, academic or ecclesiastical activity. It is spring, and the shepherds come down from the mountains to gather in the shade and to sing the praises of the cuckoo, the representative of the season – not, as in the *Versus de Cuculo*, anything more precisely allegorical. The cause is taken up by Spring itself, garlanded with flowers, and Winter, with frozen hair:

> His certamen erat cuculi de carmine grande. (8)
>
> *They had a great debate about the cuckoo's song.*

The debate starts as to whether it is a good thing that the cuckoo should return, then turns into a direct conflict between the contestants. They themselves, however, carry little of the symbolic weight attached to the seasons by later pastoralists, notably Spenser: Winter presents herself as the season of rest, and Spring makes no attempt to answer her by associating her with age or death. Winter accuses Spring of being the season of war, but this theme, which became widespread in pastoral of the later Middle Ages, is again not developed. Spring wins the contest on the grounds that Winter lives off the produce of the summer months, but the shepherds' celebration of Spring is less an adjudgment of victory than a eulogy of the renewing year:

> Collibus in nostris erumpant germina laeta,
> Pascua sint pecori, requies et dulcis in arvis,
> Et virides rami praestent umbracula fessis,
> Uberibus plenis veniantque ad mulctra capellae,
> Et volucres varia Phoebum sub voce salutent.
> Quapropter citius cuculus nunc ecce venito! (47–52)
>
> *May the seeds burst open for joy in our hills; may there be grazing for the herds and sweet rest in the fields, may green branches provide shade for the weary, the goats come full-uddered to the milkpails and the birds greet the sun with their different songs. Lo, then, cuckoo, come quickly now!*

The poem is the earliest example – and a fine one – of the close association of pastoral with the movement and contrast of the seasons. Spring, and the month of May in particular – the month of the coming of the cuckoo – is the ideal setting for the mode, but it is only given its full significance when it is set against the harshness of winter. The presence of winter works in the same way as does the idea of war and deprivation in Virgil's first eclogue or Sidney's *Apology*, to make an ironic contrast with the golden pastoral world.

There is one other eclogue that, like Modin's *Ecloga* and the *Conflictus*, stands midway between Classical bucolic and a mediaeval approach to pastoral. This is the *Ecloga Duarum Sanctimonialium* of Paschasius Radbertus,[16] dating from a few years later in the ninth century; it is a lament for St. Adalhard, Paschasius' predecessor as Abbot of Corbie, with which Paschasius concluded his Life of the saint. The poets at Charlemagne's court had preferred the panegyric function of pastoral when they wrote about the contemporary scene, and its elegiac possibilities had been ignored even though the Classical tradition was substantial – Virgil's fifth eclogue was to be imitated time and again, and he in turn was repeating what Theocritus and Moschus had done. Paschasius derives the structural movement of his poem, from mourning and lament to rejoicing, from Virgil: the pattern is taken up many times later, cursorily by Petrarch, more powerfully by Marot, Spenser, Milton and many other ecloguists.[17] The poem takes the form of a dialogue between mother and daughter, Fillis and Galathea, Fillis representing the original abbey of Corbie, Galathea the new foundation on the Weser that Adalhard had set up in 822. The personifications are already beginning to foreshadow the cryptic allegory of Petrarch and his imitators, with Paschasius declaring that he named Galathea 'on account of the fairness of her face', Fillis 'on account of her love of charity'. The pastoral metaphor here is no longer all-pervasive: it is drawn on when it is useful for an image or an idea but it does not provide the imaginative basis for the poem. Galathea speaks first and calls on all things to lament the death of Menalchas, at once the Virgilian shepherd, 'formosi pecoris custos formosior ipse',[18] and the Christian 'sanctissime pastor' of his flock at Corbie. Unlike Petrarch, Paschasius does not make his work rely on its inner meaning to be comprehensible: the poem continually widens out to a lament for the mortality of all things, to lyrical passages of summons to adorn the tomb with flowers and of prophecy from Isaiah, and to the triumphant climax of a vision of Heaven. Fillis's apostrophe to death is an elaboration of the theme of *tempus edax rerum* that is so often called into use in pastoral: time and death, like winter, are the ironic contrast to the golden world – *et in Arcadia ego*.[19] Death knows no mercy or favour; it cannot be turned aside by bribery.

Omnibus una manes sors inrevocabilis horae, (65)

[*You, death,*] *are the one fate that awaits all things at the irrevocable hour.*

The lyrical second section of the poem, spoken mostly by Fillis, begins the movement from this bleak sense of doom towards the final celebration of Heaven. Menalchas is assured of glory, and in Paschasius' free paraphrase of Isaiah (lv.12–13) the Virgilian Golden Age and the Eastern paradise seem to merge:

Sancta tibi hinc veniunt plaudentia ligna decoris,
Exultant inibi myrtus, abies sive pinus,
Vitis et uva, nitens etiam pinguescit oliva,
Ac tamquam paradysus et hortus deliciarum
Inriguis nutiris aquis de vertice caeli. (95–9)

Hence the sacred trees come clapping their hands at your glory, there the myrtle trees rejoice, the fir and the pine; the grape of the vine and the bright olive flourish, and like paradise or a garden of delights you will be fed with refreshing streams from highest heaven.

Galathea is still despairing, but Fillis's hope rises ever more strongly:

Beatus amor tantum mihi crescit in illo,
Quantum vere novo se mundus floribus auget. (135–6)

Blessed love for him grows in me as abundantly as the earth enriches itself with flowers at the coming of spring.

The spring image replaces the darkness of death stressed at the beginning of the poem, and both speakers unite in rejoicing. Menalchas is safe in the 'ethereis campis' (151) whither he will lead them too. Fillis describes the City of God, with the Lord Himself ever-present among the bands of apostles, prophets, patriarchs and martyrs: there is no attempt to make Heaven a pastoral scene, as the Byzantine artists were doing and as Jean de

Meung and Boccaccio were to do, though the themes of eternal life and eternal spring link closely with what has gone before:

> Vita perennis ovat, virtutum pascua florent;
> Angelicae gratulantur oves, caelestia vernant. (163–4)

> *The everlasting vine rejoices, the meadows flourish in their strength; angelic flocks give thanks, the heavenly bodies rejoice in their youth.*

The eclogue closes as Galathea urges Fillis to strew yet more flowers, not now on the tomb as a rite due to the dead, but everywhere, as if their joy were for a bridal or a triumph:

> Sparge viam violis, virtutum floribus arvum,
> Pinge rosis callem, plateis lilia sterne. (180–81)

> *Strew the way with violets and the field with flowers of virtues; adorn the hill tracks with roses, scatter lilies in the streets.*

It is as if the everlasting spring of Heaven had become a present reality on earth.

The poets of the Carolingian Renaissance were well aware of the range of possibilities contained in the *Bucolics,* and although no eclogue cycle was written at this period their separate poems indicate this consciousness: panegyric was not, as has been suggested,[20] the only or even the primary use they saw for the eclogue. They drew on Virgil just as much for the triumphant elegy, for the plea of poet to patron, for light allegory, for their stress on the value of poetry itself – all themes that were to be taken up again later in the Middle Ages. There is one other poem from this early period that contains many ideas that were to be developed further in mediaeval pastoral while itself retaining a Classical formal outline and approach. This is not an eclogue but an elegant and sophisticated little piece of mock-heroic in elegiacs on the death of a ram belonging to Bishop Hartgar, Sedulius Scotus' *De Quodam Verbece a Cane Discerpto.*[21] All the usual Virgilian tags are here, though appropriately there are more from the *Aeneid* than the *Bucolics.* The poem opens with an account of the creation of sheep, and of one particularly splendid wether – the subject is twisted just enough not to make the line inevitable –

> Egregii pecoris custos praeclarior ipse, (25)

> *Guardian of an illustrious flock, himself more splendid.*

The gods' love for sheep is given a special mention,

> Namque ferunt Lunam lanarum vellus amasse,
> Pan deus Arcadiae vellere lusit eam. (35–6)

> *For they say Luna herself loved woolly fleeces, Pan the god of Arcadia sported with her on a fleece.*

Fortune, however, 'bonis semper contraria rebus' (41), soon frowns on Tityrus, as the animal is called. It is carried off by a thief; when the dogs run out to attack him, the man drops the wether and makes his escape, and the dogs threaten to attack the sheep instead. It tries to calm them by identifying itself:

> 'Gnoscite me famulum praesulis Hartgarii.
> Non sum latro malus, non sum furunculus ille,
> Sed sum multo pius, dux gregis eximius.' (66–8)

> *'Know that I am one of bishop Hartgar's household. I am not an evil robber, that petty thief; I am a law-abiding sheep, the outstanding leader of the flock.'*

One dog begins the attack, however, and the others follow; when the sheep falls dead, the nymphs, the woods and the flocks lament. 'Iustus quid meruit, simplex, sine fraude maligna?' Sedulius asks (105) – 'Was this what you deserved, simple and free from evil deceit as you were?'; and he goes on to a passage of praise for the simple life, specifically reminiscent of the *Georgics*[22] though the theme itself is pastoral:

> Illi pastus erat sollemnicus herba per agros
>   Ad dulcem potum limphida Mosa dabat;
> Non ostri vestes rubei cupiebat avarus,
>   Sed contentus erat pellicia tunica;
> Nonque superbus equo lustrabat amoena virecta,
>   Sed propriis pedibus rite migrabat iter;
> Non mendosus erat nec inania verba locutus:
>   Báá seu béé mystica verba dabat.   (109–16)

> *He fed simply on the grass of the fields, the clear Meuse provided him with sweet drink; he did not, miser-like, desire clothes of purple from the bramble, but was content with his fleecy covering; he did not proudly ride over the pleasant sward on horseback, but made his way in due order on his own feet. He did not speak false or empty words: he uttered only the mystic phrase, 'Baa-aa.'*

There is nothing of a fantasy Golden Age about this sheep: his fellow-beasts in *Pollio* have their wool ready-dyed, but that belongs with all the elaborate art Sedulius is mocking. Immediately after this delicate spoof, Sedulius takes up another theme that has been present in the poem without being allowed to develop: the idea of the sheep as 'multo pius', 'simplex, sine fraude maligna', the type of the sacrificed Christ.

> Agnus ut altithronus pro peccatoribus acrem
>   Gustavit mortem filius ipse dei:
> Carpens mortis iter canibus laceratus iniquis
>   Pro latrone malo sic, pie multo, peris.
> Quomodo pro Isaac aries sacer hostia factus:
>   Sic tu pro misero victima grata manes.   (117–22)

> *As the Lamb enthroned on high, the Son of God Himself, tasted bitter death for sinners, so you, most righteous one, took the way of death, being torn to pieces by evil dogs, and died for the wicked thief. As the sacred ram was sacrificed in Isaac's place, so you were a willing victim on behalf of the wretched man.*

The whole tone of the fable makes it impossible to take this as other than mock-heroic – the analogy with the story is too accurate not to be witty – but it is mock-heroic become serious. Sedulius returns to the earlier tone for the concluding Epitaphium:

> Te (fateor) cupii; viduam matremque cupisco,
>   Fratres atque tuos semper amabo. Vale.   (139–40)

> *I desired you, I confess; I still desire your widow and mother, and I shall always love your brothers. Farewell.*

It is not, after all, the noble spirit of the beast that is the motive of his attachment to it.

The Carolingians' sensitivity to Virgil's poetry is probably the characteristic that most clearly distinguishes their pastoral writings from those of the later Middle Ages. New themes, especially Christian ideas, were imported into the bucolic by many of these early poets, but they are still in touch with a vital Classical poetic tradition. The dearth of pastoral in the succeeding centuries, and the completely new form it took under Petrarch's hands, are

an indication of the increasing conceptual distance between Virgil and the
men who read him. They were unable to imagine that so great an authority
could be anything less than enormously weighty, and they read the *Bucolics*
accordingly; the lightness of touch in the poems, the sophistication and the
sheer delight in poetry for its own sake were only generally recognized again
in the Renaissance, when the same qualities were valued. Only two poets of
High Middle Ages show the same closeness to Virgil as the Carolingians
displayed, and the gulf between those two illustrates in an extreme form the
bewilderment that could be caused by the pure art of the *Bucolics*. Martius
Valerius and Metellus of Tegernsee probably both belong to the same period,
the twelfth-century Renaissance. To Valerius belongs the honour of having
written the only eclogue series of the Middle Ages comparable in treatment,
and even in poetic quality, with the eclogues of antiquity; while Metellus'
cycle, the most closely dependent on Virgil of all the mediaeval eclogues,
displays a deadness and a monumental poetic ineptitude that reveal a vast
distance between himself and his model.

Valerius' eclogues were only discovered in this century, and not published
until comparatively recently.[23] Nothing is known about the author; even his
name – Martius, Marcius or Marcus Valerius – is uncertain, and in any case
it is probably a pseudonym.[24] His dates and his country of origin are matters
of speculation: one of the two MSS containing his poems is written in a
French hand of around 1200, but this in itself tells us little. The poems themselves have a very few features in common with other twelfth-century poetry
and lack many other characteristics of that age. In one respect in particular
he was exceptional: he had access to complete copies of Calpurnius and
Nemesianus, apparently being the only poet to use their work between the
Carolingians and Boccaccio. It is not impossible that he did in fact belong
to the ninth or tenth century, though the totally Classical quality of his
eclogues, untouched by allegory, personification or propaganda of any sort,
makes them exceptional in any age. The language and content of the five
poems, a pastoral *Prologus* in elegiacs and four true eclogues, are consistently
close to ancient practice, and yet they are always original and move independently of his three pastoral authorities: imitation has found its proper place.
He is creating, not copying, just as Virgil used Theocritus or Calpurnius
Virgil, though the opening line of the first eclogue declares his allegiance:

> Cidne, sub algenti recubas dum molliter umbra...

Virgil's 'Tityre, tu patulae recubans sub tegmine fagi' haunted almost every
writer of eclogues for centuries: to imitate it is not just a matter of copying
the master but a way of announcing your intentions, declaring yourself a
pastoral poet – particularly important when the eclogue was not one of the
usual current poetic forms. Valerius sets out his own attitude to pastoral in
the *Prologus* – at least, the attitude he assumes for the occasion: it consists
largely of the combined declaration of modesty and of the worth of pastoral
that is so common among both the Carolingians and the Elizabethans.

> Tityrus a molli surrexit in ardua clivo,
>> Cuius grandisonas vicit avena tubas.
> Nos tenui labor est stipulas implere susurro
>> Et vix est humili colle tenere gradum. (7–10)

> *Tityrus climbed from the gentle slope to the heights, and the sound of his reed surpassed
> mighty trumpets. It is an effort for me to fill my pipe with a poor murmur, and I can
> scarcely keep my footing on a low hill.*

This passage is followed almost at once by eight lines of prosodic acrobatics in which each line consists of two or three words only: Valerius will not even wait for the eclogues proper to display his skill. He has an exceptionally clear idea of the rôle of the shepherd as poet; only Dante in the whole of the Middle Ages can write anything comparable with the image of the shepherd struggling to play his pipe, and even he is more directly allusive. For Valerius the metaphor has an immediate imaginative significance without any need for the precise allegorical transposition of details. Poetry itself is a major theme in his eclogues, too. The first two are lyrical laments, one in dialogue, one monologue; the third is a singing-match in true Classical style; and the fourth contains the song of Apollo, the very god of poetry. The scope of these poems, as well as their quality, is an indication of Valerius' confidence in handling the pastoral mode, whatever mediaeval rhetorical practice may lead him to say in the prologue – and, indeed, whatever inadequacy he may genuinely have felt before his master Tityrus.

The first two eclogues are both laments over unhappy love. Cidnus confesses to Ladon his love for Sistis – a love so overwhelming that he cannot move to the hill pastures, his flocks are suffering and he is incapable of taking the usual care of them. Although it is so marked a theme of Classical and Renaissance pastoral, love is a rare subject for the eclogue in the Middle Ages – only Boccaccio, in two youthful poems that seem to have caused him some shame in later life, takes up the theme apart from Valerius – and Valerius' treatment of the subject is an interesting anticipation of the expression of love through the Petrarchan paradox, of which the Renaissance pastoralists were so fond. The poem opens, like Virgil's first eclogue, with one shepherd lying in the shade; but this is contrasted not with the other shepherd's hardship but with the burning passion of love within himself.

> O utinam...estusque meos hec pelleret umbra!
> Sed ferit interno non simplex flamma calore.　　　　　　　　　(I.26–9)

> *If only this shade would drive away the heat I feel! but an unnatural flame kills me, burning within.*

He is incapable of putting Sistis out of his mind, and, like Virgil's Tityrus before the beneficent Octavian, he calls on the natural world for *impossibilia* to image forth his condition:

> Ver fugit ante rosas estusque refugit aristas,
> Autumnus volucres vitabit, bruma pruinas,
> Sistis amata sui quam cedat pectore Cidni.　　　　　　　　　(79–81)

> *Spring will drive away the roses and summer the ears of corn, autumn will shun the insects and winter the frosts, before his beloved Sistis gives up her place in Cidnus' heart.*

Valerius uses similar techniques again in the following poem, *Versus Iarbe Pastoris de Amica*. Iarbas' love, Eufilis, is pretending to love Nicotis in order to arouse his jealousy, and Iarbas himself retreats to a cave to lament.

> Ver favet ecce, vides, et spirant floribus agri
> Et pecus omne nova gaudens spatiatur in herba;
> Te procul unus ego sordere rosaria credo
> Et calet umbra michi suntque aspera prata iacenti.　　　　　　(II.20–3)

Lo, you see the spring flourishing and the fields alive with flowers; the whole flock is scattered over the fresh grass, delighting in it; only I, far from you, find no pleasure in the rose-arbours, the shade burns me and the meadows are rough to lie in.

It is exceptional at this period to find the landscape used in this way, as an extension of the shepherd's own mind – not the pathetic fallacy in this case, but its direct opposite, which itself implies a consciousness of its existence: shepherd and countryside should be in harmony, and it is the distance from this ideal state that highlights Iarbas' condition. Cidnus identifies the stability of his love with the natural order of the seasons, Iarbas sees himself as cut off from the pastoral world. These are the first post-Classical examples of the interplay of shepherd and setting, of the idea of the landscape of the mind.

Other details in these poems are also interesting forshadowings of what the Renaissance poets were to do with pastoral. Cidnus describes how he first made the acquaintance of Sistis, as Mantuan, by far the most popular of the Renaissance Latin ecloguists, makes his shepherd-lovers narrate their first meetings with their girls; there is only a hint of this in Virgil. The madness of love that Virgil's Corydon wryly mocks himself for suffering – 'Quae te dementia cepit?' – is stressed by both Cidnus and Iarbas, Cidnus as he admits to the obsession that prevents him from looking after his flock, Iarbas as he asks himself desperately, 'Sed quo ferar amens?', 'Where will this madness drive me?' He considers killing himself, and even imagines the epitaph on his tomb and the shepherds coming to read it. Like Corydon, he eventually pulls himself together and goes back to his duties, and Valerius tells us in a final couplet that the omens look good for him and Eufilis to live happily ever after; Mantuan's Amyntas has none of the Classical sense of proportion, and after predicting his epitaph does indeed kill himself – or at least goes mad and ranges the woods until he dies, when his bones are picked clean by wild creatures. The whole idea of the pastoral world as the setting for unfulfilled love is typical of the Classical bucolic tradition, reinforced later by the tenets of Petrarchan love-poetry; in mediaeval vernacular pastoral, where love is a perpetually recurring theme, it is almost invariably happy, in explicit contrast to the sufferings of courtly love.

Valerius' third eclogue is a singing-match between Meris and Mopsus. Meris' he-goat has strayed into Mopsus' herd, and a quarrel develops when he claims it back. He says he will call it to him with his pipe; Meris laughs at his musical self-confidence, and they challenge each other to sing. The match is amoebaean, each singer taking two hexameters in turn, and ends (like Virgil's) with riddles from each of them. The judge, Ligurgus, declares a draw. The last poem, entitled *Carmen Apollonis*, is based on Virgil's sixth eclogue, the song of Silenus; but Valerius sets out to write not only the poetry of a god but divine poetry at its best. He does – like Virgil – avoid the worst of the problem by recounting the song in indirect speech and in general terms; and he adds too that Apollo had lost the highest of his skill in becoming human. He had abandoned his divine form, so the myth ran, to work for a while as a shepherd for Admetus; Valerius refers to the incident in the *Versus Iarbe*, when Iarbas first laments because Eufilis is worthy of the gods, then comforts himself by remembering that Apollo became a shepherd. The myth is mentioned time and again in later pastoral as justifying the estate of the herdsman. Valerius sets his fourth eclogue in the very time when Apollo was on earth; he is tired with driving bulls, and lies down to rest. Pan and a Napaea – the term may here be used as a proper name – come on him and ask him to sing; and the countryside falls silent to listen.

> Utque canit, rigidi mollescit culmen Olimpi
> Duraque blandisonis animantur saxa camenis
> Marmoribusque pares herent ad carmina tigres;
> It nemus et tacitis refluus stetit amnis in undis
> Omnis silva silet, ventorum flabra quiescunt;
> Ne tremefacta comas invita remurmuret, arbos
> Accubat et strictis condensat frondibus umbras;
> Astupet omnis ager, reprimunt convitia cantus
> Atque oblita nefas posuit philomena querelas. (18–26)

As he sang, the peak of frozen Olympus melted, the hard rocks were brought to life by the sweet music and the tigers froze like marble statues at the song; the woods moved and the river turned back and stood still, its waves silent; the whole forest was quiet, the gusts of wind fell silent; the trees bowed down lest they should involuntarily murmur in reply when their foliage was stirred, and drew in their shadow as they gathered their branches close; the ploughed land lay still in wonder. The song made all sound cease, and the nightingale, forgetting her wrong, abandoned her laments.

The first part of Apollo's song deals with three subjects, each in three parts – the perfect number, reflecting the divine nature of the singer. First he sings of the triple qualities in man of life, sense and reason, properties held in common with, in turn, plants, beasts and gods; then of events past, present and future; finally of the invention of language, of laws and of poetry. So much has been for Pan; next Apollo sings for the nymph, recounting a series of mythological love-stories (derived from Ovid). He finally comes to the story of his own beloved, Daphne, and falls silent in grief. It is an ending of remarkable grace and delicacy.

With every other ecloguist of the Middle Ages, it is possible to identify a set of attitudes and assumptions typical of his period. The bucolic, the commentaries declared, was allusive; moreover, said the Church fathers, it was a divinely chosen medium for Christian thought. Valerius, however, recreates the Classical eclogue in theme and in treatment – in technical details, such as his free use of narrative or monologue or dialogue, where other writers were concentrating on dialogue alone; in essential spirit, as further meanings give way to pure poetry. He apparently ignores contemporary critical theory unless it coincides with his own conception of pastoral: his style is simple and unfigured in a *stylus humilis* that itself helps to draw him closer to his models.

Metellus of Tegernsee, probably his contemporary, is at the opposite extreme, not just because his poetry is so extraordinarily bad but because so many of his faults arise from an over-literal interpretation of current critical thought. The *Bucolica Quirinalium*[25] are a slavish rewriting of the *Bucolics*, line by line, sometimes almost word by word, 'in praise of the glorious martyr, the blessed Quirinus', who was the patron saint of the foundation at Tegernsee. Despite their closeness to Virgil, the poems are both religious and allegorical; and Metellus does his utmost wherever he can to make his hexameters leonine. His very first line,

> Tityre, tu magni recubans in margine stagni,

> *Tityrus, lying on the bank of a large stagnant pool,*

sufficiently illustrates his method. To make matters worse, Metellus knows (and points out in his prologue) that the word *bucolic* is derived from 'custodibus boum', cowherds – a point repeated by both Servius and Isidore of

Seville,[26] either of whom he might easily have read; but he makes a funda-
mental mistake in confusing bucolic poetry with bovine, and the entire cycle
tells of how ten different oxen or calves or cows vowed to Quirinus went
astray in one way or another and were miraculously recovered by the saint.
Each eclogue is headed by a summary of the argument and a statement as to
who represents whom. The first will serve as an example for them all:

> Concerning a beautiful calf, which was vowed to the blessed Quirinus by
> a peasant, but was put in with the master's own herds. Whereupon one
> night the whole herd, apart from this calf, perished.
> Allegorically, Tityrus is the man at Tegernsee responsible for receiving the
> animals brought as offerings. Melibeus is a certain man who once scorned
> the blessed Quirinus and who is struck with paralysis in the last eclogue and
> converted after being cured.[27]

In spite of this kind of framework Metellus manages to follow the formal
outline of each eclogue, so that he even produces a couple of singing-matches
of a rather peculiar kind. The third eclogue, for instance, is based on a rather
complicated story of how an ox vowed to the saint was stolen, bought by
another man and ran off to the shrine of its own accord – all this happening
before the poem opens. The match is held to decide the ownership, and
consists of a succession of Biblical, theological or pastoral snippets. The
contest in the seventh eclogue is not really a singing-match at all, even in
intention: it starts as an argument between master and servant – a kind of
literal *conflictus* – and ends as a sort of dialogue hymn. The eighth poem,
which in Virgil consists of two successive songs each with a recurring refrain,
loses even this trace of a poetic basis and becomes simply two speeches with
repeated lines, one spoken by a thief as he tries to kill the ox he has stolen (but
which had of course been previously vowed to Quirinus), the second by the
priest to whom he finally hands it over. All the eclogues are heavily didactic:
apart from the direct moral contained in each story, Metellus is at pains to
make his rustics exchange additional *sententiae*, and he adds comments of his
own to highlight the issues. When, in the second eclogue, wolves carry off a
heifer vowed to the saint but never handed over, he marvels at the miracle
and sees it as a source of renewed faith. The fourth poem is the most catastrophic of all, for Metellus was quite unable to find either subject or
significance to match the theme, and the idea of the return of the Golden Age
can hardly have any counterpart in this kind of bucolic material. Virgil had
pictured the return of Astraea, the Virgin of justice, and the descent of the
messianic child from Heaven,

> Iam redit et Virgo, redeunt Saturnia regna;
> Iam nova progenies caelo demittitur alto; (IV.6–7)

and he urges the infant to smile as it recognizes its mother:

> Incipe, parve puer, risu cognoscere matrem. (IV.60)

Metellus' infant, however, is inevitably a calf, of surpassing beauty, and he
apostrophizes it accordingly.

> Iam nova progenies maculis insignis et albo
> Ac niveo miscens orbes nigros quasi carbo
> Aut rutilo fulgens pecori decus addidit ingens.
> Iam redit et largo data pignore matris imago.
> Incipe, taure tener, mugitu noscere matrem. (20–3)

Now a new offspring is born, outstanding for its markings, that mingles patches as black as coal with the white and snowy, or shining red imparted a great beauty to the herd. Now the image of the mother returns in abundant form in the child. Begin, little bull, to acknowledge your mother with a moo.

Perhaps the most remarkable thing about Metellus is that he could have read so much Classical poetry so closely – he subjects Horace's *Odes* to the same procedure – and yet show such total insensitivity to it. He is completely lacking in the skill shown in different ways by Valerius and the Carolingians of transmuting such poetry into new literature of his own. He is less a dwarf on a giant's shoulder than a dwarf under a giant's foot – the giant, Virgil, crushing him all the harder for the weight of commentary he carried. Poetry evokes no artistic or imaginative response in Metellus, and the concept of pastoral means nothing to him whatsoever.

It is perhaps unfair to the Middle Ages to take Metellus' misreading of the *Bucolics* as typical, but it is true that no other period could have provided the intellectual climate in which such an interpretation could be made. Metellus is a product of his age; and the attitude of other scholars, commentators and later poets to the *Bucolics* themselves and to the pastoral mode in general suggests plainly that they were as much a source of bewilderment as inspiration. Apparently nobody – not even Dante – read Virgil with the same clarity of response as Valerius until the high Renaissance. Over the centuries, mediaeval writers developed their own understanding of pastoral – an interpretation so far from Virgil himself that it left them free, for better or for worse, to create a completely new kind of eclogue.

II. *The Mediaeval Interpretation*

There were five forces, of unequal strength, at work in the re-shaping of Classical pastoral into mediaeval, and they all helped to obscure the real nature of the Latin eclogue and to suggest new forms and uses. The first was the stylistic theory that had been grafted onto the *Bucolics* since at least the time of Servius, which laid down that pastoral should be written in low style; this had comparatively little effect on actual poetic practice in the Middle Ages, however frequently scholars and theorists mentioned it, and it only becomes crucial in the Renaissance. The one poet who does appear to pay some attention to the theory is Valerius, the least typically mediaeval of them all. The second factor affecting the eclogue tradition was the development of vernacular pastoral literature in France, and from the thirteenth century onwards there is clear evidence that some Latin and French poets saw themselves as working in the same mode. Thirdly, the eclogue came to be regarded as a vehicle for satire – an idea of considerable importance for the later history of pastoral. Fourthly, Christian thought of one kind or another came to dominate the contents; one form of this is the metaphor of Christ, or the pope, bishop or priest, as shepherd of his flock. Connected with this, and by far the most important of the five, was the tendency of the mode towards allegory. It is a characteristic of pastoral of every age that it spreads out to include a wide variety of non-pastoral subjects – that is always implied by its metaphorical relationship to the real world; but the typical Latin eclogue of the Middle Ages took this to the point where true pastoral subject-matter ceased to exist, where the bucolic framework was a medium for saying something entirely different. There is only tenuous Classical authority for this assumption that allegory was a proper approach to pastoral, even less that it should be the only correct treatment. Servius admits that Virgil's eclogues do have a tendency towards allegory while those of Theocritus are 'simplex', but he believes that they should be understood literally as far as possible; and his commentary repeatedly includes such notes as, 'It is better for us to take this at face value; for some people mistakenly look for allegory.'[28] He clearly has a considerable opposition to contend with; but he himself helps to strengthen their position at times, not only by preserving the allegorical interpretations he refutes, but also by adding some of his own. He never seems to believe absolutely in his own position, qualifying his statements as soon as he has made them: 'Allegories are to be refuted in the eclogue, except where, as we have noted above, they arise from some necessity concerning lost lands.'[29] The opposing viewpoint is represented by figures such as Fulgentius, who went so far as to ascribe a mystic quality to the philosophy of the *Bucolics*.[30] As long as this attitude was kept in check by a wide and sympathetic knowledge of the Classics, the eclogue could remain Virgilian in tone; but gradually, in theory and in practice, a new kind of pastoral was created.

There is already allegory of a kind in the classicist eclogues of the Carolingians – in the personifications of the *Conflictus Veris et Hiemis*, in the poetic and political allusions of Modoin's poem. He himself describes his eclogue in the prologue as a 'veiled song', *carmine velato*, though the veil is always transparent. This kind of open allusion, of representation of political life in terms of the pastoral world, was not taken up again until the Renaissance humanists turned their hand to the eclogue, and they often still prefer the thicker obscurity in which Petrarch hid his intentions. The poets of the ninth century, Sedulius and Paschasius Radbertus in particular, also played their part in introducing the metaphor of the Good Shepherd into pastoral. The theme had already been treated in detail from the Biblical side, in sermons or treatises by many of the Church Fathers, and in poetry by Prudentius and others;[31] the first Christian eclogue, by Endelechius, was written in the same early period. The actual equation of the Classical and Biblical shepherd is found in art, in the catacombs or Byzantine wall-paintings and mosaics, where Christ is often depicted with a lyre or panpipes, but it did not occur in literature until later. It seems to have been Sedulius who was the first to identify the shepherd of bucolic and the shepherd of the church from the poetic side. In his series of poems to bishop Hartgar[32] he repeatedly describes himself as celebrating the *bonus pastor* on his *pastorea fistola*, and on occasion he goes so far as to give himself and Hartgar pastoral names. None of the poems is actually an eclogue, however, and although the imagery of sheep is used many times it is never developed with any consistency. It is only in Paschasius' poem that the Christian pastor is given a fully pastoral context, and the choice of name – Menalcas – is in keeping with this. The identification occurs later in the Middle Ages too: in the twelfth-century Feast of Fools song,

> Gregis pastor Tityrus
> Noster est episcopus,[33]

or more strikingly in a lament for the death of Robert Grosseteste, bishop of Lincoln, which occurred in 1253. This poem was written by a certain Hubert, who may have been a friar in the bishop's service.[34] It is again not strictly an eclogue, though it borrows many phrases and images from pastoral: Lincoln's sun has set; the sheep have lost their careful shepherd and are no longer safe from the wolf; the pastoral landscape is spoiled by tares and thorns. Grosse-teste himself is the Biblical Good Shepherd, and he is also given the name of Tytirus, the archetypal shepherd of the eclogue. There are not many occasions, all the same, when Classical and ecclesiastical pastoral are con-nected; and it seldom, if ever, happens from the other side – that a homilist discussing Christ or the rôle of His ministers should make the identification. This is in marked contrast to the mediaeval vernacular tradition, where the literary and Biblical shepherd are very closely connected. Hubert may none the less have gone no further than the contemporary *artes poeticae* for his stimulus: he displays a good knowledge of them in many ways, and he would have found in them both shepherd metaphors and, in John of Garland's recent work, instructions as to the correct name and setting to use when writing about the *pastor*. Hubert may have put two and two together in an unusually skilful way. The only actual eclogues of the whole of the Middle Ages that really use the Good Shepherd metaphor are Paschasius' lament and one very influential poem by Petrarch, his sixth eclogue, in which he con-demns the state of the Church; there are also a couple of rather perfunctory lines in John of Garland's own eclogue. Although its roots are mediaeval, the theme only comes into its own as part of the eclogue at the Renaissance.

The belief that the eclogue was an appropriate medium for satire, or at least stringent social criticism, had been a critical commonplace for several centuries before the first series of invective eclogues was actually written by Petrarch. It had been accepted for some time that the word *eclogue* was derived from αἰγ- and λογος, and so meant 'goatish speech' or, later, 'goat-herds' talk'; the first mention of this derivation is found in a ninth-century life of Virgil.[35] Some two hundred years later Bernard of Utrecht took the logical next step and gave the derivation an inner significance as well: '*Egloga* is derived from goats, as if one were to say egle-logos, that is, goatish speech, either because it is concerned with shepherds or because it deplores the foul-ness of the vices symbolized by that animal.'[36] The false etymology itself becomes a reason for the satirical use of the genre; and this was occasionally reinforced by the Biblical imagery of the sheep and the goats. The religious allegory that is perhaps the most characteristic form of mediaeval Latin pastoral made the eclogue an obvious medium of ecclesiastical satire and of theological instruction: Christian doctrine could be transferred into a literary genre that had Classical authority – and indeed, it was believed, Classical authority for containing Christian ideas, in the Fourth Eclogue – providing a mixture ready to hand of the *utile* (the doctrinal ingredient) with the *dulce* (the pastoral imagery and the art form itself). The balance of Classical and Christian depends largely on the individual author, though the Christian tends to win in the later Middle Ages: Sedulius, for instance, uses the Christian imagery primarily to serve his immediate poetic purpose in his poem on Hartgar's wether, while Metellus uses Virgil to bolster the adoration of Quirinus.

The use of the eclogue for religious propaganda and apology – not as yet strictly allegorical – goes back as far as the late fourth or early fifth century, to the *Carmen de Mortibus Boum* of Severus Sanctus Endelechius,[37] a professor of rhetoric at Rome and friend of St. Paulinus of Nola. The poem is written in asclepiadic stanzas, not hexameters, and consists of dialogue alone. That Endelechius himself thought of the poem as an eclogue is confirmed by the names he gives his characters: Bucolus, Aegon and Tityrus. Together they form a pastoral triad: Tityrus for the shepherd, Bucolus the cowherd, and Aegon from αἰγ-, 'goat'. Donatus, in his commentary on the *Bucolics* attached to the end of his Life of Virgil, classifies the bucolic into three types according to the nature of the animal the speakers are herding, and the classification was already a commonplace by this period. Apart from this, the poem has little in common with Virgilian pastoral, except perhaps for the opening, in which Aegon finds Bucolus grieving and asks him the cause – a recurrent eclogue introduction. After some hesitation, Bucolus admits that although he was once mighty in flocks, 'gregibus potens', so that the countryside was covered with them, he has lost them all in a cattle-plague. Aegon has heard of the widespread disaster, but he expresses his surprise that so good a herdsman as Bucolus, familiar with diseases and their remedies, could not have taken action to avoid it. Bucolus replies that the plague advanced too fast: oxen fell in the yoke, calves sucked death from their mothers, beasts fell like snowflakes or

> Quam multis foliis silva cadentibus
> Nudatur, gelidis tacta Aquilonibus, (85–6)

As the wood is stripped by the multitude of falling leaves at the touch of the cold North wind...

The herdsmen are amazed to see Tityrus coming towards them with a flock still apparently in perfect health. Bucolus asks him how he has preserved them, and Tityrus replies that the sign of the cross, marked on each beast's forehead, is a guaranteed apotropaic, 'cunctarum pecudum certa salus' (110). Not surprisingly, the other two herdsmen express a keen interest in the new religion, especially when Tityrus goes on to assure them that faith is all that is needed and not offerings and sacrifices – a point of which a Protestant editor of the early seventeenth century strongly approved.[38] Bucolus decides to abandon his old error and take up the new religion, and Aegon declares his intention of joining the others:

> Nam cur addubitem, quin homini quoque
> Signum prosit idem perpete saeculo,
> Quo vis morbida vincitur? (130–2)

For why should I doubt that the same sign that overcame the power of the plague would do just as much good to man, world without end?

The superstition of signing animals with the cross is probably as old as Christianity itself; Endelechius does at least argue forward from there a little, and it is possible that he had deeper allegorical meanings in mind – perhaps that only the Christian can be a good shepherd, perhaps that the Cross of baptism preserves the flock of the faithful from the onslaughts of the devil. The absence of any pointer towards such an interpretation within the poem, however, tells strongly against it. As an eclogue the poem is unique for its age;[39] it has far less in common with Classical bucolic than with later works such as the *Ecloga Theoduli* in its use of pastoral for Christian apologia, or with late mediaeval pastoral in its association of the mode with plague or disaster.

The *Ecloga Theoduli*, of the ninth or tenth century,[40] combines Christian doctrine with allegory, though this is still not taken far beyond personification; the poet is at pains not to depart too far from Classical pastoral. It consists of a contest between Pseustis, 'liar', an Athenian goatherd, and Alithia, 'truth', a shepherdess of the seed of David. Their occupations are the nearest Theodulus comes to allegory proper: given the Christian context, the goatherd must inevitably be the representative of the damned, even before his name is mentioned. The debate is judged by 'mater Fronesis', 'understanding'. The opening scene-setting of the summer countryside, and the structure of the poem with the challenge, promising of prizes, appointing of a judge, the contest and the nightfall close, are all Virgilian themes; the debate itself is not in this tradition, but the transition is made easily as the opening theme is Pseustis' account of the Saturnian Golden Age. Alithia counters with an account of Paradise and the Fall of Man, and from then on the arguments are mythological and Biblical, carefully matched – Daedalus and Icarus against Abraham and Isaac, the long night of Alcmene and Jove against the sun standing still upon Gibeon – but containing no pastoral material until almost the end, when a transition back from Christian material to the eclogue setting is made through the metaphor of Christ as the Lamb and Satan as the wolf. Pseustis is urging Alithia to yield and describes the approaching nightfall:

> Sponte sua tauri cupiunt ad tecta reverti;
> Vesper oves cithiso, capras depellit ab ulmo;
> Ni matura redis, lupus insidiabitur agnis. (293–5)

> *The bulls want to make their way back to their stalls of their own accord; evening drives the sheep from the clover and the goats from the elm. If you do not return in good time, the wolf will entrap the lambs.*

Alithia replies:

> Si vos terret, oves, lupus ad caulas redeuntes,
> Cornibus elatis illum, mea cura, petatis,
> Quem sine fraude pius paschalis vicerat agnus.
> Fige, dies, cursum, ne perdet virgo triumphum. (297–300)

> *If the wolf frightens you, my sheep, as you are returning to your folds, make for him, my charge, with horns held high, for the righteous paschal lamb devoid of sin overcame him. Complete your course, o day, and let not the virgin lose her triumph.*

Fronesis, predictably, gives Alithia the victory. The poem was imitated by Warnerius of Bâle in the late eleventh century in his *Synodicus*, a *conflictus* between characters representing the Old and New Testaments; but this poem has crossed the dividing line between eclogue and debate, and apart from an open-air setting it contains no pastoral references or material.

The *Ecloga Theoduli* is the only mediaeval eclogue that came to be generally known and so had any widespread influence on later pastoral. It was often used as a schoolbook,[41] since it possessed the great advantage – from the pedagogic point of view – of teaching pagan mythology in a Christian context, so that the corrupting influences of real pagan authors could be kept at bay. It was generally used at elementary level, but Conrad of Hirsau lists it among the more advanced works on the grounds that it requires understanding on three levels: 'First in this work the teacher should lay down the literal sense, then the letter itself must be expounded through allegory, then the reader's life related to it through a moral explanation.'[42] The personifications of the poem appear straightforward beside Petrarch's convoluted allegories, but Conrad obviously sees more in it than this – in fact, he thinks of Theodulus as being more allegórical than Virgil; his attitude to the *Bucolics* is comparable to that of Servius, with allegory being a possible rather than a necessary method of approach. By the time he was writing, Theodulus and Virgil were the only known examples of the eclogue genre, and commentators and rhetoricians had no other material to draw on. Theodulus had to be read allegorically, Virgil could be and generally was; and later ecloguists proceeded to imitate what they considered to be the correct form.

That Theodulus was himself working within a tradition that laid increasing emphasis on allegory is illustrated by a more or less contemporary eclogue by Radbod, who became bishop of Utrecht in 899 or 900, the *Egloga de Virtutibus Lebuini*.[43] This poem shows the early stages of the development of a kind of pastoral where the surface meaning is nothing without the inner significance – a development that was to be taken much further by John of Garland and Petrarch, though Radbod does at least give the reader plenty of information about his method of procedure and what it all means. The eclogue is a mixture of panegyric and moral instruction. It starts with an account of the coming of Lebuin, one of the eighth-century missionaries to the Saxons and Friesians, from England to the Rhine, but the accompanying landscape descriptions soon become explicitly ambiguous with a reference to allegorical vines (*allegoricis vitibus*) in the fields. Radbod does not leave his readers to puzzle for long, however, and the abundant landscape soon resolves itself into its appropriate significances.

> Nam pepigit vites, cum multos codicis almi
> Ornavit gemmis (vinum hinc potare salubre est);
> Triticeam posuit messem, cum pectora munda
> Esse dedit castumque deo subnexuit agmen;
> Porro autem arboreas studuit plantare novellas,
> Robora cum fidei statuit, cum pacis olivam
> Crescere, cum fructus fecit pollere perennes. (28–34)

> *For he planted vines when he adorned many a nourishing book with precious stones (to drink wine from such a source brings health); he made his harvest of wheat when he declared hearts to be cleansed and brought a pious troop under God's command; and moreover he conscientiously planted new trees when he strengthened the oak of faith, when he made the olive of peace to flourish and unfailing fruit to grow firm.*

This reads like the glossing of a Biblical text, and Radbod presumably derives his method from this; but he seems also to have at the back of his mind the idea of abundance of Golden Age pastoral, as if the efforts of one man could help to bring about the Messianic era. The fallen world may not bring forth abundantly of its own accord, but at least Christian activity can go some way towards restoring the fruitfulness of Eden. The christianized idea of the Golden Age, here and elsewhere, looks both backward and forward: historically Eden and the age of Astraea are identified (as they are in Theodulus), but the redemption of mankind by Christ foreshadows a return to perfection parallel with the return of Saturn's reign prophesied by Virgil. The theme recurs perpetually in later pastoral. Radbod also takes up another recurring but narrower theme later in the poem, when he discusses the appropriateness of the name Lebuin, or Liafwin, 'carus amicus', in a passage on human and divine love. He has no need to choose an allegorical name for his protagonist: it is provided for him already. This section is the equivalent of the careful choice of significant names for their pastoral characters made by writers from Paschasius Radbertus and Theodulus to Boccaccio and Petrarch, and later to Fairfax and Quarles. Radbod concludes his poem with what was already something of a pastoral commonplace, an apology lest he offend delicate ears with his hoarse reed.

All the same, it is not immediately clear why Radbod should have chosen to call his poem an *egloga;* it contains very little strictly pastoral subject-matter, and the identification of Classical and Christian pastor is never made. Its principal connection with the whole pastoral tradition, in fact, is its allegorical treatment, and it seems most likely to be this that Radbod had in mind. The association of pastoral and allegory was made even clearer in the following centuries; by the thirteenth century it appears that pastoral terminology, completely independent of the eclogue, was regarded as a natural medium for allegory, and the authors of some *artes poeticae* make the most of it even when they are not concerned at all with the pastoral mode itself. When Geoffroi de Vinsauf comes to discuss metaphorical tropes in his *Poetria Nova*, the very first example he gives of a phrase with a further meaning is, 'Pastores praedantur oves':[44] the satirical image of the bad shepherd is the first metaphor that comes to his mind. John of Garland's *Poetria*, completed around 1234,[45] abounds with pastoral images referring not only to the priest but also to various other people, situations or personifications, and culminating in a full-scale eclogue of moral allegory. In the *Prologue* he describes the Parisian Master of Arts as a shepherd watching over his flock of scholars as they feed on the *pascua* of learning. He gives a number of pastoral examples of proverbs; and in the section headed 'De arte inveniendi nomina substantiva' he illustrates the principle of consistency of terminology with three pastoral examples ('materia de Pastore'), a quotation from the *Bucolics*, his own eclogue, and a couplet on the Incarnation taken from another of his poems, the *Epithalamium Beate Maria Virginis*:

> Ex oue procedit pastor, procedit ab agna
> Dux aries, agnum mistica lana parit. (p. 24)

The shepherd comes forth from the sheep, the ram, leader of the flock, from the ewe-lamb; the mystic fleece gives birth to the Lamb.

If the lines seem overdone as mystic paradox, the images of Christ as Lamb and Shepherd and of the Virgin as Gideon's fleece are ready-made to be drawn into the pastoral mode, to be set alongside Virgil. John sets out the same principle of consistency in more detail in his Wheel of Virgil, where the appropriate names and properties are laid down for each style, the high (heroic), middling and low (pastoral), as exemplified by the three works of Virgil and supplemented where Virgil fails him by common logic or Christian Latin. The list for the *humilis stylus* gives the leisured shepherd, 'pastor ociosus', as the typical character, Titirus and Melibeus as suitable names, the sheep as the representative animal, the crook (*baculus*) as the distinguishing mark of office, the pasture as the setting and the beech as the appropriate tree.[46] *Baculus* is actually the Christian form of the word, and though John could have found *baculum* in Ovid or the pseudo-Virgilian *Culex* it never appears in the *Bucolics*. None of this prevents his believing either that low style is associated with low subject-matter, or that pastoral is essentially metaphorical, or allegorical when extended. His eclogue is a didactic religious allegory, but it has none of the basis of conventional symbolism of his Incarnation couplet: it is as cryptic in itself as anything of Petrarch's. He writes it specifically as an example of what an eclogue is; and it is of particular importance as illustrating what a learned literary critic and established poet thought the pastoral mode to be. In addition, the poem is especially interesting since for the first time in the history of the eclogue vernacular pastoral is

making its influence apparent. John explicitly takes Virgil as his authority
for bucolic; but when he actually comes to writing, the pastourelle bulks
equally large.[47] This use of the vernacular tradition could be subconscious;
but whether this was so or not, it still indicates that vernacular shepherd
literature, even in its lightest and most lyrical form, was coming to be
recognized as truly pastoral and so identified with the Classical tradition.
That John does use it deliberately is suggested by its importance in the
eclogue – the poem is in fact almost incomprehensible unless the pastourelle
basis, with its first-person narration, is assumed; and it is possible too that he
uses it in another of his works, the *Stella Maris*, where the Virgin is depicted
as a shepherdess saving the flock of faithful sheep from wolves:

> Virgo mater est pastoris,
> Servans oves a raptoris
>   Faucibus pastoria.
> Illi cedunt lupi fortes,
> Per quam prede sunt exsortes
>   Noctis in vigilia.[48]

> *She is the virgin mother of the shepherd, a shepherdess keeping her sheep safe from the*
> *ravager's jaws. The strong wolves yield to her through whom their prey is preserved in*
> *the night watches.*

Here the consistency of metaphor creates something close to an allegorical
pastourelle to the Virgin: it is in the lyric, not the eclogue or the Bible, that
shepherdess and wolf are to be found in conjunction. 'Pastoria' for 'shepherdess' is in fact a mediaeval coinage, to fit a character not known to the
Classical world. In another celebration of the Virgin, his *Epithalamium*, John
turns to the pastoral of Virgil and Ovid to identify her with Astraea, the
Virgin of the Fourth Eclogue and goddess of the Golden Age.[49]

As anxious as Polonius not to miss anything out, John describes his eclogue
as 'elegiac-amabaean-bucolic-ethical', and then explains what this means
(it is *ama*baean, for instance, because it is *ama*tory) and gives a very necessary
outline of the plot:

> The subject of these lines is how a young man raped a nymph, whose lover
> was Coridon. The flesh is signified by the nymph, the world or the devil by
> the young man who corrupts her, and reason by her true lover. It is spoken
> by the character personifying the world:[50]

– and there follows the poem. The meaning is not always obvious, whether
literal or allegorical, and the scribes of the various surviving manuscripts
sometimes seem to have been puzzled themselves. The personal narration of
the *mundus uel diabolus* is essential to an understanding of the poem, and it is as
well that John mentions it before he starts since the first-person verbs do not
begin to appear until half way through the work, apart from in the refrain
line at the end of each of the twelve-line stanzas,

> Sim licet in laqueo, liber amator eo,

> *Though I am in a snare, yet as a lover I walk free.*

The work in fact bears much more resemblance to a pastourelle than to an
eclogue, both in form – the stanza with refrain – and in subject, the seduction of the shepherdess from her true lover by the narrator. That the poem
should have a plot at all distinguishes it from Classical bucolic, which is
characteristically a meditation on a situation, and groups it with pastoral such

as Metellus' or with the various vernacular genres that used the mode. The thick allegorical cloak, however, is borrowed straight from the tradition of bucolic commentary. The poem opens, like any pastourelle, with a description of spring and birdsong, and then describes the shepherdess herself, spinning and singing as she watches her sheep – though the beech under which she sits is derived from the *Bucolics* and the Wheel of Virgil.

> Phillis oues pauit, sub fago se recreauit
>   Ducens fila colo sola uirente solo,
> Et breuiter tacta decantat Daphnidis acta:
>   Quam bene sub legem traxerit ipse gregem;
> Daphnin predones canit illa fugasse leones. (413–7)

> *Phillis is grazing her sheep, spinning thread on a distaff and resting by herself under a beech on the fresh green earth. She sings of the deeds of Daphnis, lightly touching on them, how well he led his flock under his rule; she sings how Daphnis put to flight the marauding lions.*

One would expect Daphnis to be Phillis' lover, in the way that Marion sings of Robin in Adam de la Halle's *Jeu de Robin et Marion*, but here, as the next stanza and a supporting note in one manuscript make clear, Daphnis is God Himself, presented as the Good Shepherd. Phillis continues her song in praise of Christ, 'Daphnidis natus', but she is interrupted by the seduction of the narrator-devil:

> Dum sic gratatur pastoria, sicque iocatur,
>   Candoris niuei mulceo pectus ei, (425–6)

> *While the shepherdess celebrates and rejoices in this way, I caress her breast of snowy white*

– worldly temptation, in other words, is creeping up on her while she least expects it. It is significant that she is called *pastoria* here, never (unlike in the heading) *nimpha*: like the Virgin, she belongs more to the pastourelle than bucolic. John apparently uses 'nimpha' as loosely as the late Renaissance pastoralists, with no mythological implications. At this juncture of the poem the devil's rival, Reason, appears in the shape of the true lover Coridon, 'who soothes himself with his pipe' – the vernacular shepherd's customary skill in music is being put to allegorical use. Also like the shepherd-lover in the pastourelle, he comes too late. There follows a struggle between shepherdess and shepherd that ends with Coridon being pushed into the mud and Phillis scorning him for his dreary morality, more in keeping with the elderly than with a lover:

> Ludere nos iuuenes ne prohibete, senes!
> Istos per colles cum mecum ludere nolles
>   Lusorem tenui rusticitate tui. (436–8)

> *Don't you old men try to stop us having fun while we are young! Since you would not make love with me in these hills, because of your boorishness, I have taken a man who will.*

Coridon tries to win her back by promising pastoral gifts, of a sheepskin or even some sheep, but she mocks him sharply for his peasant's amatory clumsiness compared with the skill of her seducer – again, both are commonplaces of the pastourelle, though conventionally it is the wooer who offers presents.

> Sequar hunc qui nouit amare,
> Nec solet in ludis dulcibus esse rudis.
> Est iuuenis letus, saliens, probus et requietus;
> Est Coridon uilis tegmine, pelle, pilis. (443–6)

I will follow this man, who knows how to love and is not clumsy in sweet love-play. This young man pleases me, he is agile, skilful and always ready for more; Coridon is churlish in his clothing, with rough skin and untidy hair.

The narrator then outlines the nature of love in a courtly paradox even more paradoxical than the refrain:

> Sic uir amo quod amor, ergo non hamo nec hamor,
> Hamo sic hamor quem mihi tendit amor. (451–2)

Like a man, I love because I am loved – I neither fish nor get caught; so I am taken with the hook that love offers me.

Amo and *hamo* were believed to be etymologically identical in the Middle Ages, a fact that makes the lines even more convoluted. In the allegorical context they suggest that just as love is voluntary but irresistible, so the flesh gives itself over to sin of its own free will. The mixture of linguistic and theological scholarship with vernacular conventions is typical of the whole poem. The eclogue ends with a couplet that draws the moral in more literal terms:

> Sic Caro mechatur, Ratio dum subpeditatur;
> Est Mundus mechus, Carnis inane decus. (455–6)

So the Flesh commits adultery while Reason is trodden underfoot; the World is the adulterer, the beauty of the Flesh is worthless.

John certainly fulfils his promise to write ethical bucolic with the greatest faithfulness. Every detail of his shepherd world carries its own moral – indeed, is created for the sake of the moral. The pastoral setting has no imaginative force of its own; it exists purely as a didactic construct.

John was apparently rather proud of his eclogue. It is the first full-length poem in the *Poetria*, and to place it in such a work would ensure a wider circulation for it than would otherwise be likely. He quotes it ostensibly to illustrate a specific point, words suited to the matter, *verba cognata materie*, but it is hardly essential to the argument. As in his other example of the same point, the Incarnation couplet, he is concerned entirely with the consistency of the words used, not with how well the phraseology really suits the underlying subject. It is possible that he conceived the poem as an allegorical pastourelle in Classical guise rather than as an eclogue; but the title of 'carmen bucolicum' makes the claim that the poem is indeed an eclogue, with all the appropriate stylistic features. John's place in Paris put him close to the intellectual centre of his age, but he is never notable for originality of thought; so it seems fair to take his poem as characteristic of the scholarly view of bucolic in the thirteenth century. The developments it illustrates in the theory of pastoral are certainly typical. The influence of vernacular pastoral on even so strictly a Classical genre as the eclogue is particularly significant in France. More important for the eclogue tradition as a whole is the assumption that a *carmen bucolicum* should be *ethicum*, should argue a cause and state a moral. The connection of the eclogue with the debate is reduced to the author's own polemical stance; and the conflict is transmuted here into something rather closer to a psychomachia, the struggle of good and evil within the soul allegorized as an actual brawl. The essence of the debate was a balancing of arguments; the essence of the polemical eclogue is moralistic, with a sharp distinction between good and evil – a conception far removed from the rival art of the Virgilian singing-match. Another development, equally important, is the fusion of pastoral with allegory, to the point where the surface narrative ceases to have any coherent meaning apart from its inner significance. John is still not taking this aspect very far, but for the first time there is a complete division between the words on the page and the author's intended statement. Both this and the polemic emphasis were to be taken much further in the following century in Italy, despite the fact that the early humanists claimed to look to Virgil alone as their model and inspiration.

The next eclogues to be written were composed some ninety years later, by the poet who had the greatest love for Virgil of anyone in the Middle Ages: Dante. His two eclogues take the form of pastoral epistles, written to the 'amiable pedant' Giovanni de Virgilio in 1319 and 1321; and Giovanni, who welcomed them with enormous enthusiasm as representing a Classical revival, was inspired to write one in reply as well.[51] He was happy to recognize Dante as the direct descendant of Virgil: in a pastoral poem written to Albertino Mussato after Dante's death he declares that the shepherd's pipes had never been sounded, at least by Italian poets, until they themselves competed on them –

> Fistula non posthac nostris inflata poetis
> donec ea mecum certaret Tityrus olim.[52]

He is presenting their correspondence as a kind of singing-match. Dante had given himself the name Tityrus in his eclogues, recognizing himself both as the supreme shepherd-poet and as Virgil's heir. Virgil is indeed his guide in Arcadia, as in Hell and Purgatory; although the poems are allegorical in that they allude to his own life and occupations and companions, the Classical inspiration is genuine. He is as fully in control of his medium as his master was, and pastoral in his hands becomes a sophisticated game. The *Divine Comedy* was by this time almost finished and the early parts already widely acclaimed, though his decision to write in the vernacular still worried many scholars, not least Giovanni. He wrote to Dante urging him to write in Latin, and to come to Bologna to receive the laurel crown. The pastoral form of Dante's reply is a kind of guarantee of his regard for the Classics. He pictures himself receiving the message as he numbers his goats under an oak. His companion Melibeus (possibly Dino Perini) urges him to go to Bologna, reminding him of the brevity of life – *vitae summa brevis*, one of the recurring themes of pastoral of all ages:

> Respice tempus
> Tityre quam velox; (I.45–6)

but Dante declares that he wants the crown only when he has completed his great poem, and meantime he answers Giovanni's objections to his writing in Italian with a promise of ten measures of milk from his favourite ewe, that is, ten cantos of the *Paradiso*. Even this detail is taken from Virgil by way of Servius, who comments on 'Aurea decem mala misi' (III.71), Menalcas' sending of ten apples to Amyntas,

> There are some people who would like this bit to be an allegory about giving Augustus the ten eclogues; which is superfluous, for what need is there for allegory here?[53]

The second half of the gloss, inevitably, was ignored; and in any case, Dante's pastoral metaphor requires something of the kind, on the principle of appropriate terminology such as John of Garland describes. The very fact that the poem does have such a detailed personal reference prevents it from being totally absorbed into the pastoral world; for all its consistency, the setting here is an artistic stage backcloth, a poet's intellectual amusement. The distance between the poetic characters and real shepherds is typical of the post-Classical eclogue; and it is the first step too towards the Renaissance fashion of having the principal characters merely adopt the disguise of shepherds for the sake of the plot, on the grounds that the pastoral world is a good setting for poetry. Dante and Valerius alone in the Middle Ages have some understanding of the idea of the shepherd-poet, which was to become such a key theme of Renaissance pastoral.

Giovanni was delighted with his letter. He wrote an enthusiastic answer in the same mode, though it owes rather more direct debt to Virgil. He imagines himself busy with the various occupations of the shepherd when Dante's song is wafted to him on the wind, and he promptly decides to reply in kind. He will abandon the city for the open air; he will forget learned style and high theme and sing 'depostis calamis majoribus', a recollection of the familiar Virgilian 'paulo maiora canamus'. He expresses his indignation at Dante's exile – conveniently, another Classical theme – and promises a splendid series of pastoral delights at Bologna, with springs, sweet-smelling herbs, pepper, mushrooms, garlic and honey, and gifts of roes ('silvestres capreas') and lynx-hides. He gives the poem a nightfall close, conventional even in Virgil. A scholiast rapidly got to work on the eclogue to explain its allegorical potentialities; whether Giovanni intended all of them is perhaps a different matter, though his mind does seem to have worked in that way. The *juvenci*, *agnae* and *capellae* with which Giovanni is occupied at the opening are explained as being three ages or orders of scholars; and even the mushrooms become 'dicta antiquorum magistrorum'.[54]

It was about a year before the reply came, again in eclogue form. Giovanni received it after Dante's death, and it is possible that he did not write it himself: it is described within the poem itself as having been overheard by Iolas (used elsewhere for Guido da Polenta) and written down by an intermediary – 'Ille quidem nobis et nos tibi Mopse poimus' (97). Both Boccaccio and the scholiast accept it as Dante's work, however. At midday, Tityrus and Alphesiboeus withdraw to the shade of a grove; Meliboeus arrives with Giovanni's eclogue, but as he raises his pipe to his lips to repeat it the pipe sings it of its own accord. Alphesiboeus warns Tityrus against taking up the invitation, foreseeing that nature will mourn for his absence as it would a death:

Te juga te saltus nostri te flumina flebunt
absentem,   (IV.57–8)

Our mountain-ridges, lowland pastures and rivers will lament your absence

– the lines are an echo of Virgil (I.39–40), and are themselves echoed even more clearly in nature's lament over Lycidas:

Thee, shepherd, thee the woods and desert caves
With wild thyme and the gadding vine o'ergrown
And all their echoes mourn.

It may be a coincidence, but it is not inconceivable that Milton could have seen a manuscript of the poems on his visit to Italy (they were not printed until the eighteenth century). Tityrus is principally discouraged from going by the thought of Polyphemus, Robert of Naples; and the poem ends, like Giovanni's, with nightfall. This poem illustrates a problem that recurs frequently in Petrarch's eclogues: it is often difficult to square the geography of Italy or the political situation with the pastoral disguise. Dante does at least have the justification that his eclogues are written as epistles, letters in pastoral form in a clearly understood personal and historical context, and the allegory follows from this. Dante has enough sympathy for the mode to make the poems pleasant reading quite apart from any questions of interpretation. Giovanni saw them as a great achievement, and he made a special reference to them in the poem he intended as Dante's epitaph.[55]

Petrarch's eclogues, written mostly in 1346–50 and polished up for the neat copy he made in 1357,[56] are an entirely different matter from Dante's. They are very difficult poems indeed, not because of the quality of the poetry itself but because of the complexity of the subject-matter covered by the thick disguise of pastoral allegory – a complexity that continually strains the pastoral mode beyond any previously recognized limits. Where Dante is supremely in control of the mode, Petrarch gives the impression of being all but overwhelmed by it. The problem of interpretation is crucial for these poems; the commentators (among them that indefatigable interpreter of texts, Benvenuto da Imola) set to work in Petrarch's own lifetime, and devoted an enormous amount of time and effort to explaining the master. The obscurity was entirely intentional. For Petrarch, allegory was the essence of pastoral; allegory so cryptic that the meaning was held entirely in the poet's own mind, so that not even initiates could understand it completely without his assistance: 'The nature of this kind of poetry is such that, unless it is expounded by the same man who composed it, the meaning can perhaps be guessed but it is impossible to understand it all.'[57] He never suggests that this definition of pastoral is a new development. His personal copy of the *Bucolics* contains an autograph commentary of his own on the first eclogue, interlined with it, consisting of the same kind of word by word allegorical explication that his own commentators provided for him.[58] Petrarch's work is the logical conclusion of the whole mediaeval tendency to pastoral allegory exemplified by John of Garland. Boccaccio was never so extreme in his interpretation of the mode, perhaps because his first stimulus to pastoral was not Petrarch but Dante; he made an effort to continue the genre of pastoral correspondence with Cecco di Mileto, and one of the principal manuscripts of Dante's eclogues is in his own hand. He also had the advantage of knowing the minor Classical ecloguists, as Petrarch did not—at least until after he had finished his *Bucolicum Carmen*. Petrarch's work influenced him deeply, however, when he came into contact with it in 1350, and he revised his earlier eclogues accordingly and made his later ones more obscure. He never doubted the essentially allegorical nature of pastoral, and when he described the history of the eclogue he expressed it entirely in terms of the degree of further meaning admitted by various poets.

> Theocritus, a poet of Syracuse, was the first, we are told by ancient writers, to develop the pastoral mode in Greek poetry, and he intended nothing beyond what the outer meaning of the words conveyed. After him Virgil wrote in Latin, but he concealed some further meanings beneath the surface, though he did not invariably want us to understand anything else under the names of his characters. After him others also wrote, but they are

insignificant and not worthy of attention [presumably he does not count Dante's eclogues as his major works], with the exception of my famous teacher Francis Petrarch, who has raised the style a little above what is usual and who continually gives his speakers significant names according to the subjects of his eclogues. Of these writers I have followed Virgil, in that I have not always been concerned to conceal a further meaning in all my characters' names.[59]

Virgil might have recognized himself as little in Boccaccio's work as in any other mediaeval eclogues, but it is true that Boccaccio never goes in for Petrarch's extreme mystification. He did not condemn it either: it is one of the matters that was on his mind when he came to write on poetry in Book XIV of the *Genealogia Deorum*, and he devotes a whole chapter to the thesis that 'poetic obscurity is not to be condemned'. Petrarch's eclogues become the test case for the justification of poetry as being deeply meaningful, as he argues that 'it is foolish to believe that poets do not mean to convey anything beyond the outer shell of their stories':

> Who would be so crazy as to think that that most famous and Christian gentleman, Francis Petrarch...spent as many sleepless nights, as many pious meditations, as many hours, days and years as we can rightly believe to have been expended, if we think the seriousness of his Bucolics, its poetic richness, its carefully-devised beauty of words, exist to represent Gallus beseeching Tyrhenus for instruction in playing the pipes, or Pamphylus and Mitio and others quarrelling with each other to be merely ranting shepherds?[60]

– whereas in fact they are concerned respectively with the nature of poetic inspiration and the state of the Church. Pastoral, according to this point of view, is no longer the humblest form of poetry but an esoteric medium of highly wrought art.

It follows from this interpretation of the pastoral mode that the break with the actual shepherd world is complete: Petrarch at least does not allow anyone resembling a realistic herdsman to make an appearance in his work. As Boccaccio says, he raises low style, beyond what was usual; and he accordingly also leaves behind low subject-matter. The shepherds who appear in his eclogues are popes and cardinals, personifications of the papal curia, of aspiring poets, of the great Italian families; and the shepherds they in turn refer to are contemporary monarchs or great figures from the past such as Julius Caesar and Cicero. Pastoral becomes almost indistinguishable from the heroic. There had been a tendency in the late Classical era to identify the three works of Virgil with the contemplative, sensual and active lives, and the equation of pastoral and contemplative in particular was fully developed later; but Petrarch's shepherds never pause to meditate. The place of Petrarchan bucolic is in the thick of every controversy, or thundering condemnation of every contemporary abuse. He himself seems never to have felt the deep attraction of the pastoral world. He apparently thought of the literal herdsman's life as distasteful, arduous and hazardous – he speaks of the risks the shepherd runs of encountering all sorts of nasty accidents while searching for stray animals,[61] and the bad shepherd Mitio of his sixth eclogue feels a disgust for the tasks of sheepkeeping that has the ring of conviction. These lines illustrate Petrarch's complex attitude to pastoral as well as any. Mitio (who represents Pope Clement VI) rejects the Good Shepherd's teaching,

> semperque in fontibus egras
> Mersat oves, tondere iubens, ne vellera lappe
> Intricent, prohibens ipsis a sepibus hircos, (VI.187–9)

and how he should always dip the diseased sheep in running water, ordering them to be shorn lest their fleeces get entangled with goose-grass, and keeping the goats from the hedges.

The passage, inevitably, has in fact nothing to do with the herdsman's activities, as Benvenuto explains: 'Christ always commands that prelates should busy themselves with their cure of souls, and He orders the sick little ones – that is, sinners – to be frequently dipped in virtues; and Christ Himself orders those same sinners to be shorn...keeping away lascivious goats and driving them from the doors of the Church.'[62] The pastoral metaphor is never for a single word an end in itself, always the medium of some other greater concern.

Boccaccio's approach to the mode, as he himself acknowledged, is rather more relaxed. The first two poems of his *Bucolicum Carmen* are not allegorical at all; they are tales of shepherd love modelled on Virgil, an exercise that rather embarrassed him later when he had moved on to higher things. They were written before any of Petrarch's, and were not susceptible to the Petrarchan revision he inflicted on his later compositions. Even his more obscure allegories retain some links with the countryside, often stronger than in these two wearisomely artificial poems. The account in his tenth eclogue of the shepherd Micon's activities, which include milking the ewes, dipping and shearing the sheep and music-making,[63] is particularly striking, but the immediate stimulus to this passage is a similar account in Calpurnius' fifth eclogue. Boccaccio will only write in this way when the subject-matter is sufficiently picturesque to be compatible with learned poetic; and his descriptions of shepherd hardship, like Petrarch's, always have political implications. Just how far Boccaccio is from anything approximating to a real peasant is indicated by a passage in his hymn on the life of Christ in Ecloga XI, *Pantheon*, where Glaucus

> cantabat odoros
> pastores puero portantes thura sabeos
> advenisse quidem celeris ad presepia passu,
> sydere dante viam montana per ardua claro, (173–6)

sang how the shepherds came with swift step to the manger bearing fragrant incense of Saba, a bright star showing the way over high mountains.

Even in this context shepherds cannot be allowed to represent themselves: these are the Magi, the kings; the heroic, not the humble. The passage is a measure of the distance between this extreme of bucolic and vernacular pastoral. There the Bethlehem herdsmen are the culmination and justification of the shepherd life; here they could be nothing but an embarrassment.

The subjects both poets chose for their eclogues follow from their allegorical conception of pastoral. Petrarch was the great innovator in theme; Boccaccio followed him closely in his choice of political material, but he never indulges in Petrarch's extended virulent attacks on the Church. The themes that would usually be expected in pastoral have little or no place in their work. Country life is virtually excluded because they are not in the least concerned with the countryside; anything so low would mar the deadly seriousness they inflicted on the eclogue form. Love would be an unworthy subject for the same reason, and Boccaccio dismisses his first two eclogues as valueless. When Laura makes her appearance in Petrarch's eclogues she has very little of the woman left about her. She is poetic glory, the laurel crown, poetry itself, even Love in the abstract, and she is described through hyperbole and paradox that surpass even the *Rime* and that are designed to define her as something beyond the human. There is nothing of pastoral idyllicism in any of their eclogues; the setting is the fallen world in an age of war and plague, and even Boccaccio's two love-poems describe suffering rather than fulfilment. The themes of the Golden Age, as an ethical or an erotic ideal, and of the value of the simple life are also generally absent; and the concept of the good shepherd makes its only positive appearance in Mitio's scorn for the whole idea. Nevertheless, these themes are so much an essential part of the pastoral tradition that their very absence is intended to shock the reader. Once the conventions of any genre – whether eclogue, romance or novel – are sufficiently clearly established and widely known, any departure from them becomes a deliberate act, and their omission as significant as their inclusion. Pastoral should present an ideal world, the shepherd ought to care for his flock; and the conditions of distress that prevail in fourteenth-century Italy are a damning indictment of Church and State.

There is a group of three eclogues in Boccaccio's work, the fourth, fifth and sixth, that shows this process at work particularly clearly, because for almost the only time in the work of either poet the idealism against which the pastoral world of the first two poems should be judged does finally become explicit in the third. They are all concerned with the condition of Naples, 'which state, in keeping with pastoral tradition, I call a "grove"'[64] – a pastoral tradition, he might add, derived on slender authority from Dante. As humanist eclogues go, these poems are comparatively straightforward, though the political situation they refer to was convoluted in the extreme. Louis of Taranto had fled from Naples after an attack by Louis of Hungary in 1347–8; his opponent was himself forced to withdraw by the onslaught of the Black Death, and the exiled leader returned later that year. In the fourth eclogue Boccaccio describes how Dorus, the fleeing prince, is offered a refuge in the pastoral world by Montanus, but the refuge, as he admits, is not particularly desirable. It is a life of hardship, not ease; the shepherds are suffering from the oppression of Poliphemus (Louis of Hungary), who kills the lambs, strips bare the trees and fleeces the sheep. The following poem recounts a lament, in which the dead or dying landscape is contrasted with the peace and prosperity of the Golden Age – not so much the Classical version as the just and wise rule of Tytirus, Robert of Naples, who had died in 1343. (He had not looked so good in his lifetime: he was Dante's Polyphemus, taking the rôle of the tyrant that Boccaccio gives to Louis of Hungary.) Now the flocks and shepherds alike are scattered and killed by the plague. The sixth eclogue, the one panegyric of these cycles, was written to celebrate the return of Louis of Taranto under the name of Alcestus; that Boccaccio managed to break out of the death-and-destruction pattern at all is probably due here to his use of Calpurnius' first eclogue, the poem Modoin drew on to eulogize Charlemagne. Boccaccio promises the return of the Golden Age of justice,

Astream silvis revocavit abactam, (VI.109)

He has recalled the exiled Astraea to the woods,

and prophesies that Alcestus' deeds will be inscribed on the trees for future ages to read. Petrarch's own avoidance of panegyric is not due to total political disillusionment; he just prefers to stress the dark side of life, where Boccaccio balances the two. The nearest he comes to genuine eulogy – and just how far away he still is is illustrated by the examples themselves – is in his second eclogue, which recounts a lament for the good and admirable ruler Argus (Robert of Naples again) and for the landscape which is lapsing into chaos from its former glory; and the fifth, which he sent to Cola di Rienzo to congratulate him on his assumption of power in Rome in 1347, but where his enthusiasm for the new regime is subordinated to his disgust at the selfish faction-fighting that had preceded it. The situation cries out for panegyric; Petrarch provides a satire.

Petrarch's two bitterly anti-ecclesiastical eclogues, the sixth and seventh, are an even more striking example of how unstated but conventional pastoral values can be brought into play to affect the argument, though here they act purely negatively: there is scarcely any positive statement of the ideal to redress the balance. The two eclogues probably started their existence as a single poem; the 'plot' is continuous from one to the other. The sixth, *Pastorum Pathos*, is a dialogue between Mitio (Clement VI) and Pamphilus, St. Peter. Pamphilus' opening line suggests the theme of the poem, of responsibility neglected and social ills:

> Quis nemus omne vagis lacerandum prebuit hircis?

> *Who has given over the woods to be despoiled by straying goats?*

The goats' nibbling trees, especially vines, was a perpetual concern of shepherds: Mantuan's have to prevent it, pictures of herdsmen from Giotto onwards often include it as a detail of the background, and it appears in one of the illustrations in the *Kalender of Shepherdes*[65] (in the woodcut to Spenser's 'February' the goat is unnaturalistically replaced by a cow). Besides this, Petrarch's readers would already have discovered that neither groves nor goats are what they seem: here they are the Church and the cardinals. Mitio mocks at Pamphilus' appearance in an aside, rather like a stage Vice, and he certainly does appear rather odd: he is clutching a rock and a formidable key, *nodosa repagula*, for the purpose of identification (a rare concession from Petrarch), as if he were in a stained-glass window or a dramatic procession.[66] In any case, Mitio finds a shepherd's tasks much too wearisome to be receptive to anything the saint might have to say – 'Pastorum sors dura nimis!' None the less he greets Pamphilus fawningly, only to hear further accusations. There is nothing of pastoral harmony or content about the countryside the saint describes, and the passage depends on the reader's consciousness of the distance between the ideal and the actual.

> Cui grex pascendus in herba?
> Intempestivis perierunt mortibus agni;
> Defessi periere boves, hircique supersunt,
> Immundique sues, quos luxus et otia tendunt.   (VI.25–8)

> *Whose flock is to graze on the grass? The lambs have died unseasonable deaths, the oxen have perished exhausted, and there survive the goats and foul swine swollen with debauchery and sloth.*

Pastoral *otium*, the idyllic state of leisure, is taken to an extreme approaching deadly sin – a theme picked up again later. Mitio's speech of defence again relies on the reader's consciousness, not only of the duties of the good shepherd and the idea of pastoral peace, but of the temperate climate of the Golden Age.

> Te forte magistro,
> Segnior haud gregibus mors ac lupus ingruat albis?
> Nequicquam baculoque minax vultuque venires;
> Nil tibi tristis hiems (quanquam cessura rigori
> Illa tuo), nil ver dubium, nil morbidus auster,
> Nil tibi de proprio violenta remitteret estas. (38–43)

> *Perhaps if you were in charge death would come more slowly on the white flocks or the wolf be slower to attack? It would be no use your coming and threatening with your crook and pulling faces; sad winter would yield nothing of its severity to you (although it may be surpassed by your own), nor would the uncertain spring, nor the fever-laden south wind, nor fierce summer.*

Pamphilus points out that he was once a shepherd, under Nereus, Nero. Mitio concedes this, with a sharp reminder as to what happened to the flock of the faithful then. Pamphilus justifies himself on the grounds that he sent the fleeces to his master (the theme of the shepherd being worthy of his hire, a perpetually recurring motif of Good Shepherd pastoral), and asks whether Mitio can say as much. He replies,

> Servo aurum, teneris quod compensavimus agnis, (62)

> *I store up gold, with which we make up for the young lambs*

(a reference, Benvenuto says, to the sale of high ecclesiastical posts to young children), and once again the pastoral tradition is brought in as a silent witness to the ethical values of the care of the flock, and, even more, simplicity. A herdsman should have nothing to do with gold. That Mitio should deck his wife with jewels, as he boasts, is not the duty of a shepherd; it represents a total inversion of values. To lie at ease with her in the shade is no longer a sign of pastoral content but a flagrant dereliction of responsibility. Their freedom from care, taking no thought for the morrow, becomes an ugly parody:

> Sedeo iaceoque supinus,
> Multa canens que dictat amor, nec crastina curans;
> Commissique gregis ludos et prelia cerno. (78–80)

> *I sit or lie back, singing of many things as love dictates, and taking no thought for the morrow; I look on at the games and battles of the flock in another's charge.*

The tasks of sheepkeeping are all thoroughly distasteful too; though his list of them only serves to show up his own lack of care. It is the same contrast, only more extreme, between the two views of the shepherd's life that Spenser uses in his ecclesiastical eclogues, especially 'May'. The seventh poem, *Grex Infectus et Suffectus*, continues the same themes in a dialogue between Mitio and his *amica* Epy, who stands for the papal curia at Avignon. The main subject here is the appointment of a new group of cardinals, characterized as usual as goats and with a particularly nasty assemblage of goatish vices; but the wretched condition of the flock is again mentioned, a reference to the Black Death as well as their spiritual state, and the motif of *vitae summa brevis*, touched on in the previous eclogue, becomes increasingly important. Elsewhere for Petrarch, and for Boccaccio, the mutability of the pastoral world is a motive for seeking God; here the Church itself is shown as having no such consciousness. Epy declares that their love can never end –

> Nulla dies, Mitio, nostros abrumpat amores   (VII.4)

– a line cynical both in the pastoral context and when set against Pamphilus' veiled warning of the Second Coming at the end of the previous poem. Mitio does indeed feel the threat of time, but he is determined to forget all such considerations in pleasure.

> Quid non longa rapit, seclis fugientibus, etas?...
> Ludere consilium, nec euntis temporis horam
> Perdere segnitie, curasque repellere inanes.   (80, 83–4)

> *What does time not at length seize as the years slip away? My advice is to take pleasure, not to waste the present moment of passing time doing nothing, and to drive away imaginary worries.*

The spiritual leaders, the Church itself, are entirely limited to this world; their attempt to ignore time is a mockery of poignant pastoral bliss, poignant because mortal, and a bitter indictment of their failure to look to eternity.

Boccaccio makes use of the same motif of time, though without the complications of ecclesiastical satire, in his fifteenth eclogue, *Phylostropos*, the last apart from the dedicatory poem. The subject is the conversion from love of earthly to love of heavenly things; more specifically, the speakers, Phylostropus and Typhlus, represent Petrarch and Boccaccio themselves. The poem opens strikingly as Phylostropus speaks of the approach of winter:

> Lusimus et sertis nimium nymphisque vacatum est;
> instat hyemps...   (XV.1–2)

> *Our play is over and the abundance of garlands and nymphs has gone; winter is upon us...*

Typhlus at first ignores his warnings, preferring to see winter as part of the cyclical movement of the seasons, to be dissolved by spring, but his friend insists on the fragility of all things mortal.

> Rapit omnia tempus:
> quas Amon vestit silvas, denudit Orion,
> et sub sole cadit quicquid sub sole creatum est.   (147–9)

> *Time snatches away all things: the woods that Amon clothes are stripped by Orion, and whatever was created beneath the sun dies beneath the sun.*

The only place of refuge is Heaven, and with Typhlus given strength by Soter (who redeemed the pastoral world with his blood, 'qui sanguine silvas/ infectosque greges pridem purgavit' (139–40)) the two set off together toward the light. Both Boccaccio and Petrarch make an absolute distinction between the world of pastoral and Heaven. In a number of vernacular works, it is in pastoral that the frontiers of earth and Heaven overlap; for the early humanists, the pastoral world is mortal, liable to misery and corruption, even, in Petrarch, evil in itself. Petrarch raises the issue in his very first eclogue, a dialogue between himself, the poet wandering in the hostile world, and Monicus, his brother Gherardo, who summons him to salvation within monastery walls. There can be no security in the setting of the pastoral landscape. The quality of the real world preserved most consistently in the pastoral metaphor of the Petrarchan eclogue is its mortality, even its taint of original sin. When Boccaccio does describe a pastoral Heaven it never merges with its earthly image, as it begins to do in the *Roman de la Rose* or some of the mystery plays. The passage comes in the fourteenth eclogue, *Olympia*, and is spoken by Olympia herself, the soul of his dead child Violante. She describes a mountain that belongs to the tradition of literary paradises – the tradition of Lactantius' home of the phoenix or Alan of Lille's *sedes Naturae*:

Est in secessu pecori mons invius aegro,   (XIV.170)

Far away there is a mountain, inaccessible to sickly flocks,

– and even in that opening line the separation of the place from the corrupt earthly shepherd world is made clear. It has the temperateness of the Golden Age associated with Paradise, and here too at last is freedom from mortality, corruption and disease. It is ruled by Archesilas, who holds in his lap a Lamb on which the inhabitants of the place feed. He is surrounded by worshipping bands of garlanded satyrs (representing angels – the pastoral metaphor begins to get confused at this juncture), of martyrs and innocents. Olympia describes how she herself was taken to Parthenos, the Virgin, 'the shepherds' sure hope of salvation' (252), who in her turn is worshipped by fauns and nymphs. The bliss of the innocents themselves is described in pastoral terms:

Nos pueri legimus flores factisque corollis
cingimus intonsos crines letisque choreis
ambimus silvam fontes rivosque sonoros.   (263–5)

We children pick flowers and make them into garlands to set on our flowing hair; and in joyful bands we wander around the woods, the springs and the rushing rivers.

But this is not the pastoral world exalted to a divine plane. The eclogue had opened with an idyllic dawn, but this is itself the beginning of the divine vision, not the usual state of the world. The earth is a place of tears and mourning. Sylvius, Boccaccio himself, tries to offer his daughter the pleasant life of the *Bucolics*:

Nos omnes teget illa domus, somnosque quietos
herba dabit viridis, cespesque sub ylice mensam;
vitreus is large prestabit pocula rivus;
castaneas mites et poma recentia nobis
rustica silva feret, teneros grex fertilis edos
lacque simul pressum,   (133–8)

That lodging will house us all, the green grass will give us quiet sleep and the turf beneath the holm-oak will be our table; this glassy river will provide us liberally with drink, the country woods will furnish us with soft chestnuts and fresh apples, the fertile flock with young kids and cheese;

but the delicate simplicity of such a life can have no appeal to one who has enjoyed the eternal spring of Heaven. Olympia tells her father how to reach the mountain, then vanishes, leaving him plunged into yet deeper unhappiness at losing her a second time.

The Virgilian pattern of elegy, of lament balanced by celebration, is used twice by Petrarch, and his example helped to make it one of the most important pastoral forms of the Renaissance. His tenth and eleventh eclogues are an attempt to come to terms with Laura's death in the course of the great plague. His emotional reaction, his desperate grief, are given expression in the *Rime*; in his bucolics she maintains her rôle as a symbol, and a symbol almost totally dissociated from the woman herself. The subject of the tenth eclogue, *Laurea Occidens*, is the nature of the forces that made him a poet, and it consists principally of a wearisome list of all his Classical reading (described allusively, as usual); but the central image is the laurel itself, symbol of his poetic inspiration, which has been torn down by storms. He is reassured at the end, and his continuance as a poet guaranteed, by being told that it has in fact been taken by the gods and planted in the Elysian fields. The following poem, *Galathea*, is again patterned as lament and comfort, but the detail of the structure is unusual. It opens with two sisters coming to Galathea's tomb, one, Niobe, lamenting, the other, Fusca, trying to restrain her. Niobe celebrates Galathea as the most beautiful being created by Nature, as outshining the sun, and yet now reduced to nothing. Fusca at last calls on her to stop:

> Nempe hesterna dies ulla nequit arte reverti;
> Mors adimit curas, mors omnia vincla resolvit. (XI.47–8)

> *The past day cannot possibly be recalled by any art. Death takes away troubles, death loosens all bonds.*

This cynicism is broken by the appearance of Fulgida, 'bright Reason that drives away grief',[67] coming to restore the just balance in the mind from Niobe, the spirit overcome with sorrow, and Fusca, total disillusionment, the mind unenlightened by faith or hope. She blames them on two grounds: that Galathea's mortality was the seed of immortality, and that love is not destroyed by loss. Galathea, leaving the beauty of her mortal body in the clutch of death,

> Libera iamque polos et regia tecta tonantis
> Ipsa quidem superumque choros mensasque frequentat...
> Nuda, domum repetens, e carcere fugit amato. (79–80, 88)

> *Now she is released to dwell in the heavens and the royal palaces of the Thunderer; she attends the joyful assemblies of the gods and has a place at their table...Naked, seeking its home, her spirit fled from its beloved prison.*

Niobe, understanding at last, responds,

> Nuda quidem minime, quam gloria vestit, (89)

> *Not naked at all, for glory clothes her.*

There is no question now of forgetting Galathea: her name will continue to be the source of poetic inspiration, the poetry itself that will make the stars leave their places and the bees their honey.

The differences between Petrarch's approach to Laura's death here and Paschasius' to Adalhard's are typical of the changes that the pastoral mode itself had undergone. It is possible that Petrarch knew the *Ecloga Duarum Sanctimonialium* – if he did, the contrast is all the more striking. For Paschasius, the Christian promise of Heaven provided a cause for rejoicing even at a time of sorrow; it is not that lamentation is a wrong response, but that something greater, beyond the human sphere, has been offered. In Petrarch's eclogue, the whole drama is played out in the mind, as it moves from darkness to illumination. There is certainly psychological validity in this presentation – the same development, from the initial response to death as resentment and grief that cannot see beyond themselves to the recovery of reason and its reminder of faith, is described lyrically and intensely in the *Rime* – but Petrarch has none of Paschasius' detachment. Niobe and Fusca, as their names indicate, are wrong, and can never be anything else because they are personifications of bad qualities: Fusca has to drop out of the poem altogether once enlightenment has come. Petrarch cannot for a moment cease to write polemic. It is at the basis of every one of his eclogues on whatever subject, not only in the poems of political or ecclesiastical comment but here in what purports to be a lament for the death of his lady. The lament is itself part of the disguise. Laura is not the true subject, as a woman or as poetic inspiration; the basis of the poem is ethical, and Galathea is little more than the image around which the moral meaning of the work is arranged. She is a necessary symbol of the aim of human aspiration, but the polemical structure of the piece is finally of more importance. There is a quality of foregone conclusion about practically all of these eclogues, Boccaccio's as well as Petrarch's; and the fact that this quality is shared by John of Garland's *carmen bucolicon* and the *Ecloga Theoduli* indicates that this interpretation of the genre was not a new development in the fourteenth century. The basis of the eclogue is no longer idyll, but contention. The move from singing-match to *conflictus* shows the same shift; the centre of attention passes from the quality of the poetry to the quality of the argument. The only attempt at a singing-match in the fourteenth-century eclogue cycles, in Boccaccio's *Laurea* (XIII), is a contest between a shepherd-poet and a shepherd-merchant as to which occupation is the more worthwhile. The Classical trappings, the offering of prizes and so on, are altogether subordinate to the argument. Boccaccio may have set out initially to write a singing-match rather than to argue the rival causes of commerce and the arts, but he cannot release the pastoral form from its associations with polemic in order to return to pure poetry. Most of the eclogues of both poets, in fact, read as if they were an extension of the concept of a debate. There is always a cause at stake, and the dialogue form of the poems arranges itself naturally into proposer and opponent, thesis and antithesis. The syllogism is very seldom completed, however: Petrarch in particular makes one side carry the full moral significance of each poem. Where the moral emphasis is not so clear-cut, as in Monicus' appeal to him in his first eclogue to abandon poetry for the monastic life or in Boccaccio's singing-match, the issue is usually left unresolved.

It is a characteristic of vernacular pastoral of the late Middle Ages that it should pass very easily into social comment and criticism. In the Petrarchan eclogue this tendency is fully realized: the primary purpose of pastoral is as a vehicle for ethical, political or ecclesiastical comment. The developments in Latin and the vernaculars, although more or less contemporary, appear not to be directly related; they depend primarily on the inherent tendency of pastoral to call out its opposite – just as the pastoral mode itself is the product of a courtly or urban society. Early mediaeval Latin pastoral had moved towards allegory and argument, but Petrarch's use of the genre for criticism and satire was an innovation that was to have an extensive influence in the Renaissance, especially with the support it received from the vernacular tradition. The main difference between the kinds of criticism expressed in the two traditions is that the vernacular, with its insistent realism, tends to concentrate on moral and social matters of universal concern such as would affect the countryside, matters such as oppression, economic decline and the effects of war, while the Petrarchan eclogue is concerned with higher political considerations, faction-fighting, rebellions and deaths, recriminations against the cardinals *en masse* and individually. Vernacular writers talk about the bad priest, Petrarch about the bad Pope. Petrarch sets himself up as the conscience of Europe; the vernacular shepherds speak with the voice of the suffering Common Man. The commons, if they appear in Petrarch at all, are not shepherds but sheep. There is, however, no absolute distinction between the two types, and by the fifteenth century Petrarchan pastoral was occasionally affecting the vernacular tradition directly; it was not always so great a jump. Where Petrarch does stand alone is in the almost totally pessimistic view of life he puts across in his eclogues, untouched by Dante's gently humorous sophistication or the vernacular idealism. The *Bucolics* themselves are not entirely idyllic, but he takes his themes far beyond anything justifiable by Classical imitation or authority. It is in the nature of the Petrarchan world to be perpetually on the brink of disaster, suffering from attack, death, papal misgovernment, neglect, disloyalty, or, when poetry is the subject, lack of appreciation. The very ideas of the Good Shepherd and the Golden Age are used to show up how deeply the fallen world is embedded in corruption.

The subjects chosen by Petrarch and Boccaccio as being suitable for pastoral – poetry itself, elegies, matters of contemporary interest – are not so very different from those of Virgil or the Carolingians in outline, but the mode itself had travelled a long way in the course of the centuries. The shepherd world itself is interpreted in a highly specialized sense; and although it reflects the complexities of life and society, it does not provide a simple image – the pastoral metaphor, in fact, can become merely an additional complicating factor in an obscurely allusive and closely-textured poem. Allegory is not a resonance behind the poetry but its very fabric. The eclogue genre, always scholarly, is now arcane. There is nothing left of the idyll or of anything remotely escapist: the place of the pastoral is in the thick of every contemporary controversy. The Petrarchan eclogue is the end of a development: it could be imitated – unfortunately it was – but not taken further. He had a succession of followers in the fourteenth century, none approaching him in poetic merit, but occasionally (for lack of commentators) managing to pass him in cryptic obscurity.[68] Many of their works are now lost. The stimulus did not last long, however; and the dead hand of allegory very nearly killed the genre. The only possible advance was to go backwards, even to start again – to rediscover the Virgil who was an idyllic shepherd-poet after the manner of the newly-found Theocritus, not an intellectual obscurantist. It took a hundred years before the fresh air of the Renaissance made such a reading possible, and even then this interpretation of the eclogue was still only one of several now facing the poet. Petrarch remained one of the key influences on Renaissance pastoral. The limitations of subject-matter exemplified by Virgil and implied in stylistic theory were broken – if not for good and all, at least for three centuries. Petrarch was the first man to realize that pastoral could be used as a weapon in matters concerning the highest human institutions, Church and State.

II

THE VERNACULAR TRADITIONS

The most striking thing about the vernacular pastoral tradition in the Middle Ages is that it is about shepherds – a subject that even Theocritus had treated with caution, Virgil largely avoids, Petrarch and Pope never dream of. The Latin eclogue was getting further and further from anything resembling a real herdsman, but French and English writers took the realistic shepherd and saw in him a subject of enormous artistic potential. He was interesting in himself; and he could be made the symbol of the simple or the good life, of the teacher, the priest or the prince, the lover, Man, Christ Himself. The shepherd's first task is to look after his sheep – a point not immediately gathered from the *Bucolics* – and the pastoral ideal is therefore an image not of withdrawal from the world but of social responsibility. The basis for metaphor in this context is the realistic shepherd, not a literary theory. The duties of the good shepherd are literal before they are allegorical; if Christ told Peter to feed His sheep, Peter's successor has a range of duties coextensive with those of the actual herdsman. The realism does not in the least mean that shepherds are confined to their existence as peasants – a condition far less interesting to the mediaeval mind than the modern, and which has little or nothing to do with pastoral.[1] It became increasingly rare to write about shepherds in the Middle Ages without having them trailing clouds of further meanings. The commonest and best known type of shepherd literature, the pastourelle, is most often just light-hearted fantasy; but the very earliest surviving vernacular pastourelles, the two by the Provençal troubadour Marcabru,[2] are in this respect already fully pastoral: the shepherd world is being used to provide an objective viewpoint outside courtly society and critical of it, and the starting point is the figure of the more or less realistic shepherdess. What are now accepted as the basic concepts of pastoral – the contrast of country life with the court or city, the presentation of a simplified image of society or ideas – were handed down to the Renaissance not through John of Garland or Petrarch, nor even primarily through Mantuan, but through other genres that are none the less truly pastoral for having no direct connection with Classical bucolic. The very fact that the early Latin pastourelles do not show the same development towards pastoral significance is an indication of the specifically vernacular nature of this movement in its origins; but it was not long before poets in both traditions were recognizing their common ground. Vernacular poets who know Virgil will link their own work with the *Bucolics* as casually as John of Garland writes a pastourelle eclogue. The identity of the two was generally accepted by the Renaissance.

Realism is a relative concept, and this is especially true of mediaeval literary conventions compared with modern ones. To use a shepherd metaphorically – or to describe the shepherd world in isolation at all – is non-naturalistic; and the basically realistic treatment itself becomes an artistic convention. It is just these conventions that make it possible to talk about vernacular pastoral: writer after writer in the Middle Ages takes up the same essential subject, the shepherd, and treats him in essentially the same ways, consciously working in a literary tradition that cuts across all the usual generic classifications of mediaeval literature and culture into religious or secular, drama or lyric, romance, carol, homily, royal entry and so on. Pastoral, in fact, is operating in its distinctive way as a mode of thought or presentation, a particular optic on the world, which for the first time is not channelled through the eclogue alone but can be drawn on in any literary form. The contemporary French term for this kind of pastoral was *bergerie* – a word that itself embraces both the realistic and artistic aspects of the shepherd world. It can mean simply 'sheepkeeping'; it can be used as the collective term for shepherds or shepherd society; or it can have a more specific meaning within its larger literary sense, as a description of shepherd life, or as a pastoral morality play (the *bergerie moralisée*). Every work of *bergerie* shares in the same group of conventions, and it was through the development of these that it became a single coherent literary tradition with as much sense of its own identity as any more formal genre. The range of conventions was narrower in England than in France, apparently in reflection of actual conditions: shepherdesses appear scarcely to have been known – the first usages of the word are unequivocally courtly in context, and occur in writers closely familiar with French literature;[3] the climate does not lend itself to idyllic lyricism; wolves were known about principally from the Bible. There was none the less a common tradition of *bergerie* in England and France, working within the same conventions and growing out of the same concepts, and the two literatures belong together. As with so much literary history in the Middle Ages, England tended to follow where France led, and *bergerie* literature was never produced in the same quantity this side of the Channel; but it was not a question of poor imitation, or of translation. Pastoral was as much a native tradition in England as any of the literary forms this country shared with the continent, from the romance to rhyme itself, and it is treated with the same degree of independence.

Pastoral first appears within a few decades of the very beginnings of Provençal vernacular literature. Marcabru was writing around 1150; and pastourelles, probably of the simple love-adventure type, were composed even earlier – the Life of Cercamon, another early troubadour, notes that he 'made verses and pastourelles in the ancient manner',[4] a phrase that pushes their origins back beyond any surviving Provençal literature. The same kind of specifically pastoral use of the pastourelle such as Marcabru makes first occurs in French around 1200. The thirteenth century was the age of the great flowering of the French pastourelle; it also saw the first explicit connection of French pastoral with Latin by Jean de Meung in his continuation of the *Roman de la Rose* – a connection just a few years later than John of Garland's linking of the eclogue and pastourelle – and the first *bergerie* drama, Adam de la Halle's *Jeu de Robin et Marion*. There may perhaps have been shepherd plays in England too by 1300, though the earliest surviving texts are somewhat later. The most striking development in the fourteenth century in France was the elevation of the shepherd into an ideal, an image of the idyllic simple life set in explicit contrast to the court; and from this period onwards *bergerie* really came into its own, giving writers a very wide range of conventions to draw on – a width only exceeded in Elizabethan England. The fifteenth century opened with Christine de Pisan's delicate love-narrative the *Dit de la Pastoure*; 'Bucarius' – the name is presumably a pseudonym – completed his monumental pastoral allegory on the civil wars between the Burgundians and the Armagnacs, the *Pastoralet*, around 1422; the shepherd scenes of the Nativity plays reached their highest point in the *Passions* of Marcadé early in the century and Greban in 1452 and in the Rouen *Nativité* of 1474; *bergeries moralisées* were written in considerable numbers, and shepherds became increasingly common figures in street pageants and court entertainments. The court was fascinated by the herdsman; René of Anjou in particular was deeply attracted by the shepherd world, and he went so far as to produce the ultimate paradox, taken up by the Elizabethans too, of the pastoral tournament, the *Pas d'Armes de la Bergière* of 1449. English literature and entertainment, weak throughout the fifteenth century, never came near to matching this quantity or range of output: *bergerie* is thinly scattered among lyrics and poetic homilies, and even the great literary flowering of the reign of Richard II produced little apart from the metrical romance of *King Edward and the Shepherd*. English *bergerie* reaches its perfection, however, in the mystery plays, and in the work of the Wakefield Master in particular, whose shepherds represent the very best of the native English part of the tradition.[5] There is some *bergerie* literature from Scotland too: Henryson's delightful lyric of *Robene and Makyne*, from late in the fifteenth century, and a long shepherd scene in the prose *Complaynt of Scotlande*, written in the mid-sixteenth but entirely mediaeval in content and spirit. The progress of Renaissance culture from Italy northwards can almost be dated by the changes that occurred in the treatment of pastoral itself: the mid-fifteenth century in Italy, around 1530 in France, 1550 in England, even later in Scotland.

Mediaeval vernacular pastoral covers a large range of tones and themes, from the idyllic to the boorish, the mystic to the obscene; works written in only a small range from opposite ends of the spectrum may appear to have little in common, but they are all working within the same conventions. Rustic ignorance shades into innocence, the revel can degenerate into a brawl or be refined to an idyll, the portrayal of pastoral peace is only one step from the criticism of its disruption through social injustice or war. Almost every work touches on many others at some point of the spectrum, and it is these thematic connections – which are inevitably obscured by a chronological account of *bergerie* – that are especially interesting, both for what they show mediaeval writers used pastoral to do and for the use Renaissance poets made of them. It was a commonplace of mediaeval Biblical exegesis that a text could be interpreted on four levels. The details vary, but the most commonly accepted divisions were the literal, the allegorical or doctrinal, the moral (tropological), and the anagogical (the mystical, or concerned with the Four Last Things, Death, Judgement, Heaven and Hell):

> Littera gesta docet, quid credas allegoria,
> Moralis quid agas, quo tendas anagogia.[6]

Such detailed interpretation was consistently applied only to the Bible, and very few mediaeval allegories attempt more than one level beyond the literal at any one time; but the divisions do indicate the type and range of significance recognised in the Middle Ages, and the different treatment given to *bergerie* by different poets corresponds remarkably closely to this scheme. It must be emphasised that this is not due to my own choice of classification, nor to a deliberate attempt by the poets to write in accordance with a theory designed for something else; the analogy derives simply from a common way of looking at the world and at literature. This chapter will follow through each level in turn. First are the basic conventions themselves and various treatments of them; second, the rôle of the shepherd as teacher; third, allegory and metaphor growing out of these; and lastly, the supreme development of *bergerie* as it becomes an image of Heaven. In the literature itself the themes never appear as imposed classifications. They spring from the nature of the pastoral mode itself, and from the potentialities that mediaeval poets saw in the image of the shepherd world.

I. *The Conventions of* Bergerie

In 1379, the French king Charles V commissioned a treatise on the theory and practice of sheepkeeping from an experienced shepherd named Jehan de Brie. The original work is now lost, but a shortened version, entitled *Le Vray Régime et Gouvernement des Bergers et Bergères*, was printed in the early sixteenth century and went through many editions; it came to be known simply as *Le Bon Berger*.[7] It influenced the later Shepherds' Calendars, and parts were even transferred whole into some late editions of that work; but where the calendars are encyclopaedic, the *Bon Berger* keeps strictly to its subject of the shepherd. Much of the work is concerned with the herdsman's duties month by month, weather prediction, information about herbs, the recognition and cure of diseases; other sections describe the shepherd's clothing and equipment, his diet and his ideal character. The work offers a complete portrait of the mediaeval shepherd, drawn essentially from life; and it is a portrait that can be matched, or even given extra detail, by dozens of literary and artistic works that make no such direct claim to experience. The figure of the shepherd came to exercise such a hold on the imagination that the ordinary details of his life became a literary convention. The very fact that Charles should have shown an interest in sheepkeeping indicates the fascination the subject held.

Pastoral literature tends to concentrate on the hours when the shepherd is not directly concerned with his flocks, and this is true of the Middle Ages as of Classical and Renaissance works; but in *bergerie* literature his care for the sheep is never forgotten. The commonplace tasks that Mitio scorns in Petrarch provide a constant background to the vernacular tradition, French and English. If no work goes into quite such extensive detail on the herdsman's duties as Jehan de Brie gives, there are few that neglect them altogether. The Virgilian shepherd did little but fold his flock in the evening, the Biblical shepherd kept watch against wolves and searched for missing sheep; in addition, the mediaeval literary *berger* typically shears the animals, smears them with tar against the scab, shelters them from the worst of the weather and searches out good pasture. One of the most courtly French poems, Christine de Pisan's *Dit de la Pastoure*, written in 1403, gives an even more comprehensive list, including milking the ewes, making sure the lambs suck and changing the hay in the mangers.[8] Often the tasks are set out in detail as one shepherd instructs his younger companions – as happens at enormous length and on different subjects in the *Kalender of Shepherdes* itself. There are episodes of this kind in the *Pastoralet*,⁹ the Rouen *Nativité*,¹⁰ Jean Lemaire de Belges' elaborately artificial retelling of the story of Troy,¹¹ and in the 'prolixt orison' of the chief shepherd in the *Complaynt of Scotlande*¹² – though there the sheep themselves do not get a lot of space. According to Lemaire, the tasks of the young Paris (who was brought up as a shepherd after being exposed as the result of a prophecy that he would cause the fall of Troy) included making wicker hurdles for the sheepfolds and reed baskets for cheeses, and constructing the little wooden huts on wheels, 'logettes ou maisonettes', in which shepherds took shelter in the season when the flocks spent all their time in the open fields; these are illustrated occasionally in mediaeval paintings of shepherds, and in the Rouen *Nativité* a *logette* serves as a stage property and is finally presented to Christ by the shepherd who owns it. English works of *bergerie* do not go into the same detail on the herdsman's tasks, though the underlying sense of his care for his sheep is just as important. One of the characters in the Chester *Adoration of the Shepherds* declares,

> Ashamed am I not to showe
> No poynt that longeth to my crafte,¹³

though he keeps his account brief. The most detailed descriptions of sheep-keeping in English tend to be negative – to be a list of all the things that the bad shepherd (generally allegorical) fails to do or does wrongly, pastoral sins of omission and commission.

The shepherd's appearance is described with even more attention than his activities, and lists of his clothing and gear are a widespread commonplace of *bergerie* in the late fourteenth and the fifteenth century. Christine de Pisan's shepherds are equipped with crook and pouch, knife, shears, tarbox, awl and needle and thread – all items mentioned by Jehan de Brie; and other works go into still greater detail. Froissart's *Pastourelles* – pastoral *ballades* describes their nature better, since they have nothing to do with the love-adventure type of lyric – contain several such passages, and he also mentions the point stressed by Jehan that the smaller items of gear are attached to the belt.¹⁴ This close attention to fact extends into the *bergeries moralisées* as well, so that Foy, in the *Moralité de l'Alliance de Foy et Loyalté*, 'The Marriage of Faith and Troth', is characterized by his perfection as a herdsman:

> Vecy Foy, le pasteur soubtilh,
> qui poinchon at et escorgie,
> flieme et pannetiere laichie,
> waghe, iupilh et cappel gry,
> alesne, forche, aguyel et fy
> por ses soleir rataconneir,
> porueü, et sens plus parleir,
> de ce que pasteur doit auoir.¹⁵

> *Here is Faith, the skilful shepherd, who is equipped with punch and belt, scalpel, pouch with fastenings, leggings, tunic and grey hat, awl, shears, needle and thread for clouting his shoes, and to cut a long story short with everything the shepherd ought to have.*

Other standard items are added in the description of the shepherdess Loyalté that follows: she has a tarbox, bagpipe, flute and crook. Such detailed accounts are not confined to lengthy works: there are lyrics that seem to consist of little else.

Lés un bosket
Vi Robechon.
Mout y ot joli vallet;
Houziaus ot
Oins et chapiau vert, sourcot
Griset
Et chaperon.
Il n'estoit pas sans son chienet;
Fretel,
Coutel
Ot et baston;
Sounete avoit,
Son flaiol ot, si flaioloit.[16]

Beside a copse I saw young Robin. He was a very fine young man; he had boots of soft leather, a green hat, grey surcoat and hood. He was not without his dog; he had pipes, knife and staff; he had his bell and his flute, and he was playing on it.

There are few French mediaeval shepherds, in fact, however, casually mentioned, who do not have at least some of these properties; and the same convention of listing equipment existed in English. In the metrical romance of *King Edward and the Shepherd*, probably of the late fourteenth century, the shepherd Adam's gear for his visit to court is described in as much detail as the arming of a knight – which it might indeed be parodying:

In russet clothyng he tyret hym þo,	(*dressed; then*)
In kyrtil and in curtebye,	(*short cloak*)
And a blak furred hode	
þat wel fast to his cheke stode,	
þe typet myght not wrye.	
þe mytans clutt forgate he noʒt;	
þe slyng cumys not out of his thoʒt.[17]	

The 'mytans clutt' are perhaps home-made patchwork mittens of the kind Jehan describes; it is mentioned that they 'hang be his spayre' (869), presumably from his belt. His staff and hat, which he refuses to give up or remove even in the presence of the King, receive a special mention. Jolly Wat, of a carol written down in the early sixteenth century but possibly older, belongs to the same tradition:

The shepherd vpon a hill he satt;
He had on hym hys tabard and his hat,
His tarbox, hys pype and hys flagat.[18]

The action of this poem is so close to the Nativity plays of the mystery cycles that it seems likely that the description would apply to the way the shepherds were presented on stage. Wat also has a dog tied to his girdle, like Jehan's shepherd and many others in poetry and in art.

Artistic representations of shepherds generally work within the same convention of detailed realism, and literature and painting corroborate and illuminate each other. We know, for instance, that the *logette* tended to look more like a bathing-machine than a caravan; and the word *wages* (variously spelt), referring to an article of clothing worn somewhere below the waist – just where has puzzled the lexicographers – would seem from paintings to refer to the puttee-like leggings worn by many shepherds, the only distinctive item of dress to be repeatedly drawn. They are probably the same as the English 'cockers', mentioned as typical of the shepherd's clothing by Barclay and Drayton. Jehan de Brie mentions the shepherd's gloves; Arnoul Greban

Plate I

The Holkham Bible Picture-Book, B.M. MS Add. 47682 f. 13ʳ
(reproduced by permission of the British Library Board)

Plate II La Main Chaude (tapestry, Victoria and Albert Museum; reproduced by courtesy of the Trustees)

specifies that they are two-fingered mittens, a type illustrated in some Books of Hours and in the scene of the Annunciation to the Shepherds in the early fourteenth-century Anglo-Norman Holkham Bible Picture Book (Plate I).[19] Shepherds were a popular subject for art in both religious and secular contexts, especially in northern France and Flanders. One of the standard subjects for the illumination of Tierce in the Hours of the Virgin was the Annunciation to the Shepherds, and even in this context shepherds and shepherdesses are often portrayed in minute detail, with particular care being given to their musical instruments. Working within the same tradition but on an altogether larger scale is Hugo van der Goes' painting of the Adoration in the Uffizi, or the vast secular Flemish tapestry called 'La Main Chaude' (Plate II), dating from the early sixteenth century and now in the Victoria and Albert Museum, which shows a country game among shepherds and shepherdesses who are fully equipped with belts, pouches and the whole range of attachments – combs, shears, tarboxes, needlecases, a knife, recorders, even a rosary; and their crooks are lying on the ground beside them. The items most frequently mentioned in poetry and drama and portrayed in art of every kind – illuminations, tapestries, stained glass and altarpieces – are the crook, pouch, hat and bagpipe. The 'houlette' and 'pannetiere' were the shepherd's badge of office – Jehan compares the crook to the crozier or the scribe's pens as the shepherd's characteristic and essential tool. It may have been from this tradition that John of Garland derives the *baculus* for his Wheel of Virgil; he certainly did not get it from Virgil himself. These basic items were used as the distinguishing marks of the shepherd in pageants or entertainments such as René of Anjou's pastoral tournament, though there, as the poet who describes it has to admit, the *pastours jousteurs* hardly looked like shepherds because of their armour.[20] The shepherd's appearance was not subject to rapid changes of fashion: the equipment is necessary for the job, the clothes are designed for warmth and protection, in England as in France. The herdsmen in the Holkham Bible Picture-Book illustrate many of the features still characteristic of the shepherd several centuries later; the bagpipe is mentioned in twelfth-century pastourelles and seventeenth-century eclogues, the slope-brimmed sou'wester-shaped hats worn by two of the Holkham shepherds are listed by Jehan as vital for protection against rain, sun and cold. The hat even becomes one of the marks of the Good Shepherd in the *Pastoralet*:

> Bons bergiers, Michiel ou Michault,
> Ait chapel contre le grant chault
> D'esté et le grant froid d'yver, (5777-9)

> *The good shepherd, Michiel or Michault, will have a hat to guard against the great heat of summer and the great cold of winter;*

and it makes its appearance too in drama in England, when the Secundus Pastor of the Coventry *Pageant of the Shearmen and Taylors* presents his to Christ:

> Holde, take thow here my hat on thy hedde!
> And now off won thyng thow art well sped,
> For weddur thow hast noo nede to complayne,
> For wynd, ne sun, hayle, snoo and rayne.[21]

The Holkham shepherds themselves clearly have close connections with drama, even though the earliest surviving dramatic texts are so much later:

the caption to one picture of them has them attempting to imitate the angels' song, as the herdsmen do in many of the cycle plays, and presumably, like Jolly Wat, they illustrate the way the shepherds of the pageants would have been presented.

It is possible that both 'Jolly Wat' and 'Jolly Robin', and conceivably also 'Colin', were traditional names for the shepherd in England, as 'Robin' was in France. A Robin figures in the fragmentary lyric 'Joly cheperte of Aschell downe'; Henryson calls his shepherd Robin and his shepherdess Makyne. In 1447 a payment was made to 'ij ludentibus Joly Wat and Malkyn':[22] it sounds as if it might be a kind of English dramatic pastourelle. There are however no English names comparable in popularity with the French Robin and Marion, who appear in dozens of lyrics from the early thirteenth century onwards. Their companions too have conventional names: Aloris, Gombaut, Ysambert, Rifflart and Gautier (English 'Walter', 'Wat') for the men, Peronelle for a girl.

Jolly Wat carries two musical instruments; Jehan de Brie concludes his list of essential equipment with six, including two varieties of bagpipe. The mediaeval shepherd may not be cast as a poet, like Tityrus and Colin Clout, but he is an inveterate musician. Froissart describes the shepherd's accoutrements in these terms:

> Sacheaus trellis et panetiere
> Lacié au costé d'un cordel,
> Aloyere, bourse et coutel,
> Escorgies, boites aussi,
> Et cloquettes de Saint Remi,
> Pipes, canemeaus et flagos
> Et musettes à bourdons gros...
> Ongement à oindre brebis.[23]

> *A netted bag and pouch fastened on the side with a cord, wallet, purse and knife, leather belt, boots too, and St. Remi's bells, recorders, corn-pipes, flutes and bagpipes with large drones...tar to smear the sheep.*

The bells and bagpipes and corn-pipes are just as characteristic of the shepherd as the pouch or tarbox. Chaucer's only lines of *bergerie* spring out of the mention of musical instruments:

> Many flowte and liltyng horn,
> And pipes made of grene corn,
> As han thise lytel herde-gromes
> That kepen bestis in the bromes.

Gavin Douglas and Spenser both borrowed these phrases from Chaucer,[24] and Lydgate developed the musical idea further in his lines on the daisy, that flowers

> On bankys hy a-mong the bromys,
> Wher as these lytylle herdegromys
> Floutyn al the longe day,
> Bothe in aprylle and in may,
> In here smale recorderys,
> In floutys and in rede sperys.[25]

Eight instruments are listed in the shepherd interlude in the *Complaynt of Scotlande*: the drone bagpipe, 'ane pipe maid of ane bleddir and of ane reid', a 'pipe maid of ane gait horne', trump, corn-pipe, recorder, fiddle and whistle.[26] Pictorial representations of shepherds cover almost as large a range.

Almost every manuscript illumination of a shepherd shows him with at least a bagpipe, including an Italian Renaissance manuscript of Virgil's *Bucolics*;[27] and a greater number of instruments is common – the Adoration scene in fifteenth-century stained glass at East Harling church in Norfolk shows three different kinds of pipe.[28] An ivory Gospel-book cover of the Aachen palace school survives from the early ninth century, showing in the lower border the Annunciation to three shepherds, one with double pipes.[29] The bagpipe was always the most characteristic instrument of the shepherd, however. The Feast of the Pheasant held at the Burgundian court in 1454 included an *entremets* of twenty-eight different musicians in a pie, the very first being a shepherd with his bagpipe;[30] and Mantuan gives a detailed account of a shepherd playing the instrument at a country feast.[31] An anonymous sixteenth-century poet in *Tottel's Miscellany* even epitomizes Apollo's metamorphosis into a shepherd in terms of musical instruments:

> For loue Appollo (his Godhead set aside)
> Was seruant to the kyng of Thessaley,
> Whose daughter was so pleasant in his eye
> That bothe his harpe and sawtrey he defide,
> And bagpipe, solace of the rurall bride,
> Did puffe and blowe, and on the holtes hy
> His cattell kept with that rude melody.[32]

The passage is a loose translation of three lines from Seneca, where the god is given the much more elegant *calamus* – in this case apparently the panpipes.

When the shepherds do not play, they sing. They sing in the *Jeu de Robin et Marion* and in dozens of pastourelles; they sing in almost every English mystery play. Even the brief scene of Joachim among the shepherds in the Ludus Coventriae *Joachim and Anna* ends with one shepherd promising,

> We xal make us so mery.now þis is be-stad
> þat a myle on ʒour wey.ʒe xal here us synge.[33]

The English Nativity shepherds all attempt to imitate the angels' song, from the time of the Holkham Bible Picture-Book onwards; and they are often given additional songs as well. The shepherds of the Wakefield *Secunda Pastorum* sing a three-part song (Shakespeare's shepherd revellers in *The Winter's Tale* are still 'three-part song-men all'), and that their interest is theoretical as well as practical is indicated by their discussion of the rhythmical mensuration of the *Gloria*; and Mak, the sheep-stealer, appears to be marked out as a bad shepherd by his lack of skill in music as much as anything else.[34] In the Coventry *Pageant of the Shearmen and Taylors* the herdsmen sing two stanzas of a shepherd carol:

> Ase I out rode this enders night,
> Of thre ioli sheppardes I saw a sight,
> And all a-bowte there fold a star shone bright;
> They sange terli terlow;
> So mereli the sheppards ther pipes can blow.[35]

A high proportion of noëls, as Christmas songs of this kind are called (*carol* of course refers to the form rather than the season), describe the shepherds, often stressing their singing, music and dancing. They were widespread on both sides of the Channel – they merited their own anthology in France in 1483 – and they have close connections with the pageants and *mystères*:[36] *Jolly Wat* is itself a noël, again in carol form. Of French plays in general, Howard Mayer Brown comments, 'A shepherd almost never appears on any kind of fifteenth- or sixteenth-century stage without at least talking about music.'[37] They often have songs explicitly assigned to them, and in addition their dialogue is often put into rondeau form, but there is no indication as to whether these were intended to be sung:[38] it is a formal device that is widespread in all fifteenth-century drama, whoever the speakers. The Rouen *Nativité* contains a number of part songs in the shepherd scenes, including a five-part 'Requiescant in pace'; and when the new shepherd boy Anathot asks for instructions in the art of *bergerie* from an older herdsman, his master starts off with a music lesson packed with technical terms – *dyapente, dyatesseron, sexquialtera* – that leave the boy utterly bewildered.[39]

Besides making music, the second universal occupation of the shepherd is eating. Anathot imagines for a moment that 'l'art' (of music) refers to 'lard' (bacon). When Aucassin and Nicolette in turn come upon a group of shepherds, they find them with a cloth spread on the grass and a meal in progress.[40] A list of food is as widespread a commonplace as a list of equipment. Philippe de Vitry's Franc Gontier and Helaine eat

Fromage frais, lait, beurre, fromagee,	(*cream cheese*)
Cresme, mattons, pomme, nois, prune, poire,	(*curds*)
Aulx et oignons, eschalogne froiee,	(*shallot*)
Sur crouste bise.[41]	(*brown bread*)

These are the basic, more or less realistic items (however unlikely their abundance may be); Adam de la Halle's shepherds in the *Jeu de Robin et Marion* add a pasty, ham and chicken,[42] Froissart for one exceptionally splendid meal allows his herdsmen in addition beef, mutton and wine.[43] The more idyllic *bergerie* works are closer to *Franc Gontier* in advocating a pastoral simplicity of diet, though it is always plentiful. The lovers in *Regnault et Jehanneton*, traditionally though doubtfully attributed to René of Anjou,[44] eat bacon, cheese, nuts, apples, mushrooms and onions and drink milk; like the shepherds of *Aucassin* or *Robin et Marion*, they have a tablecloth, and their dog Bricquet has to be scolded for walking on it. Many of the Nativity shepherd plays, French and English, contain an actual feast on stage. The early fifteenth-century *Passion de Semur* even has two – though 'feast' is perhaps the wrong word here: on both occasions the shepherds are thoroughly disgusted with the food prepared by their wives. The first meal, taken between the Annunciation and the visit to Bethlehem – a moment that suggests more eagerness to eat than to go to the stable – apparently consists of scrambled eggs, which they suspect to be curdled milk; the second, after their return, is broth with the odd feather floating in it, and this as much as his sight of Christ seems to be instrumental in making the Second Shepherd decide to withdraw from the world.[45] By contrast, there is a monstrous proliferation of food equal to Froissart's in the Chester play and the Wakefield *Prima Pastorum* – so monstrous that it has been suggested that the latter is a figment of the shepherds' imagination;[46] and Adam in *King Edward and the Shepherd* has a hilariously well-stocked larder. The author of the *Complaynt of Scotlande*, with more realism but with typical concern for fine detail, lists thirteen different milk products eaten for breakfast by his shepherds with their rye bread and scones. The *topos* of the shepherd feast perhaps lies behind one verse of the Feast of Fools song 'Gregis pastor Tityrus':

Veneremur Tityrum,
Qui nos propter baculum
Invitat ad epulum.

Let us honour Tityrus, who invites us to his feast because of his crook.

Feasting and music are combined with games and dancing in the shepherd
revels that are the subject of so many pastourelles and similar poems. *Bergerie*
poetry of this kind was developed principally in northern France and
Flanders,[47] and is most typical of this area throughout the Middle Ages. Adam
de la Halle himself was from Arras, and the second half of the *Jeu de Robin et
Marion* consists of revels of this kind; he is working as much from the pastourelle here as in the first part, where Sire Aubert tries to seduce Marion. The
feasting and games he describes, even the choosing of a 'king', are commonplaces of *bergerie* literature.

A l'entree dous tens novel
s'asamblerent par un matin
pastorelles et pastorel:
roi ont fait dou plus bel.[48]

*Shepherdesses and shepherds came together one morning early in spring; the fairest they
made king.*

Christine de Pisan's shepherds amuse themselves with a wide variety of
pastimes, from swords and bucklers in summer to nine-men's morris in
winter.[49] Even Cain and Abel play games as they watch their beasts in the
Anglo-Norman Queen Mary's Psalter, contemporary with the Holkham
Bible.[50] A chapter in Eloi Damerval's *Livre de la Diablerie* (1508), an attack
on all the estates of the world except peasants in general and shepherds in
particular, is headed, 'Comment les pastoureaulx et pastourelles ensemble se
jouent en divers jeux', and he lists ten games by name as well as describing
various other pastimes such as making swings from the branches.[51] One of the
best pictures in the original manuscript of *Regnault et Jehanneton*, where each
page contains about fourteen lines of text with an accompanying illustration,
shows a shepherd tumbling off such a swing.[52] The tapestry of La Main
Chaude shows the shepherds playing a kind of forfeits, and miniatures of the
Annunciation to the Shepherds sometimes abandon much or all of their
religious impact in favour of drawing more secular *bergerie* scenes of shepherds
and shepherdesses carolling or giving garlands to their lovers.[53] The garland
is the love-token of the shepherd world, sometimes exchanged, more typically
given by shepherdess to shepherd as the courtly lady gives a knight her
favour. Several shepherdesses in the pastourelles are found lamenting
because

Robin d'autrui ke de mi
prist chapel de glai,   (Bartsch II.7)

Robin has taken a green chaplet from someone other than me.

Froissart varies the giving of garlands by having the shepherds run a beauty
contest among the shepherdesses, with a rose or a turtle-dove as the prize
(X, XX). Springtime, and especially May, is the season for most of the
pastourelles, and in several poems festivities are being held to celebrate 'le
premier jour de mai'.[54]

Bergerie, the depiction of the shepherd world in accordance with these
conventions, is found in many literary genres in the later Middle Ages, but

the earliest form in which it appears was the pastourelle. The association of the lyric describing the single shepherdess and the poem describing shepherd society was always close; Adam de la Halle passes from one to the other without a break. The earliest *bergerie* lyrics are themselves elaborated love-adventures where the knight joins the revels and tries, successfully or otherwise, to seduce one of the girls. The connection of *bergerie* and pastourelle is indicated by Froissart's choice of the latter word to describe poems of the former type; and there are various motets where a pastourelle proper and a *bergerie* lyric accompany each other. Many of the conventions of treatment of the shepherd make their first appearance in the pastourelles and the poems closely connected with them; and the first-person narrative lyric is the most typical form of *bergerie*. It is therefore worth taking a brief look at the genre of the pastourelle itself and its place in the development of pastoral – a place it continued to occupy in the Renaissance, though it was never again the dominant form.

The mere presence of a shepherdess will not make a work pastoral, and this holds true in particular if, as seems most likely, the pastourelle is of folk origin[55] – pastoral is always the self-conscious product of court or city. It is in some of the courtly pastourelles that the deliberate contrast of court and country is first made in the Middle Ages. The genre was at its peak in the thirteenth century, and although it tended not to take the attention of serious poets after this – at least not in its simple love-adventure form – it did not die out. There are at least as many surviving from the fifteenth century as from the thirteenth, and the form then found its way into printed songbooks; and as folksong the tradition has probably been continuous from early Middle Ages to the present. In England the genre was affected principally by the non-existence of shepherdesses, who only make their appearance in poems of this type after the introduction of Arcadian pastoral in the late sixteenth century. The earliest extant English pastourelles provide no occupation for the girl;[56] she may not even be of low class. In folksong, however, she was probably defined more specifically, as a milkmaid.

> 'Where are you going to, my pretty maid?'
> 'I'm going a-milking, Sir,' she said

– this is its most familiar form now, still retaining the love-debate and the man's eventual discomfiture. This particular version is based on a nineteenth-century expurgation of a seventeenth-century folksong; the earliest poem of the kind extant is a song from the court of Henry VIII,

> Hey troly loly lo! Mayde, whether go you?
> I go to the medowe to mylke my cow.[57]

The tradition can be taken back even further: it must have been thoroughly familiar to Malory as a motif, presumably from folksong, for he adds a key phrase to his source in Torre's mother's account of how the boy was begotten:

> When she was a mayde *and wente to mylke hir kyne*, ther mette with me a sterne knyght, and half be force he had my maydynhed.[58]

The shepherdess never came near to ousting the milkmaid as the heroine of the love-debate and attempted or successful seduction in English ballads and broadsides. There is only one explicit reference to the shepherdess pastourelle in England in the Middle Ages; and that is made by Gower, who was probably as closely acquainted with French literature as any Englishman of his time. In the course of his description of the sins of love in the *Confessio Amantis* he comes to Avarice and the robber-lovers who seize love wherever they find it, like a highwayman, 'in wode and field':

> Yee, though sche were a Scheperdesse,
> Yit wol the lord of wantounesse
> Assaie, althogh sche be unmete,
> For other mennes good is swete.[59]

This shepherdess, like so many of the French ones, already has a lover (or husband) of her own; and the man has a wife, to whom he rides home afterwards with tall stories of his splendid hunting. The substitution of morality for fantasy is characteristic both of Gower and of the whole English tradition. The most typical feature of the pastourelle, its structure, is also the most widespread. The *chanson d'aventure* framework (that is, the first-person narration), and the overheard conversation or complaint that often follows, occur in many *bergerie* or even pastoral contexts independently of any connection with a love-adventure: Boccaccio's fifth eclogue takes this form, for instance, as do some English satirical poems, *Regnault et Jehanneton* and many poems of moral or political comment.

These are the raw materials from which *bergerie* literature was built: conventions of matter, the descriptions, tasks, names, music, revels; and conventions of form, the pastourelle, the love debate or the overheard complaint. It is the poet's attitude towards his material that can turn *bergerie* into pastoral, when he uses the shepherd world to criticize or comment on a more sophisticated society. Almost every way of presenting the shepherd has two sides to it, the comic and the idyllic, mocking the rustic or criticizing the courtly; and sometimes both can happen at once. Adam de la Halle's Sire Aubert first accosts Marion to ask her if she has seen the heron he is pursuing, but she cannot make head or tail of his hunting terminology or tell the difference between 'heron' and 'herring'; and the resulting word-play makes them both appear comic, she for her ignorance, he for his refinement. It is the same process as in *The Winter's Tale* when the Old Shepherd whispers to his son, 'Advocate's a court word for pheasant' (IV.iv.737). In *King Edward and the Shepherd*, a work comparatively lacking in artistic sophistication, the peasant Adam will voice his opinion on the pretentiousness of the court with all the final conviction of common sense:

> This court is noȝt but pride;
> I ne can of no sich fare:
> These hye halles, þei are so bare!
> Why ar þei made so wyde? (727–30)

The comedy reflects partly on him, but his criticism is made none the less from the pastoral standpoint – the 'pride' is opposed to his own humbleness, the pomp of the architecture to the ideals of simplicity and sufficiency. The pastoral idealism of many works, that scorns wealth when compared with love or contentment, is balanced in others by the shepherds' shrewdness in extracting money: the memories of the herdsmen in *Aucassin et Nicolette* are only stirred once cash has been exchanged, and the shepherd in the famous *Farce de Maistre Pierre Pathelin* is the only character to have a financial advantage of any kind at the end of the play. Froissart gives his shepherds a properly uncourtly interest in cash values that turns into gentle satire on courtly activities, as they discuss the new fashion of the 'houpelande' and decide that although they are none too sure what it is (in fact the voluminous outer garment that had just come into fashion) it would certainly cost too much to wear (I); or as they comment on a royal wedding of 1389,

> La touse ait à cousin
> Le pape, qui a maint florin
> Et qui peut donner des beaus dons. (XIV.40–2)

> *The lass is the cousin of the Pope, who has lots of money and can give fine presents.*

There is no need for country simplicity to be idealized for it to become the platform for shrewd comment.

There was certainly a demand for *bergerie* comedy unmixed with any further implications, and this could provide the *raison d'être* of a shepherd scene, especially in drama. An interlude consisting of two shepherds arguing with each other and concocting impossibly grandiose shemes closes each half of the late fourteenth-century *Estoire de Griseldis*, a dramatized version of the story of Patient Griselda possibly written by Philippe de Mézières.[60] The shepherds here spend their time mocking each other with misunderstandings and word-play and insults, with the slower-witted always at the mercy of the other. When the first shepherd comes in with the news of the story's happy ending, his companion prevents him from telling it with some twenty lines of puns and misapprehensions, until the first shepherd utters the word 'feste'. This puts the second shepherd into as co-operative a frame of mind as the mention of money does the herdsmen of *Aucassin*. The same kind of thing happens in England too, for instance in the *Prima Pastorum* when the third shepherd empties his bag of meal in order to compare his companions' wits to the empty sack. Actual punning is unusual in English: the lad's speech in the Chester play when he is invited to eat,

> Fye on your loynes and your liverye,
> your lyverastes, livers and longes, (202–3)

is almost the only example. There are plenty of comic *bergerie* scenes in both French and English nativity plays, some of quite crude slapstick; these sometimes appear to be interpolations, suggesting the growth of a demand for rustic comedy later than the original texts. The English plays generally assimilate such comedy best into their essentially religious subject-matter, perhaps because of the antiquity of the comic *bergerie* tradition that the Holkham Bible Picture-Book illustrates. This particular episode, the imitation of the *Gloria*, is an especially clear example of the kind of effect the dramatists could make through the exploitation of comic ignorance, and also of how they put firm restrictions on its use so that it furthers the religious aim of the work rather than being at cross-purposes with it. The Holkham shepherds at first dismiss the angel's song as incomprehensible –

> Li un dist Glum glo ceo ne est rien

– but by the time they reach the stable one is singing 'Gloria in excelsis deo et in terra'; the later plays make it clear that this is not contradiction but enlightenment. The Chester shepherds argue for over fifty lines as to what the song was, the Tertius Pastor trying to claim his greater age as authority for his own version, but they do pick up some words, they translate 'pax', and their attempts at wise remarks do hit the mark almost in spite of themselves:

> Hee sange alsoe of a 'Deo'
> me thought that heled my hart. (430–1)

The episode is not always treated with such theological purposefulness, and the incident became an expected part of the play – it had to be put into the *Ludus Coventriae*, and the shepherds there never get further with their interpretation than

> It was gle glo glas glum; (85)

but even here Man is attempting to respond, however inadequately, to Heaven.

The shepherd is a *vilain*, a clown, the epitome of ignorance, yet ignorance is only a short step from innocence. One extreme is the shepherd's reply to Nicolette's courteous greeting:

> 'Dix vos benie!' fait li uns qui plus fu enparlés des autres. (XVIII)
>
> *'God bless you!' said the one who was more articulate than the others.*

At the other extreme are the shepherds of Greban's *Mystère de la Passion*, whose lack of knowledge of everything outside their own society is a sign of their purity, their fitness to receive the news of Christ's birth. Rifflart, who has been into town and seen the procedures for the census in operation with the officials on a scaffold in the market-place, breaks down in the middle of telling his companions about it when he cannot think of the title of one of the officers:

> Ainsi que j'esgardoye amont,
> vint ung de ceulx, ne sçay qu'i sont,
> ceulx qui font les gens enfermer –
> haro! aidez moy a nommer –
> qui portent ces batons d'argent,
> c'est, chose – (4787–92)
>
> *As I was looking up, one of those people came, I don't know who they are – the ones who put people in prison – goodness! help me to remember their name – who carry those silver sticks – they're – thingummy –*

and finally one of his companions comes to his rescue with the word 'sergent'; and Ysambert, a few lines later, cannot think of the title 'empereur'. Rustic ignorance becomes a measure of the simplicity of their life. The same principle lies behind the presentation of the Berger in a morality play written just a few years earlier, probably in 1440, *Mestier et Marchandise*.[61] Mestier and Marchandise themselves are personifications of crafts and commerce; the Berger represents the life of the fields – as if the shepherd were already sufficiently familiar as an allegorical figure not to need any further abstraction. All three are suffering from 'le Temps', the hardship of the times, the Berger most acutely; but he still does not know what the word means, since for him it is always midday or might just as well be. He may be familiar with hunger and hardship, but there is a simplicity and joy about his life that the others lack; he declares his preference for poverty with happiness over 'soulcy et argent'. He alone leads a life of peace and contentment amid the bustle of daily living. There are plenty of accounts of the knight finding the shepherdess, of Nicolette or Spenser's Calidore coming on the herdsman, but the shepherd's point of view is seldom given. He is the fixed point in a world of roaming chevaliers, story-telling pilgrims, travelling friars, merchants on business excursions, all the journeyings that make up the great bulk of mediaeval literature from the lyric *chansons d'aventure* to saints' lives or romances or the *Canterbury Tales*:

Je suys la a les regarder
Passer; les uns, en chavauchant,
Vont chantant, les aultres preschant,
En contant de leurs aventures,
Et je repose a mes patures,
En l'ombre d'un beau bisonnet,
Avec quelque sadin grongnet,
Chantant ou jouant quelque jeu.
Je dis bon jour, je dis adieu,
Ou Dieu gard le gentil bergier.   (p. 46)

*I stay there watching them go by; some go singing as they ride, others preaching or
telling stories about themselves, and I rest in the meadow in the pleasant shade of a bush
with a sweet-sounding bagpipe, singing or playing games. I say good day, I say goodbye,
or God keep the noble shepherd!*

This is the vernacular equivalent of the Classical *otium*; and it is the first step
towards making the shepherd a symbol of the contemplative life.

The Berger may have to go hungry, but he has something to make up for it:
love.

L'une foys j'ey la pance heureuse,
L'aultre non, mais ce m'est tout un.
Berger de pensee amoureuse
Ne cherche jamais grand desjun.   (p. 46)

*One time my belly is nice and full, another time not, but it's all the same to me: a
shepherd with his thoughts on love never wants much to eat.*

Love is an all but essential part of French *bergerie* literature, and two English
shepherd love-lyrics, 'Joly cheperte of Aschell down' and 'Ie haue so longe
kepe schepe on the grene', which take the theme very much for granted,
suggest it may have been more widespread than one might imagine in
English too.[62] In French it is the subject where the contrast between comic,
realistic and idyllic is most marked. The *vilain*, the churl, is at the bottom of
the social order; the peasant girl who resists a knight can fairly be raped, at
least according to Andreas Capellanus' scheme of things. In many pastourelles
the love-adventure moves close to the fabliau with its accompanying comedy,
as the knight assures the girl who is pleading to be released because she is a
virgin that her mother survived it, or when a clerk informs his shepherdess
that he is a 'maistre' who can make anyone who scorns love eat grass.[63] A
knight's love must be superior to a rustic's, according to one conventional
line of thought – the idea used by John of Garland as Phillis tells Coridon
what she thinks of his prowess as a lover – and there is a wry humour in the
shepherd's belated discovery that his *amie* too lacks courtly virtues:

Robins siet sous lo pin,
et tient lo chief enclin
et jure saint Martin
k'iawe nen est pas vin
ne cuers de femme fins.   (Bartsch II.12)

*Robin sits under the pine with his head bowed; and he swears by St. Martin that water
is not wine, nor woman's heart refined.*

The shepherds whose revel degenerates into a brawl are asking for the knight
to take advantage of the situation to make off with one of the shepherdesses
while the opportunity offers; and if he misses his chance he is mocked for it:

Pendre deu hom sa soldada
Sempre que l'es autreyada;
Car qui temps a, e temps aten,
Pert son temps trop nesciamen.[64]

*A man must take his pay while it's offered; for he who has an opportunity and waits
for another, loses it most foolishly.*

Variations on the proverb are found continually in pastourelle-type ballads
down the centuries – the British versions are usually variations on the
formula used by Henryson in *Robene and Makyne*, which he himself describes
as proverbial:

The man that will nocht quhen he may
Sall haif nocht quhen he wald. (91–2)

The mockery can easily turn from the shepherd onto the knight; the chevalier
of the pastourelles is baffled in one way or another at least as often as he is
successful, and the means by which the shepherdess repels his advances and
the arguments she uses will sometimes depend on the different values of court
and country – become fully pastoral, in fact. The knight's fine protestations
of love are mere courtly counters, and a peasant girl's common sense, or her
understanding of true human values that the knight's sophistication over-
looks, will show them up for the false coin they are.

This is the case in one of the earliest surviving vernacular pastourelles,
Marcabru's 'L'autrier, jost' una sebissa'. The debate between himself and
the shepherdess is not a mere opposition of will and denial: it is a confronta-
tion of different values, and a criticism of the knight's attitude to love and
rank. He starts by commenting on her exposure to the weather – a remark
that is itself significant in defining their relationship: he is protected from the
harsher facts of life by his social status, she has to rely on her own resources.
He tries to claim her as an equal in love:

Ben concosc al trespassatge
Qu'ab aital toza vilana
Pot hom far ric compaignatge
ab amistat de coratge, (p. 140)

*I know well that from coming on such a fair peasant girl a man can make a valuable
friendship of heartfelt love*

– but she immediately shows this up as special pleading: he is a fool to
suggest it, and she will not exchange her virginity for nothing better than
being called a whore. He tries to appeal to Nature instead – since his courtliness has been refuted by her practicality, perhaps an appeal to basic instinct
will work; but she answers by reminding him of the need for 'mezura', a
supremely courtly rule of life, in this case meaning the law of like with like.
He is conquered not only by her common sense but on his own ground of
courtly ideals.

Marcabru tries to flatter his shepherdess by telling her she is too beautiful
for her station, but he does not pretend that her life can have anything to
offer him. A different kind of comment on the knight emerges from an
anonymous French pastourelle where his visions of an idyllic pastoral life are
shattered by the girl's more practical approach. He declares,

Pour vous que tant par ai chiere
voudrai je devenir pastor,
si vous donrai riche don,

escarlate et pelicon,
la cainture de deus tors:
s'irons cueillir la violete
et si serons riches d'amors,
et si serez plus joliete
que l'aloete au point du jor. (Bartsch II.68)

For you whom I love so dearly I would like to become a shepherd, and I will give you rich gifts, scarlet cloth and a fur cloak and a girdle with a double buckle; we shall go gathering violets [a common euphemism for making love], *and we shall be rich in love; and you will be blither than the lark at daybreak.*

She pretends to agree, but then slips away to her father. There is no debate, but it is obvious what she thinks of his protestations. The narrator's vision of pastoral life and love, however, was not confined to him alone; and ideal love is much more central to *bergerie* than are the casual love-adventures of the simpler pastourelles.

This kind of love is presented through a group of conventions that set it in direct opposition to the conventions of courtly love. *Fine amours* is primarily a matter of courtship and almost invariably demands long service and much suffering; pastoral love is spontaneous, joyous and fulfilled. Joy, in fact, is the quality that can sometimes raise the pastourelle towards the pastoral, when physical pleasure is absorbed in something greater. 'The search for *Jois*,' writes L. T. Topsfield of the troubadours, 'appears to be more important than the experience of *Amors*, which is merely the means by which *Jois* or "individual happiness" can be found. The degree of *Jois* which can be gained is determined by the quality of the *Amors* which is experienced...[They] are searching for a *Jois* which will be supreme, lasting and beneficial and will go beyond the limits of everyday experience.'[65] This is the peak of the courtly love experience; what is remarkable is to find it removed altogether from the context of the court, where nobility of blood and refinement of feeling match each other, and translated to the countryside and the peasant. One of the Arrageois poets, Richart de Semilli, gives the idea one of its finest expressions. He sees Robin and Marion delighting in their love, but he is cut off from such a kind of loving by his rank; and he comments enviously on

la grant joie que cil fesoit...
qui onques amors servies n'avoit, (Bartsch III.11)

the great joy he made who had never served love.

Robin himself emphasises the overwhelming value of this kind of pastoral love, as unaffected by the cult of Amors as it is by the material advantages of rank:

J'ai mult plus de joie et de delit
que li rois de France n'en a, ce cuit.
S'il a sa richece, je la li cuit,
et j'ai m'amiete et jor et nuit,
ne ja ne departiron.

I have much more joy and pleasure than the king of France, I believe. If he's got wealth, let him keep it; I have my sweetheart both day and night, and we shall never be parted.

True love is found not at court, where the art of love is studied, but where love is spontaneous and fulfilled. Foy and Loyalté, in the *bergerie moralisée* named after them, are best represented as shepherd and shepherdess in love. Moniot de Paris, another pastourelle poet, recognizes true love only in his Robin and Marguerot:

Cil est bien enamoras
qui d'amors a joie entiere,
cil a amors droituriere.   (Bartsch III.44)

He is well in love who gets entire joy from loving; he has true love indeed.

This idea of pastoral love can occur in contexts that would seem likely to rule out any possibility of it. Guillaume de Machaut includes a description of lovers of all kinds, including the rustics Robin and Marote and their companions, in his *Dit dou Lyon*, which he wrote in 1342, in the century following the great age of the pastourelle. His introductory account of the peasants is far from flattering: their ugliness is beyond a painter's skill, and it is of a piece with their diet of cheese, cabbages and turnips. But their love, however inarticulately or inadequately expressed it may be, seems genuine, and they too derive 'grant joie' from it.[66] In all these works there is perhaps an assumption that the love is permanent, but this is not necessarily the case: the joy of spontaneous free association in love can be its own reward. In a pastourelle by Gui d'Ussel this is enough to heal the bitterness of both shepherdess and knight who have found their lovers disloyal.[67] Guido Cavalcanti's famous pastourelle, 'In un boschetto', follows the pattern of the usual love-adventure, but in the course of it a new spiritual dimension is opened:

Tanto vi sentio gioia e dolzore
che'l dio d'amore   mi parea vedere.[68]

There I felt such joy and sweetness that I seemed to look on the god of love himself.

The terms are courtly; the experience of love, by definition, is not. The pastoral world is being held up to the court as a pattern to which by its nature it cannot attain.

Even in poems that are specifically courtly, the attraction of pastoral for fulfilled love sometimes makes itself felt, as if the joy and spontaneity of consummation break through the courtly framework to the natural world beyond. A strikingly beautiful example of this occurs in one of the most unexpected places – unexpected because the work presents almost a pattern of courtliness: Chaucer's *Troilus and Criseyde*. Troilus spends the first two and a half books enduring the first part of his 'double sorwe', the sorrow of unfulfilled love; but at the moment when the lovers at last come together, when the courtly formalities give way to love-play and their grief turns to joy, the imagery moves to the pastoral world, and beyond that to the place where the shepherd is silent and only the heart sings.

And as the newe abaysed nyghtyngale,
That stynteth first whan she bygynneth to synge,
Whan that she hereth any herde tale,
Or in the hegges any wyght stirynge,
And after siker doth hire vois out rynge,
Right so Criseyde, whan hire drede stente,
Opned hire herte, and tolde hym hire entente.   (III.1233–9)

The 'herde' brings with him all his associations of joy and freedom in love. The same kind of thing happens in *Aucassin et Nicolette*, only there it is a physical journey rather than a metaphorical one: their love has its moment of bliss in the country – in the shepherd world, no matter how differently the shepherds may have been presented – and it is only there that the barriers to their love can be surmounted. They sleep together in Nicolette's 'loge' of flowers and leaves, through which Aucassin can see the stars. The naturalness of love and its idyllic natural setting combine to make a single ideal: as a fifteenth-century lyric puts it,

> Je luy faiz courtine
> D'une blanche espine
> Et d'une aultre flour
> Qu'on appelle rose;
> C'est bien aultre chose
> Que d'aymer par amour.[69]

I made her a curtain of hawthorn, and of another flower called the rose; it is a very different thing from courtly love.

The encounter in this poem is again casual; but the love is given value and resonance by its setting, as it is in Cavalcanti, or *Aucassin*, or in Chaucer's imagery.

The setting in which the mediaeval shepherd or shepherdess is placed is again conventional in two ways, one naturalistic, the other idyllic; in either case, it emphasises the separation of the shepherd world from the court. Marcabru's shepherdess is exposed to the hardships of the weather, but that fact itself gives her a kind of superiority that he, with his more sheltered existence, cannot match. The shepherds in many of the mystery plays, French as well as English, are suffering from the cold of the night, before the Annunciation turns their minds to greater matters. The English tradition, not surprisingly, concentrates most on the hardness of the shepherd's life, on the 'styffe stormes'[70] he has to endure and from which he must protect his sheep; and to the First Shepherd of the *Prima Pastorum* the weather is only one symptom of the troubled state of the world:

> Here is mekyll vnceyll, and long has it last: (*misery*)
> Now in hert, now in heyll, now in weytt, now in blast;
> Now in care,
> Now in comforth againe;
> Now in fayre, now in rane. (3–7)

Greban's shepherds may dress themselves carefully for their night's watch, with mittens and warm boots, but they have spent the day singing of the 'doulce saison', of lambs and gathering flowers and music-making.

None the less, the conventional realism of shepherd descriptions (the *treatment* of the shepherd world is often non-naturalistic, as the idealization of love illustrates) had its weakest hold on the setting of *bergerie*. Spring is the shepherds' season just as it is the season for the pastourelle:

> L'autrier a doulz mois de mai,
> ke nest la verdure,
> ke cil oixelet sont gai,
> plain d'envoixeure,
> sors mon chaval l'ambleure
> m'alai chevalchant,
> s'oi pastoure chantant
> de jolit cuer amerous... (Bartsch II.8)

The other day in the sweet month of May, when foliage springs into life and the birds are blithe and full of joy, I was riding my way on horseback at a gentle pace when I heard a shepherdess singing from a heart made gay by love...

The setting alone takes *bergerie* half way towards becoming idyllic pastoral, and in the mid-fourteenth century Philippe de Vitry completed the process in

Les Dictz de Franc Gontier. Gontier himself is in fact not a shepherd but a woodcutter; but the ideas he embodies – and indeed explicitly states, for the bulk of the poem consists of his exposition of the supreme value of the simple life – were even then so inseparable from the pastoral tradition that his original occupation was soon forgotten and he became proverbial as the ideal contented shepherd:

> Je recontray le Frant Gontier,
> C'est le plus beau des pastureaux,

runs a song in a later *bergerie moralisée.*[71] Gontier's life epitomizes all the motifs of the appeal and value of idyllic pastoral. The poem is a *chanson d'aventure*, where the courtly outsider is given a glimpse into a perfect pastoral world; and the perfection includes the landscape itself. Gontier and his love Helaine are sitting

> Soubz feuille vert, sur herbe delitable,
> Lez ru bruiant et prez clere fontaine,   *(stream)*

with birds singing all around them: again, it is the classic setting for the pastourelle, but it has a wider significance than that. It begins to take on the connotations of the Earthly Paradise or the Golden Age, of human bliss in a harmonious world. Although it occurs in a vast range of literary contexts in the Middle Ages, the whole concept of the *locus amoenus*, the idyllic landscape, is related to pastoral;[72] and it certainly always plays an essential part in creating the wholeness of the pastoral ideal. The author of a later Franc Gontier poem, the *Banquet du Bois*, which describes the May revels held by Gontier for the other shepherds, goes so far as to use the technical rhetorical term:

> Soubz aubépine bien flourie et flairant,
> En *lieu amène*, comme en ung paradis…[73]

Christine de Pisan's shepherdess is found in the ideal natural setting,

> Ou lieu avoit moult bel estre,
> Bois feuillu tout environ,
> Et l'erbe jusqu'au giron,
> Par placetes drue et basse;
> De flouretes a grant masse
> Diverses ot et planté,
> Sus la fontaine planté
> Arbres beaulz de moult belle ombre
> Que soleil ne feist encombre,   (461–8)

> *Where there was a most beautiful spot, with leafy woods all around and grass running right up to the river-bank with thick short tufts; there was an abundance of flowers of various kinds, and growing above the spring were many fine trees whose delightful shade was never disturbed by the sun.*

Froissart's shepherd world includes a fountain of love set

> en lieu plaisant,
> Bel et ombru et verdoiant.   (XI.8–9)

The ideal outdoor setting of the romance is usually a garden: here Nature creates a harmony of her own. The natural spontaneity of love is in keeping with the landscape: Gontier and Helaine, Regnault and Jehanneton, Robin and Marguerot, are a part of the idyllic natural life. After the feasting and games of the *Banquet du Bois* the shepherds and their loves slip away to the woods; and the poet comments,

Je n'en dis plus; de Adam sommes et de Eve (p. 222)

– it is more Eden, in the context, than original sin.

The idyllic aspects of *bergerie* were increasingly emphasised in courtly French poetry in the fifteenth century. The *Banquet* is deliberately nostalgic: Gontier is calling the 'pastours de jadis' to join his revels, for contemporary *pastourie* is pitifully depressed. With that comment the poet explicitly relinquishes any claim to realism: he is creating a fictional Golden Age of *bergerie*, presented as a countrified version of court life. The feast is elaborated with various *entremectz*, the shepherds love 'par amours fines', even 'secretement'; the wolf itself has become 'seigneur Ysangrins'. Pastoral could be both picturesque and fashionable, and the extent of the vogue is indicated by the increased production of courtly *bergerie* literature and art. A good number of elaborate shepherd tapestries were produced over this period, a few still surviving, many more listed in inventories; and the fashion had an appeal in England as well as France – Henry V owned one such tapestry and Henry VIII three.[74] Pastoral, especially as exemplified by *Franc Gontier*, is an indictment of the court, but the court sometimes threatened to adopt all the trappings while ignoring the moral core. René of Anjou seems to have turned his court into a kind of mock-pastoral – a fact that inspired Chastellain to list a king playing shepherd among the wonders of the world of his time[75] – but it is not clear how far he took this beyond poetry, pageantry and an interest in the detailed running of his estates; in any case he found the idea intensely appealing. That a king should want to associate himself with shepherds at all, however, is what seems to astonish Chastellain. Even if they had been adopted by the court in some form, they were still base. If René organized a pastoral tournament, an account of the Jousts of Saint-Inglevert, held in 1390, gives a different view of the relationship of *bergerie* with the chivalric life. The narrator of the poem overhears a group of shepherds talking about the tournament (at which three French knights took on the challenges of thirty-six foreign knights in the course of a week). One shepherdess asks her lover why he did not take part himself, and

che pastour à qui ne pleust mie,
Respondi: Ch'est ungs prileus tours
De la jouster, par saint Hellie![76]

The shepherd didn't like the idea at all, and answered, 'It's a nasty dangerous business to joust there, by St. Eloy!'

Heroic pastoral is a contradiction in terms. There is a double irony when a shepherdess names her pet dogs Tristan, Hector and Rollant, and then in a splendid display of lack of fine feeling laments their absence as much as her lover's;[77] and when a group of Flemish knights prepared for battle before St-Omer in 1487 dressed as shepherds with crook and pouch, it was in answer to the French mock that 'Flamens n'estoient que bergiers, come mal habile au mestier d'armes' – 'Flemings are mere shepherds in their lack of skill in arms'.[78]

On one level, then, the court accepted, even valued, the shepherd; on another, it despised him. Some of the most interesting works of *bergerie* are concerned with exploring tensions of this kind, between the base and the idyllic. Christine de Pisan makes them the thematic structure of the *Dit de la Pastoure*, which is a kind of pastoral *lai*, recounting an 'aventure' of Amours. The pastoral world she portrays appears to have all the qualities that should make it ideal – beautiful countryside, love, singing and dancing, freedom from care; but it is disturbed, and eventually irretrievably damaged, by the irruption into it of courtly life and all its values. It seems at the outset to epitomize the courtly-idyllic view of the shepherd, but true courtliness shows up the distance between them. The poem is narrated by the shepherdess Marotele herself, in a reversal of the usual pastourelle allocation of rôles. She describes her life, with its round of duties, its music and revelling, and her companions, among whom

> N'il n'y avoit si povrete
> Qui ne fust riche d'ami, (148–9)

> *There was no lass so poor as not to be rich in her lover.*

She alone has always refused her suitors, and is happy by herself. While she is watching her sheep one day, however, a lord – 'Monseigneur' – and his train appear; and her astonishment at his revelation of the courtly world is as great as the young Perceval's when he first saw a knight. The lord makes her sing to them, and the song Christine gives her summarizes the aristocratic view of *bergerie*:

> Qui verroit ces bergieretes
> Et ces jolis pastoureaulx
> Entr'amer par amouretes
> Et faire de flours chapeaulz,
>
> Il diroit qu'il n'est sentier
> Ne voye qui soit si pure,
> Jamais d'autre n'aroit cure. (631–7)

> *Whoever saw these shepherdesses and merry shepherds loving each other and making garlands of flowers, he would say there was no other way of life so good; he would never care for any other.*

The lord is strongly attracted by the pastoral world, but in the poem as a whole the insufficiency of the pastoral ideal is shown up. Not only his clothing and trappings and rank, but, much more importantly, his *courtoisie*, are new experiences for the girl. After her first meeting with him one of the shepherds describes to her the feast she has missed, and the perennial *bergerie* delight in food suddenly seems spiritually poverty-stricken beside the emotional experience she has just had. The traditional themes of *bergerie* are used to damage it as an ideal. Marotele takes her friend Lorete to meet the lord; and afterwards she asks her a question that shows up the limitations of the shepherd world:

> N'est il gracieux et gent
> Et plaisant a toute gent?
> Sont pastoureaulz de tel sorte? (1258–60)

> *Isn't he gracious and courteous, and delightful to people of all kinds? Are shepherds like that?*

She herself, by the terms of the poem, has to be capable of a courtesy equalling his, but this too distinguishes her from the people around her. The best in each of the two worlds, the pastoral and the courtly, are for a while fused and complete each other. But however attractive the idea is, it is an impossibility, even within the literary conventions in which Christine writes. She will not take the escape route of making Marotele into Pastorella or Perdita, of producing some noble antecedents for the shepherdess and so revealing true courtliness in the *bergerie* setting: the two are finally incompatible. The lord has to go, and his departure and absence mean a kind of breaking of Arcadia, a destruction of pastoral peace and content. The pastoral ideal is in a way reversed: it is in the prince that the shepherdess has found her 'paradiz terrestre'; he has become the ground of her existence:

> Sanz luy n'ay envie
> De vivre; il est la pasture
> Sans qui de vivre n'ay cure. (2260–2)

> *I have no wish to live without him; he is the pasture without which I care nothing for life.*

The images are themselves drawn from the pastoral world – it is at once the world that has failed her, whose limitations she has at last realized and to which she cannot return with any pleasure, and the symbol of the joy that she cannot attain.

Christine says at the beginning of her poem that the story is allusive – that it refers in some way to actual events. In *Regnault et Jehanneton* the allusion is an open secret: it is about the love of René of Anjou and his second wife, Jeanne de Laval. In this poem the problem of the inadequacy of the world of *bergerie* is solved by transmuting it into a delicate world of the imagination. It is a conventional work in many ways: there is the spring setting, a first-person narrator who overhears the lovers' conversation, the simple feast, true and faithful love. The most striking thing about it is its creation of *bergerie* through art, in a way that makes it the forerunner of Renaissance pastoral. There is plenty of room for idyllic realism – the ploughman calling to the oxen by name, the shepherd walking through an ideal landscape and tracing nests from the birdsong – but equally important are the brilliant iconographic set-pieces: the birds catching fish in the *fontaine*, the turtle-doves on the single green branch of a dead stump, the last rays of sun on the tower of the church which is the narrator-pilgrim's goal. The poem turns into a *débat* as to which of the two lovers loves the most; the narrator offers himself as judge, and says he will give his judgement on the following day. In the morning he returns to the place where he met the lovers, but there is no one there and his calls go unanswered. It is as if the poetry had created a golden moment of the imagination too fine for reality.

Works of this kind have obviously moved a long way from the literal truth to life of Jehan de Brie: the centre of interest is no longer in the shepherd as peasant, but in the pastoral as art. The distinction was too marked not to need some kind of explanation or excuse to link the two. Classical bucolic might have provided the means, but comparatively few vernacular pastoralists before the later fifteenth century show any signs of using this even though, when they do, they seem to have a more genuine appreciation of Virgil than the Latin scholars: Jean de Meung leads into his passage of *bergerie* in the *Roman de la Rose* with a splendid and totally non-allegorical account of the Saturnian Golden Age, and there is a singing-match in the *Pastoralet* where it is the quality of the song and not the quality of the argument that matters. It is possible that the author of *Regnault et Jehanneton* had some acquaintance with the Latin eclogue, both mediaeval, in the *conflictus* theme, and Classical, in his suggestion of the interrelationship of pastoral and poetry. One way of making the bridge, of linking nature and art, became conventional in *bergerie*: that was to list a series of *exempla* of shepherds who were also princes, or kings, or patriarchs, or even gods. 'Ce labeur cy nest pas seulement Royal,' as Jean Lemaire de Belges' master shepherd put it, 'mais plustost vne occupation deïfique'[79] – not only royal, but divine. The shepherd may appear base, but there is more to *bergerie* than that, or Christ Himself would not have chosen the title of shepherd. Paris, Orpheus and Apollo were all herdsmen; so were Abel, Jacob, Moses and David. The *Moralité du Petit et du Grand*[80] opens by citing Tityrus and Melibeus, Orpheus, Pseustis and Alithea (from Theodulus), and then later Jacob, Moses and Paris, who is both the Classical figure and the city. Biblical *exempla* are generally more widespread than Classical. One chapter of Jehan de Brie's work is devoted to 'l'honneur et estat du bergier', and he announces,

> Le mestier de la garde des œilles est moult honnorable et de grant auctorite.
> Ce peult on prouver appertement par nature et par la saincte escripture.
>
> (p. 38)

> *The profession of sheep-keeping is very honourable and of great authority. That can be clearly proved by nature and by Holy Scripture.*

He goes on to cite Abel, the Patriarchs and also Cyrus; and he dedicates the whole work to the 'tres-bon et souverain pasteur le createur de toutes choses' – Christ must always be the supreme justification for pastoral. The chief shepherd in the Rouen *Nativité* tells his companions how the Patriarchs were shepherds, how David as a shepherd boy killed Goliath with stones from his *pennetiere*, and how Abel was at once virgin, martyr, priest and shepherd; and they conclude that

> Telle assemblee de gens de bien
> Anoblit treffort nostre estat,   (II p. 310)

> *Such a collection of notable people greatly ennobles our profession.*

Abel appears as a different kind of ideal shepherd in the *Banquet du Bois*, where he is described as the leader of *bergerie* revels. The master shepherd in the *Complaynt of Scotlande* gives a list running to several pages and including David, Apollo, numerous Roman public figures, Paris, the Patriarchs and later also the shepherds of the *Bucolics*.[81] Some Renaissance humanists borrowed the *topos*: Mantuan has a list of mixed Biblical and pagan *exempla* in his seventh eclogue – a list from which Spenser borrowed for 'July'; and Iohannes Oporinus prefaced his anthology of a hundred and fifty-six Latin eclogues published in 1546 with a justification of pastoral by reference to the Bethlehem shepherds, Christ, Peter, herdsmen who became kings, Pan and Apollo.[82] The idea remained a commonplace throughout the Elizabethan age. *Bergerie* could claim formidable authority for making the shepherd something more than a clown.

II. *The Shepherd as Teacher*

If 'shepherd' could be used almost as a synonym for 'peasant' as a term of abuse, it could also mean the opposite, 'wise man'. Almost every section of the *Kalender of Shepherdes*, the almanac translated from the fifteenth-century French *Compost et Kalendrier des Bergiers*, opens with the phrase, 'Shepherds know –'; and if this particular usage arises directly out of the form of the work, it was certainly not a new departure to make the shepherd the mouthpiece of wisdom and instruction. The practice was encouraged by the Christian metaphor of the pastor and by the connection of the simple pastoral life with the ethical ideal; but it goes beyond these associations, so that the shepherd is wise by virtue of his office. Where Sidney describes the poet as a *vates*, a prophet, the prophetic function in the Middle Ages belonged more to the shepherd. Boccaccio tells of how Dante's mother had a dream before his birth in which her son appeared as a shepherd; and Boccaccio interprets this as a sign that he would become, not a great poet, but a great teacher.[83]

The simplest form of this device is the convention, already mentioned, of making the master shepherd give instruction in the art of *bergerie*, but the realistic limitations are seldom adhered to, just as *bergerie* itself is seldom merely naturalistic. The ethical aspects of the shepherd world are always important, and it was an easy step from writing in praise of the simple life to making the shepherd speak its praise himself. Franc Gontier's detailed account of the good of country life compared with the evil of the court is the *locus classicus* in the Middle Ages, and Deschamps was quick to follow in Philippe de Vitry's footsteps with Robin and his love Marion substituted for Gontier and Helaine. Robin declares,

> Juge ne craim qui me puist faire paine
> Selon raison: je n'ay rien offensé.
> Je t'aime fort, tu moy d'amour certaine.
> Pas ne doubte que soie empoisonné.
> Tirant ne craing: je ne scay homme armé
> Qui me peust oster une laitue.[84]

> *I fear no judge who could punish me, and rightly, for I have done no wrong. I love you dearly, and you me, with faithful love. I have not the slightest fear of being poisoned. I fear no tyrant; I know of no man at arms who could take a lettuce from me.*

Robin here is not explicitly a shepherd: the only occupation to which Deschamps refers is, like Gontier's, woodcutting, and though this sounds more like a hobby it does provide the opportunity for telling how Robin had gone to court with some wood and there seen for himself

> qu'a ces cours ont de dueil et de paine
> Ces curiaux!

> *What misery and hardship courtiers have at these courts!*

He is the first of a long line of shepherds who have looked in on the life of the court – or the city – and rejected it, not through theory but through direct experience; the idea recurs in Mantuan, Barclay, Tasso, Spenser and many lesser writers. The descriptions and the themes of Deschamps' poem, as well as the names, are all central to the pastoral tradition in spite of the reference to woodcutting; and the *ballade* has the refrain,

> J'ai Franc Vouloir, le seigneur de ce monde,

> *I have Free Will, the lord of this world,*

suggesting the shepherd's link with the earthly paradise before the Fall. Deschamps obviously found his creation attractive: he wrote another longer poem along similar lines, the *Lay de la Franchise*, comparing the May revels of the court with Robin and Marion's simple festivities.[85] Here again, Robin (this time certainly a herdsman) expounds the security of the simple life, where it is possible to eat and drink without fear of poison, and concludes that he is richer than 'roy ne palazin'. Many poets stressed the shepherd's freedom: he may not have the status given by literal wealth or rank, but he has liberty and therefore 'empire':

> Bergier qui a pennetiere
> bien cloant, ferme et entiere,
> c'est ung petit roy.[86]

The shepherd with his well-fastened pouch is a king in little.

The poet of the *Banquet du Bois* spells out the pastoral ethic so as to make the setting and the shepherd's life a single expression of natural perfection:

> Au lez d'un bois si plaisant qu'on peut dire,
> Sur l'erbe vert, auprès d'une fontaine,
> Fust Franc Gontier, et la tint son empire
> Et son bancquet, en joye moult haultaine,
> Sans quelque orgueil, sans rigueur, sans attaine
> Et sans envie, car de ce n'ont ilz cure,
> Contens des biens que leur donne Nature.
>
> Biens ont assez, car ilz ont suffisaunce;
> De deuil n'ont cure, ne de merencolie.   (*melancholy*) (p. 213)

These are ideals as old as civilization, when men first moved from the country to the town; but the specific stimulus for passages like this can often be found in Horace or the *Georgics*. Many of these late mediaeval poets were familiar with the Classics; Nicholas de Clemenges even translated *Franc Gontier* into Latin, omitting the typically vernacular *chanson d'aventure* opening, and it makes a tolerable eclogue.[87] Many of these poems make their principal point negatively – that the country is good because the court is bad; Deschamps' Robin says nothing at all about his own life. It was easy for this idea to lose its pastoral associations altogether, and several scholars of the late fourteenth century took up the theme of condemnation of the court with the minimum of corresponding praise for the simple life. Alain Chartier wrote an epistle on the subject, *Le Curial*, perhaps translated from a Latin original, and this was widely circulated and eventually printed; Caxton made an English translation in 1484. Aeneas Silvius Piccolomini, the Italian humanist who later became Pope Pius II, probably knew it when he wrote his own tract on the wretchedness of courtiers, the *Epistola de Curialium Miseriis*; and from there the theme found its way back into pastoral, for Barclay made this work the basis of the first eclogues to be written in English.[88] The subject is one of the commonplaces of Renaissance pastoral – in the shepherd interlude in Tasso's *Gerusalemme Liberata*, several times in Spenser, Nicholas Breton, Shakespeare any many others.

That the shepherd should expound the pastoral ethical system and declare it superior to the courtly was a result, not the cause, of the tradition that the shepherd should teach. The connection of some of these works with the *Georgics* does not mean that it was Classical influence that makes Robin teach morality to the courtier: the idea that the shepherd or shepherdess could be the mouthpiece of wisdom is an integral part of the vernacular tradition of pastoral. How the idea originated is impossible to tell; it is already in existence in the earliest vernacular texts, Marcabru's pastourelles. The shepherdess in 'L'autrier, jost' una sebissa' has much to teach the narrator in the way of human values; and his other pastourelle, 'L'autrier, a l'issida d'abriu', is an even more remarkable piece in its use of the girl for instruction. The narrator makes the usual approaches to the shepherdess, but she replies that her mind is too much on other matters, in this case the current decline of morals:

> Pretz e Jovens e Jois dechai
> C'om en autre no.is pot fiar, (p. 134)

> *Worthiness and Youth and Joy are in decay, so that no one can trust another.*

The knight presumably slinks away overcome by all this, for the poem ends with the end of her tirade and we hear no more from him – the pastourelle form, in fact, is the excuse for the attack on morals. Marcabru's other shepherdess had answered the knight's protestations with cool common sense; but this girl is concerned with courtly values – *pretz, jovens* and *jois* are all key words of the romance or the *lai*. The shepherdess has moved onto the knight's own level of courtliness, and above him in moral authority. In some pastourelles she can become his equal or superior even on questions of love: she can sit down to a courtly debate on Amors,[89] or accuse him of 'pechie' in wooing her when his heart is set on another lady.[90] Moniot de Paris and Richart de Semilli learn the nature of true love from watching shepherd lovers of a less courtly kind, but other herdsmen lecture the knight on the nature of *fine amours* itself. In literature, at least, it is quite in order for a knight unhappy in love to stop his horse beside a shepherd and ask him how to achieve the happiness and fulfilment that the shepherd himself seems to have; and Robin never advocates an abandonment of the court, but an even more loyal adherence to the values of love itself. He may himself have found joy, but he knows about suffering as well:

> Nus n'en puet avoir grant joie
> s'il n'en sueffre paine,[91]

> *No one can have great joy if he does not endure grief for it.*

It is a small step from this to making the pastourelle fully allegorical, with the first-person character being instructed in love by personifications. As he rides along the 'sentier d'amours' in one poem, he meets

> Bone-Amor floretes coillant,
> En sa compaignie
> Sen et cortoisie, (Bartsch II.2)

> *Courtly Love gathering flowers, with Fine Feeling and Courtesy in his company.*

He asks them, 'Ke font fin amant?', 'How do true lovers act?', almost 'What makes a courtly lover?'; and after he has been instructed a girl sings a 'chanson pastorelle' to entertain him. Dante included a sonnet based on the same situation in the *Vita Nuova*: its close relationship with the French pastourelle, with its typical opening,

> L'autre ier chevauchai mon chemin, (Bartsch III.19)

is established in the first line:

> Cavalcando l'altr'ier per un cammino,
> pensoso de l'andar che mi sgradia
> trovai Amore in mezzo de la via.[92]

As I was riding my way the other day, pensive because the journey was painful to me, I met Love in the middle of the road.

The pastourelle form contains the potential for instruction in love from the shepherd and from Love himself. The idea that love ennobles the character and heightens the sensibility, conventional as a concept in courtly literature, is transferred to the shepherd world, setting herdsman and courtier on an equal plane. Even Henryson's Makyne becomes an expert in the fine details of love, instructing the ignorant Robene in the ABC of 'luvis lair':

Be heynd, courtas and fair of feir,	*(noble; action)*
Wyse, hardy and fre;	*(generous)*

and he in his turn is taught by his own love to fear the 'janglour', the gossip who breaks the secrecy enjoined by love, just as the most courtly of the French or Provençal shepherds fear the *mesdisans* or the *lauzenjadors*.[93]

If love can endow the shepherd with courtly fine feeling, hardship enables him to speak with the voice of the Common Man. This is a constantly recurring principle of *bergerie* literature, and again its first occurrence is in an early pastourelle, Jean Bodel's 'Contre le dous tans novel'.[94] As in Marcabru's second poem, the shepherdess is too much distressed to accept the offer of love, but this time it is because of the disruption caused by

> des eschis
> ki l'iaue ont passee

> *the base outlaws who have crossed the water*

– the French who pursued the Flemings across the Lys in 1199 and pillaged the country, 'ki trop l'ont gastee'. Her complaint foreshadows a number of shepherd laments against the overrunning of France by English soldiers during the Hundred Years' War: there were several *bergeries moralisées* devoted to this, and Deschamps wrote some *balades* on the subject. Two of his poems are concerned with the value of Calais in the peace negotiations with England, both in the form of overheard conversations between shepherds: *bergerie* is now being used as a political implement. He acknowledges that the pastoral peace of the countryside has been wrecked – as one speaker puts it,

Je n'ose descouchier le matin	*(get up)*
Pour les Anglois qui nous sont destruisans[95]	

– but still declares that the town is more important. In the *envoys* to these poems he urges the same principle of resistance in his own voice. Froissart uses the same means of putting forward military policy in his twelfth *Pastourelle*, again written after a French crossing of the Lys, when he is urging the King to press home his attack; one of his shepherds declares that there can never be peace in the country

Se le pooir des flours de lys	*(power)*
Ne vient la chose refourmer	

– a 'reformation' aimed at 'l'orgoeil de Bruges et de Gand'. The poem is a fine example of the topical use of *bergerie*: the allusions are so precise that it can be dated within a week.[96] The shepherd form is a way of pointing the allusions, not, as in Petrarch, disguising them. The shepherd's suffering here receives less emphasis than the policy they are advocating; usually it is the other way around – the moralities tend to be principally expositions of hardship and pleas for good government, which may have been written with reference to a particular situation but which are relevant outside that as well. The convention of making the shepherd the critic of society extends well beyond specific events; it underlies the whole concept of the *bergerie moralisée*, and is so pervasive as to make its way even into the *Banquet du Bois*. Gontier laments the non-idyllic state of contemporary 'pastourie', where unemployment and poverty abound; and, he adds,

> Les pauvres gens ne veult-on mais aydier. (p. 207)

In an anonymous play of the late fifteenth century, *La Patience de Job*, there is a scene between Robin, Marote and an unnamed shepherd and a ploughman, in which the ploughman's complaint of the hardship he and his kind suffer is endorsed and given a wider social application by the shepherd:

> Nous sommez tous de l'arche Noé
> Et cuyde selon mon savoir
> Que chascun honme deust avoir
> Autant de biens l'ung conme l'aultre,
> Et nous en avons si grant faulte.
> Les grans seigneurs ont tous les biens
> Et le pauvre peuple n'a riens
> Forsquez paine et adversité.[97]
>
> *We all came from Noah's ark; and as far as I can make out every man should have as much as any other, but we are going very short. The great lords have all the goods; and the poor have nothing but trouble and hardship.*

The same use of the shepherd, as a mouthpiece of complaint against social injustice, is particularly characteristic of English shepherd literature. There are only a few poems where the theme occupies the whole work, but whenever a shepherd is introduced the potential for criticism is created, and many writers take advantage of it. This happens even in *King Edward and the Shepherd*: Adam is suffering from the exactions of corrupt officials who take his beasts 'and payen but a stik of tre', a worthless wooden tally-stick (31–6); and his daughter has been raped and his hens stolen by outlaws (149–68). The passages are particularly striking as they are in contradiction to the main plot of the poem, which depends on Adam's abundance of food and drink, but they do not read as if Adam means them merely to mislead the King. They seem to reflect genuine social abuses, but ones more appropriate for the shepherd to complain of in his rôle as Common Man rather than for the particular individual Adam. In the *Secunda Pastorum* too one of the herdsmen speaks of the oppression of the poor and of the abuses of 'maintained' men:

> We are so hamyd, *(hamstrung)*
> Fortaxed and ramyd, *(beaten down)*
> We are mayde handtamyd
> With thyse gentlery-men. (15–18)

The shepherd will tell the truth about society, and he can do so because he is familiar with its ills at first hand. His experience extends beyond his low estate to become a keen awareness of the evil of society in general; and there is one short poem that consists of nothing but an indictment by a shepherd of the state of the world.

> As I me lend to a lend, *(walked along a ploughland)*
> I herd a schepperde makyn a schowte;
> He gronyd and seyde with sory syghyng,
> 'A! Lord, how gos þis word abowte! *(world)*

'It gos ful wrong, ho so it wyst;
  A frend ho may ken fro his foo?
To hom I may trewely trost –
  In fayth, I fynde but fewe of þo.'⁹⁶   (*those*)

His particular complaint is about 'half frends', and all those

  þat false are and fayr euer speke,

but this extends to include the universal lack of steadfastness:

Now wel, now wo; now frend, now foo;
  Now lef, now þef; now in, now out;
Now cum, now go; now to, now fro;
  A! Lord, how gos þis word abowte!

The shepherds' laments in the *Prima Pastorum* run along very similar lines –

Here is mekyll vnceyll, and long has it last: (*misery*)
Now in hert, now in heyll, now in weytt, now in blast,
Now in care,
Now in comforth againe;
Now in fayre, now in rane;
Now in hart full fane,
And after full sare.

Thus this world, as I say, farys on ylk syde;   (3–10)

and they pray too for deliverance from 'robers and thefys' and 'bosters and bragers' (52, 55). This is the postlapsarian world, and the shepherd, with his associations of Paradise and the moral ideal, is the man with the authority to denounce its ills. In the mystery plays in particular, these associations are made explicit.

The shepherds of the English Nativities are often also given substantial amounts of more directly didactic material, principally a summary of the Messianic prophecies. This is fairly rare in the French *mystères* – the Rouen play is the only notable example – but the York and *Ludus Coventriae* cycles devote the opening section of their shepherd scenes to long expositions of the prophets, even before the Angel has appeared. The Wakefield Master manages to comprehend the convention of instruction within the convention of clownishness: one shepherd has to drown out his companion's singing in order to deliver his speech –

We fynde by the prophecy – let be youre dyn!   (*Secunda* 674)

– and another who quotes Virgil's 'Iam nova progenies' brings forth a violent reaction:

Weme! tord! what speke ye here in myn eeres?
Tell vs no clergé! I hold you of the freres.   (*Prima* 388–9)

He persists, however, declaring, 'I shall you teche.' The shepherd is beginning to turn into the pastor.

Even before the shepherd becomes allegorical, the tradition of the Good Shepherd constantly affects the way he is portrayed. The literal herdsman as well as the spiritual pastor could look to Christ as his overlord; Jehan de Brie dedicates his sheepkeeping treatise 'a la gloire, louenge et a l'honneur du tres-bon et souverain pasteur'. There is a considerable amount of moral instruction in the work as well as practical, much of it based on the Biblical definitions of the Good Shepherd, and he devotes a special section to the need for moral uprightness in the herdsman. The shepherd in the *Pastoralet* who delivers a speech to his companions summarizing 'aulcuns des tours de bergerie' makes the same double emphasis, practical and moral:

> Pastours qui voelt son bien acroistre,
> Doibt soy et puis son foucq cognoistre,
> Adfin de soy bien ordener
> Et de son foucq à droit mener.
> Bons bergiers, Michiel ou Michault,
> Ait chapel contre le grant chault
> D'esté et le grant froit d'yver... (5773–9)

> *The shepherd who wishes to increase his holding must know first himself, then his flock, in order to rule himself well and lead his flock properly. The good shepherd should have a hat to guard against the great heat of summer and the cold of winter...*

An early sixteenth-century poem formerly ascribed to Marot, *Le Sermon du Bon Pasteur et du Mauvais* – perhaps better described by its manuscript title *Le Pasteur Evangelique*[99] – turns the pastor back into the shepherd so that he may preach a long sermon to his sheep. The narrator goes for a walk in the fields around Paris one Lent to see the shepherds taking their 'repos' beside their flocks; and

> Lors ung i'en vey sur ung tertre monté
> Que charitable amour auoit dompté
> Songneusement gardant son petit nombre
> Qui la estoit tappy a terre en l'umbre,
> Et le paissoit de l'escripture saincte. (f. 2ʳ)

> *Then I saw one of them who had climbed onto a hillock, whom divine love had mastered, carefully watching his small flock as they lay there on the ground in the shade; and he grazed them on the holy Scriptures.*

The author clearly found a particular appropriateness in giving the sermon such a setting; it is hard to tell whether it is the shepherd or the pastor who is the allegorical figure. Either has the right to teach.

The shepherd first appears as the instructor in detailed Christian morals as early as the second century, in *The Pastor of Hermas*,[100] one of the most popular works of the early Church. It was written in Greek, and later translated into Latin, but it remained best known in the Eastern Church; and there was no continuing tradition of the Christian shepherd-teacher to link up with the late mediaeval treatises along the same lines. Of these treatises the *Compost et Kalendrier des Bergiers*, first published in French in 1493 and in English ten years later, was the most popular and the most compendious, spiritual and moral instruction being only two of the items gathered into its encyclopaedic embrace. There was some sort of association of shepherds with calendars even before this date – when Greban's herdsmen decide what gifts to present to Christ, gifts that are almost invariably typical of *bergerie*, one of them chooses to give a 'kalendrier de bois'. The bulk of the *Compost* itself has almost as little to do with shepherds as any other almanac: it is mostly a very long way from Jehan de Brie's treatise, though they do have a few practical topics such as weather prediction in common, and it was not until 1602 that it occurred to anybody to combine the two.[101] The *Kalender of Shepherdes* consists principally of lengthy and deeply learned instruction given by the Master Shepherd on such matters as astrology and astronomy, health, the ages of man in parallel with the months and seasons, the punishments in Hell for various sins and so on. The author of the *Complaynt of Scotlande* obviously liked the idea, and most of his shepherd interlude consists of a similar dissertation of inordinate length by the 'prencipal scheiphirde', who declares that

> Phisic, astronomye and natural philosophie, var fyrst prettikit and doctrinet be vs that ar scheiphirdis, for our faculte knauis the natur and the vertu of the sternis and planetis of the spere, and of the circlis contenit in the samyn.

(p. 46)

The author makes a determined attempt to make even the most abstruse information relevant to the shepherds themselves; and he is also typically anxious to include every possible aspect of the *bergerie* conventions he can bring in. The whole idea of instruction is one of these; so is the section in the course of the speech on famous shepherds who made good. So, paradoxically, are the ideas of the shepherd's ignorance and his pastimes, so that

> Quhen the scheiphird hed endit his prolixt orison to the laif of the scheip-heirdis, i meruellit nocht litil quhen i herd ane rustic pastour of bestialite, distitut of vrbanite, and of speculatione of natural philosophe, indoctryne his nychtbours as he had studeit ptholome, auerois, aristotel, galien, ypocrites or cicero, quhilk var expert practicians in methamatic art. Than the scheiphirdis vyf said, my veil belouit hisband, i pray the to decist fra that tideus melan-colic orison, quhilk surpassis thy ingyne,

and she suggests story-telling and singing as more agreeable ways of passing the time. There are, after all, more congenial things for shepherds to do than to teach or be taught.

III. '*Sur ung texte font plusieurs gloses*'

'There are many interpretations of a single text': the quotation comes not from a commentary on the Bible but from the poem that concludes the *Bon Berger*. Even from such a practical handbook as this, we are told – perhaps by Jehan de Brie himself, perhaps by his sixteenth-century editor –, 'les pasteurs portans crosse et mitre', prelates and bishops, can learn to care the better for their flocks. The literal realism of the work does not prevent the ideal shepherd it portrays from being allegorical as well. It became increasingly unlikely as the Middle Ages advanced that a shepherd in literature would be merely a herdsman. In sheer quantity, mediaeval didactic pastoral at least equals the idyllic; and although the shepherd himself could by convention teach directly, most comment and instruction worked through allegory. The range of allegorical possibilities was limited only by the poet's imagination; the priest is only one of many characters symbolized by the shepherd. Boccaccio's discussion of the nature of shepherds in his life of Dante gives some idea of the kind of interpretation they could be given.

> There are, in my judgement, two kinds of shepherds: those of the body and those of the soul. There are likewise two kinds of shepherds of the body, one being those who lead their sheep, cattle and other animals through the woods and meadows, the other being emperors, kings and fathers of families, who have to keep the people in their care with justice and in peace, and to find a source of food for their subjects and sons at appropriate times. Spiritual shepherds can likewise be said to be of two kinds, one being those who feed the souls of the living on spiritual food, that is, the Word of God, and those are prelates, preachers and priests; the other being those who first become expert in some branch of learning, and then teach others by reading or writing.[102]

The passage is much more applicable to the vernacular use of the shepherd than to Boccaccio's own eclogues, where, even if he writes about a king, the actual shepherd metaphor – the image of the Prince as guardian of and provider for his people – generally gets lost, if it is not forgotten altogether. In French and English, the literal shepherd always provides the starting-point for the allegory to develop from. The prince, the priest and the teacher can be presented as shepherds because their tasks, metaphorically speaking, are the same. The only exceptions, where the shepherds do not have these precise allegorical functions, occur in the *bergeries moralisées*, where the instruction is acted out in shepherd guise rather than being spoken directly, and so there anything that can be presented as a morality figure can take shepherd form, from Plat Pays (open country inviting invasion) to Foy or Paris or Peuple Pensif. Even these characters tend to have a dual rôle: they are the abstraction itself, and they also speak with the voice of the shepherd as suffering common man.

Bergerie allegory is rarely so precisely historical as mediaeval Latin pastoral; if it is working from specific events or within a specific situation, they are generalized and moralized so as to become more widely applicable. The eclogue closest in spirit to vernacular pastoral is also the closest in form, John of Garland's allegory of the seduction of the flesh by the devil. Most *bergerie* allegory appears to develop out of the shepherd's rôle as representative of the Common Man or out of the part he is given in the Bible, and vernacular authors seldom stop to state any theory they may have on the matter: *bergerie* appears to move naturally into allegory, in rather the same way as pastoral sprang to the minds of the authors of the *artes poeticae* when they came to deal with metaphor. In the twelfth-century calendar of Philipe de Thaün, for instance, he begins a 'Reprehensio allegorice per proverbia' with shepherd imagery:

> Que ferat pasturel
> Ki nen at nul drapel?
> Cum guarderat berbiz
> Ki nen at nul pastiz?[103]

> *What can a shepherd do when he has no clothing? How is he to keep sheep when he has no pasture?*

In spite of the generally accepted closeness of the connection, two writers do speak directly about the principles of their work: Christine de Pisan and 'Bucarius', author of the *Pastoralet*. Christine declares that the *Dit de la Pastoure* has an inner meaning for those able to discover it:

> Et m'est avis, qui veult drois
> Y visier, qu'on peult entendre
> Qu'a aultre chose veult tendre
> Que le texte ne desclot,
> Car aucune fois on clot
> En parabole couverte
> Matiere a tous non ouverte,
> Qui semble estre truffe ou fable,
> Ou sentence gist notable.   (24–32)

> *In my opinion, whoever wants to aim correctly can understand that it is about something other than the text itself discloses; for many times one conceals subject-matter that is not to be generally known in a secret parable which seems to be nonsense or fiction while there is really an important meaning.*

Barclay and Puttenham were to set out the theory of pastoral in almost identical terms:

Betwene Shepherdes, as it were but a fable,
To write of matters both true and profitable,

or 'matters such as perchance had not bene safe to haue beene disclosed in
any other sort'.[104] It is a surprise, after such an opening, to find the idyllic
story of Marotele. Whatever inner meaning it may have, it is certainly not
the closely-textured allegory of Petrarch where every word carries a herculean
load of secondary meanings. The 'sentence' of the *Dit* is closer to the
'sentence' of a romance, in that it conveys an emotional 'moral' through the
development of the story, though presumably it also has some particular
topical allusion. The allegory of the *Pastoralet* is much more detailed, though
Bucarius' account of his procedure is similar to Christine's. He sets out to

> trouver couverte voie
> Sans apertement révéler
> Les fais de quoy je voel parler,
> Qui sont bien digne de mémore:
> Sy m'estoet laissier droit histore
> Et torner aux fables couvertes
> Ou seront dittes et ouvertes
> Les paix, les gherres et les tours
> Des bergieres et des pastours
> Qui sont de haulte extraction, (8–17)

find a secret way of telling the deeds I want to describe without revealing them openly,
worthy of remembrance as they are; and so I had to abandon straight history and turn
to secret fables, in which are told and revealed the treaties, wars and actions of the
nobly-born shepherdesses and shepherds.

In his 'tres-brief exposition' at the end, in which he provides a key to all the
names, he apologizes for revealing matters 'par pastourie couvert' (8844).
It is not impossible that Petrarch's work gave him the idea for writing
political allegory in pastoral form, but his approach is entirely different – not
least in that his aim is to be understood, to see the civil wars in the perspective
of the shepherd world and so see them in a new way. His self-consciousness
about the way in which he is using the pastoral mode is more likely to be due
to his familiarity with Virgil than with Petrarch. Also, he is at his happiest in
the genre of pastoral allegory when he can be least allegorical: the poem
passes at every opportunity into interludes of song or dance or descriptions of
the season or the setting. The one French poet who worked directly under the
influence of Petrarch was Jean Molinet, who wrote his two pastoral poems
some sixty years later, towards the end of the fifteenth century. In form they
belong to the vernacular tradition of lyric *bergerie*, not with the bucolic; but
the complication of the allegory is entirely Petrarchan. *L'Arbre de Bourgonne*
describes the death of Charles, duke of Burgundy, as a tree falling, Petrarch's
metaphor in his second eclogue; and *Le Bergier sans Soulas*, a political allegory,
reads like a successful attempt to equal Petrarch's thickest obscurity.[105] One
manuscript includes a Latin key to the poem, which informs the reader who
or what represents whom, but even with this it is hard to make out the point
of many of the verses. Much of the language is ornately aureate, and this adds
considerably to the tediousness of the work. Like Petrarch, but in marked
contrast to Bucarius, Molinet fails to use the shepherd imagery dynamically –
it is cipher, not symbol.

The one characteristic that much vernacular allegorical pastoral has in
common with the Petrarchan eclogue is a preference for non-idyllic subject
matter: war, corruption in public life or the Church, bad government.

Petrarch sometimes implicitly contrasts such a state of affairs with ideal pastoral; in the vernacular, explicit comparison is continually being made with what *bergerie* should be like. The complaint of Jean Bodel's shepherdess, accusing the narrator of belonging to the invading army, is all the more striking by contrast with the usual sweetness of the pastourelle setting. In one of the finest of the *bergeries moralisées* of the fifteenth century, *Mieulx-que-Devant*[106] (a title that, as in most moralities, indicates the nature of the plot – matters are at last showing signs of improvement), the shepherds who open the play, Plat Pays and Peuple Pensif, the open countryside and its suffering inhabitants, describe a desolate scene where singing has ceased,

> Dessus ces beaulx champs
> Sont faillis les chans
> Des bergiers de nom, (p. 54)

where men at arms kill the sheep and cattle, where

> Il n'y a plus avril ne may,

and the sound of the trumpet terrifies the peasants – traditionally a sound never heard in the pastoral world. The shepherd is no longer king in his own realm:

> Qui règne sur les champs?
> – Gendarmes. (p. 56)

The hedges have been fired; one of the shepherds has even had stolen his 'chappeau jausne de Pasques'. They themselves are helpless, and all they can do is appeal to the 'bergerete franche' for aid: not an allegorical figure this time, but a recollection of the shepherdess of Domrémi, Joan of Arc. Life gradually improves: first a shepherdess named Bonne Esperance appears singing, the first sign of the recovery of *bergerie*; she is followed by Mieulx-que-Devant himself, again singing, who promises relief from the soldiers and from crushing taxation. Moreover, he declares,

> Roger Bon-Temps je vois suyvant,
> Faisant chapeaulx de fleurs nouvelles; (p. 60)

the garlands are a promise of the return of spring to the countryside. The interlude of hardship is almost at an end, and the shepherd world will once again return to its idyllic state. The emphasis, however, is on the hardship; and the depiction of the ideal is the foil to set that off. An unpublished *bergerie moralisée* of around 1437, the *Moralité du Petit et du Grand*, opens with the same pattern being set out, as the two shepherds of the title lament the present condition of the shepherd world in comparison with the Golden Age of the past – a Golden Age at once fully Classical,

> le aige doré
> Que Saturne amena aux hommes,

the world of Tityrus, Orpheus and Pseustis and Alithea, and also the golden world of *bergerie* where

> Bergiers s'esbatoient,
> Gros flaiol fleutoient,
> Bergieres chantoient, (f. 1ʳ)

and where the shepherds could shear their flocks and sell the wool in peace. The play tells, at some length, how Petit and Grand, representing basically the commons and the nobility, are directed by Dame Justice to uproot the *englantier*, the wild English rose that has taken root in France, blocking the fountain of Justice and wounding the shepherds with its thorns. Justice herself is not a shepherd; Conseill, 'counsel', her right-hand man, significantly enough is; – the teacher personified. Justice offers them the choice of numerous wise judges to help to preserve the fountain, but they dislike the sound of them all until she comes to Paris, who was not only a shepherd himself but had judged the goddesses by rather more congenial standards than her other examples had shown. Paris then makes his appearance, being transformed from the mythological figure into the city, and is left to administer the waters of justice with a promise that peace will reign henceforth.

The heading given to the *Pastoralet* announces that it will tell of 'la désolation du roialme de France', and it works in a similar way. It presents first of all a scene of idyllic pastoral: Bucarius describes himself as riding out in May to the Bois de Vénus and seeing the shepherds' revels there; and he comments,

> C'estoit un droit paradis,
> Se cest deduit durast toudis,   (355–6)

> *It would have been a very paradise if this delight had lasted for ever.*

The conditional mood is important: the paradise is shattered by the civil wars of the Burgundians and Armagnacs. The delight of *bergerie* itself is here of two kinds: there is the genuine carefree joy of the unnamed herdsmen – the commons – which is combined with care for their flocks, as the long exposition of the art of sheepkeeping proves; and there is the irresponsible carelessness of many of the leading shepherds. When Tristifer (Louis, duke of Orléans) sings of how his *bergiere* has given him a garland of may, the effect is ironic: his mistress is the Queen, and so the relationship is based on treachery and unfaithfulness, the opposite of the traditional simplicity and truth. The nobles take their enjoyment at the flock's expense and think only of their own pleasure; and as conditions deteriorate, they come to be as harmful to their sheep as the wolves (1984–8). Tristifer shears them four times a year; Lupal and Pompal, the Armagnac leaders, shear them twelve times, and the flocks die of cold. Even so, in the intervals of peace and at every treaty genuine *bergerie* revels continue in the setting of a timeless May – a perpetual reminder of the 'natural' state of the shepherd world, of which the war is a perversion. The sacking of the *parc* of Compiègne strikes all the more horribly against this background:

> Le parc pillent et tout despendent,
> Et des pastoriaux les uns pendent,
> Les aultres voelent decoler
> Et les bergières violer,
> Dont maint cry amer et dolent,
> Sicom en enfer le pulent,
> Y oy-l'en.   (5319–25)

> *They sacked the sheepwalk and utterly ravaged it; they hanged some of the shepherds and meant to behead others and rape the shepherdesses, whose bitter and grief-stricken cries could be heard like the horrors of hell.*

The contrast with the 'droit paradis' that France could be is complete.

Many authors suffer some difficulty in keeping their allegory consistent. The shepherd, by long custom, is the common man, who rejoices or who suffers; he is also, by natural metaphor, the prince with the commons as his sheep. Bucarius solves the problem to some degree by creaming off the 'pastours roiaux et gentils' from the others, but the commons have to lead a werewolf existence as sometimes shepherds, sometimes sheep, sometimes very nearly both at once. Generally the rôles of the shepherd are familiar enough for there not to be any confusion, even though he complicates matters further at one point by including an allegory within the allegory, a beast-fable about the seduction of the ewe by the wolf – the kind of 'tale of Wolues and Sheepe' that Sidney includes in his description of pastoral. Elsewhere the same shepherds occasionally have to take on both functions, as prince and commons, at once: in the *Bergerie de l'Agneau de France*, of 1485, the shepherds represent the three princes of the blood closest to the young Charles VIII (the lamb of the title), but they also speak as the suffering commons:

> Selon les gens le temps est gouverné. (8)

In the *Moralité de l'Alliance de Foy et Loyalté*, a more generalized political morality dating probably from the late fourteenth century, the conflict of rôle is between the realistic complaint of the suffering commons and the ideal life implied by the characters' names, the 'faith and troth' of Elizabethan pastoral. Loyalté laments that she dare not lead her sheep to pasture for fear of wolves, interpreted by Foy as 'gens d'arme'; but he goes on to remind her that now they have become shepherds they have no need to fear. Both characters have left public life and 'les III Estas' because they found there Covetousness, Ambition, Presumption, Avarice and Pride; and, Foy explains,

> Partant, devien-ge pastureil,
> ne iamais, qui soit laid ne bel,
> le miens cors ne les seruirat,
> tant qu'il ayent cele gent la. (244–7)

> *Coming away, I became a shepherd; and I shall never serve them with my body while that crew are there, for foul or fair.*

Corruption and war, by this account, are absolutely incompatible with true *bergerie*. Foy, Loyalté and Paix, together with Prudence, Honeur and Amour, sit down to feast together – on cheese, brown bread, apples, tart and cheese-cake – and the play ends with the marriage of the ideal shepherd and shep-herdess, each described in careful detail.

By implication, the shepherd always represented peace, even when he was complaining of war. The angels of the Annunciation had foretold 'Pax in terra' to the shepherds, and the scene formed a favourite pageant for royal entries: it was played for Charles VII at Paris in 1437 after the English had been driven out, at Bruges in 1440 and at Ghent in 1458.[107] Deschamps is satirical about the contrast with actuality:

> La paix fut destinee a ceaulx
> Qui volunté aroient bonne en eaulx...
> Le contraire faisons, si qu'en ce temps
> Nous ne devons ne bien ne paix avoir.[108]

> *Peace was destined for those who were men of good will ... We are the opposite, so that in this age we may have neither good nor peace.*

The theme of peace on earth was equally often presented at royal entries through secular *bergerie* scenes, with France itself as the setting, just as the whole country is the setting for the political *bergeries moralisées* or the *Pastoralet*. Pierre Gringore, one of the most accomplished dramatists and pageant-designers of the early sixteenth century, used the idea three times, in 1501, 1504 and 1514, this last occasion being when the English Princess Mary entered Paris as Queen of France.[109] One of his tableaux for her entry was designed to illustrate the peace brought by the two Virgins Mary: there was the Annunciation to the Virgin at the top of the pageant, a king and queen seated in the centre with Justice and Truth on either side of them, and at the bottom 'ung iardin nommé le iardin de france' containing shepherds and shepherdesses singing. For the visit of Philip the Fair to Paris in 1502, 'a shepherd representing Paris stood at the gate of a close to show that peace reigned in Paris'.[110] The political shepherd moralities and the tableaux are often very close in theme: the shepherds in both are associated with peace, with justice, with 'Bon Temps'.[111] The treaty of Valenciennes of 1493 was celebrated by a play performed before Margaret of Austria, 'and this play was based on the desertion of the countryside, which was beginning to recover, all in *bergerie*'.[112] The play itself has not survived, but in theme it was clearly very close to *Mieulx-que-Devant*.

The shepherd with his flock was an obvious metaphor for the prince as well as for the common man. Greban's shepherds have the self-sufficiency of the 'petit roy'; and the herdsman's life was a living allegory – in the words of Jean Lemaire's master shepherd, 'Your way of life is no other than the true model of a kingdom, and a kind of political government of a common-wealth.'[113] Many *bergerie* pageants were designed to emphasise the king's rôle as shepherd of his people. The young Charles VIII, the lamb of the *Bergerie de l'Agneau*, was welcomed into Rouen with a series of shepherd pageants: in one, shepherds and shepherdesses sang a four-part rondeau on the theme

> Resioys sommes au repos pacifique,[114]
>
> *We are made happy in rest and peace;*

in another they played a short scene, 'which matter based on *pastourerie* was a fiction modelled on bucolics, being a gathering of shepherds coming together to welcome the said shepherd'.[115] Classical pastoral and *bergerie* festivities are becoming identified, not to say confused. The pageants concluded with a plea to the 'grans pasteurs' to maintain justice in the state. Charles himself is both shepherd and lamb: a mechanical *agnus Dei* is compared with the King's own 'ioenne aage'. Many entertainments of this kind read more like an attempt at sympathetic magic than simple compliment, as if the presentation of the desired good would play its part in bringing it to pass. Louis XII was welcomed into Paris after his coronation in 1498 with a tableau showing him as the Good Shepherd bringing Peace, Good Times and Rejoicing to the French people[116] – a broad hint as to what they expected of him, and an indication of the close metaphorical relationship of their political ideal with the ideal of the shepherd world. The second *entremectz* at the wedding feast of Margaret of York and the duke of Burgundy in 1468 consisted of a lion entering the hall carrying on its back the dwarf Madame de Beaugrant dressed in rich cloth of gold and with pouch, crook and 'tous habillemens de bergiere'. The lion made a circuit of the hall, singing a song of welcome in two parts, tenor and treble, and opening and closing its mouth in time to the music; the need for hearing the words clearly would presumably mean that the parts were taken by singers at the side of the hall, not by the front and back legs.

> Bien viegne la belle bergiere
> De qui la beaulté et maniere
> Nous rend soulace et esperance!...
> C'est nostre paix et asseurance.

A lord then presented the shepherdess to the new duchess, 'en souvenance des nobles bargieres qui par cy devant ont esté pastoures et gardes de brebis de pardeça', 'in memory of the noble shepherdesses who have hitherto been the guardians of the sheep in this country'.[117] Margaret, like her predecessors, must be the shepherdess and guardian of her people. She, like Louis XII and Charles VIII, has not yet had time to show her mettle: they are only just entering on their reigns, and the tableaux provide an image on which they should model themselves.

The same ideas could also serve for compliments in the course of a reign, and for an elegy at the end. Martial d'Auvergne drew on them several times in his *Vigilles du Roy Charles VII*,[118] a poem commemorating the death of the king who had won back France from the English; and the hopes expressed in *Mieulx-que-Devant* and the *Moralité du Petit et du Grand* – which he may have known[119] – are now described as fulfilled: there had been plenty, peace and 'bon temps' in his reign; the *gens d'armes* had been 'gracieulx' to the shepherds; there had been feasting, dancing, music and birdsong, turning into the idyllic 'vie du franc Gontier' (I.85). Pierre II of Bourbon was celebrated in a similar way by Jean Lemaire de Belges: seven shepherds and shepherdesses with Classical names, representing the provinces under his rule, sing his praises and describe the abundance of the countryside; they call on their companions to make music to honour him and describe how he has chased away wolves and other wild beasts from his 'parcs'. The whole poem is an elegy for Pierre's death, but this particular section, where the shepherds introduce themselves and refer to the symbolic colouring of their clothes, looks as if it is the text of a pageant written for presentation in his lifetime and inserted into the elegy later.[120] Lemaire refers to the Duke as Pan in this poem, identifying him as the shepherds' patron and protector; Marot uses the name later to refer to François I, and he also picks up the themes of elegiac *bergerie* for his eclogue on the death of Loyse de Savoie.[121]

The ideal of society that the prince should aim to create – a world of peace, security and sufficiency – was familiar from *bergerie* literature of every kind; and like the literal shepherd, his first duty was to care for his flock. He must live for the sheep, not off them; to fleece the sheep – a recurrent image for burdensome taxation, in both secular and religious contexts[122] – or, even worse, to kill them, characterizes the bad herdsman, the bad prince and the bad priest alike. Jean Meschinot takes up these themes in discussing the prince's rôle as shepherd of his people in *Les Lunettes des Princes*, one of the most popular – and one of the most mediaeval in tone – of the books of advice to rulers fashionable in the early Renaissance; it was in fact written during the flourishing of *bergerie* under the Rhétoriqueurs, the group of poets led by Molinet and including Jean Lemaire, in the late fifteenth century.[123] He reminds the prince that, like the hired shepherd, he is answerable for his charge:

> Seigneur, tu es de Dieu bergier,
> Garde ses bestes loyaulment.   (663–4)

To be a hireling, the *mercenarius* of the Bible, more often defines the bad shepherd; in this context it is an additional incentive to diligence. If the prince acts more like the wolf than the shepherd, God will punish him as the human employer punishes a brutal herdsman.

> S'aulcun garde ma brebis,
> Puis la touze, escorche ou la tue,
> J'ay sens plus froit que mabre bis
> Si par moy sa peau n'est batue:
> Ceste chose bien debatue,
> Vous qui estes de Dieu pastours,
> De faultes ne faictes pas tours.   (642–8)

If anyone is keeping a sheep of mine, then fleeces, injures or kills it, my feelings are colder than grey marble if I don't beat his hide. So much is obvious; so, you who are God's shepherds, do not commit such evil deeds in the guise of exploits.

The prince must imitate the Good Shepherd of the Bible, in service to his flock, in humility and in following Christ. The contrast between ideal and actual was an obvious source of satire, and Barthélemy Aneau took up the theme when the Emperor Charles V visited France at Advent in 1539. He calls for celebrations to honour the royal entry of 'l'Empereur, le Roy, le grant seigneur'; but this turns out not to refer to Charles after all.

> Est ce Charles d'Austriche?
> Nenny, nenny, c'est bien ung aultre riche
> De beaucoup plus, et plus haute maison:
> C'est l'aigneau doulx, simple, sans fraude ou triche.
> Charles n'en ha sinon que la toison.[124]

'Charles bears no resemblance to the Lamb except for the fleece': he was the head of the Order of the Golden Fleece, but Aneau is coming very close to suggesting too that he is a wolf in sheep's clothing.

All the metaphors that can be applied to the prince can refer equally well to the priest; and the concept of the Good Shepherd came to be connected with *bergerie* traditions and conventions to the point where the priest is not so much presented as the shepherd as the shepherd begins to turn into the priest. The 'pasteur evangelique' is found, in the course of a spring walk, preaching to his flock as they lie in the shade; and in estates poetry, 'the literature of social classes',[125] the two are practically identified. It would be impossible for Chaucer to include a shepherd in the General Prologue to the *Canterbury Tales* as well as the Parson: he has described the one in describing the other. When Lydgate gives an account of each estate in turn from the prince downwards, he follows his description of the ploughman with these lines:

> So as the shepperde waccith upon the sheep
> The hoote somyr, the coolde wynterys nyght,
> Spiritual heerdys shulde take keep
> In Crystes foolde[126]

– again, shepherd and pastor are conflated. In both these instances, however, the imagery goes only a little way beyond the Biblical – Chaucer's sheep 'encombred in the myre', Lydgate's hard climate – and the idea never really takes wing. It is metaphor, not allegory, and it is not in the poet's interest to let the idea take over. Sermons and tracts tend to treat the theme even more strictly, uses of it being short and perfunctory; and it is entirely absent from John Bromyard's encyclopaedic *Summa Praedicantium*. The idea is given its fullest expression, not in writings about the priest, but in writings about the shepherd. The imagery as used by any poet may borrow from *bergerie* conventions; and the *bergerie* tradition itself found a new symbolic richness in the association.

As an example of the way in which the realistic shepherd became metaphorical, Jehan de Brie's *Bon Berger* is notable because of its non-allegorical character. He describes the all-important shepherd's hat, made of felt, with its broad brim folded up in front to form a pocket into which scraps of wool may be put so that his master loses nothing; and then he contrasts the prelate's hat, modelled on the shepherd's but with significant differences:

> Prelates' hats are made of costlier stuff than felt, and also, they are not bent back and folded in front. Perhaps this is because they do not wish to bring any profit to their master who has given them the charge they hold: for prelates fleece and take willingly and keep all the profit for themselves, it is said.[127]

The criticism of the bad priest springs from the study of the good shepherd; and the higher clergy in particular stand condemned by the contrast. There is a passage in the C-text of *Piers Plowman* attacking the easy-going bishops who allow irreligious hermits and such men to discredit the Church; and Langland enters completely into the shepherd world, letting the lines take their force from the metaphor itself, to the point where the allegory takes on a life of its own: the call to the herdsman, 'Hoow! hurde!', cannot be transferred back to a literal level of meaning. The prelates sleep instead of watching, as the shepherd should:

> *Vigilare* were fairour   for thow hast gret charge.
> For meny waker wolues   ben broke in-to foldes;
> Thyne berkeres ben all blynde   that bryngeth forth thy lambren,   (*watchdogs*)
> *Dispergentur oues*   thi dogge dar nat berke;
> The tarre is vntydy   that to thyne sheep by-longeth,
> Hure salue ys of *supersedeas*   in someneres boxes;   (=*writs*)
> Thyne sheep are ner al shabbyd   the wolf shiteth woolle...   (*scabby*)
> Hoow! hurde! wher is thyn hounde   and thyn hardy herte,
> For to wyrie the wolf   that thy woolle fouleth?
> Ich leyue, for thy lacchesse   thow leest meny wederes,   (*negligence*)
> And ful many fayre flus   falsliche wasshe!   (*fleeces*)
> When thy lord loketh to haue   alouance for hus bestes,
> And of the monye thow haddist ther-myd   hus meoble to saue,   (*property*)
> And the woolle worth weye   woo ys the thenne!   (*is weighed*)
> *Redde rationem uillicacionis tue*   other in arerage falle!
> Thyn hyre, hurde, as ich hope   hath nouht to quyty thy dette.[128]   (*believe*)

This is not allegory in the strictest sense – certainly not in the Petrarchan sense: occasionally the allusion is precise, and is pointed out – the reference to the summoners' writs, for instance; but over all, the poetic method is to create an analogy in another world, to transform the prelate's duties into the shepherd's, and see his failings in the perspective of pastoral. The metaphor continues right up to the Day of Judgement, when the bishop, like Meschinot's prince, has to answer before his master for his care of the flock and to pay his hire. The imagery brings the prelate's tasks within easy grasp; it also serves to elevate the shepherd, to present his life *sub specie aeternitatis*.

The touchstone for the quality of the Christian pastor becomes the actual shepherd, whose care and whose humbleness provide a model for every churchman from the pope downwards. The same tasks that are used to characterize the herdsman are brought in evidence against the clergy. Chaucer never wrote a story for his Ploughman, the Parson-shepherd's brother, but the omission was repaired later by the inclusion in many sixteenth-century editions of his works of the poem known as the *Plowman's Tale*, in origin almost certainly a Lollard tract of c. 1400.[129] It consists of a debate between a Griffon, supporter of the Pope, and a 'Pellicane withouten pryde' who does most of the talking, speaking on behalf of the Lollards and indicting the wealth and corruption of the Church, often in the pastoral imagery of the Bible, sometimes in terms of the literal or the ideal herdsman. The good shepherd is described as having nothing to do with 'lordshippes', for his life should be one of simplicity; he will treat his flock with loving care, protect them from wolves, smear them against the scab, carry them 'till his bak bend', keep them from the worst of the weather. The bad shepherd, on the other hand, takes a purely materialistic interest in his flock: he

> culleth the sheep as doth the cook;
> Of hem they taken the woll untrend. (593-4)

Similar themes are found repeatedly in French and Latin throughout the Middle Ages, but the idea seems to have taken the firmest hold in England. There is little elaborate development of *bergerie* as the image of the priest in French until the Reformation, in the eclogues attributed to Marot; and mediaeval poets occupied with more than one language tend to concentrate most on the idea when they are writing in English. There is a passage of some twenty lines in Robert Mannyng of Brunne's *Handlyng Synne* (1303), describing the shepherd-priest's duties and his responsibilities to his master – lines for which there is only the briefest hint in the French poem he was translating.[130] Gower makes brief attacks on the clergy in each of his three major poems, Latin, French and English; but only in the English, in the Prologue to the *Confessio Amantis*, does the idea really take life as an extended metaphor:

> Lo, thus tobroke is Cristes folde...
> The scharpe pricke in stede of salve
> Thei usen now, wherof the hele
> Thei hurte of that thei scholden hele;
> And what schep that is full of wulle
> Upon his back, thei toose and pulle,
> Whil ther is eny thing to pile.[131]

To use the image of the shepherd at all implies the ideal of selfless care for the flock; and there is no more rigorous, or more accurate, criterion for distinguishing the good priest from the bad. The idea remained a commonplace of pastoral literature for several centuries, and was given fresh impetus by the Reformation. Spenser's ecclesiastical eclogues and Milton's *Lycidas* are probably the best known instances, but they are certainly not the only, nor the most detailed, examples.

If the priest is defined by analogy with the shepherd, the reverse can happen too: the ideal herdsman can be distinguished from the bad by criteria that gain in force from their perpetual use in religious contexts. There is something of this process at work in the Wakefield *Secunda Pastorum*, where the dramatist brings onto the stage two contrasting groups of shepherds: the herdsmen who are chosen to see Christ, and Mak the sheep-stealer and his wife Gyll. Mak's shortcomings as a shepherd are all too obvious – most of them, at least: his lack of skill in music is a more subtle touch. Over the whole action of the play, however, the division between himself and the others is gradually established in religious terms: the shepherds who are to be called to Bethlehem will search for the lost sheep until it is found; Mak's only aim is to eat it, and he is excluded from the mystery of the Incarnation. The Chester dramatist takes the idea still further. He lays particular emphasis at the start of the play on his shepherds' care for their flocks, and at the end they agree to take up various forms of the religious life – to become pastors, shepherds of men: the good shepherd turns into the priest.

The connection of the pastoral world with the Redemption goes beyond allegory to become *figura*, symbolism of a kind where the earthly image is only a poor representation of the ideas it embodies, yet where those ideas are brought within reach by the image itself. Christ was the supreme good shepherd, the ideal at which prince, priest and herdsman alike should aim.

> Lorde of all Schepherdes, blessed mote thou be, for thou louedest more the Scheep, than her Wole; for thou fedest thy Scheep both in Body and in Soule; and, for Loue of thy Scheep, thou toke thy Deth to bring thy Scheep out of Wolues Mouthes.[132]

The shepherds who come to the manger in Aneau's *Chant Pastoural* can address the infant Christ,

> O bon pasteur, de tous pasteurs le maistre!   (sig. b.iv^a)

and they beseech Him to protect the lambs from wolves with His crook, the Cross. It is the presentation of the shepherd as the image of Christ and of Christ as the shepherd that is the culmination of mediaeval *bergerie*. The mode may be concerned with war, corruption and hardship; it also embraces the means whereby all these can be overcome, as the shepherd world turns into Paradise.

IV. *The Apotheosis of Pastoral*

The shepherd, by long tradition, was particularly close to God. Bacon describes 'the two simplest and most primitive trades of life' figured by Abel and Cain,

> that of the shepherd, (who, by reason of his leisure, rest in place, and living in view of heaven, is a lively image of a contemplative life,) and that of the husbandman: where we see again the favour and election of God went to the shepherd, and not to the tiller of the ground.[133]

In the Middle Ages the idea was accorded more than just literary recognition. Twice, in 1251 and again in 1320, popular crusades were preached in France specifically to shepherds, movements which were named 'Pastoureaux'.[134] Joan of Arc, who had carried out all the varied labours of the country girl, was established in the popular imagination within her own lifetime as having been a shepherdess, and the *Mystère du Siège d'Orléans*, of the mid-fifteenth century, speaks of her as 'God's shepherdess'.[135] In literature the Nativity plays are the prime example of God's especial favour to herdsmen, but the idea is widespread elsewhere: Joachim in the *Ludus Coventriae* receives comfort from the angel after the shepherds have promised to pray for him; the Nativity theme is extended to the political sphere as the shepherd becomes the embodiment of *pax in terra* for royal entries. Marguerite de Navarre was only taking a mediaeval theme to its logical conclusion when she made the

Bergère in her *Comédie jouée au Mont de Marsan* 'la Ravie de l'amour de Dieu', a mystic who is so absorbed in the love of God that she is beyond the scope of Reason. One of the Bergère's songs is a fragment from one of Marguerite's own *Chansons Spirituelles* (XXVII),

> O bergere, ma mye,
> Je ne vis que d'amours

– pastoral love has become the image of divine. She returned to pastoral persistently in her writings; among them is a Nativity play in which the shepherds have a leading part and are treated in a way that shows her sentitivity to the potential of *bergerie*: they are good shepherds, working hard and caring for their sheep; and they are also contemplatives, admiring God in His works and especially in the stars.[136]

The mystery plays were moving steadily towards this kind of ideal through-out the Middle Ages. The earliest shepherd plays do not count as pastoral at all: the shepherds perform the rôle they are allotted in the Bible, perhaps with some liturgical elaboration but with no sense of their belonging to a world of their own that exists in a special relationship to the real world. The *Officium Pastorum*, the liturgical drama of the shepherds, is based on the Gospel narrative and on the *Quem quaeritis* trope, and although in some versions the shepherds also sing hymns these belong with the liturgical context rather than with the dramatic action. The earliest non-liturgical plays, of the thirteenth century, again find no special inspiration in the shepherd world: the Benediktbeuern Christmas play, in which the shepherd scene takes the form of a debate, a kind of psychomachia with the herdsmen placed between the angel annunciant and the devil who wants to dissuade them from taking any notice, still gives the shepherds themselves very little to do; [137] and the Provençal *Esposalizi de Nostra Dona* (c. 1270–75) scarcely goes beyond the Gospel narrative except to add the gift of a lamb.[138] These plays still antedate the earliest secular *bergerie* drama, the *Jeu de Robin et Marion*; and it was only in the fourteenth century – though perhaps at the very beginning, if the evidence of the Holkham Bible Picture-Book is taken into account – that dramatists really began to treat the shepherd scenes as *bergerie* and so to develop the special relationship of the shepherd with God. The earliest surviving French shepherd Nativity is the Ste. Geneviève play of the early or middle fourteenth century,[139] and this does not go beyond the 'literal' *bergerie* conventions of music and horseplay; there is a coarse comic scene between the shepherds, and in this play alone there is no real adoration – the shepherds look on from a distance, insult each other, and return playing an *estampie*

> Pour Marion, ma doulce amie. (1979)

Relating treatment to date of composition is a problem for all these early plays: these parts of the piece may be an interpolation, presumably included in response to public demand; and while there is some evidence that the shepherd plays are the oldest part of the English mystery cycles,[140] there is little precise indication as to how close the original texts were to those that survive. Fifteenth-century dramatists, such as the Wakefield Master in England and Marcadé and Greban in France, made their shepherd scenes increasingly elaborate and increasingly capable of carrying crucial signifi-cances. They all show a concern for making their shepherds fit to receive the first news of Christ's birth: their care for their sheep is stressed, often they repeat the Messianic prophecies even before the Annunciation is made, and most of the French authors make some effort to present the shepherd world as innocent and joyful, untainted by sin, in a way that recalls the connection of pastoral with the unfallen world, the Golden Age or Eden. In France shepherdesses as well as shepherds go to adore the infant, and in France and England the herdsmen take with them gifts characteristic of their way of life: a flute, apples and nuts 'qui nous demorat hier a soppeir',[141] a hat, crook or tarbox, a nuthook, Greban's 'kalendrier de bois'. The shepherds' attributes are hallowed by Christ's acceptance of them, just as their lives are hallowed by His coming. Occasionally the gifts take on a symbolic significance parallel to the gold, frankincense and myrrh, but when this happens the meaning is always spelt out, and there is no indication that the gifts in the other plays carry any symbolism apart from representing the shepherd world. Marcadé's *Passion* was the first play to make the further development.[142] Here Robechon gives Christ his pouch,

> Car je sçay bien selon les prophéties
> Que pélerin seras en verité
> Pour rassembler les œuilles peries, (2294–6)

For I know well according to the prophecies that you will be the true pilgrim who will gather together the lost sheep.

Gombaut gives his crook to the One Who is

> Le vray pastour de grant auctorité; (2306)

and Gontier gives an apple, as a sphere an image of God's infinite goodness. The Virgin promises them Heaven in terms especially suited to the shepherd:

> Lassus en glore infinitive
> Arez joye *contemplative*. (2324–5)

The language the shepherds use as they present these gifts is elaborate, high style, as if they are elevated and inspired by their adoration. Once they are outside the stable the standard *bergerie* simplicity asserts itself again: their moment of sublime understanding is gone, and Robechon declares,

> Il sera de grant dignité
> S'il vit! (2359–60)

The Rouen *Nativité* combines the two approaches at the manger itself: the first three shepherds present a rather un-shepherdly clock, symbolizing eternity, for Christ is God; bread and wine, symbolizing His priestly function; and birds in a cage, representing kingship. The next shepherd then gives his mobile cabin, his *loge*, because Christ is the Shepherd and also poorly housed; and he shows off its features – where to put the dog and so on – with great pride. Finally the lad Anathot (the one who had so much trouble with his music lesson) promises complete service, himself, and then backs up the declaration by presenting his new crook, his pouch and his musical instrument, which he is just about to blow in the baby's ear when the others manage to stop him.

The English shepherd mysteries are most concerned with making the shepherds themselves a living image of God's Providence. They are shown as being worthy of the Annunciation – the Chester herdsmen boast of their healing skills, the shepherds of the *Secunda Pastorum* are defined as 'good' shepherds by their search for the lost sheep – but the society in which they are set is far from being one of idyllic innocence. It is the fallen world, a world of hardship and oppression; and in the coming of Christ Man's redemption is acted out. This presentation is generally more realistic than in French; but the realism serves a theological and symbolic purpose. As V. A. Kolve has pointed out in his detailed discussion of these plays, their action is perpetually related to wider theological issues: the Chester shepherd's skill in healing parallels Christ's power to heal; the ease with which the lad, the *Gartius*, throws his masters in the wrestling-match, is associated with the verse in the Magnificat on the deposition of the mighty; Christ's coming re-establishes peace and joy in the world; the feasting is an analogy of the end of the Advent fast, and perhaps even suggests the Eucharist; their singing is the worship due from man to God.[143] Even though some of these ideas may go beyond what the dramatist intended, they still indicate the richness of meaning of these plays; and that it should be the shepherd pageants that do carry the deepest significance is characteristic of the mediaeval pastoral tradition. The themes that Kolve picks out are almost all drawn from conventional *bergerie* material. The whole action becomes figural, important in itself (the dramatic vigour of the plays establishes that beyond any doubt) yet in essence only the key to something greater. The openings of the Wakefield plays, with the shepherd's grumbles about the weather, mutability, hardship and oppression, are designed as a foil for the events of the Nativity, through which Man is redeemed, freed from temporal distress, and given joy, peace and the stability of

> For ay his blys ful euen
> Contynuying. (*Prima* 488–9)

Christ alone can 'kepe you fro woe' (*Sec.* 742). The Coventry *Pageant of the Shearman and Taylors* uses the same contrast, and gives the closing promise of bliss even more immediate force. Its shepherd scene opens with one of the herdsmen alone and lost in the winter night:

> Then forto goo wyst I nott whyddur,
> But trawellid on this loo hyddur and thyddur. (*hill*) (230–1)

The events of Christmas night bring light and purpose to the shepherds – literally, in the appearance of the star and of the angels with the glory of the Lord shining round about them, and in the instructions to go to Bethlehem; and spiritually in their overwhelming joy that is described later by two *profetae*, and in their winning of Heaven:

> He graunt them hevyn ther-in to dwell;
> In ar the gon with joie and myrthe,
> And there songe hit is 'Neowell'. (472–4)

The music of *bergerie* is consecrated as an expression of divine worship and rejoicing, even as it is in their inadequate attempts in many of the plays to respond to the angels' 'Gloria'. The human response to divine grace is inevitably inadequate; it is also essential that it should be made. The Coventry shepherds' singing as they enter Heaven is a guarantee of its acceptability. The same is true of the shepherds' prayers for abundance in the Hesse Christmas play,[144] one of the very few instances of *bergerie* literature in German. Their prayers are an image of the men's spiritual hunger, and they recognize Christ as the creating God Who can answer their need.

If the Redemption is presented in action in these plays, it is suggested in more typological fashion through the connection of the pastoral world with the Golden Age, past and to come. Both the idyllic innocence of Greban's shepherds, and the sense of the world grown old and evil in the Wakefield plays, are a part of this; and in the *Prima Pastorum* the idea becomes explicit, as the shepherd expounding Virgil's prophecy declares

> that Saturne shall bend
> vnto vs
> With peasse and plente,
> With ryches and menee,
> Good luf and charyte
> Blendyd amanges vs. (398–403)

The typological parallel of the Golden Age and Eden was a commonplace of mediaeval thought, and it is found in several pastoral contexts: Theodulus uses it to make the transition from bucolic to theology in his eclogue; in an illumination in a fifteenth-century manuscript of the *Roman de la Rose*, illustrating Genius's comparison of the Shepherd's Park with the Golden Age and his account of the world's degeneration, the peaceful, primitive life of Saturn's reign is shown along with the seeds of its destruction, as one man climbs a tree to pluck a fruit.[145] Deschamps' Robin with his 'Franc Vouloir' is associated with unfallen man. Shepherds are also specifically connected with Eden, and through that the Redemption. There is an allegorical lyric by the thirteenth-century German poet Meister Alexander describing how as children they gathered strawberries, playing and dancing in a state of idyllic innocence; and it is a shepherd who calls out to warn them of serpents – a warning that is all too true, for their *gfeterlin* (presumably a reference to Adam) has been bitten and is condemned to be forever 'suren unde unsælic', 'in pain and accursed'.[146] The further connection with the Redemption is again seen at its most striking in Germany, this time in a work of art – an illumination by Berthold Furtmeyr in a missal made for the Archbishop of Salzburg in 1481 (Plate III).[147] The main scene is the Tree of Life and Death: on the left is the Virgin Mary plucking Mass wafers from the tree, on which there hangs a crucifix, and giving them to believers; on the right is Eve offering the forbidden fruit to sinners, with a skull in the tree above her. Below this picture are three medallions depicting shepherds, each with a label. The first, where the herdsman is standing watching his sheep, is headed:

> Prudencia: Quid honorabilius quam mea bene regere,
>
> *Prudence: What is more worthy of honour than to rule my own?*

The second shepherd, complete with broad-brimmed hat and pouch, is raking the grass for forage, and is headed:

> Regalitas: Quid laudabilius quam mihi commissa debita custodire,
>
> *Kingship: What is more worthy of praise than to keep watch over the duties laid on me?*

In the third medallion is a young shepherd with his hat slung back and a wallet at his waist attending to a sheep; he is the true shepherd, *Verus Pastor*, and his words are,

> Die hac (= ac) nocte meas preservabo et custodiam,
>
> *Day and night I shall keep and guard my sheep.*

Plate III

The Tree of Life and Death, Bayerische Staatsbibliothek,
Munich, Clm. 15710 f. 60ᵛ

The shepherd's knowledge of himself and his recognition of sufficiency as an ideal, his status as ruler in his own world and his care for his flock, are brought into direct relationship with the Redemption. Adam let his unruly passions win over his reason and imprudently wanted more than he was allowed; he lost his lordship of Eden; and he was redeemed by the ever-lasting love and care of the Good Shepherd, to win a pastoral Paradise.

The tendency of the Salzburg illumination is the same as that of the mystery plays: to see in religious *bergerie* a way by which mutability can be transformed into eternity, the fallen world into a renewed Paradise. The shepherds of the *Prima Pastorum* will be released from temporal hardship through the promise of eternal bliss; the Coventry herdsmen leave the bare wolds for Heaven. Mutability is a key theme of vernacular pastoral as it is of the Petrarchan eclogues: idyllic bliss will be shattered by time, war and destruction; the shepherd will be as harmful to the sheep as the wolf;

> Ah! Lord, how goes this world about!

is more than the refrain of a single poem. Bad herdsmen turn from the eternal to the corruptible:

> Ilz ont laissé le past qui ne perit
> Pour cestuy la qui en l'instant pourrit.[148]

But Heaven itself can become pastoral – the Shepherd's Park; and the good shepherds, who like the herdsmen of the pageants look towards God, will enjoy a life of eternal *bergerie*. Marguerite de Navarre expressed the point almost too succinctly in her play on the death of Pan, François I:

> Pan n'est poinct mort mais plus que jamais vit
> Avec Moyse et Jacob et David,
> Et sont aux cieulx parlans de bergerie.[149]

The prince and the patriarchs are united in a pastoral Heaven, and through their common rôle as shepherds have plenty to discuss. Marguerite called the work a 'Comédie': it ends not with death, but, like the *Divine Comedy*, in Paradise. The concept of a pastoral eternal life was widespread in the early Church – Psalm 23 is the crucial inspiration for it – and several Byzantine mosaics illustrate the theme; Gregory the Great preached on it in the course of his Sermon on the Good Shepherd,[150] where the faithful souls are presented as the Good Shepherd's flock. Two French poets make the theme their own and develop it in particularly fascinating ways: Jean de Meung, in the *Roman de la Rose*; and Bucarius, who was drawing on the *Roman*. They each make it in some sense the culmination of their work.

The passage on the Shepherd's Park in the *Roman*, spoken by Genius when he is addressing Love's forces, appears to be yet another of Jean's digressions, and it has received little critical attention except in so far as it testifies as to whether he was or was not a religious poet, a master of irony or a hypocrite. It is placed at a crucial point in the work, immediately before the final assault on the Rose; and the context of *bergerie* literature makes its form and purpose clearer. Jean was familiar with both Classical and vernacular pastoral. His knowledge of the *Bucolics* is abundantly attested by his references to them, most of which occur in the course of this passage or very close to it; and when Genius comes to the end of his address, he breaks off with,

> Que vous vois ci flajolant?
> Dreiz est que mon fretel restuie,   (20660–1)

> *Where am I taking you, fluting away like this? I must put away my pipes.*

The eclogue, in other words, is over, and the shepherd-preacher must go on to fresh pastures – in this case, the assault on the Rose. The speech starts, however, not as an eclogue but as an exhortation to love freely as Nature commands. There was only one literary mode in which such love is conventional (there are of course plenty of other isolated examples): in *bergerie*, and in particular the pastourelle. Fulfilled love, in Genius' eyes, is the only sort worth anything. Right from the beginning of his speech, he is moving within the sphere of pastoral thought, and his description of the Golden Age is a conscious part of this: he cites the *Bucolics* and *Georgics* as well as Ovid for his authorities. His principal theme, however, is the description of Heaven as the Shepherd's Park, of the bliss that awaits those who follow or who preach Nature's commands. They will become the white-fleeced flock of the Good Shepherd, feeding on the constantly springing grass and flowers. There will be no age there, and they will be free from all earthly hardships – from disease and corruption, from being fleeced or slaughtered; for the Good Shepherd prevents all harm from touching them, and Himself takes their image as the Lamb.

> Dou bon pasteur ne dout je mie,
> Qui devant sei paistre les meine,
> Qu'il ne seit vestuz de leur laine;
> Si nes despueille il ne ne plume
> Qui leur coust le pris d'une plume;
> Mais il li plaist e bon li semble
> Que sa robe la leur resemble. (19994–20000)

I have no doubt that the good shepherd who drives them before him to pasture is not clothed in their wool, nor does he rob or fleece them of anything worth so much as a feather; but it seems pleasing and good to him that his clothing should be like theirs.

An illustration of the passage in one manuscript shows Christ as the Lamb leading His sheep in procession, in a style strongly Byzantine, towards the sheepwalk where He stands watching over them as shepherd, complete with hat and crook.[151] The eternal spring of the park may be like the Golden Age, but there is an important difference: the Golden Age, like the Garden of Eden, did not last. This idea of the transitoriness of even the best of earthly things is a preparation for the next comparison Jean makes, of the park with the Garden of Mirth. Genius declares that the park surpasses the garden in all its details: the park is round, not square; the Well of Narcissus is replaced by the Water of Life, and its spring is watched over by the 'sage bergier' rather as the shepherds Paris and Conseill guard the fountain of Justice in the *Moralité du Pètit et du Grand*; and the pine beside the well gives way to the olive that bears the fruit of Salvation. Above all, the garden was earthly, and therefore mutable. There, Amant

> vit queroles qui faillirent,
> E faudront tuit cil qui les firent, (20355–6)

saw carols that fail, and all those who danced them will fail;

but those who follow Nature will know such a life in its true perfection:

> Ainz ireiz par jolieté
> Chantant en pardurableté
> Motez, conduits et chançonetes
> Par l'erbe vert seur les flouretes,
> Sous l'olivete querolant. (20655–9)

Rather you will go joyfully, singing forever songs of all kinds, carolling beneath the olive over the green grass and the flowers.

The courtly garden is nothing but the poor distorted image of the pastoral park. The sterile service paid by the lover to the Rose is against Nature, and as yet he can have no share in the landscape of the park; but those who have loved freely and gladly will have their part in its joy and its revels, 'both everlasting and true',

> Les beaus jeus, e les granz joies,
> E pardurables e veroies. (20379–80)

The highest bliss Jean can imagine is *bergerie* become 'pardurable'.

The extended *bergerie* of the *Pastoralet* allows Bucarius to develop the same pastoral themes that Jean de Meung uses in greater detail and with wider implications. Mutability is in a way the theme of the whole work: there is no safety, no stability, no joy that is not wrecked almost as soon as it is begun. The pattern is enacted through the events of the poem time and again, and in addition it is given its sharpest expression in a debate between an old and a young shepherd, somewhat similar to Spenser's 'February'. The old man warns the youth,

> N'aime pas trop ta couleur fine.
> Les flourettes enmi la prée
> S'amatissent à la vesprée,
> Et, que pis est, par pluie ou vent,
> Devant le vespre bien souvent.
> Jonèce, force, ne beaulté
> N'ont contre la mort séureté. (2376–82)

> *Do not be too fond of your splendid colour. The flowers in the meadow fade in the evening, or, what is worse, often before evening in rain or wind. Not youth, strength nor beauty offers any security against death.*

'Couleur fine' is the phrase used by Jean de Meung to describe the ever-blooming flowers of Paradise; and ordinary as the words are, the echo could still be intentionally ironic. The young shepherd, named Elesis in the poem, represents Jean, duke of Alençon; he was killed in the course of the civil wars at the battle of Roussaville, and Bucarius lists him aong the dead as 'Elesis, le berger jonet', a phrase that recalls this passage. He is one who in spite of his youth and beauty has died in the storm, 'devant le vespre'. The fragility of moral good, and the corruption within the superficially idyllic Bois de Vénus, are essential preliminaries to Bucarius' account of the Shepherd's Park; almost every incident in the work, in fact, reflects on it in some way, and the chapter in which it is placed is particularly carefully constructed so as to reach a richly meaningful culmination in the description of the pastoral Heaven. The chapter opens with the shepherd world in a state of intense suffering; the sheep have been left without protection for wolves to attack; and the sacking of Compiègne, the main political event of the section, follows swiftly. The city, in Bucarius' allegorical vocabulary, is a *parc*, and the sack represents the destruction of the pastoral world, turning it into an image of hell, 'sicom en enfer' (5324). Yet peace is made once more, and the shepherds revel and carol and dance to celebrate the treaty. During the festivities they sing a *lay* in honour of pastoral life.

> Bien dient en lor chanterie
> Que n'est estat que bergerie,
> Mais qu'il soient sans tricherie;
> C'est le vray, n'est pas menterie.

Pastours qui a joly jupel,
Houle, panetiere et chapel,
Belle amie et plaisant tropel,
Et bon pastourage en champel;

Pastours qui a hoch et forcettes,
Boiste pendant à lanierettes,
Et alennes bien déliettes,
Lignoel en ponte de soiettes;

Pastours qui a par les praïaux
Botes ou solers a noïaux,
N'a pas cure d'aultres joïaux:
Beaux est ly mestiers et roïaux.   (5617–32)

They say well in their songs that keeping sheep is the only walk of life to be free from treachery; that is the truth, it is no lie.

The shepherd who has a gay tunic, staff, pouch and hat, a fair sweetheart and a fine flock, and good pasture in the fields; who has a crook and shears, tarbox hanging from a strap, a case of fine awls, and thread sharp as bristles; who has boots or shoes fastened with buttons, as he goes through the meadow – he does not care for other jewels: the craft is fair and royal.

The shepherd pipes down the meadows, he eats butter and brown bread, he counts his flock on their return to the fold, he sleeps soundly without a care in the world. The final stanza introduces a new theme:

Honnour, loenge e plus encore
Soit au souverain roy de glore,
Et paix aux pastours qui dès ore
Auront bonne et loial memore!   (5657–60)

It is a paraphrase of the 'Gloria in excelsis' of the Annunciation to the Shepherds. Just how far it is from the actual current state of affairs is indicated by the appearance immediately afterwards of Hayne, Hate, within the shepherd world – a contrast that again emphasises the corruption of the earth, and its mutability. But Bucarius is also suggesting how these can be transcended. He is taking *bergerie* up through the four ascending levels of interpretation – levels that bring the inner meaning of the text steadily closer to God. There is comparatively little allusive historical allegory at this point to blur the patterns, and he can work it out purely in the more general moral terms that suit *bergerie* best. The festivities, and the description of the shepherd's life in the song, act on the literal level, as a narrative presentation of the shepherd world. The allegorical level, associated in Biblical exegesis with doctrine, is given in the song in the words of the angel to the shepherds. The moral level follows, as an old shepherd gets up and instructs his fellows in 'aulcuns des tours de bergerie', relevant to the prince and the priest as well as the herdsman. The shepherd, he declares, must know himself, he must care for his flock and keep them from wolves, he must be properly equipped; and he may also sit in the shade piping for his *amie*. The speech is the pastoral equivalent of Genius' dissertation on keeping the natural law, and it ends in the same way. The herdsman must set his mind on the Lamb, the Shepherd who heals His sheep at their death and whitens their fleeces; he must think of the park that encloses all that is infinitely fairer than any sheepwalk,

Et lors ses champs oubliera,
Et par ainsy en fin ira,
Tout esbatant et faisant festes,
Mener toutes ses blanches bestes
En ce beau parc et remanoir
Avoec l'Aignel qui n'est pas noir.   (5830–4)

And then he will forget his fields, and instead he will at last go rejoicing and revelling to lead all his white sheep into the beautiful park and to dwell with the Lamb who has no trace of black.

The image of the 'beau parc' is doubly emphasised by the earlier sack of the *parc* of Compiègne. The shrieks of Hell can have no place here; as in the *Roman de la Rose*, Heaven is *bergerie* made everlasting. Bucarius finds in the pastoral metaphor both the anagogical culmination of man's life and the way to attain it. 'Quo tendas' – the end of all things is the *bergerie* revel become the joyful adoration of the Lamb, the Good Shepherd, in a pasture eternally fair, eternally secure.

III

THE TRANSITION:
MIDDLE AGES TO RENAISSANCE

I. *Italy: New directions*

The Middle Ages were not dead centuries for pastoral literature. It was then that the foundations of the great achievements of Renaissance pastoral were laid; and in some respects the tradition reached its peak in this period – nobody after Petrarch imagined the bucolic to be such an arcane and intellectually demanding medium; the barriers between earth and heaven were seldom so insubstantial as in the Coventry *Pageant of the Shearmen and Taylors*. But the pastoral of the Renaissance is a different phenomenon from either *bergerie* or the Petrarchan eclogue, just as all three are different from the Virgilian bucolic; and perhaps the most decisive single difference is the Renaissance attitude to art itself. The enormously increased richness of understanding of the point of creative and imaginative activity was especially important in pastoral; and if the move away from *bergerie* realism ultimately spelt the death sentence of the shepherd pastoral, it was the development of its artistic potential that enabled the mode to reach its highest forms of expression. The change from mediaeval to Renaissance styles of pastoral is clear and unmistakable, but there is no break in tradition; and while a few poets are concerned to create an almost entirely new kind of pastoral, the tools of every writer had been forged in the Middle Ages.

The pattern of change varied from country to country. In France the rich tradition of pastoral continued almost unbroken from the fifteenth to the sixteenth century; in England the early sixteenth century saw a slowly but steadily increasing interest in the mode. The biggest changes came in Italy. Very little vernacular Italian pastoral had been written before the fifteenth century, but this does not mean that the *bergerie* conventions had no effect there; strangely enough, it was only in the Renaissance itself, when Italian poets were discovering the idyllic and escapist extremes of pastoral, that the simpler themes of *bergerie* were widely used, and then principally as a foil for the high lyricism that expressed those extremes. The seriousness and the social involvement of the northern vernacular traditions were never adopted, however; and although the eclogue often still took the form of political allusion and panegyric, it lost almost completely the moral edge that Petrarch, or even John of Garland, had given it. The most striking example of these tendencies, and the most significant, is Sannazaro's *Arcadia*, which gave Europe a model of abstracted love-melancholy played out in a pastoral world of the imagination; the most striking exception is Mantuan's cycle of ten rustic and sententious eclogues, which owe as much to the Middle Ages as to the new humanism, and which were drilled into practically every schoolboy of the next century.

The only surviving Italian pastoral poems of the Middle Ages are two idyllic pastourelle-type lyrics: Cavalcanti's 'In un boschetto', of the late thirteenth century, with its delicate expression of the joys of love;[1] and Franco Sacchetti's description of a meeting with some hill shepherdesses, 'O vaghe montanine pasturelle', written before 1377.[2] Here the narrator attempts to persuade the girls that their beauty deserves riches, honour and love, asking them whether they can ever be content with poverty and the wild woods:

> Deh, ditemi se voi vi contentate
> Di star ne' boschi così poverelle?

But *content* is just the ideal they most enjoy in their present life. They have no desire for riches; their dances and songs and flowers and garlands – 'balli canti e fiori e ghirlandelle' – are all they want, and in the envoy to the poem Sacchetti sighs romantically for such a life for himself. The poem has some resemblances in outline to Marcabru's 'L'autrier, jost' una sebissa', in the narrator's interrogation of the shepherdesses, but their replies assume a non-existent ideal world of eternal flowery fields, not the winter world of hardship and moral common sense; its praise of the simple life is in some ways parallel to the almost contemporary *Franc Gontier*, but it has none of the criticism of ambition and court life. The poem is already close to the escapist Arcadian pastoral; and it enjoyed a new popularity in the Renaissance in a shortened version attributed to Politian.[3]

The cruder side of *bergerie* does appear in Italy, but in a rather different context: in a nativity play of the later fifteenth century, the *Rappresentazione della Natività di Cristo*.[4] The lack of any earlier texts makes it impossible to say whether this play was part of an older Italian dramatic tradition; but it is certainly close to the French plays, and close to them at the 'ignorant' rather than the 'innocent' end of the spectrum, where the conventions of music and feasting are not given meaning by symbolism of any kind, and the shepherds themselves are in no way presented as especially fitted to hear the first news of Christ's birth. The shepherd boy is actually left behind to guard the sheep, much against his will, under threats of beating; and the shepherds pause to eat twice – once after the Annunciation to prepare themselves for the journey; and again in the stable itself, when one of them remarks,

> Io son di quelli che vo' un po' mangiare,   (p. 197)
>
> *Anyone else for a bite to eat?*

and at Joseph's invitation they eat some of the cheese they had brought as a gift to Christ. The play went through numerous editions, and was still being reprinted in the seventeenth century. The shepherds do, it is true, play a more genuinely worshipful rôle before Christ than in the crudest of the French nativities such as the Ste. Geneviève drama; but the *Rappresentazione*, and the rewriting of Sacchetti's poem only a few years later, illustrate particularly clearly the kind of process at work in Italian Renaissance pastoral. The seriousness and symbolism of the *bergerie* traditions, all the middle ground between caricatured realism and the idyllic, are ignored, and instead the literature becomes polarized into the crude and the cultured, the clownish and the aristocratic. Even the most Classical of pastoral forms, the eclogue itself, illustrates the division. In the early sixteenth century the Italian bucolics fall into four main types: the politically allusive, almost invariably panegyric; the elegiac; the love poems, usually laments of a Virgilian-type shepherd for unrequited passion; and the rustic, often written in dialect and describing revels and feasting such as are familiar from French *bergerie*.[5] The eclogue form encourages a somewhat idyllic treatment even of revels, but in more fully dramatized genres, *contrasti* and dialogues and actual plays, the crudity of the rustics becomes more marked. Shepherds themselves, however, had increasingly Arcadian associations; and accordingly the bumpkins tend to become mere peasants of unspecified occupation,[6] sometimes being contrasted with the idyllic kind of shepherd within a single work. The *Batecchio* of Fumoso, a *maggio* or May play written for the Congrega dei Rozzi of Siena in about 1548–9,[7] illustrates the kind of mingling of traditions that could occur. There are two 'levels' of characters: the nymphs and shepherds, who spend most of their time singing in the shade; and the *villani*, who are perpetually concocting plots to abduct various women. Mixed in with all this are other themes reminiscent of the *bergeries moralisées*: the peasants complain about the 'soldati', the Spaniards whom Charles V had installed in Siena after the city had put itself under his protection; and the closing song in praise of May,

> Ben venga Maggio
> che di Speranza è figlio,

and the prologue and epilogue spoken by Speranza herself, are strikingly close to the association of Spring and Bonne Esperance in *Mieulx-que-Devant*. The whole connection of May with pastoral is traditional, almost archetypal, though whether this play has any links with the folk *maggio* is not known – if it has, they are certainly well disguised. By contrast with these *motifs* that the play shares with the *bergerie* tradition are others that are of specifically Italian origin: the nymphs look back to works such as Boccaccio's mythological *favola boschereccia*, *Ameto*; and the coarseness of the peasants' love-interests has no connection with the simple truth of the mediaeval shepherd-lover. The two levels stand in juxtaposition to each other: they are interwoven, not combined, and the effect is one of contrast rather than harmony. The *villani* have ceased to be pastoral in any but the remotest historical sense; and the shepherds have lost all touch with their origins in the fields, and instead inhabit the same semi-mythological world as the nymphs.

The association of shepherd and 'nymph' (usually a synonym for 'shepherdess': only a few writers, notably Montemayor, keep the two separate), with all that it implies, epitomizes more clearly than anything else the underlying vapidity of this kind of pastoral: the kind that ruled supreme in Italy from the sixteenth century, and that came to dominate all Europe in the seventeenth and eighteenth. It is one – and at this stage only one – of the strands in Elizabethan pastoral; and although by the early seventeenth century the English songbooks abound in nymph-and-shepherd lyrics, its influence on major literature was still very small. Much more important was another gift from Italy: the idea of the pastoral world as a symbol of the poet's imagination. There is scarcely anything parallel to this in the whole range of mediaeval pastoral – perhaps because of the universal lack of interest in the workings of poetic inspiration; Martius Valerius is in this as in so much else the honourable exception. The idea appears, unheralded and unexplained, in the course of Giusto de' Conti's *La Bella Mano*, a collection of sonnets, sestine and canzoni on love composed around 1420.[8] It ends with four 'capitoli' that explore the relationship between the lover and the landscape; and in the third the lover has turned into the shepherd. The piece opens where an eclogue usually ends, at nightfall; and the shepherd, instead of leading home his flock, urges them to return alone.

> Itene a casa, e noi lasciate al bosco,
> Pasciute pecorelle: e voi d'intorno
> Pastori, omai venite a pianger nosco.

> *Go hence home and leave me in the forest, my full-fed flock; and you shepherds who dwell around, now come and lament with me.*

The theme of unfulfilled love, the great theme of Petrarch's *Rime*, is also making practically its first appearance in pastoral outside the Latin eclogue, and again its development was to be out of all proportion to such an insignificant beginning. Virgil's Coridon provided Classical authority for the theme, but only Valerius and the young Boccaccio had used the idea in the Middle Ages. In the fifteenth century it at last became possible to add Theocritus' Cyclops to the list of love-sick pastoral figures; and the pastoral of Virgil, Theocritus, Petrarch and de' Conti himself all worked on the imagination of Iacobo Sannazaro to produce the first great work of Italian pastoral, the *Arcadia*. The double inspiration from modern Italy and ancient Rome is indicated in the second eclogue of the work:

> Itene all'ombra degli ameni faggi,
> pasciute pecorelle, omai che 'l sole
> sul mezzo giorno indrizza i caldi raggi.[9]

> *Go hence to the shade of the pleasant beeches, my full-fed flock, now that the sun sends down its hot midday rays.*

The shadowy beeches are Virgil's – the very first line that so many pastoral poets echoed to declare their allegiance; the phrasing echoes both Virgil (X.77) and de' Conti; and then only a few lines later Sannazaro lets his poetry run a more turgid course in an obscure passage of Petrarchan socio-political satire, in an indictment of wolves, thieves and all the things that make the pastoral world corrupt. The other kind of influence from Petrarch, from the *Rime*, shows itself in a number of ways: in the exploration of landscape as it relates to the poet; in the elevation of love-melancholy to the ideal poetic state of mind; in the interest in the poet himself. Here again the idea is partly Classical – both Theocritus and Virgil had appeared as characters in their own eclogues, as Sannazaro appears as Sincero in the *Arcadia*; but the subjectivity of the presentation, the process of projecting the poet's own mind, goes far beyond Classical authority, and beyond Petrarch himself in its intensity. The form of the work, alternating sections of prose and verse, is derived from yet another source, Boccaccio's *Ameto*: a work that is pastoral only by hindsight, and by the accident of containing an eclogue. The mythological setting of this piece, with its abundance of nymphs and its almost neoplatonic treatment of love, make it something of an anachronism for the fourteenth century; there is nothing resembling it in the pastoral proper of the period, and the fact that Sannazaro received from it a stimulus so different from anything the Middle Ages had apparently experienced is an index of the different interpretation of pastoral in the Renaissance.

The *Arcadia* is composed of twelve *prose* and twelve eclogues, with a prologue and epilogue in which Sannazaro comments on the nature of the work
he has produced – again an indication of his artistic self-consciousness. Some
of the eclogues may have been written independently first, and the whole
scheme developed later. The work was probably complete as far as the tenth
eclogue by 1489; an unauthorized version was printed in 1502, and Sannazaro added the last section for publication two years later. Although what
little story the work has is continued through both parts,[10] the centre of
inspiration for the final addition has moved from the *Bucolics* to the *Aeneid*:
the setting is almost reluctantly pastoral, and the themes – funeral games and
a kind of underworld visit to the sources of the earth's rivers – are closer to
the heroic. It was Sannazaro's pastoral vision, however, that captured the
imagination of Europe, and made the work seminal for Renaissance literature.
Arcadia, for him, becomes something of a symbol of the nature of poetry
untouched by real life. Virgil had transformed the barren Greek uplands
into an idyllic land of the imagination;[11] Sannazaro practically identifies the
two, imagination and land, and the identification seems to have fulfilled
some particular need of the age for symbolic expression – an expression of the
relationship between love of beauty in all its forms, such as characterizes the
Renaissance. The great weakness of the vision, its escapism, was also one of
its greatest attractions; and it did serve Sidney as an incentive to recreate
the Arcadian world in a more serious form. The pastoral tradition as Sannazaro knew it certainly did not authorize such a retreat from harsh reality, and
oddly enough he almost admits as much: the eclogue at this period could not
simply ignore the Petrarchan vision of the fallen world, and several times – in
the second, sixth and tenth eclogues, sometimes at considerable length – the
poetry turns into obscurely allusive allegory on the corruption of the times,
sometimes apparently with some particular political reference, sometimes in
the more general moral terms of *bergerie* satire:

> Nel mondo oggi gli amici non si trovano,
> la fede è morta e regnano le 'nvidie,
> e i mal costumi ognor più si rinovano. (VI.4–6)
>
> *In the world today no friends are to be found; faith is dead and envy reigns supreme,*
> *and evil practices are ever on the increase.*

But Sannazaro will never commit himself to such a view of the world. On
each occasion the listening shepherds applaud the singers and praise their
verses; their delight, and not the bitterness of the words, is given all the
emphasis. The tenth eclogue contains the most concerted attack on the
pastoral world and the present 'duro tempo' compared with the past Golden
Age: the shepherds eat acorns out of mere poverty, not out of primitive
innocence; the gods, the demigods, the birds and the flowers are wasting
away; Astraea has fled the earth; and the shepherd-poets are dead –

> Dafni, Mopso e Menalca, oimè, son morti. (X.109)

But the effect of all this is so cushioned that it strikes as hard as thistledown.
Its immediate context is a discussion, in beautiful verses, on whether or not
poetry has declined; and the speech on the state of the world is not uttered
by Sannazaro himself, either directly as author or by Sincero within the work,
nor even by one of the other characters, but is reported in the course of the
eclogue. Caracciol, the wise shepherd who uttered it originally, may have had

all the characteristics of the healer and teacher such as helped to raise the herdsman to his position of moral authority (40–45), but still the song is only heard at third remove, repeated by Selvaggio and recorded by Sincero-Sannazaro; and when Sincero describes his own reactions to the eclogue at the beginning of the next *prosa*, he simply ignores the main bulk of the poem and comments only on the account of his homeland in the opening lines. It is as if the unpleasantness of the 'real' world were brought in simply in order to be discounted – to be framed and rendered innocuous, even picturesque, by poetry.

The Arcadian version of pastoral was enormously influential. Over the course of the next century or so it came to displace the mediaeval traditions almost entirely; and even now the immediate associations of the word 'pastoral' derive more from Sannazaro than from any other single writer. The *Bucolics* themselves were obscured for centuries by Arcadian preconceptions as much as they had previously been by allegory. Many of the great works of Renaissance pastoral take almost all their inspiration for their portrayal of the shepherd world from Sannazaro; Montemayor's *Diana* (written in Spanish but rapidly translated into a number of languages, including English), Tasso's *Aminta* and Guarini's *Pastor Fido*, with the *Arcadia* the four works most influential in the sixteenth and seventeenth centuries, all transfer their action to a mythological world of temples and nymphs, where love is the only event of any importance and that is a sickness that languishes in poetry and must be cured by magic or the gods. The underlying assumptions about the mode have moved from allegory to romance; and if there is any one Classical parallel it is not the *Bucolics* but the newly-discovered *Daphnis and Chloe* of Longus, a late Greek romance that tells of the pseudo-innocent awakening to love of a pseudo-shepherd and shepherdess, who turn out eventually to be long-lost noble children. The whole process is almost the direct opposite of the mediaeval uses of pastoral, whether in eclogue or *bergerie* form; and the features that are most characteristic of Arcadian pastoral are a complete inversion of the ideas that the earlier traditions had attempted to express.

The first of these characteristics, and perhaps the most immediately striking, is the overwhelming importance of love in the Arcadian tradition, to the point where the plots scarcely admit of anything else. Love, moreover, is almost invariably rejected, miserable and self-regarding, and if the lover – or lovers, for the plots are usually sustained by a multiplication of such unhappy love-stories – do finally win their mistresses, it is due to supernatural intervention or to equally remarkable upheavals of plot. Both the tone and the structure look backwards, to Petrarch's *Rime* and to the romances, but not to any earlier pastoral. Mediaeval bucolic generally rejected all idea of love; and the *bergerie* tradition took an entirely different attitude. There, love is joyous and fulfilled; it represents a complete rejection of the courtly conventions of suffering and service, and in its spontaneity it comes close to representing Nature and indicting Art. Love there is the highest earthly expression of pastoral bliss, which the outsider can rarely do more than envy. The principal genre for expressing all this is the lyric: it is impossible to make a 'plot' out of achieved love such as could sustain any form of greater scope, and the reader or listener is invited not to trace the uneven path of true love, or the still more uneven path of false love, but to look in on, and wonder at, the perfection of joy.

The second characteristic of Arcadian pastoral is closely connected with its Petrarchan presentation of love, for Petrarchism is also an attitude to poetry and the poet. Arcadia is not realistic; it is the poet's invention, his own realm, and so his own imagination. The landscape becomes an extension of his mind and a means of exploring it; there is a sense in which the clouds have no alternative but to weep with him. Mediaeval pastoral, on the other hand, had studied the poet in the world, but not the world within the poet. The changing seasons had been a symbol of mutability which the pastoral metaphor could overcome. There was all too much painful realism in this world; but pastoral also offered an image of eternal stability. The Arcadian tradition, taken to its extreme, is both escapist and introverted; the mediaeval tradition, as exemplified both by allegorical *bergerie* and by the Petrarch of the *Bucolicum Carmen*, found its meaning at the centre of social concerns. The values of Arcadian pastoral are the values of art, and their importance and their weakness both lie in that fact. It was up to the poet what he made of them. The values of mediaeval pastoral were much more directly moral: the social responsibility of the herdsman, 'faith and troth', the rejection of greed, pride, hypocrisy and ambition, the eternal reward bestowed by the Good Shepherd on the good shepherd.

The third feature that most clearly distinguishes the Arcadian from the *bergerie* tradition is that not only does pastoral become aristocratic but the shepherd becomes an aristocrat. The Petrarchan eclogue had done something analogous to this, but there it is a transposition rather than a journey that is in question: the actual world ceases to exist while the action is played out on the allegorical plane. In Arcadia, the best shepherd will turn out to be a noble youth taking time off, the best shepherdess to have been snatched from her royal cradle fifteen years before. The apparent fusion of aristocratic and shepherd worlds always proves illusory; the distinction between them remains absolute, their identity an author's fiction. In *bergerie* literature the relationship between the two was repeatedly examined, and in a rather more critical way – in the pastourelles, royal pageantry, the *Dit de la Pastoure*, the *Estoire de Griseldis*. Griseldis was the one mediaeval shepherdess who married a lord, and there is a clear suggestion that her excellence is due to her upbringing, not that her courtesy had survived in spite of it. Even here, however, the point of the story depends on the contrast of the two worlds, and elsewhere the possibility of a real link is always simply rejected. The Arcadian shepherd world, artificial as it is, can never quite dispense with the fact that shepherds are peasants and so cannot be the equals of the princes and gentlemen. It does its best all the same: realism becomes merely decorative, to be appreciated rather patronizingly from a safe distance by both author and reader, and the sheep accordingly become just peaceful white blobs on the landscape. Both sheep and aristocrat had rather different functions in the Middle Ages: the best prince was the shepherd who paid most attention to his flock.

The inhabitants of Arcadia do not come from the real world. Whatever else the mediaeval shepherdess may have been, she was always flesh and blood; by the time Tasso was writing *Aminta* or Fletcher *The Faithful Shepherdess*, 'nymph' and 'shepherdess' were virtually synonymous. The villain in *bergerie* is the wolf, the oppressor or the pillaging soldier, in Petrarch political enemies or the Avignon papacy; in Arcadia it is more likely to be the satyr, and the object of his attack is not the sheep or the shepherd but the shepherdess. The concern with human issues, whether expressed through the fantasies of the pastourelles or the bitter engagement of the eclogue, is replaced by a teasing and only semi-human eroticism.

In spite of the popularity of Sannazaro's work, Arcadian pastoral did not have an immediate victory: in Italy its effect was felt very quickly, but in England the history of pastoral in the sixteenth century is best summarized as a battle between the two traditions – perhaps even as a love-affair. The *Arcadia* was, in any case, not the only influential pastoral work to be produced in Italy at the end of the fifteenth century. There was another that was if anything even more widely known, and which represents a rather different tradition: the *Adolescentia*, the ten eclogues of Baptista Spagnuolo Mantuanus. At the time these works were written, it was Mantuan rather than Sannazaro who was more in the main stream of pastoral: both works make some innovations, but where Sannazaro is breaking new ground in genre, tone and the whole use to which pastoral was put, Mantuan uses traditionally recognized forms and themes in a new way.

The eclogue was the commonest form of pastoral in Italy at this period, in both Latin and Italian. There had been an interval of almost a century after Petrarch's followers had played his kind of bucolic to its bitterest end before the genre recovered; it was not until the 1460's that the breath of the gentler humanism of the Renaissance brought it back to life,[12] and it revived in a mutated form. Virgil was rediscovered: not Virgil the prophet or moralist, even less Virgil the mystic or arcane allegorist, but the artistic poet of idyllic rural life. He was still believed to be concerned with political matters, with Christian prophecy, with panegyric, but these no longer involved a divorce from his ostensible subject-matter; and the influence of the *Bucolics* read with the minimum of gloss lent respectability to the figure of the shepherd. Mediaeval traditions could not simply be forgotten in favour of a pure and sterile Classicism, but the traditions that the Renaissance ecloguists drew on were wider than Petrarch would ever have allowed. Three poems in Latin, among the very first of the revival, illustrate this changed attitude to the eclogue. Two, by Tito Strozzi, are a celebration of the seasons, spoken by an old shepherd as a judgement on a debate as to their rival merits between his two young companions[13] – themes that look back to the Classics, but through the poetry of the Carolingians; and the third, by Francesco Patrizi, is an eclogue on the Nativity written for Pope Pius II,[14] presenting in semi-dramatic form the reactions of Lycidas and Menalcas to the events of the first Christmas night, and transforming the typical *bergerie* subject into a Virgilian bucolic. Allegory and polemic have here disappeared, giving way to the shepherd: not yet actually a realistic peasant, but something not too far away.

Naturalism was in no sense the aim of these poets, however: it was the artistic potential of the eclogue that ensured its popularity in that most art-conscious of all ages. Pastoral is a mode that invites beautiful poetry: Theocritus and Virgil knew as much, and Martius Valerius, but it was Strozzi and Sannazaro and their contemporaries who fully responded to the invitation. The return of the singing-match, where the quality of the poetry and not the quality of the argument is the issue, is an indication of the change in interest. The eclogue could still be put to practical use, but in situations where good poetry could be shown off at its best: panegyric, not satire, becomes the typical allusive form. Even the eclogues with the most serious

intentions, such as those on the life of Christ,[15] are not didactic in the mediaeval sense: they are artistic variations on a familiar theme – perhaps even
artistic exercises – and are intended to instruct, or to point a moral, only in
the loosest sense. The invention of new settings for the eclogue is the result of
the same process, a desire to extend its artistic possibilities. Sannazaro had
created a new type of shepherd pastoral in Italian; he invented the piscatorial
in Latin, substituting a stereotyped fisher world for a stereotyped shepherd
world within the confines of the eclogue. These poems, like the *Arcadia*,
became immediately popular, but their influence was much smaller than
that of the *Adolescentia*. It is almost as if the artistic eclogues of the early
Renaissance were out of their time as far as other countries were concerned:
it was Mantuan, with his moral aphorisms and his rustic peasants, who ranks
alongside Virgil as the pattern for bucolic in northern Europe.

The first eight of Mantuan's eclogues belong in origin to the 1460's, when
he was a student – hence the title *Adolescentia*. This was the first decade of the
revived eclogue, when each poet was able to set his own tone and style for his
work; and although he probably revised them extensively before publishing
them in 1498, along with two more poems to bring the number up to the
Virgilian total, they remain almost entirely distinct from the more idyllic
tendencies of the general run of Italian eclogues: less Renaissance, in fact,
and more mediaeval. Rustic realism and the corruption of the world are
much more central to these eclogues than beautiful landscapes or Golden
Age panegyric; and Mantuan is of key importance for the way in which he
helped to pass on these mediaeval approaches to pastoral to succeeding
generations. His work was especially influential since educationalists seized
on it immediately, for it was simple enough to use, like the *Ecloga Theoduli*, as
a schoolbook, and with the gloss of Iodocus Badius Ascensius, produced only
a couple of years after the poems were first published, it became a standard
textbook in most countries of Europe.[16] He was rated extraordinarily highly:
he was hailed in his time as a second Virgil, by one tourist even as a poet
twice as good as Virgil;[17] and Alexander Barclay, in his list of authorities for
the eclogue form which he composed within some fifteen years of the publication of the *Adolescentia*, describes him as

> the most famous Baptist Mantuan,
> The best of that sort since Poetes first began. (Prol. 33–4)

Mantuan himself was well versed in the *Bucolics*, but there is almost as little
idyllicism in his eclogues as in Petrarch's. His descriptions of shade, the
spring and flowers are short and casual, and overshadowed by the emphasis
he lays on the hardships of the shepherd's life, by accounts of cold winters,
hard labour, floods and hailstorms. Love is baffled by practical considerations
or by the lover's own will to destruction; and instead of elevating love to the
centre and aim of existence, as the Arcadian tradition would have it, Mantuan
firmly degrades the emotion with a wry comment that rapidly became
proverbial, 'Semel insanivimus omnes' (I.118), 'We have all been mad
once'. There is less panegyric than abuse – of townsmen, of churchmen,
doctors, even countrymen, and also, and most notably, women. For him as
for Boccaccio, the pastoral world can be perfected only in Heaven,[18] and
there is no direct point of contact between the two. The earth is a place of
suffering and distress, to be ended only through common mortality:

> Omnia longa dies abolet; cum vivere cessas,
> omnia sic abeunt, ut lux cum sole recedit. (VI.173–4)

The day wipes out all things at length; when you cease to live, all things pass away, as the light fades with the sun.

The poems are set in the fallen world, and the real world: the characters are not exotic swains from a land of the imagination but earthly peasants, who work, feel the cold, marry, go behind a bush *ad ventrem levandum* (IV.87), play football, feast and dance to the bagpipes. Just as in the *bergerie* tradition, however, this superficial naturalism does not prevent Mantuan from treating a much larger range of subjects than strict realism would allow, though it does keep him within moderate bounds. He includes a poem (V) on the perennially popular subject of the lack of patronage – Barclay and Marot and Spenser were to take up the theme in imitation; but his shepherd-poet is not the Petrarchan laureate nor the inspired *vates* of the Renaissance, but the mediaeval music-maker, who can no longer sing because he is hungry and cold and cannot afford a knife to trim his corn-pipe. Mantuan will expatiate on the evils of the town, but the shepherd who describes them knows about them through experience, through having sold his goats' milk within the city walls. Mantuan's shepherds, represent what they may, rarely need to step out of their primary literal existence. The language they speak may be Latin – a contradiction that he tried, none too successfully, to make up for[19] – but the imagery and the stories they tell are homely: the married sister of Faustus' sweetheart watches him as a cat watches a mouse that wants the bacon; Eve, ashamed lest the excessive number of her children should make her seem to have been lustful, hides half of them in the straw when God comes visiting. When the situations are borrowed from purely artistic conventions, as in the acute love-melancholy, madness and eventual death of Amyntas in the second and third eclogues, there is still something to keep the reader in touch with ordinary life: we never hear Amyntas lamenting directly, his sufferings are all transmitted through the moralising and practical peasants who tell or listen to the story. The choice of a Classical name for him, in contrast to most of the other characters, itself indicates the different level of experience: the first eclogue was about the joyful outcome of 'honest' love, and describes the normal processes of wooing and marriage; the second is a companion-piece on the madness of love, 'amoris insania', and the finest examples lie to hand not in life but in literature. The process is the opposite of Sannazaro's in the *Arcadia*, where the eclogues may hint at actual events and the darker side of life, but the impact is cushioned by poetry and the golden mythological world; here, the love-melancholy of the Classical shepherd in his world of poetry and nymphs is set in the perspective of down-to-earth commentary, of reminders of the need to provide for one's old age and so on.

All these eclogues are didactic. The shepherd is still the teacher, not perhaps being endowed with the wisdom of some of his predecessors but certainly having a neat way of turning a moral epigram. Mantuan's method of writing is to develop a situation – his eclogues, like Metellus' or John of Garland's, frequently have plots, even if the action is recounted rather than presented – and then to comment on it: the moral is not inherent in the situation, as it is in the more strictly allegorical eclogues. Mantuan's distance from pure allegory is illustrated by his mention of a gift of ten apples as a love-token. The commentators had for centuries assumed that Virgil's line on this subject referred to the *Bucolics* themselves, and Dante borrowed and adapted the idea; in Mantuan, the apples remain apples, but they are made the opportunity for a remark on how women's tastes in presents have become more expensive:

> Ventum est a gramine ad aurum. (III.86)
>
> *But now from grasse to golde*
> *They are ascended.*[20]

The structure of many of the poems also helps to point the general moral. The two Amyntas eclogues are preceded by accounts of disasters due to excesses in nature, the flooding of the Po and a violent hailstorm, which provide an analogy to the excesses of the shepherd's love very different from the usual kind of pastoral pathetic fallacy; and the seventh eclogue, which tells how the Virgin appeared to a herdsman named Pollux, opens with an account of the gods' especial favour to shepherds – in contrast to ploughmen, and with all the mediaeval *exempla*, of Paris, Abraham, Moses, Apollo, the Bethlehem shepherds and Christ Himself, cited in evidence. The literalism of the first six eclogues was perhaps beginning to be rather a constriction by this time: the landscape of the earth that the Virgin (not as yet identified) describes to Pollux, with its snakes in the grass and men transformed to beasts, is a marked change of level from the first part of Pollux's story, where he has left home to escape the oppression of his father and stepmother (the *noverca* of the *Bucolics*). If Pollux will go to Mount Carmel, the Virgin tells him – in other words, join the Carmelite order – then he will eventually enjoy the true pastoral countryside of Heaven. The suggestions of allegory in the landscape are carried over to the next eclogue, with its debate on the rival merits of hills and plains – a debate continued in more explicitly allegorical terms by Spenser and others. The poem continues with the next instalment of the story of Pollux, but lest the theme should risk becoming too sublime Mantuan makes his shepherds even more rustic than usual, getting their words wrong or losing the thread of what they were saying. The poem ends with a list of the feasts of the Virgin, which Pollux has learnt through watching the stars: an amalgamation of the calendar and contemplation themes.

The last two eclogues, composed some time later, no longer even attempt to preserve the illusion of realism, though the central concern is still instruction rather than art. *Bergerie* has given way to the mediaeval bucolic tradition: satire and allegory are the order of the day, and the pastoral setting is simply a transposition from a literal level of meaning, with no dynamism, or scarcely even existence, of its own. The ninth poem opens ostensibly as a continuation of the discussion of hills and plains, but quickly resolves into an attack on the corruption of Rome, and then changes into a panegyric of Falco – Falcone de' Sinibaldi, papal treasurer and a candidate for the papacy itself. He is described as having all the attributes of the good shepherd of every kind: he is rich in flocks; he is a better poet than Orpheus; he can heal diseases and restore moisture to the barren land. The final poem is even more of an occasional piece, and still more firmly in the polemic tradition. It is a debate – even a quarrel; certainly not a singing-match – between shepherds representing rival factions of the Carmelite order, with a decisive victory for the party Mantuan himself held with. In form and subject the poem has moved a long way from the semi-naturalism of the earlier eclogues, but it highlights Mantuan's rejection of the subjective use of pastoral as the expression of the poet's own artistic imagination in favour of longer-estabished traditions. The *Adolescentia* represents a synthesis of the Classical and the mediaeval eclogue with *bergerie*, along with a bow to the Renaissance fashion of love-melancholy in the story of Amyntas. Mantuan made the Virgilian bucolic a contemporary form – contemporary not just because it could deal with topics of current concern but because its characters and settings were recognizable in modern terms; and by writing of fifteenth-century peasants in Latin he made the actual shepherd a fit subject of scholarly attention.

II. *France before the Pléiade*

The new humanism that restored Virgil to the eclogue was not so desperately needed in France as in Italy; the first echoes of Virgil to be heard in French pastoral occur in Jean de Meung, in the thirteenth century. *Bergerie* literature had shown an increasing tendency to take note of the *Bucolics* in the fifteenth century – it shows in the Classicism of Bucarius, in Pinel's pageants of 1485 'traictee sur bucoliques', even in Molinet's abstruse mythologizing; and the Rhétoriqueurs, the 'school' of Molinet and his followers, pursued their own peculiar brand of humanism in pastoral. After them, however, there was a lull of around two decades in the writing of formal pastoral; and when Marot turned his attention to the mode in his eclogue on the death of Loyse de Savoie in 1531, the first formal eclogue to be written in French, he was able to look at it with a new perspective. The pastoral of the Rhétoriqueurs often reads like an anxious attempt to include everything – picturesque *bergerie*, allegory, Virgilian imitation, panegyric, elaborate style; Marot is if anything even more eclectic, but far more relaxed. His principal models are Classical – Virgil, and to some extent Theocritus; but he draws heavily too on Jean Lemaire de Belges, and he uses the full range of allusion that the vernacular tradition had made available. He owes comparatively little to the recent developments in Italian and neo-Latin pastoral, even though a number of Italian ecloguists, notably Andrelini in the 1490's and Alamanni and Belmisseri in his own time, worked at the French court.[21] His allegiances are indicated most clearly by his juvenile translation of Virgil's first eclogue, and by his choice of a pastoral pseudonym for himself in 1539: not Tityrus, but Robin – the piper of his own homeland, not the master of the Classical tradition. The name has a double appropriateness in that 'Marot' was a common abbreviation of 'Marion', so it becomes almost an allusive pun. At least one of his pastoral imitators thought a more Virgilian title would have been more fitting, linking Marot with Maro;[22] Marot's avoidance of this may have been deliberate. As a Renaissance poet, he was bound to honour the Classics; as a French poet, he valued vernacular traditions as well.

The *Eglogue sur le Trespas de ma Dame Loyse de Savoye*[23] is a dialogue between Colin and Thenot, who presumably represent contemporary poets – they start by congratulating each other on the quality of their poetry – but apparently not Marot himself. Thenot offers Colin twelve quinces and a double pipe in return for a song mourning 'la Bergere Loyse'; and the bulk of the poem, as in Spenser's imitation in 'November', consists of Colin's lament. The poem is allusive rather than strictly allegorical, with the openness of reference characteristic of political *bergerie* as demonstrated in tableaux for royal entries and so on; and the imagery is often reminiscent of those as well. Loyse was the shepherdess who kept safe the sheepwalk of France:

> Tant bien sçavoit son Parc clorre et fermer
> Qu'on n'a point veu les Loups y faire entrer (147–8)

– specifically a reference to her regency; and she is remembered too as 'la Bergere de Paix' (240), the peace characteristic of ideal *bergerie*. The structure of the lament follows the long-established pattern of the move from grief at her death to rejoicing at her present state in the 'champs Elisiens'; but here even this form represents a synthesis, for Marot is drawing as much on Lemaire, and on the *bergerie* traditions of heaven that he uses, as on Virgil or Theocritus. To choose to write an eclogue in French at all indicates something of a double allegiance, and Marot carries this through in the details of the poem. French and Latin provide language and form; both traditions provide the contents. Marot's later eclogues lean more towards one tradition or the other: two of them are genethliaca, birth-poems, closely imitated from Virgil's fourth eclogue, and they have lost almost all their pastoral connections in the transposition; the other, the *Eglogue de Marot au Roy, soubz les noms de Pan et Robin*, written in 1539, belongs more closely to the vernacular tradition. This is the work that inspired the *Shepheardes Calender* more than any other single poem; and as such it possesses an importance even greater than its intrinsic poetic value.

The *Eglogue au Roy* in essence is about the poet and poetry, and that in itself marks it out immediately as a Renaissance work; but Marot develops the theme through the traditional vernacular imagery of the shepherd, and through the idea of the changing seasons. Pan himself, representing François I, is drawn as his name indicates from Classical and neo-Classical traditions: as in the *Bucolics*, he is the shepherds' patron, who listens to their songs; and as in Servius' gloss, he holds a septuple pipe representing the harmony of the planets, and here also the seven liberal arts. Marot portrays himself, however, not as Tityrus but as 'petit Robinet', and he gives an account of his life in the same terms. In the spring of his youth, 'le printemps de ma jeunesse folle', he had gone birds'-nesting and nutting, had made cages for birds and chased wolves; and he had learnt to sing 'en mode pastoralle', at once the classic starting-point for the aspiring poet and the appropriate term for music-making in such an environment. In his summer, 'quant...mes jours vindrent en leur esté', life became more serious and his songs more skilled: he learnt the duties of the good shepherd, how to predict the weather, to know herbs, to recognize and cure sheep diseases:

> Et a cognoistre et guerir plusieurs maulx,
> Qui quelque fois gastoient les animaulx
> De noz pastiz; (131–3)

he fell in love; and the nymphs and fauns wept at the sound of his music – a reminder that he is, after all, a poet in the great Classical tradition. But now he is in the autumn of his life, and care threatens to drive away his inspiration as the wolf the lamb. He prays to Pan for protection for himself and his flock:

> Il me suffit que mon trouppeau preserves
> Des loups, des ours, des lyons, des loucerves,
> Et moy du froid, car l'yver, qui s'appreste,
> A commencé à neger sur ma teste. (235–8)

Marot is obviously not limiting himself to naturalistic *bergerie*, even as an allusive transposition from real life. But the pastoral mode, in all its variety, can provide him with images for his nature as a poet – as a French poet of the Renaissance, with all the interests in neo-Classical humanism and his own native background that that suggests. The eclogue is about himself as poet, but it is not subjective in the way that Sannazaro is subjective; and the over-riding natural imagery is not the landscape of the mind but the season of man's life – not the internal, but the universal. The contrasts of spring and winter, of age and youth, had been perpetually recurring themes of pastoral throughout the Middle Ages; it was Marot who combined all these to relate to a single subject – to himself, to the poet, to Man.

It is the personal aspect of the *Eglogue au Roy*, and its interest in poetry as an art, that mark it out as a Renaissance work, and that helped Spenser on his way towards his new understanding of pastoral; but the poem did not immediately open up a whole new concept of the mode, even in France. Probably the first poem to have been inspired by it, the *Complaincte d'un Pastoreau Chrestien*,[24] represents a return to the pure mediaeval tradition of allegorical *bergerie*; and though the poem is described as being 'en forme d'eglogue rustique', the eclogue structure is well disguised by the fact that the poem is not only a complaint but an *overheard* complaint – a typically vernacular pattern; the nightfall close is the only part directly reminiscent of Classical eclogue. The *Complaincte* may be Marot's own work, and was certainly accepted as his in the sixteenth century: it follows the same outline as the *Eglogue au Roy*, the prayer to Pan, but it is not just a religious imitation of the *Eglogue* such as would necessarily suggest a reworking by a different author. Pan is no longer the king, the shepherds' patron, but God, their protector, and in keeping with the *bergerie* tradition his chief concern is for their basic task of sheepkeeping: it is he

> qui seule de toutes pars
> Vas conservant noz loges et noz parcz,
> Et noz brebis estans es bergeries
> Gardes si bien qu'elles ne sont peries. (29–32)

The subject of the shepherd's lament is the decline of *bergerie* in all its forms: 'faux pasteurs' scatter the righteous; only 'pitoyables chantz' are heard in the fields; he has flung away his bagpipe for grief, and has left Marion and their child in order to mourn. The sheep are stolen; or they are given poor pasture, or straw instead of grain; or they are injured by bad herdsmen who are no better than foxes,

> Ce sont renardz qui soubz simples habitz
> Vont devorant les plus tendres brebis. (161–2)

The shepherds themselves are prevented from singing and making music in honour of Pan: not this time a reference to poetry, but specifically to Protestant worship. The age-old use of pastoral for religious and ecclesiastical allegory is being developed as a medium for Reformation propaganda; and in contrast to the *Eglogue au Roy* the central issue has moved back from the poetic to the polemic. The *Pasteur Evangelique*, also ascribed to Marot though rather more doubtfully, is even more clearly in the *bergerie* tradition – it does not claim at all to be an eclogue – but it indicates again how central pastoral imagery still was to religious debate. The new interest in the *Bucolics* could be called into the service of pastoral polemic, but it did not replace it.

The revival of the eclogue did not entail the demise of other pastoral genres, and the traditional vernacular forms – lyric, noël, mystery play, royal entry – tend to follow almost exactly the same patterns in the early sixteenth century as they had done a century earlier, though with a sophistication that marks them as belonging to a more art-conscious age. Marot himself wrote a *ballade* on the Nativity shepherds[25] that is entirely in keeping with *bergerie* conventions, and which emphasizes the separation of that tradition from more exalted poetics by rhyming in -c all the way through – a type of rhyme described by Sebillet in his *Art Poétique Françoys* as 'pauvre, a cause de son indigence et imbécillité'.[26] Barthélemy Aneau's *Chant Natal*, containing both a *Chant Pastoural* on the Nativity and a *mystère par personnages*, appeared in 1539, and Marguerite de Navarre's own *Comédie de la Nativité* was perhaps written about the same time; but both writers base their work firmly on *bergerie* conventions. Aneau's Ruben has to blow his nose before he kisses Christ; and Marguerite's shepherds and shepherdesses, despite their allegorically significant names – Sophron (Prudent), Nephalle (Watchful) and so on – go to the stable thinking that even if the door is shut

Nous le verrons au moins par vn pertuis   (665)

– exactly the kind of widely-illustrated iconographic detail that is so typical of the earlier plays. This use of old conventions does not indicate any lack of artistry or sophistication in the writers themselves. Aneau was a literary theoretician as well as a practising poet, and his *Dixain de la uenue de Iesuchrist et de Charles le quint*, his *bergerie* epigram on the Lamb and the Golden Fleece,[27] has a sharpness of expression that distinguishes it as a Renaissance piece; and Marguerite, in making her mystic 'ravie de l'amour de Dieu' in the *Comédie jouée au Mont de Marsan* a shepherdess,[28] was making actual a potential in *bergerie* that had never been so strikingly realized before. She was familiar with the French neo-Classicism of Marot too: her play on the death of François I, her brother, owes something to both his *Eglogue au Roy* and his elegy for Loyse. François becomes Pan; and the structure, the move from grief to rejoicing, follows the eclogue pattern. The actual form of the work is dramatic, however, in keeping with the *bergerie* tradition; and its intermingling of songs with the spoken word also comes from long-established French dramatic practice. Like Marot, she is making a synthesis of vernacular, Classical and Renaissance pastoral, and with the same result of enabling her work to carry more significance than an eclogue alone could have done. Pan himself is a good shepherd, characterized by his care for his flocks; and the fanciful ideas of pagan afterlife are altered to bring them closer to the Christian image of the Shepherd's Park, where the king can meet the patriarchs to discuss sheepkeeping. The two other works of Marguerite's in which she draws on pastoral traditions represent the opposite extremes of the mode: *La Fable du faulx Cuyder* is a mythological story in the Italian style about a metamorphosis involving nymphs and satyrs, based on Sannazaro's *Salices*, and is pastoral only in the loosest sense; and a long passage of pastoral allegory in the *Complainte pour un detenu Prisonnier* describes the Christian pastor in terms of the Good Shepherd, who has never injured or killed any of his flock, and who has led them to the green pastures that are only accessible by way of Christ.[29]

Marot set the pattern for the fusion of pastoral traditions, but Marguerite and Aneau are both working independently, using him as a model when it seems appropriate but not just imitating him. The other pastoralists of the 1530's and 40's were doing much the same thing: their works move within the whole range covered by the mode from Italian-style mythologizing to the austere morality of what might be called *bergerie engagée*.[30] The native tradition was not in the least despised: Rabelais himself, who mocks practically every other literary or conceptual motif of the age, is still prepared to make the shepherds with their revels and feasting into an idyllic society qualified only by the existence of the crazy outside world that impinges on them.[31] The Latin eclogues written in France at this same period show none of the same broad-mindedness: mediaeval conventions are abandoned altogether in favour of Italian or neo-Classical, and with them go the last links with the real shepherd; their pastoral is an art without any pretence of nature. In the following decades even pastoral written in French moved the same way. The subject-matter still covered a much wider range than Virgil would ever have admitted – 'mortz de Princes, calamitéz de temps, mutations de Republiques, joyeus succés et evenemens de fortune, louenges Pöétiques, et téles choses ou pareilles,' as Sebillet puts it[32] – but it is much narrower than in the previous century: pastoral becomes exclusively the plaything of the court, and the fields and the fresh air, the labour and the responsibility, are shut out.

III. *England before Spenser*

The publication of the *Shepheardes Calender* in 1579 inaugurated a new era of English pastoral, and of English poetry; but its influence was due less to the fact of innovation than to the fact of tradition. Sidney's *Apologie* shows very clearly the general longing for genuinely native poetry that would stand comparison with what was being produced in France and Italy: 'That Poesie thus embraced in all other places, should onely finde in our time a hard welcome in England, I thinke the verie earth laments it, and therefore deckes our soyle with fewer Lawrels then it was accustomed. For heretofore, Poets have in England also flourished.'[33] In choosing the pastoral mode for the first expression of the new poetry, Spenser was not rejecting English traditions in favour of Classical or continental: he is declaring the potential of the English language to challenge comparison with French or Italian, but he makes it work through English poetic and cultural traditions. The whole sixteenth century had shown a slight but persistent interest in pastoral, quickening in the two decades preceding the publication of the *Calender*; and the records of pastoral shows, the poems and eclogues that antedate Spenser are an index not only of this steadily increasing interest but of the widening circle of influence writers were prepared to admit.

The *Bucolics* had been available throughout the Middle Ages, but the Wakefield Master is the only English poet to draw on them at all for *bergerie*. Petrarch's eclogues were known in England in the fifteenth century, and the last of them, on the Hundred Years' War, was put to political use in a treatise supporting the English claim to the throne of France;[34] but there is no sign of any comparable poetic influence. It only becomes possible to trace specific sources of imitation after the major continental poets of the Renaissance were being read in England; and then the process of imitation is never simple, for the English tradition itself was too firmly established to be disregarded.

The vernacular conventions of *bergerie* were the most unscholarly of all the influences on Elizabethan pastoral, and they are in many ways the most elusive to trace since they provided a background that was taken for granted: Virgil or Sannazaro or Mantuan or Marot would be deliberately imitated so that a reader might recognize and appreciate the artistic tradition in which the poet was working, but it is only rarely that the same process of imitation can actually be documented from the native tradition. Most often the resemblances are of the general 'family' type rather than specifically of father to son: a court entertainment of 1558, for instance, required a coat, hood, cap and girdle 'for a shepperd mynstrell to the Cloynes'[35] – a shepherd who is obviously related to the music-makers Jolly Wat, the Wakefield shepherds and the French Robins rather than to the poets Tityrus or Sincero, but it is impossible to cite a precise authority for him. He belongs to a cultural context – to an artistic school rather than being painted after a given master. Probably the most pervasive idea of the shepherd came through folk-songs, and much of the evidence has been lost, just as it is no more than a chance reference in Malory that indicates the existence of the English milk-maid pastourelle in the Middle Ages. Jolly Wat himself is probably the best example of this tradition:

> The sheperd vpon a hill he satt;
> He had on hym his tabard and his hat,
> Hys tarbox, hys pype and hys flagat.
> Hys name was called Joly, Joly Wat,
>> For he was a gud herdes boy.
>> Vith hoy!
> For in hys pype he made so mych joy.

The piping had always been a traditional part of pastoral; but Sidney's 'shepheards boy piping, as though he should never be old',[36] is closer to this than to Sannazaro's shepherds tuning up for their formal eclogues. A stylized hill often seems to have been the setting for the shepherds on the pageant-wagons[37] as it was in manuscript illuminations, and it remains a conventional setting in much Elizabethan pastoral even though it may be inconvenient or unlikely from the point of view of plot.[38] In a poem by John Wootton, included in *Englands Helicon*, the anthology of pastoral lyrics first published in 1600, the themes are moving towards the eclogue:

> Jolly sheepheard, sheepheard on a hill,
>> on a hill so merrily,
>> on a hill so cherily,
> Feare not sheepheard there to pipe thy fill.[39]

He is also drawing on another popular song, widely known in the Elizabethan era but probably dating back much further:

> Jolly shepherd and upon a hill as he sate,
> So loud he blew his little horn, and kept right well his gate.
>> Early in a morning,
>> Late in an evening,
> And ever blew this little boy, so merrily piping:
> Tere liter lo.[40]

There are several other versions: one is given to the shepherd's boy Mopso in the play of *The Maydes Metamorphosis*,[41] where he, a forester's boy and a courtier's servant each enter singing songs characteristic of their rôles. The courtier's servant sings 'Fortune my foe'; the forester's starts, 'Can you blow the little horn', with words reminiscent of the forester songs of the court of Henry VIII; and Mopso, the shepherd's boy, sings,

Terlitelo, terlitelo, tertitelee, terlo.
So merrily this sheapheards Boy
His horne that he can blow,
Early in a morning, late, late in an euening...

These songs all look back to the mediaeval carols, to Jolly Wat and the
traditional refrain of the shepherd noëls,

They sang terli, terlow,
So mereli the sheppards ther pipes can blow.[42]

The carols themselves may well have sprung from secular folksong. It is a
tradition that links the centuries: the shepherd piping on the hill is the
archetype for the Elizabethans as in the Middle Ages.

The English mediaeval conventions of pastoral were as vital as they had
ever been in the early sixteenth century. *Jolly Wat* itself is found in Richard
Hill's commonplace book, a manuscript compiled c. 1508–36 and including
many old or traditional pieces.[43] The mystery plays were still being performed
until well into Elizabeth's reign: the Chester and Wakefield cycles were last
performed about 1575. The reign of Henry VIII saw a succession of works
of many different types in the mediaeval style. The *Kalender of Shepherdes*, in a
succession of translations from its French original, went through five editions
before 1528. Cardinal Wolsey organized a masque for the Christmas
festivities of 1526/7 which included 'six old men clad in the pastoral fashion,
but the material was cloth of silver and white satin'; this particular occasion
started with the King arriving with a dozen or so companions also masked,
and Cavendish may be conflating the two parts of the entertainment when he
speaks of Henry appearing at Hampton Court with 'a dozyn of other
maskars all in garmentes lyke shepherdes made of fynne Clothe of gold and
fyn Crymosyn Satten'.[44] The 'shepehokes vj' recorded in the inventory of
properties of the Revels Office made on the accession of Edward VI may be
a relic of this occasion.[45] A shepherd also appeared at least twice in the midsummer shows of the London livery companies;[46] and occasions such as these
were the forerunners of the much more elaborate pastoral disguisings and
street pageants of Elizabeth's reign. The use of pastoral for ecclesiastical
criticism was also very much alive. Skelton, under the *persona* of Colyn Clout,
condemns bad prelates in the imagery used by Gower or the author of the
Plowman's Tale:

They take no hede
Theyr sely shepe to fede,
But plucke away and pull
The fleces of theyr wull;
Vnethes they leue a locke
Of wull amonges theyr flocke,

and only 'two or thre' bishops take any care to keep the sheep away from
the goats or the wolves.[47] Another poem in Richard Hill's commonplace book
which has as its theme, repeated in varying form in the last line of each verse,
'Kepe well the shepe of cristis folde', is an attack on the pope and the prelates spoken by a real shepherd:

As I gan wandre in on evenyng,
Betwen the cornys be syde a balke,
I sawe the dew in dale gan spryng
And herd men a bowt yer shepe gan walke.

Than on of them to me gan talke,
Fful carefully clothed from the cold:
Thes prelates full still ther shuld stalke,
To kepe yer shepe well in the fold.[48]

As in 'As I me lend', the attack gains extra point from the nature of the
speaker: as a true shepherd he can speak objectively but with the authority
that comes from a full knowledge of his craft, and the hardship and care of
his own life make a pointed contrast with the pride and wealth of the
Christian pastors. The clergy, he declares, provide only 'sede of synne'
instead of 'gras of grace' for their sheep to feed on; and their sheep, like those
of Langland's prelates, are 'skabbyd', a condition that indicates a basic lack
of care. Papal magnificence comes in for especial condemnation, for

Peter rode never to rially,
But kept ye shep well in the fold.

As in the Middle Ages, the literal shepherd is made the measure of the
allegorical pastor; it is only the scurrilous language used about the pope
('ffor fere in hell yat his tayle reke') that suggests that the poem is a Reformation work rather than mediaeval. Poems and pageants of these kinds could
generally just as well have been produced in the late fourteenth or fifteenth
century as the sixteenth. There is only one reference from this period to a
work based on Classical bucolic, and since the work itself has not survived it
is impossible to know how it was treated: this is Skelton's 'diuise' of 'how
Iollas louyd goodly Phillis', based on Virgil's second eclogue.[49]

Barclay's eclogues were written in the very early years of Henry's reign;
he probably put them into their final form in about 1513–4.[50] Although he
chooses to write in the eclogue form – the first time it had been done in
English, and some twenty years before Marot did the same in French – and
although his principal direct sources are two Italian humanists, Aeneas
Silvius Piccolomini (later Pope Pius II, for whom Patrizi wrote his Nativity
eclogue) and Mantuan, pastoral for him still means the *bergerie* traditions.
The description of Cornix in the first lines of the first eclogue establishes this
allegiance at once: the hood, felt hat, cockers (French *wages*, high boots or
leggings), bottle, pipe, crook and wallet with its bread and cheese are all
familiar from many other descriptions of shepherds, though Cornix's poverty,
and touches such as the wooden spoon, take them beyond the conventional:

At diuers holes his heare grewe through his hode,
A stiffe patched felt hanging ouer his eyne,
His costly clothing was thredebare kendall grene,
His patched cockers skant reached to his knee,
In the side of his felte there stacke a spone of tree,
A botle his cote on the one side had torne,
For hanging the eare was nere a sunder worne.
In his one hande alway his pipe he bare,
Whereof the sound him released of his care,
His wallet with bread and chese, so then he stood
(A hooke in his hande) in the middest of his good.   (I.146–56)

Barclay's principal contribution to the bucolic was to naturalize his shepherds,
to make the eclogue rustic; Mantuan had pointed the way, again working
from *bergerie* traditions, but his shepherds still talk Latin, with all that that
implies, and Arcadia and allegory are often not so very far away. Barclay
does not take Spenser's step of giving his characters rustic names – they are

still the Amyntas, Minalcas and Cornix of Virgil or Mantuan – but they are unequivocally English peasants, firmly localized in the Fens around Ely where he was writing. He is the first English pastoralist of any importance to whom it is possible to ascribe a name and an artistic personality, and so in his work it is possible to trace for the first time just what an English poet of some learning expected the pastoral mode to be. His immediate stimulus was probably the appearance of the *Adolescentia*, at this date a brand-new work. It was not printed in London until 1519; but other publications – Winkyn de Worde's editions of the *Ecloga Theoduli* in 1509 and of the *Bucolics* in 1512 (the order of appearance is not insignificant) – suggest an increasing interest in the eclogue. It was, in fact, at once hallowed by authority and tradition, and a fresh and exciting literary form with a new range of potential ideas contained in it. Barclay was fully aware of both aspects of the genre. In his *Prologe* he lists the great pastoral poets of the past (itself something of a pastoral convention): Theocritus, Virgil, Mantuan, Petrarch and Theodulus (not Boccaccio, as is sometimes stated) all receive a mention, Mantuan in particularly glowing terms. Theocritus he will almost certainly have known only by name; and a first-hand knowledge of Petrarch is hard to square with his description of his bucolic style as 'playne and mery' (Prol. 36). In spite of this citation of authorities and his adherence to Mantuan and Aeneas Silvius, Barclay is more of an innovator than one might expect. For a start, his eclogues are of unprecedented length – each poem averages some twelve times the length of Virgil's; and the title of 'eclogue' refers more to their nature as shepherd dialogues than anything else. Second, but much more important, is his treatment of his sources: not simply a translation, nor an imitation, but a transposition into English pastoral conventions.

Even at this period Barclay is aware of many of the problems Spenser was to tackle in the *Shepheardes Calender*, though he never finds the dynamic solutions of the Elizabethans. He is very conscious both of the high mission of pastoral literature and of its differences from rustic life, but he makes a constant effort to reconcile the two. The English poetic tradition provided a realistic image of the shepherd, but the subjects Barclay chooses do not make it easy to carry this realism through: the first three poems are on 'the miseryes of Courtiers and Courtes of all princes in generall', borrowed from Aeneas' *Epistola de Curialium Miseriis*; the fourth, 'treating of the behauour of Riche men agaynst Poetes', is based on Mantuan's fifth eclogue, with an inset aureate poem that owes something to Jean Lemaire de Belges; and the fifth, from Mantuan's sixth, is a 'disputation of Citizens and men of the Countrey'. The realism is in any case – as in almost all *bergerie* literature – limited by conventions that imply the opposite: the descriptions Barclay gives of his shepherds' clothing, food and pastimes may be factual enough, but the basis of the work is didactic, that one shepherd will instruct the other and so the readers in general. When instruction of this kind concerns sheep-keeping, even astronomy, some illusion of realism can be maintained without straining the suspension of disbelief too far; and Barclay does his best to make things easy for the reader even in the face of the themes he has chosen. He is careful to explain his characters' knowledge naturalistically: they have been to sermons and heard learned clerks preaching, Aeneas becomes 'shepherde Siluius' (I.737) to justify his intrusion into the pastoral world. Cornix, the shepherd who expounds the miseries of court life, had acquired his inside information through selling coal there in his youth. Deschamps' Robin had

a similar onlooker's experience of the court, and so had Mantuan's Cornix
and Barclay's own Faustus of the evils of the town: Barclay writes,

> Milke and butter he thither brought to sell,
> But neuer thought he in citie for to dwell,
> For well he noted the mad enormitie,
> Enuy, fraude, malice and such iniquitie
> Which reigne in cities, therefore he led his life
> Upland in village without debate and strife.   (V.29–34)

Uncultured as he may be, the shepherd is not talking of matters beyond his
knowledge: he has seen, and seen that it is bad. His moral authority derives
not from abstract theory but from 'practise and science' (I.158). Again in the
mediaeval tradition, this is reinforced by endowing the figure of the realistic
shepherd with a status derived from authoritative *exempla* (V.445–52).
Barclay takes over Abel, the Patriarchs, Paris and Apollo from Mantuan;
he elaborates the Bethlehem shepherds and Christ's own naming of Himself
as 'shepherde or pastour' with the care typical of the *bergerie* conventions;
and for good measure he adds Pan, Silenus, Orpheus, 'ioly Tyterus', Saul
and David. His shepherds' references, in fact, are impeccable.

The pastoral mode always provides a fixed point for social criticism,
explicit or implicit, to start from, and the themes of the eclogues make the
most of this. Criticism of the court may appear an unlikely subject for a
rustic eclogue, but it is almost pastoral by implication: it is an attack on the
life that is everything the shepherd's is not. This is the kind of generalized
moral statement that *bergerie* excelled in making, and Barclay emphasizes the
austerity of the shepherd world to drive the point home; he will not criticize
by contrast with a fictitious idyll. Aeneas himself refers occasionally to the
'rusticus', but paradoxically in such a way that the conditions Barclay
accepts for his work exclude any possibility of his exploiting these references.
They belong to a different pastoral world, Arcadia rather than the Fens.
Aeneas reports how when Gyges consulted the oracle as to who was the
happy man, 'The oracle scorned kingly wealth and trappings, and replied
that a certain Arcadian named Aglaus was happy; he cultivated a small
plot, and his desires had never gone beyond the bounds of his land.'[51]
Barclay omits this passage – he could hardly put it into the mouth of a
shepherd anyway – and he also has to omit the whole idea behind it, of
country life as the good life free from care, from ambition and all the other
ills Aeneas describes. His shepherds are all too well acquainted with poverty
that thrusts them down below the pastoral ideal of sufficiency and content.
Mantuan had included in his third eclogue a section on the hardships of the
shepherd's life (ll. 17–21); Barclay translates the lines, intensifying their
effect, and places them near the beginning of his first eclogue as the key to all
that follows.

> But see with what sweat, what busines and payne
> Our simple liuing we labour to obtayne:
> Behold what illes the shepheardes must endure
> For flocke and housholde bare liuing to procure,
> In feruent heate we must intende our folde,
> And in the winter almost we frese for colde:
> Upon the harde ground or on the flintes browne
> We slepe, when other lye on a bed of downe.   (I.219–26)

The realism of the presentation of the pastoral world makes the condemnation of court life carry more conviction than it does in the *Epistola*. Whenever

Aeneas speaks of the country it is almost always in idealized terms, taken from literature rather than life, as in the passage on Aglaus. His contrast of courtiers with country folk among their sheep eating chestnuts and apples and drinking water from the brook, 'ruricolas qui medias inter oues castaneas molles et mitia poma cum lacte uorantes nitidi fluminis undas exhauriunt' (p. 51), is drawn not from personal observation, as his descriptions of the court are, but from Virgil's first eclogue:

> sunt nobis mitia poma,
> castaneae molles et pressi copia lactis. (80–1)

The passage is too deeply embedded in Aeneas' text to be cut out easily, but Barclay changes the whole emphasis of it. If court life is described realistically, so is country life, and yet still the pastoral is preferable. Cornix's statement carries a weight of conviction that Aeneas' lacks, because it takes so much more into account. Barclay is talking about practical ethics rather than literary fictions. He renders the passage,

> Shepherdes haue not so wretched liues as they,
> Though they liue poorely on cruddes, chese and whey,
> On apples, plummes, and drinke clere water deepe,
> As it were lordes reigning among their sheepe. (II.1045–8)

He does not claim that drinking water is anything but 'poore', but the sense of the integrity of the life comes over more strikingly. The ideals of pastoral contentment and sufficiency are never made idyllic. Tasso's old shepherd describes the pastoral life as being spent walking around the countryside contemplating the works of Nature and letting her provide.[52] Minalcas, Barclay's poverty-stricken shepherd-poet, declares,

> I aske no treasure nor store of worldly good,
> But a quiet life, and onely cloth and foode,
> With homely lodging to keep me warme and drye, (IV.453–5)

a request that presupposes the cold and rain outside.

Barclay's eclogues are more purely English than any other eclogue cycle of the century; only Drayton comes anywhere near him. He is continually adapting phrases from his sources to bring them nearer home: Aeneas' shepherd's diet loses its chestnuts; the climate is harder; the geography is localized. He also makes continual minor changes to keep the pastoral setting in mind. The instability of princes' liking is described,

> Then is thy fauour not worth a shepes pelt; (I.1030)

court music (specifically of Cornysh and his contemporaries) is described as being better than the shepherd's characteristic bagpipe (II. 267). The jingle he uses to translate Mantuan's lines beginning, 'Non habitant colubri quaedam Balearibus arva' (VI.219–25) is naturalized almost into an Ely nursery-rhyme:

> As many todes as breede in Irelande,
> And as many Gripes as breede in Englande,
> As many Cuckowes as sing in Ianuary,
> And Nightingales as sing in February,
> And as many whales as swimmeth in the fen,
> So many be there in Cities of good men. (V.939–44)

These are the tones and phrasing of folk verse, of 'As many red herrings as grow in the wood', and the passage is a particularly good example of

Barclay's extension of a sense of realism to the style of his poetry, or matching his art to the subject. The abundance of proverbs in the work serves the same purpose: they are connected with the whole eclogue genre by Conrad of Hirsau because of their common need for allegorical interpretation,[53] but Barclay rejects such abstruse scholasticism in favour of the simple appeal of the homely style. Even God is made to speak in this way, and the images He uses are again homely rather than sublime: He addresses the younger children of Eve, dragged out of the straw where she had hidden them in order to receive His blessing,

> None can a pitcher turne to a siluer pece,
> Nor make goodly silke of a gotes flece,
> And harde is also to make withouten fayle
> A bright two hande sworde of a cowes tayle.
> No more will I make, howbeit that I can,
> Of a vile villayne a noble gentleman. (V.359–64)

The speech has no parallel in the original episode in Mantuan. Barclay preserves the same kind of decorum when he moves into the ecclesiastical sphere. The imagery of the Good Shepherd used to describe 'Shepheard Roger' – Roger Westminster, former prior of Ely – is familiar and realistic: he salves the sheep's sores and rescues them from brambles; it acquires an epigrammatic sharpness as Coridon tells how he 'was no wolfe poore lambes to deuour ' (III.500); and it becomes almost an Aesopian fable in the transparent farmyard allegory about Alcock, bishop of Ely, and Foxe, bishop of Winchester (and the probable inventor of 'Morton's Fork'):

> This cocke was no more abashed of the foxe
> Then is a lion abashed of an oxe. (I.527–8)

Barclay does not reject allegory, but his aim is to make it familiar, not arcane. It is by means such as these that he can make the court, the city and the Church fitting subjects for herdsmen to discuss.

Barclay's insistence on the Englishness of his eclogues is carried through in the deference he pays to Chaucer. His sources may be Italian, but he looks to the greatest English poet as his master; and the debt becomes explicit in the Argument to the fifth eclogue, which reads like the General Prologue to the *Canterbury Tales* condensed for two characters: there is the seasonal description (winter, not spring, but made into a companion-piece of Chaucer's), then the men themselves, described with the Chaucerian eye for significant detail or juxtaposition. Chaucer had not described a real shepherd, only the allegorical pastor; and Barclay repairs the omission.

> In colde Ianuary when fire is comfortable,
> And that the fieldes be nere intollerable,
> When shepe and pastours leaueth fielde and folde,
> And drawe to cotes for to eschue the colde,
> What time the verdure of ground and euery tree,
> By frost and stormes is priuate of beautee,
> And euery small birde thinketh the winter longe,
> Which well appeareth by ceasing of their songe.
> At this same season two herdes freshe of age
> At time appoynted met both in one cotage,
> The first hight Faustus, the second Amintas,
> Harde was to knowe which better husband was,
> For eche of them both set more by his pleasour
> Then by aboundaunce of riches or treasour.

Amintas was formall and proper in his geare,
A man on his cloke should not espye a heare,
Nor of his clothing one wrinkle stande a wry,
In London he learned to go so manerly,
High on his bonet stacke a fayre brouche of tinne,
His purses lining was simple, poore and thinne:
But a lordes stomake and a beggers pouche
Full ill accordeth, suche was this comely slouche,
In the towne and citie so long ietted had he
That from thence he fled for det and pouertie,
No wafrer, tauerne, alehouse or tauerner,
To him was there hid while he was hosteler...
About all London there was no proper prim
But long time had bene familier with him,
But when coyne fayled no more fauour had he.   (V.1–32)

Barclay never speaks of his debt to the English Tityrus in the way Spenser does, but he does pay him the compliment of imitation.[54] His reputation as an early Tudor poet has been almost completely overshadowed by that of Skelton, but Barclay is more in the mainstream of English poetic traditions. In his eclogues he is attempting to adapt these to a time-hallowed art form that had never yet been tried out in his language. The attempt is only a partial success; but the challenge was to be taken up again, on exactly the same terms, in the *Shepheardes Calender*.

It is only towards the end of Henry VIII's reign that the first signs of any influence from the new Arcadian style of pastoral appear. There are just a few traces in Surrey's 'In winters just returne', a poem which tells how a shepherd, going out on a winter morning to unfold his sheep, hears the lament of a rejected lover, tries to prevent his suicide and finally buries him in a tomb beside Troilus'.[55] The first person narration, the realism of the shepherd attending to his duties 'in misty morning darke' and the particular relationship of shepherd and courtier all suggest the mediaeval tradition; but the interest in despised affection, the lover's suicide and the unexpected intrusion of the legendary setting are typical of Italian Arcadianism. The poem was first published in *Tottel's Miscellany*; the same collection includes the thoroughly mediaeval description of Apollo playing the bagpipes,[56] and also another fully pastoral poem, *Harpelus' Complaynt*,[57] which shows a much stronger Italian influence. The names are neo-Classical – the shepherdess Phillida, the rejected suitor Harpelus, his rival Corin; and if the theme of the shepherdess rejecting one lover for another is found in the pastourelle, Harpelus' threats of death and the epitaph he composes for himself belong with Mantuan's Amyntas, and the terms in which he laments come from the tradition of Petrarchan love-poetry:

What reason is it that cruelty
With beauty should haue part,
Or els that such great tyranny
Should dwell in womans hart?

In other ways the poem is strikingly English. The rhythm is the rhythm of the ballads, or of that entirely mediaeval pastoral lyric *Robene and Makyne*; and Phillida, with her skill in spinning and singing and her delight in making garlands for Corin, is a figure from idyllic French *bergerie* making her first appearance in England. It was perhaps this combination that made the poem so popular: it found its way into *Englands Helicon*, along with an 'aunswere' probably by Munday; it was imitated by Sir David Murray; and it also descended to the broadside.

The first real signs of a sustained interest in the eclogue form occur just after these first traces of Italian pastoral. Barclay, it must be admitted, had not started a fashion for bucolic; and it is only from the middle of the century that its composition became at all widespread. Puttenham states in his *Arte of English Poesie* (III.xiii) that he himself wrote an eclogue to Edward VI, addressing him as Elpine – a name possibly derived from Sannazaro's Elpino, 'hopeful', and in any case parallel to it, for Edward was 'a Prince of great hope'. The poem is no longer extant, but from the five lines Puttenham quotes it seems that it may have been an allegory of the ship of state – a piscatory eclogue, perhaps, rather than a true pastoral; but since Elpine is apparently standing on the land asking questions about the ship, he may have been presented as the shepherd with his traditional ignorance of the sea. The poem was certainly a mixture of moral and political allegory and allusive panegyric, in a typical bucolic fashion. Barnabe Googe produced his eclogue cycle, the only other original English bucolic before Spenser, in 1563;[58] Turberville published his translation of Mantuan in 1567; Fleming's translation of the *Bucolics* was printed in 1575; and Barclay's own eclogues were reprinted at the end of the 1570 edition of his *Ship of Fools*. Theocritus was not even partially translated until 1588, when *Sixe Jdillia* (not all in fact genuine Theocritus) was published at Oxford; and no Greek edition was printed in England for another half century. The first Anglo-Latin eclogues, three poems written by Giles Fletcher while he was a student at Cambridge in the 1560's, are a further example of the interest in the bucolic.[59] Two of these are Protestant polemic, the third is about a stormy scene of college politics – the kind of subjects that Petrarch had introduced into the eclogue, but in a post-Reformation version and with the allegory made accessible in Renaissance fashion. Mantuan and Virgil, however, were still the principal authorities at this stage. Googe widened the range of models to include Montemayor and Garcilaso de la Vega, but he tends to ignore his own native tradition except for its moral outlook, and draws all his subject-matter from continental models.

Googe's eclogue cycle is in many ways less successful than Barclay's just because he is not attempting a real synthesis of his authorities with English traditions. Almost his only concession to English is the language; for his verse form he chooses the fourteener, generally taken as the English equivalent of the hexameter – it was the metre almost invariably used for Classical translations. It has a spurious surface resemblance to the ballad metre of *Robene and Makyne* or *Harpelus' Complaynt*, especially when written with the lines divided, but it depends on the jog-trot of a reasonably correct number of syllables and not on the almost sprung-rhythm stress of the popular verse. The difference is apparent from the first lines, Googe's

> Syth Phebus now begins to flame,
> O frende Amintas deare,

as against

> Phillida was a fayr mayde
> As fresh as any floure,

and Googe only seldom, and for very brief moments, breaks away from one to the other. Most of his subjects come either from Mantuan – the state of the town (vicious), the nature of love (unpleasant) – or else from Montemayor, so that three of the poems consist principally of the recounting of extraordinarily complicated love stories. The whole tone of the cycle is quite exceptionally moralistic. Barclay is didactic, but openly so – a criticism of court life never pretends to be otherwise; Googe leads his readers along the sweet paths of romance to a lecture-theatre. The rejected lover Dametas of *Egloga Secunda*, for instance, Googe's version of Mantuan's Amyntas, laments in a long monologue of almost seductive poetry and kills himself in the last line:

> Dametas here doth dye.

But such extreme Petrarchan melancholy has its reward; the shepherds think of him at first as a martyr, 'whose soule the heauens haue' (III, p. 35), but in *Egloga Quarta* his damned spirit appears to Melibeus to utter a warning against the abuse of Reason. This serves as a definitive comment not only on the story of Dametas himself but on the description of love Googe had given in the first poem. The romance stories undergo something of the same process: Faustus, the demented noble lover of *Egloga Quinta*, turns up in the country in the next poem (he is presumably the same character, despite some narrative inconsistencies) and is lectured on the risks of Hell, the primacy of Reason and the attractions of the country life. The final poem, the eighth, sums up the general tenor: Coridon and Cornix retreat to the shade to sing

> Not of the wretched Louers lyues,
>   but of the immortal kynge.
> Who gyues vs pasture for our beasts
>   and blesseth our encrease.   (p. 71)

Cornix's song consists principally of praise of the shepherd's life, an attack on the Classical pantheon and a condemnation of all those who pursue pleasure.

What Googe is trying to do is to apply the moral outlook of the mediaeval tradition to Renaissance eclogue themes; the attempt fails, not because of the austerity of the ethic he proposes, but because there is no common ground between the two. It is one thing to criticize a bad shepherd for not being a good shepherd; it is quite another to damn a swain who has stepped out of the Italian poetic imagination for not being a Protestant with a keen sense of psychomachia. Googe is in a sense attacking Renaissance pastoral as a whole: love-sick shepherds are not good Christians; but even that statement is undermined by the attraction pastoral love-sickness holds for him, so that descriptions of it absorb over half the cycle. The one point where Googe's Protestant-moral criticism rings true is the point where the interest of many other eclogues weakens, in ecclesiastical and political allegory. The third eclogue includes an account of the return to Catholicism under Mary and the burning of the good shepherds Daphnes and Alexis, presumably Latimer and Ridley. The religious changes are described through Mantuan's imagery of the hills and valleys: the sheep, newly led to the 'pleasant Hylles', are forced to return to their 'old corrupted Grasse' in the 'stynkyng dales'. The sheep have become the measure of the shepherd: it is a much more vital use of pastoral than the declamations advocating a life of austerity.

Other forms of pastoral were also becoming known in the early years of Elizabeth's reign. The Italian and French pastoralists, especially Sannazaro and Marot, were increasingly widely read; Ronsard dedicated his *Elegies, Mascarades et Bergerie* to Elizabeth in 1565, and was reputedly given a diamond in return for a presentation copy. 'A boke intituled *lusus pastorales newly compyled*' was entered in the Stationers' Registers in 1565/6, but no copy remains. A pastoral including shepherds, wild men, nymphs and Saturn was presented by a company of Italian players at Windsor and Reading in 1574; 'a pastoral or historie of a Greeke maide' was 'enacted by the Earle of Leicester his servauntes' as part of the Christmas festivities of 1578/9; and at Christmas 1584 'a pastoral of phillyda and Chorin' was played that required, among other things, 'scarfes for the nymphes and one mountayne'.⁶⁰ Arcadian pastoral, in fact, had arrived in England, and had come to stay. But it was only one approach of many to the pastoral mode. The Renaissance provided the forms that allowed pastoral its highest development: the rediscovered eclogue, the romantic drama, the romance. It was the moral and social toughness of mediaeval pastoral, the way it was wholeheartedly committed to its subject, its firm grounding in fact, its concern with the central problems of human life – true love, righteousness, war, religion, time and death – that could give these forms their strength. The combination of the two is typical of the Elizabethan era: the first achievement of Sidney's *Arcadia* was that he managed to create such a country of the imagination without divorcing it from social responsibility. It was Italian and French pastoral that awakened the English poets to a new consciousness of their own tradition and a new excitement in it. But there was another reason, inherent in the pastoral mode itself, why it exerted such a fascination. Pastoral implies both art and nature: art, in the delight in formal poetry of Virgil and Sannazaro and every shepherd-poet; nature, in its relation to the countryside and the simple life. Alone in Europe, the Elizabethan poets – Spenser, Sidney, Shakespeare, Drayton, many others less great – realized the importance of the issue, and met the problem head on.

IV

PASTORAL DECORUM

The crux of the pastoral paradox is contained in the first two lines of Virgil's first eclogue, the lines that must have been the best known of all pastoral poetry to any poet who wished to follow in his footsteps.

> Tityre, tu patulae recubans sub tegmine fagi,
> silvestrem tenui musam meditaris avena.
>
> *Tityrus, you lie in the shade of a broad-spreading beech and play country songs on your slender* [or '*humble*'] *reed.*

Servius' gloss on the lines summarizes what any mediaeval or Renaissance poet would read into them: 'In saying "humble reed", he explicitly refers to the nature of the style which, as has been said above, he uses in pastoral.'[1] What he has said on the nature of pastoral comes in his explanation of the three styles at the very beginning of his commentary:

> There are three kinds of style, the low, the medium and the lofty [humilis, medius, grandiloquus], all of which we find in this poet. For he has the lofty style in the *Aeneid*, the middle style in the *Georgics* and the low in the *Bucolics* on account of the nature of the action and the characters: for here the characters are peasants, rejoicing in simple things, from whom nothing more elevated should be demanded.[2]

The *Rhetorica ad Herennium* had distinguished three kinds of speech, the *gravis*, *mediocris* and *attenuatus*, but it was Servius who first connected the three styles with Virgil's three works – a connection that was to be accepted by every succeeding writer, apparently without further analysis. *Stylus tenuis* was an alternative phrase for *stylus humilis*, calling to mind even more clearly the 'tenuis avena'. The slender pipe, the humble oaten reed, was the instrument on which only simple, low style tunes could be played. The *Bucolics*, however, are an example of high art, a supremely accomplished piece of work; and the poets who looked to them and imitated them found art and not simplicity. It is after all Virgil himself, the supreme master-poet of the Middle Ages and the Renaissance, who is the shepherd-singer. The identification of poet and shepherd dates back to Theocritus, and makes artistic pastoral inevitable: place the poet in a rural landscape, and fine poetry will result. The commonest occupation among the shepherds of both Theocritus and Virgil is composing songs, alone or in competition, whether they specifically represent the poet or not – the poet as author, as are Simichidas, Tityrus and Colin Clout, or the poet as type, as are Mantuan's Candidus and Barclay's Minalcas; Apollo, god of poetry, had acted the shepherd for a while, and Orpheus, the poet *par excellence*, and David, writer of the Psalms, were also both shepherds. Classical tradition, reinforced by the Bible, put pastoral poetry on the highest level; the remorselessly repeated theory insisted that eclogues were 'the basest of any other poeme in their owne proper nature'.[3] The shepherd could be the poet, the king, the god; but shepherds, it was all too well known, were illiterate and uncultured peasants. The uniquely dynamic quality of the pastoral of the Elizabethans springs largely from the way in which they were able to create a new pastoral that embraced both the poet and the peasant.

That the *Bucolics* were the principal example of the low style was scarcely questioned in the Middle Ages or the Renaissance; the tenet was repeated in dozens of critical works and would be familiar to every educated man, and so to everybody who was likely to write, or even read, an eclogue. As early as the Carolingian era it is at the basis of such typical phrases as Angilbert's reference in the *Ecloga ad Carolum Regem* to his 'humble voice' and Modoin's 'rustic songs of my harsh-voiced Muse',[4] though it was reserved for use as a conventional expression of modesty and not allowed to interfere with their poetry. In later mediaeval *artes poeticae* the theory of styles seems to have been more immediately associated with Virgil himself than with pastoral in general; the point is hard to substantiate since Virgil was almost the only writer of pastoral known to the Middle Ages, but Conrad of Hirsau makes no mention of stylistic theory when he is discussing Theodulus and reserves it for his section on Virgil. In the thirteenth century Evrard, in his *Laborintus*, gives a list of authors with a brief description of each, and Virgil appears as:

> Vergilio servit triplex stylus, et tria thema
> Praebent: bos et ager, historialis apex.[5]

> *The triple style holds its place in Virgil, and three themes are put forward: the ox and the field, and the peak of historical action.*

Petrarch in his third eclogue identifies Virgil by an even briefer tag, as 'triplicis modulator avene' (157), 'player of the triple reed', leaving it to the patient commentators to fill the reference out. It was still a commonplace of literary theory in the Renaissance: Spenser makes a passing reference to it, duly glossed by E. K., in 'October' (55–60); more typical is Abraham Fleming's account in the introduction to his translation of the *Bucolics*:

> Now, forsomuch as there bee three kinds of writing or speaking by art (according to Tullie) the first homelie and base, the second meane and indifferent, the third stately and aloft; the poet therefore very aptly doubtlesse hath vsed these three kinds of art: for his Pastoralls are written in a base, his ruralls in a meane, and his Martialls in a loftie style.

The Middle Ages and the Renaissance speak of the theory of styles with one voice; but the Renaissance poets were reading Virgil with new sympathy and appreciation, and their practice could not be bound by the theory. The eclogue was always primarily a Classical form of poetry, and new examples were only produced by variation on or imitation of authority; and authority contained both the endlessly repeated instruction to write in low style, and the model of superb poetry. On the one hand there is the demand for rusticity, on the other the example of the artistic and imaginative re-creation of idyllic life.

The demand for low style in pastoral was reinforced by another, equally basic, tenet of literary criticism: the theory of decorum, of appropriateness, first laid down by Horace in his *Ars Poetica*. He demands both that descriptions and language should suit the character, and that style should match the subject:

> singula quaeque locum teneant sortita decentem,[6]
>
> *Let each style keep the becoming place allotted to it.*

The low, unfigured style is the one that is appropriate for goatherds' or shepherds' speech. Servius had related style to subject-matter, but in the course of the Middle Ages it became even more strictly a matter of class. John of Garland defines Virgil's theory in these terms in the *Poetria*:

> There are three styles according to the three classes of men; the low style suits pastoral life, the middle suits farmers, the high noble persons who are above shepherds and farmers.[7]

The relationship of style to class was taken further by the theory that the style should fit not only the subject but the person to whom it was addressed: the high style was appropriate for writing for princes, and so on. This brings even more problems for the low, the pastoral, style; Gavin Douglas highlights them in his *Prologue* to Book IX of his translation of the *Aeneid*. First he combines the two approaches:

> The sayar eik suld weil considir thys,
> Hys mater, and quhamto it entitilit is. (27–8)

He then drops the question of 'mater', however, and concentrates on the question of audience. He is concerned with giving an explanation of the principles of high style alone, but his slighting reference towards low subject-matter perhaps goes some way towards indicating why mediaeval scholars tended to be shy of writing pastoral, especially rustic pastoral. Like John of Garland in his Wheel of Virgil, he associates each style with a different set of properties.

> 'Gyf we discryve the woddis, the treis,' quod he,
> 'Suld conform to that manis dignyte
> Quhamto our wark we direct and endyte.'
> Quhat helpis it? Full litill it wald delyte
> To write of scroggis, broym, haddir or rammale;   (*underwood; brushwood*)
> The lawrer, cedyr or the palm triumphale
> Ar mar ganand for nobillis of estait:
> The muse suld with the person aggre algait.
> Stra forto spek of gayt to gentill wight!   (*goat*) (33–41)

What conceivable interest could a nobleman have in eclogues, 'goteheards tales', 'caprinus sermo'?[8] The theory of decorum demanded that the shepherd of literature should mirror the shepherd of real life, and the low-class, uncultivated peasant would appear to offer nothing of art or of interest.

Yet the theoretical humbleness also made it an especially appropriate medium for addressing princes, as a way of turning a complimentary panegyric. Webbe sees this as one of the principal uses of pastoral, along with satire.[9] The Carolingians invoke low style to emphasise the distance between poet and subject: the high style demanded by Charlemagne's heroic qualities is beyond their power to achieve. For the same reason, Barclay makes one of his characters refuse to speak in praise of Henry VIII because as a shepherd he is limited to 'humble speech and language pastorall'[10] and the prince's due is the high, the heroic, style. In his fourth eclogue the rich shepherd Codrus tries to keep Minalcas within the same limits:

> What should a Ploughman go farther than his plough,
> What should a shepherde in wisedome wade so farre,
> Talke he of tankarde, or of his boxe of tarre　　　　　　　　(792–4)

– pastoral should be the Chester shepherds, not Virgil. But Minalcas is the shepherd-poet, and therefore able to move beyond the limitations of low style. Both the poems he recites are in aureate language, what he calls 'hye stile of eloquence' (654), and the second, the *Description of the Towre of Vertue and Honour*, is an elaborate allegory that illustrates the poet's thorough familiarity with courtly literature and Classical mythology. This is the only one of Barclay's eclogues where the shepherd is more than just a herdsman, and the move into the high style implied by the metaphor of the shepherd-poet releases Barclay from the limitations he accepts elsewhere: Henry VIII can now make his appearance. That the prince is beyond the ability of the common man to praise is a theme taken up again by the Elizabethans. Peele's *Eclogue Gratulatory*[11] is a panegyric in honour of the earl of Essex cast entirely within this framework of poetic and personal insufficiency. Palinode blames Piers for singing in honour of the Earl:

> Singest thou proud Paeans on these open plaines?
> So ill sitteth this straine, this loftie note,
> With thy rude tire, and gray russet cote.　　　　　　　　(11–13)

The grey-coated shepherd of vernacular tradition and the art-shepherd can have no point of contact. It is not enough that Elizabeth, Essex and the entire expedition to Cadiz that Peele is celebrating have become part of the pastoral world; Essex himself

> shineth on the plaines, his lustie flocke him by,
> As when Apollo kept in Arcadie,　　　　　　　　(58–9)

and even within the pastoral world itself the two extremes cannot meet. Piers eventually agrees that the 'golden flakes' of the fire of honour 'exceed the reach of Shepherds rime'. Palinode adds another item to his accusation of inadequacy in Piers:

> Honour is in him that doth it bestowe,
> Thy Reed to rough, thy seat is all to lowe.　　　　　　　　(155–6)

The *tenuis avena* is no medium for heroic poetry. None the less, it is exceptional for a poet to deny the sophistication of his intent. Francis Sabie, who published a series of eclogues in English hexameters, *Pans Pipe*, in 1595, claims that his work is not only about simple country folk but intended for them: he tells his book,

> Heu, si forte via recta peregrinus aberres
> Et Domino sumas orbus in urbe locum,
> Ridebit civis te, nescit rustica civis,
> Rustica tu cantas, rusticus ergo legat.[12]

> *If, alas, you should by chance wander a stranger from the right way and, deprived of an owner, take up your place in the city, the townsman will laugh at you, he knows nothing of country matters; you sing of country concerns, therefore let the countryman read you.*

But even before the reader reaches the eclogues themselves the fact that the words are in Latin gives him the lie: it is a scholar's irony.

The issue is complicated further because by tradition low style is an introduction to high, pastoral to the heroic; the *Bucolics* are the forerunner of the *Aeneid*. For this reason both Mantuan and Barclay stress that their

eclogues are youthful productions in an implied promise of greater things to
come. In 'October', Piers urges Cuddie,

> Abandon then the base and viler clowne,
> Lyft vp thy selfe out of the lowly dust:
> And sing of bloody Mars, of wars, of giusts;   (37–9)

and Spenser presents the *Faerie Queene* as his true achievement once his
'lowly Shepheards weeds' have been cast off. The Petrarchan poets sublimely
overrode the theory of styles to conflate the two extremes of pastoral and the
heroic. Boccaccio claims that Petrarch raised the style of pastoral slightly and
that he himself follows Virgil, but at one point he makes one of his shepherds
sing of 'pastores frigios...et danaos' (X.65–6), Trojan and Greek shepherds:
the bucolic has been raised to the level of the Trojan War, properly the
archetype for the high, the heroic, style. These poets were fully aware of the
paradox. They regarded their pastoral as an advanced and mature achievement; whatever E. K. may claim, they did not write it 'to proue theyr tender
wyngs, before they make a greater flyght'.[13] Pastoral, for them, was the
greater flight.

To write an eclogue was to declare one's self a poet working in the highest
artistic tradition, and Renaissance poets and critics alike looked to pastoral
primarily as a model not of theory but of art. Scaliger's monumental *Poetices
Libri Septem*, the *summa* of Renaissance literary theory, contains a number of
substantial sections on the theory of styles and on pastoral, but he is quite
content both to define low style as common, unadorned and unfigured speech,
with the *Bucolics* as the archetype,[14] and yet to give examples of rhetorical
colours in groups of three, one for each style, frequently drawing on Virgil's
eclogues for the third. 'Whether Virgil in his Bucolicks hath kept within
Pastorall humblenesse,' wrote Drayton, in one of the rare expressions of
doubt on the subject, 'let Scaliger...dispute;'[15] but the critic in fact remains
silent on the matter. His humanist learning does not extend to facing this
contradiction. The use of pastoral as a rhetorical, and even philosophical,
model was taken yet further by Abraham Fraunce in his two critical works
The Lawiers Logike, the original title of which was *The Shephierdes Logike*,[16] and
The Arcadian Rhetorike, both published in 1588. The uncultured herdsman
becomes the model for artistic expression.

None the less, that Art should follow Nature was the heart of critical theory
for the Elizabethans as it was for Horace,[17] and the contrast between them
could not just be casually set aside. 'He that shall translate a shephierds tale,
and vse the talke and stile of an Heroicall personage,' Turberville wrote in
the preface to his translation of Mantuan, '...in my simple iudgement ioynes
(as Horace sayth) a Horses necke and a mans hed togither.' The language
appropriate to the pastoral mode posed an acute problem. Decorum pre-
scribed low style, what E. K. in his preface to the *Shepheardes Calender* calls
'pastoral rudeness'; it is this tenet he has in mind when he praises Spenser
for his 'dewe obseruing of Decorum euerye where, in personages, in seasons,
in matter, in speach, and generally in al seemely simplycitie of handeling his
matter, and framing his words'. Ben Jonson criticized both Sidney and
Guarini because they 'keept not decorum, in making Shepherds speak as well
as [themselves] could'.[18] He could have levelled the same accusation against
Virgil. The point was in fact first raised not long after Virgil's lifetime, in the
commentary on the *Bucolics* formerly ascribed to M. Valerius Probus. The
author comments on the lack of a form of Latin comparable with the Doric

dialect used by Theocritus; Virgil has no linguistic means of making his style appear rustic.[19] The problem was even more intractable for later Latin writers. Mantuan makes an effort to introduce rustic style into his work even though to have shepherds speak in Latin, the language of culture and scholarship, was itself a contradiction. Any attempt to introduce 'pastoral rudeness' had to be painfully obvious; in his eighth eclogue he has one shepherd mock another for his peasant's ignorance of Latin:

> Rusticus es, 'crates' enim pro 'gratibus' inquis. (159)

By contrast with this it was a comparatively simple matter for the Eliza-bethans to bring the style of their pastoral close to the countryside; it was one of Spenser's more remarkable achievements to create a language of art that nevertheless appeared rustic, that was acceptable as a vehicle of serious poetry as dialect could not have been. Even so, Sidney's doubts as to the wisdom of Spenser's experiment seem to have been shared by most later pastoralists. Each revision of Drayton's eclogues left fewer linguistic aber-rations; some of Spenser's earlier followers, for instance Peele in the *Eclogue Gratulatory*, imitated his rustic language, but by the end of the century the practice was becoming rare; there are examples in some of the eclogues in Davison's *Poetical Rhapsody*, but at least one of these was composed earlier.[20]

In place of linguistic simplicity, some of the Latin ecloguists treated the shepherd's baseness more directly by showing him as incapable of coherent thought. Virgil, surprisingly, provides some authority for this, when Menalcas' memory fails him in the middle of the description of the cup that is to be one of the prizes in a singing-match:

> In medio dua signa, Conon et – quis fuit alter,
> descripsit radio totum qui gentibus orbem,
> tempora quae messor, quae curvus arator haberet? (III.40–2)

> *In the middle are two figures, Conon and – who was the other, who charted the whole celestial sphere with his rod and fixed the dates that the reaper and the bending plough-man should follow?*

Peter Ramus, in his commentary on the *Bucolics* first published in 1555, glosses this as being 'for the sake of pastoral decorum', *pastoralis decori gratia*, adding, 'because shepherds do not hear much about philosophers'. Spenser does the same kind of thing in 'July' when he makes Thomalin forget Aaron's name, and E. K. provides the same explanation: 'Whose name for more Decorum, the shepearde sayth he hath forgot, lest his remembraunce and skill in antiquities of holy writ should seeme to exceed the meanenesse of the Person.' Petrarch himself uses a similar device in his first eclogue, when he has the shepherd Monicus describe David's attributes but not name him, and then has him confuse two rivers. He explains the incident as happening 'quasi pastoria ruditate'[21] – E. K.'s 'pastorall rudeness' again; but he also gives an allegorical significance to the confusion that makes his gesture of preserving decorum seem especially exaggerated. High style, by definition, was rich in ornament, and allegory, the be-all and end-all of Petrarch's eclogues, was a difficult trope and so sufficient in itself to establish his work as high style. In all their discussions of pastoral as a useful medium for disguised political comment, the literary theorists never faced this central contradiction.

It was a long-standing tradition that pastoral was a suitable vehicle for serious subject-matter, and the belief was one of the paradoxes at the heart of the question of decorum and style. Virgil's fourth eclogue had led the way, with its opening invocation,

> Sicelides Musae, paulo maiora canamus.

> *Sicilian Muses, let us sing of somewhat higher things.*

'"Paulo" is good,' comments Servius, 'for this eclogue is allowed to depart from bucolic.'[22] Few writers were ready to slip into higher subjects with the same ease. 'The subject of Pastorals, as the language of it,' wrote Drayton, 'ought to be poor, silly and of the coursest Woofe in appearance. Neverthelesse, the most High, and most Noble Matters of the World may be shaddowed in them, and for certain sometimes are.'[23] Even so, decorum is 'not to be exceeded without leave, or without at least faire warning', and he cites Virgil's line as an example. Sannazaro's eclogue in his *Piscatorials* addressed to Ferdinand of Aragon starts with a line that in itself would have been sufficient warning of what to expect:

> Nam primum notas *velis majoribus* undas
> Currimus.[24]

> *Now we run over well-charted seas with sails spread full.*

The full spread of sail is an indication of the greater matters filling out his style. What Virgil had done as an exception to his usual practice became almost the rule itself in eclogues of the Middle Ages and Renaissance. If a preliminary apology for the baseness of the poem was in order, that the subject should actually be base was not. Barclay explains the basis of low style in the *Prologe* to his eclogues:

> It were not fitting a heard or man rurall
> To speake in termes gay and rhetoricall.
> So teacheth Horace in arte of poetry,
> That writers namely their reason should apply
> Mete speeche appropring to euery personage. (83–7)

But when he comes to speak of his own work, the pastoral paradox begins to emerge: his shepherds will speak in the appropriate 'homely language not passing their degree', but about 'courtly misery' (130–1). The shepherd world was seen as a useful and politic disguise for the poet to write about matters of contemporary concern without having to speak too openly. Puttenham departs from the usual theory of the origin of pastoral in favour of this view: he quotes the theory of genuine shepherd origins only to refute it,

> being perswaded that the Poet deuised the Eglogue long after the other drammatick poems, not of purpose to conterfait or represent the rusticall manner of loues and communication: but vnder the vaile of homely persons, and in rude speeches to insinuate and glaunce at greater matters, and such as perchance had not beene safe to haue beene disclosed in any other sort.
> (I.xviii)

Matters of state concern were not only a right and fitting subject for pastoral, but even *the* right and fitting subject. The paradox is taken still further by the confusion of styles this involves. The poet chooses to write of 'homely persons and in rude speeches' in order to disguise his high subject, but since the subject is high the style can be raised accordingly. The paradox seems never to have worried the mediaeval Latin ecloguists, and Molinet, the most Petrarchan of the French poets, positively delights in it: in his *Bergier sans Soulas* the historical characters are figured as gods, the moon or a comet, and one manuscript includes a Latin exposition of the theory and allegory of the poem in which he declares,

> In accordance with poetic custom and the low style of pastoral [stillo humili pastorali] I have filled out this little work, the quarrel of the Brabants and Flemings, to the level of the heavenly bodies or those of the air or sea.[25]

The elaborate language of the poem is an equally glaring contradiction of the theory of humble pastoral he claims to be following. Bucarius, on the other hand, whose acquaintance with Virgil and his commentators is evidenced elsewhere in the *Pastoralet*, feels the need to justify the polish of his style and its lack of the proper *humilitas*: the author, he says,

> sa basse matière excède
> En aulcuns liex ou il procède
> Par hauls mos qui font démonstrance
> De haultaine ségnefiance,   (8852–5)

exceeds his low subject in some places where he writes in high words that indicate a lofty meaning.

The paradox is still being put to deliberate use by Marvell in *Clorinda and Damon*, when Damon announces that Pan's name 'swells my slender Oate'[26] – swells it not only because he is blowing the pipe in Pan's honour, but because the style of his poetry is filled out, from the *tenuis* to the *plenus*. Despite his emphasis on the baseness of bucolic, Puttenham acknowledges the appropriateness of the 'swelling' style in Virgil's fourth eclogue.[27]

The paradox is seen at its most blatant not in English pastoral but in French, in Molinet in the fifteenth century, in Ronsard in the sixteenth. Ronsard's *Bergerie* was first published in 1565; France was well ahead of England in the production of vernacular eclogues by this time, but he still feels the need to affirm the value of the base pastoral and to explain the principles behind the composition of the work. Perhaps the title was an additional factor in the need for explanation, for it would still tend to have the wrong associations. The work takes the form of a masque written for production at court, with the royal children as principal performers – the shepherds are not even fictional mock-shepherds, but real princes. In the prologue to the work Ronsard tries to take advantage of both sides of pastoral. First he declares,

> Tousjours la nature est meilleure que l'art.
> Pour ce je me promets que le chant solitaire
> Des sauvages pasteurs doit davantage plaire,
> D'autant qu'il est naïf, sans art et sans façon,
> Qu'une plus curieuse et superbe chanson
> De ces maistres enflez d'une Muse hardie.[28]

There is no apology here for low style: it is preferable to the swelling style of deliberate art. A few lines later he is fastidiously shaking his fingers free of any imputation that might be made that he is concerned with the realistic hired shepherd.

> Ce ne sont pas bergers d'une maison champestre
> Qui mènent pour salaire aux champs les brebis paistre,
> Mais de haute famille et de race d'ayeux,
> Qui portant en la main le sceptre en divers lieux,
> Ont defendu l'Europe.

He reinforced the apologia in the 1584 edition of his eclogues, which includes the *Bergerie*, in the dedication, where he draws the parallel so well known to the Middle Ages between the prince and the shepherd, and cites David and Moses as examples. He concludes with a sweeping declaration of the high mission of pastoral:

> Rien n'est si duisant,
> Ny qui tant se conforme aux grandes seigneuries,
> Que l'estat des bergers et de leurs bergeries. (p. 916)

'Stra for to spek of gayt to gentil wight!' Gavin Douglas had written, but then he had a better idea of what a real goat was like. Jehan de Brie might have been more in sympathy with Ronsard's words, but not with his particular application of them – a panegyric of Catherine de' Medici, who, he declares from the centre of faction-torn France, has brought back the Golden Age. For all Ronsard's praise of Nature, it never gets a chance to make an appearance in any of his pastoral works.

Ronsard is invoking a higher decorum, of fine art to court politics. The shepherd of the eclogue tradition does not conform to nature. Tuberville prefaces his translation of Mantuan with an Epistle in which he tries to establish some common ground between the two. He begins by apologizing for the title 'eglogs', in case, 'being altogither of the Countrey affaires', it should seem 'ouerrude and barbarous' – in case rustic matters, in however Classical a form, might be scorned. He continues with a justification of the work on the grounds of decorum: not that real shepherds are worth reading about, but that

> Shephierds...were not in that age such siellie sottes as our Shephierdes are nowe a days, onely haueing Reason by Experience to prate of their Pastures, and folde and vnfolde their flockes: But these fellowes, whome the Poet and I haue here brought in, were well able both to moue the doubtful cause, and (if need were) to discide the proponed case. They not only knewe the Calfe from the Lambe, the Woulfe from the Mastife, but had reason to know the dyfference twixt Towne and Countrey, the oddes betwixt Vice and Vertue, and other thinges needefull and appertayning to the life of man.

He is acutely aware of the difference between Mantuan's shepherds and contemporary peasants, but he justifies them on the grounds of nature rather than art. Such an apology may appear naïve; but practically every pastoral writer of the Renaissance felt impelled to enter into the same kind of discussion, to try to bridge the gulf between the shepherd-poet and the peasant, between the normal speech of the countryside and the high matters contained within the pastoral mode. If the problem had simply been a conflict between actuality and an artistic convention, it would never have become so problematic; that the brunette heroines of mediaeval and Renaissance literature can almost be counted on the fingers of one hand is a contradiction of nature by art that was taken for granted. With pastoral, the problem goes deeper, and it involves centuries of tradition – traditions of Latin and vernacular poetry, of stylistic and poetic theory, of folksong and iconography.

Mediaeval *bergerie* owed nothing to critical theories, but it did mirror nature. The image of the shepherd of the vernacular pastoral conventions preserves decorum in a way that the characters of Virgil, Sannazaro or Ronsard never do. He is realistic, or over-rustic to the point of caricature, and he was a figure as familiar to the Elizabethans as Tityrus himself – perhaps more so, since it was a portrait they knew not through formal education but through folksongs, through mystery plays, through the bagpipe-playing figures of tapestries or stained glass or of the English countryside. Descriptions of shepherd revels, of feasts and Maygames were a distinct part of the mediaeval pastoral tradition of England and northern France, and closely associated with the idea of pastoral in the minds of ordinary people. Fletcher blamed the unpopularity of *The Faithful Shepherdess* on the fact that, being so deeply and lyrically Italianate in its approach to the mode, it quite signally failed to connect with anything the audience was expecting. Even as late as the Jacobean era, the iconographic, the comic and the festive shepherd was still the archetypal pastoral figure for most people. When Fletcher published the work in 1610 he attached to it an epistle to the reader in which he explains what the mode involves. The play

> is a pastoral tragi-comedy, which the people seeing when it was played, having ever had a singular gift in defining, concluded to be a play of country hired shepherds in grey cloaks, with curtailed dogs in strings, sometimes laughing together, and sometimes killing one another; and, missing Whitsun-ales, cream, wassail, and morris-dances, began to be angry. In their error I would not have you fall, lest you incur their censure. Understand, therefore, a pastoral to be a representation of shepherds and shepherdesses with their actions and passions, which must be such as may agree with their natures, at least not exceeding former fictions and vulgar traditions; they are not to be adorned with any art, but such improper ones as nature is said to bestow, as singing and poetry; or such as experience may teach them, as the virtues of herbs and fountains, the ordinary course of the sun, moon and stars, and such like. But you are ever to remember shepherds to be such as all the ancient poets, and modern of understanding, have received them; that is, the owners of their flocks, and not hirelings.[29]

This is Fletcher's attempt to reconcile theory and example, decorum and artistry. He is stressing the decorum of the piece as he defines pastoral as 'a representation of shepherds and shepherdesses with their actions and passions, which must be such as may agree with their natures', but he has to qualify it at once – 'at least not exceeding former fictions and vulgar traditions': not going higher than is authorized by earlier writers. The phrase 'vulgar traditions' is rather vague in the context, but it seems to mean only more or less contemporary Italian and English styles of pastoral. The rejection of art is in accordance with decorum again, but he has to make an immediate exception for singing and poetry because they are so inherently a part of the pastoral tradition; but he justifies them on the grounds of naturalness, 'such as nature is said to bestow', so that by a saving grace art is still kept out of the shepherd world. The exact meaning of the word 'improper' here has been disputed. The most likely meaning seems to be 'not properly so called' – the *OED* lists it under this heading, though with a query; the arts of singing and poetry, in fact, cannot really be *arts* if they are *natural*. (The alternative meaning given is 'confined to certain individuals, not a common property'.) It is dangerous to chase ambiguities in such a context, but there does seem to be a shadow of the meaning 'inappropriate, indecorous' – a suggestion of a consciousness that these arts do not agree with the nature of shepherds. At the same time, like Ronsard, he declares his pastoral worthy of serious attention by the fact that his characters are not 'country hired shepherds'.

If decorum is strictly followed, then the shepherd in literature will represent the antithesis of cultured art. The peasant was at the far extreme of the social scale from the monarch, to the point where Latimer could cite the 'highest prince' and the 'poorest shepherd' as the ultimate examples to show the common mortality of men,[30] and Sir Walter Raleigh, himself a pastoral poet, could express his disgust by declaring, 'I would disdayn it as miche as to keap sheepe.'[31] Comic caricature was the usual way of showing the baseness of the herdsman. Corin in the play of *Clyomon and Clamydes* is an example from the earlier Elizabethan age.[32] His name is in keeping with the exotic setting, but he lives a rich life of his own.

> Then at night when maides come to milkin, the games begin,
> But I may zay to you, my nabor Hodges maid had a clap, wel let them
>   laugh that win.
> Chave but one daughter, but chould not vor vorty pence she were so sped,
> Cha may zay to you, she lookes every night to go to bed:
> But tis no matter, the whores be so whiskish when thare under a bush,
> That thare never satisfied, til their bellies be flush.
> Well cha must abroad about my flocks, least the fengeance wolves catch
>   a lambe.   (1297–303)

It sounds like the kind of caricatured naturalism that the fabliaux exploited, yet it is if anything even more conventional: the accessibility of the milk-maid, the threat of the wolf. The rough metre and the dialect are in full accordance with the demands of style and decorum; and the courtly heroine drives the point home with her sententious comment, 'Like man, like talke, in every degree' (1335).

To make the shepherd a figure of rustic comedy alone was unusual: the pastoral tradition as a whole was too strong, and the shepherd would move towards the ideal of idyllic country life, of pastoral innocence and true love. Sir Philip Sidney in particular was aware of the two sides of pastoral, of the demand for decorum and low style and the model of art and idyllicism, and the conflict between the two is a perennial preoccupation of his: the *Arcadia* perpetually illustrates the pull between the two traditions, of decorous rusticity opposed to the art of the shepherd-poet. Arcadia itself, as it is described in the second version of the book, is one vast *locus amoenus*, a place of hills and valleys, sun and shade, birdsong and bleating lambs; 'here a shepheards boy piping, as though he should never be old: there a yong shepherdesse knitting, and withall singing, and it seemed that her voice comforted her hands to work, and her hands kept time to her voices music'.[33] In this countryside, with its harmony of landscape and society and mind, of work and art, it is appropriate for Musidorus to take up the crook in order to be near Pamela, for the shepherds to entertain themselves with singing eclogues. The *Old Arcadia* presents a slightly different picture that brings into focus the problem of decorum. The impression Sidney gives of the country is still the same, though this passage does not appear; but Strephon and Klaius, who open the revised *Arcadia* with the splendidly wrought art of their declarations of love for Urania, are in this first version not true shepherds but, like Musidorus and Pyrocles, noblemen in disguise, and Urania herself 'thought a shepherds daughter, but indeede of far greater birth'.[34] The only genuine shepherds left who play any part in the action of the first draft of the book are Damoetas and his family, the clowns of the piece. The 'real' shepherds are almost anti-Arcadian. In neither version do they even contribute to any sense of integrity or simplicity there might be about the countryside, as the shepherds around Perdita do in *The Winter's Tale*: they are foolish rather than innocent, they are coarse, unrefined, and the language Sidney uses for them is the opposite of cultured art. Miso's account of the 'good wold woman' of the village, Mopsa's popular romance of the knight and princess who elope 'without staying so much as for their breakfast', are an extension of this appropriateness of treatment; and it is made the basis of an ironic pun when Musidorus, in shepherd disguise, bribes his way into the good graces of Damoetas, 'that of all manners of stile could best conceive of golden elo-quence'.[35] Presumably Sidney felt increasingly that to confine his art-shepherds to the eclogue interludes was too rigid an attitude to decorum and cut out too much of the pastoral tradition, but by making Strephon and Klaius a true part of his pastoral world he did lay himself open to Jonson's criticism of his style as indecorous. The eclogue was at least hallowed by tradition as the medium for the shepherd-poet.

The contrast between the different kinds of shepherd can be deeply satisfying even within a single work when the author is fully in control of his medium. Spenser's 'August' is a fine example, where the shepherd-poet's artistic and highly wrought sestina is set against the country vigour of Willy and Perigot's 'roundle', based on an actual popular song:[36]

It fell vpon a holly eue,
  hey ho hollidaye,
When holly fathers wont to shrieue:
  now gynneth this roundelay.
Sitting vpon a hill so hye
  hey ho the high hyll... (53–8)

– the singing-match has returned to the countryside. Each poem is appro-priate for the different characters, and the pastoral world embraces them both. The combination of crude peasant and idyllic pastoral is less happy in a work such as William Warner's *Albions England*,[37] where one figure embraces both extremes. Curan is not even a 'real' shepherd: he is a king's son in disguise, but he adopts more of the peasant than the clothing. When he falls in love with 'a Neatherds maid', he rubs his galoshes with bacon fat to make them shine, he leaves his tarbox at the fold lest the smell should offend her, he stuffs his scrip with bread, cheese and nuts to feast her, and he pipes on 'hollow Quilles of Oten straw' in her honour.

But when he spied her his saint, he wipt his greasie shooes,
And clear'd the driuell from his beard and thus the Shephearde wooes.
  I haue, sweet Wench, a peece of cheese, as good as toothe may chaw,
And bread, and Wildings souling-well (and therewithall did draw
His Lardrie) and, in eating, see, yon crumpled Ewe (quoth he)
Did twinne this fall, and twin shouldst thou, if I might tup with thee.

This is almost as crude as Corin in *Clyomon and Clamydes;* but a few moments later he is urging his suit in more idyllic terms.

Chuse a Shepheard: with the Sun he doth his Flocke vnfold,
And all the day on Hill or Plaine he merrie chat can hold...
Well wot I, sooth they say that say more quiet nights and daies
The Shepheard sleeps and wakes then he whose Cattel he doth graize.
Beleeue me, Lasse, a King is but a man, and so am I:
Content is worth a Monarchie, and mischiefes hit the hie.

Curan knows the truth of this from the course of his own life, but it does not prevent him from fighting to regain his kingdom as soon as the opportunity offers. And the neatherd's maid turns out to be his long-lost royal sweetheart.

Spenser and Drayton, the two Elizabethan poets perhaps most responsive to native English as well as Classically derived traditions of poetry, are out-standing in the way in which they use the richness offered by the various approaches to the mode. Drayton was attracted by the iconographic portrayal of the shepherd, the detailed descriptions so common in earlier art and literature. The shepherd in the Sixth Nimphal of the *Muses' Elizium*, the most idyllic of all his pastoral poems, belongs to this tradition:

> My Tarboxe, and my Scrip, my Bagpipe, at my back,
> My sheephooke in my hand, what can I say I lacke.   (231–2)

Drayton's deep love for the English countryside makes him see the real shepherd as leading an idyllic life: the Cotswold shearing-feasts of *Poly-Olbion* or the *Pastorals* are more perfect in their way than the admitted fantasy of the *Banquet du Bois*. In the eighth eclogue of *Idea the Shepherds Garland* (the fourth of the revised *Pastorals*) he introduces a shepherd described in even more loving detail, again with mediaeval iconographic realism. The passage is introduced by a debate on pastoral decorum between Motto and Gorbo, on the contrast between subjects suitable for the shepherd-poet and heroic matters. Motto then tells the low style shepherd's tale of Dowsabell, in which Drayton aims at achieving rustic decorum through archaism as Spenser had done. *Dowsabell* echoes both the *Shepheardes Calender* and Chaucer: the language is just slightly antiquated, the tail-rhyme stanza is a deliberate re-creation of the debased form of the popular romance as exemplified by *Sir Thopas* – who himself gets a mention in the poem. The shepherd with whom Dowsabell falls in love is described sitting on a bank carolling to the woods and fields around; he looks like Tamburlaine (who himself started life as a shepherd) but he has Abel's gentleness. As for his appearance,

> This shepheard ware a sheepe gray cloke,
> Which was of the finest loke,   (*short wool*)
>   that could be cut with sheere,
> His mittens were of Bauzens skinne,   (*badger*)
> His cockers were of Cordiwin,
>   his hood of Menivere.
> His aule and lingell in a thong,   (*waxed thread*)
> His tar-boxe on his broad belt hong,
>   his breech of Coyntrie blew...
> And pyping still he spent the day,
> So mery as the Popingay.[38]

When Drayton wishes to write in strict accordance with pastoral decorum, as he indicates in the discussion that opens the eclogue, he goes back to vernacular mediaeval poetic traditions – in rhythm, in subject and in language. The smaller items of the shepherd's equipment are attached to his belt, as they had been in the Middle Ages. The grey cloak itself is one of the attributes of the shepherd expected by Fletcher's baffled audience, and which in Peele's eyes excludes the peasants from the world of the god-like shepherd.

The Classical demand for simple style found a parallel in the vernacular tradition of moral simplicity. The shepherd in his rôle of instructor speaks with a directness that scorns art; Spenser uses his most archaic and rustic language, the roughest metres, not only for his most realistic shepherds but for his moral eclogues and in *Mother Hubberds Tale*. Here the theory of styles as expounded not by Servius but in the *Rhetorica ad Herennium* and in mediaeval traditions of preaching is brought into play. Low style will be used, or will be claimed to be used, not only because it is appropriate to pastoral but because it is appropriate to moral instruction. Lodge commends his eclogues in *A Fig for Momus* to 'men of approued iudgement';[39] pastoral is a serious, not a frivolous, mode.

> Waigh not the words, but mark the worth,
> Great flouds do often issue forth
> From humble waters, and deepe skill
> May flow from an impolisht quill.
> Who waites for words, may get him hence,
> For shepheards onely sing for sence.[40]

This is more obviously true of the calendar tradition than the eclogue, and Lodge himself is using it as a kind of modesty *topos*; but in the wide context of Renaissance pastoral the idea had far-reaching implications. 'There is no greater marke for a true shepheard to be knowne by, than Humilitie': so Chettle wrote, not about style but about character.[41] One of the most widespread moral commonplaces of pastoral was that the base estate of the shepherd precluded ambition and aspiring thought by its very nature:

> We live contentedly: A thing call'd pride
> Which so corrupts the Court and every place...
> I know not what it meanes in any case.[42]

The playwrights of the Middle Ages too had known how to utilize the ignorance of the peasant in the service of God, so that Greban's shepherds, forgetting the title of the Emperor, become a symbol of the simplicity of the Golden Age before there were rulers or cities, so that the Chester herdsmen can grasp intuitively an understanding of the nature of God through their crude groping towards repeating the angels' song. Milton's shepherds in the *Hymn on the Morning of Christ's Nativity* (1629) are of the same breed: they belong to a tradition half iconographic, half of rustic eclogue, but in any case in keeping with decorum:

> The Shepherds on the Lawn,
> Or ere the point of dawn,
> Sate simply chatting in a rustick row;
> Full little thought they than
> That the mighty Pan
> Was kindly come to live with them below;
> Perhaps their loves, or els their sheep,
> Was all that did their silly thoughts so busie keep.[43]

This is how the shepherds are pictured in the Books of Hours, though perhaps their loves come as much from Mantuan's 'antiquos amores'[44] as the pastourelle tradition, and to present Christ, the Good Shepherd, as Pan the god of shepherds is a characteristic of the eclogue. Milton is also at pains to stress their purity of heart: they are 'simple', 'silly' – words often used as epithets in pastoral with a range of meaning that covers everything that is the opposite of cultured, from the stupidity and ignorance implied by Turberville's 'sillie sottes' to the innocence of Breton's Coridon as he swears his true meaning in love

> with many a pretty oath,
> Yea and nay, and faith and troth,
> Such as silly Sheepheards use,
> When they will not Love abuse.   (*EH* p. 23)

Milton's description of the shepherds is naturalistic within an artistic framework (unlike Lycidas' threnodist, who is the shepherd-poet and shepherd-moralist *par excellence*, drawn completely within the world of art); but the overall effect of the realism is designed to bring out the integrity of the pastoral life, as is Breton's 'faith and troth'. 'Only faith and troth, that's shepherd's wooing,' is a line used by Lodge in *Rosalynde*[45] that sums up what many writers of different centuries are concerned to present. The whole concept is an age-old part of pastoral tradition: it can be seen in the myth of the pastoral Golden Age, the age of Astraea; in some of the pastourelles, or in *Franc Gontier*, where faithful and joyous love is celebrated; in the *Moralité de l'Alliance de Foy et Loyalté*, where Faith and Troth, banished from the political sphere, flee to the country to take up the life of shepherds and to maintain their existence in the pastoral world. A description of a pageant devised for the royal entry of the Archduke Charles into Bruges in 1515, when the Middle Ages were just giving way to the Renaissance in northern Europe, elaborates the Astraea myth to explain that she, like Foy and Loyalté, was banished from most estates of mankind by the rise of cities, laws and 'constitutions politiques', yet

> never the less (say the poets) for her final refuge she made her dwelling among ploughmen, shepherds and peasants, who after all others at last forced her to withdraw to the heavens from where she had originally descended. So therefore ploughing and sheepkeeping are the oldest of all estates...and furthermore virtue there is purer, less corruptible.[46]

This idea of her retreat to the shepherds before she finally left the earth is not found in any Classical source; it is apparently an early Renaissance invention to explain the innocence of pastoral life. Even in the Age of Iron, the shepherd world still preserves the last traces of the age of Astraea.

The Golden Age was broken when the life of pure Nature was damaged by the invention of arts, of building, of commerce. Even in the Middle Ages, when the *vilain* was most scorned, there was a feeling that the life closest to Nature still preserved many of the things that were best in human experience; and Greban put the idea to use in the shepherd scenes of his *Mystère*, Jean de Meung promised the Golden Age and eternal spring of the Shepherd's Park to those who obeyed Nature's commands to love freely, spontaneously and abundantly. The art of courtly love itself could be a barrier to joy, to true 'faith and troth'. When Perdita rejects the grafted plants in *The Winter's Tale* she is doing the same thing, insisting on the integrity of Nature before the 'improving' influences of Art. Love itself must be simple and whole, with no glozing on either side, and she will have as little to do with the art of make-up to attract Florizel as with the false breeding of flowers. The pastoral world is essentially the world of Nature, and the intrusion of Art would damage its wholeness as it wrecked the Golden Age. Shakespeare uses realistic English pastoral such as Fletcher's audience expected, the shepherd revels and dancing, to convey part of this idea. His shepherds are not entirely limited to prose, but when the Old Shepherd does speak in blank verse it is still in a naturalistic low style, not elevated beyond his rank, for instance in his description of his wife at the feast,

> her face o' fire
> With labour and the thing she took to quench it.　　　　(IV.iv.60–1)

More important, however, in the Elizabethan pastoral paradox, is the superb poetry of Perdita and Florizel, the flower imagery, the symbol of Perdita's closeness to nature as a 'wave o' the sea', joy in love on a flower-strewn bank. The integrity of the pastoral life comes from its realism, a realism that can embrace even the arch-deceiver Autolycus; and from the art that is rooted in nature. But although they are so homely, and English, the 'real' shepherds are never anti-Arcadian, as Sidney's Damoetas and his family are. The yokels, the 'silly shepherds', as well as the mock-shepherds who speak the beautiful poetry, create the sense of pastoral harmony. Shakespeare is using the idea of the dual shepherd, rustic and artistic, and using it in accordance with the prescripts of decorum – prose and clowning for the true peasants, poetry and beauty for the high-born – but he is exploiting the differences, and the similarities, between them to create a world where the two can exist in artistic harmony, and where they can each give something to the other.

The implications and possibilities of the pastoral mode could only be worked out in practice, in the artistic creation of fictional pastoral. If the shepherd-poet is one of its leading figures, it is as much a part of the tradition that art should be used to deny art, fiction to declare truth. All these paradoxes are at work in an unusually explicit fashion in Sidney's poem *Dispraise of a Courtly Life*,[47] addressed to his friends and fellow-courtiers Dyer and Greville. He uses all the familiar pastoral themes and commonplaces, every rule relating to the mode, not as the framework but as the very fabric of the poem. It is an overheard lament, one of the standard mediaeval pastoral-related forms; the idea of the herdsman getting inside knowledge of the court is a theme derived from mediaeval, not Classical, pastoral; and the moral instruction too is characteristic of vernacular pastoral traditions. The result is a syncretic Renaissance fusion of all the disparate viewpoints and conventions contained in the mode, a serious game about the interplay of art and truth. Sidney himself seems to have a double *persona* in the poem, both as narrator and as the man lamenting his move from the pastoral world to the court. The narrator leaves the sun to walk in the woods, and there hears the former shepherd

> Rewing change of wonted state,
> Whence he was transformed late,
> Once to Shepheard's God retayning,
> Now in servile Court remaying.   (9–12)

He laments:

> 'My old mates I grieve to see,
> Voyde of me in field to bee,
> Where we once our lovely sheepe,
> Lovingly like friends did keepe,
> Oft each other's friendship proving,
> Never striving, but in loving.

> 'But may Love abiding bee
> In poore shepheard's base degree?
> It belongs to such alone
> To whom arte of Love is knowne:
> Seely shepheards are not witting
> What in art of Love is fitting.

> 'Nay, what neede the Arte to those,
> To whom we our love disclose?
> It is to be used then,
> When we doe but flatter men:
> Friendship true in hart assured,
> Is by nature's giftes procured.

> 'Therefore shepheardes wanting skill
> Can Love's duties best fulfill:
> Since they know not how to faine,
> Nor with Love to cloake Disdaine,
> Like the wiser sorte, whose learning,
> Hides their inward will of harming.

'Well was I, while under shade
Oten Reedes me musicke made,
Striving with my Mates in Song,
Mixing mirth our Songs among,
Greater was that shepheard's treasure,
Than this false, fine, Courtly pleasure.'   (19-48)

The shepherd world in its humbleness, its innocence, even its ignorance, provides the simplicity that true love, that any true relationship, demands, and which can be found nowhere else. The oaten reed, low style, *stylus tenuis*, is a part of the simple life; elaborate language itself becomes only a means of deception, of clouding open faith: Art

> is to be used then
> When we doe but flatter men.

Moral value and linguistic simplicity are equated; the poetic theory reinforces the moral statement implicit in the world of pastoral. The *tenuis avena*, the slender oaten reed, becomes the guarantee of true and open virtue.

V

PASTORAL OF THE ENGLISH RENAISSANCE

The persistent curiosity that the early Elizabethan poets had felt for pastoral suddenly turned into a fashion – almost a craze – in the later years of the reign. The pastoral mode as the Elizabethans knew it contained a remarkable variety of approach, of subject and treatment: there were the idyllic landscapes and the nymphs, the love-melancholy and the crossed paths of lovers, but these were not the only, nor the primary, matters for pastoral concern: politics and panegyric, religious comment, ecclesiastical and social satire, personal allusion, moral instruction, peasant life, prophecy, age and youth, the changing seasons and death all had a time-honoured place, and were indeed almost inseparable from the idea of pastoral itself. The real strength of the best of Elizabethan pastoral, and the point where it differs most from the later more vapid, and more stereotyped, development – or degeneration – of the mode, lies in its intense consciousness of these concerns. The first appeal of pastoral was the appeal of art: the Elizabethans use it to explore the nature of poetry and of their poetic inspiration, but it was an art that was also deeply involved in the central issues of life and society. This is the Elizabethans' real inheritance from the pastoral of the Middle Ages, and it emerges not just in a host of minor poets but in the great figures of the age as well – in Sidney, Spenser, Drayton, Shakespeare himself. It is this that made the pastoral mode so challenging in their eyes, and that makes their work important in a way that Sannazaro's, for instance, is not: there is not merely the delight in art for its own sake but the intense desire for that art to reflect back onto life.

The fashion for pastoral had been set on the Continent already, and the barrenness of English literature over the preceding hundred and fifty years meant that the Elizabethan poets had to look outside for their models; but this did not mean that the native tradition of pastoral was forgotten. Sidney and Spenser, who opened the great age of pastoral in the late 1570's, took their inspiration from different poets representing different pastoral traditions – Sidney from Sannazaro and Montemayor,[1] Spenser from Mantuan and Marot – but they both saw in the mode a potential for creating the highest English art. It was only in the seventeenth century that Italianate pastoral of the nymph-and-shepherd variety came to be of major significance in England, and it did not hold the centre of the stage undisputed until after the Restoration. The Renaissance invention of the semi-mythological romance, and plays belonging to the same world, may have set the fashion in Italy and Spain, but generally this is not what the Elizabethans were interested in: nymphs would be as discordant in Sidney's *Arcadia* or *The Winter's Tale* as they are at home in Sannazaro or Tasso's *Aminta*, for although these writers may all give their works a setting in a legendary age of gods and oracles Sidney and Shakespeare are directly concerned with mankind in a way that the others are not. The pastoral traditions of the Middle Ages reached their finest point in the literature of the Elizabethans, and if it was Italianate pastoral, with its emphasis on the poet and poetry, that made such a culmination possible, the heights could never be reached through the new traditions alone.

It is the great Elizabethans who show the fusion of traditions at its most complete: traditions derived from the Classical eclogue and its mediaeval reinterpretation, from *bergerie*, from contemporary Italy and France. In the early seventeenth century the traditions began to separate again, as the idyllic romance or drama or lyric that owed almost nothing to the Middle Ages parted from moral or satirical poems and eclogues. The years preceding the Civil War saw the end of the mediaeval tradition as an important force in pastoral – a force lost together with the cause for which it was fighting, for in the hands of several Royalist poets the mode was once again in the centre of the political arena. One of the strangest characteristics of the pastoral of these years, from 1578 till about 1640, is its self-consciousness: not just artistically – that is a feature common to almost all Renaissance pastoral – but historically. In the figure of Elizabeth herself, pastoral found a unique resting-place, a single symbol in which all the ideas it could be used to express could be united; and after her death, her reign appeared as the true age of pastoral poetry, a poetic and political Golden Age.

I. *Sidney*

As far as pastoral is concerned, Sir Philip Sidney was an exceptional figure in an exceptional age, for two reasons: because such a high proportion of his work was written within the mode, and because he himself was personally involved in the whole idea of pastoral as no other figure of the age was, except the Queen herself. Spenser's *Shepheardes Calender* is often cited as the first product of the New Poetry; but Sidney had already begun work quite independently on one of the other masterpieces of English pastoral, the *Arcadia* (which he wrote twice, though the second version was never completed), and he had written the *Lady of May*, a pastoral interlude for presentation before the Queen, in 1578, eighteen months before the *Calender* appeared. Although the two poets had certainly met by early 1579, and must have discussed their work, their approaches to pastoral remained quite distinct. Spenser was attracted by the pastoral mode all his life, but his great work, the *Faerie Queene*, is basically heroic; Sidney in his own masterwork attempts to combine the heroic and the pastoral. The combination is particularly interesting because of his own involvement in both rôles. René of Anjou with his pastoral tournament had felt something of the same urge to reconcile the two ideals; and in the extension of art into life typical of the pageantry of the age Sidney used the double *persona* for himself in his poetry and at court. In the *Arcadia* he presents himself as Philisides, who appears several times in the eclogues of the first version as a gentleman who has become a shepherd for the sake of love; in the revision he appears once only, as the Shepherd Knight – the knight who adopts a pastoral disguise for a tournament:

whose manner of entring was, with bagpipes in steed of trumpets; a shepheards boy before him for a Page, and by him a dosen apparelled like
shepherds for the fashion, though rich in stuffe, who caried his launces,
which though strong to give a launcely blow indeed, yet so were they
couloured with hooks neere the mourn, that they pretily represented
shephooks. His own furniture was drest over with wooll, so enriched with
Jewels artificially placed, that one would have thought it a mariage
between the lowest and the highest.[2]

'The lowest and the highest', the heroic and the pastoral, the opposite ends
of the spectrum of art, and Sidney cannot help commenting on the 'mariage'.
It is typical of the richness the mode appeared to offer to the Elizabethans
that the poet who was most acutely sensitive to the problem of artistic
decorum should best have combined the two. The description of Philisides at
the tournament is probably a portrait of himself as he appeared at the
Accession Day tilts of 1581. The Philisides of the *Old Arcadia* is the more
usual kind of pastoral self-portrait, of the Virgil-Tityrus, Sannazaro-Sincero
or Spenser-Colin variety, and there he gives more details of himself: a
shallowly disguised 'autobiography', remarkably close to Sincero's, in the
Fourth Eclogues; and in 'As I my little flock' in the Third Eclogues an
account of the teaching of Hubert Languet, the Protestant statesman he had
met on his tour of Europe and with whom he maintained a correspondence.
Languet in this eclogue becomes the master shepherd, noted equally for his
'clerkly reed' and moral uprightness; and Philisides recounts a song of his,
which turns out to be a beast-fable about the creation and nature of Man.
This is the only piece of fully allegorical pastoral that Sidney ever wrote, and
it fits with his description of the double meaning of 'prettie tales of Wolues
and Sheepe' in his account of pastoral in the *Apologie for Poetrie*.

The *Arcadia* as a whole seems at first sight to owe comparatively little to
mediaeval ideas of pastoral, and there are not many passages like the eclogue
on Languet that have obvious antecedents in the Middle Ages. But the
influence of mediaeval pastoral is quite strongly present, and it shows itself
principally on a larger scale: in Sidney's use of the mode to make a serious
statement on the nature of virtue, of good government, rule of one's self and
rule of a kingdom. Pastoral was not the frivolous or escapist mode that it was
later exclusively to become; Sidney is in effect restoring to it the deep social
and political concern that his direct models had cut out. The idea as he
develops it contains an element of the Platonic – the idea of personal and
political justice being images of each other; but he starts with a simpler
account of the nature of the state of Arcadia. Nobody had ever conceived of
a pastoral Arcadia as a 'state' in this sense before; Sidney bases his own
conception on the moral self-sufficiency of the shepherd world. The Arcadians
are not interested in 'the shining title of glorie'; rather, they 'are the onely
people, which as by their Justice and providence geve neither cause nor hope
to their neyghbours to annoy them' (I p. 19). Beyond that there is little to
interest the political observer within the story, and Musidorus, 'having
informed himselfe fully of the strength and riches of the country' (p. 54),
would be quite happy to leave but that love breaks in and binds him irredeem-
ably to the country and all it stands for. The Good Shepherd of the Middle
Ages had to know his flock and himself; and if the sheep are no longer
important, the pastoral world is still the place where self-knowledge can and
must be learnt. The process is not straightforward, and the princes' total
commitment to the pastoral life at first involves nothing so much as a series

of disguises and delusions – 'transformd in shew, but more transformd in minde'; the pastoral interlude in their lives is no more an unmitigated good for them than for Basilius, the king who has withdrawn from the responsibilities of state to the irresponsibility of Petit Trianon-type pastoral. Just what Sidney's final intentions were it is impossible to know; but one theme is common both to the simpler plot of the *Old Arcadia* and to the enormous addition of the war with Cecropia, in the course of which the revised version breaks off; and that is the theme of maturity through suffering. The princes' youthful conviction of self-sufficiency is first broken down by love, and then re-established on the firmer basis of painful experience. The process is more characteristic of the chivalric than the pastoral romance; but Sidney is placing the quest for true self-knowledge in the perspective of the pastoral world, where thought and contemplation are more important than action.

The most striking aspect of *bergerie*, the detailed description of shepherds and their activities, is almost entirely missing from the *Arcadia*: there is just an occasional mention of Musidorus' activities when he is disguised as a shepherd, in making hurdles or in learning how to throw 'a litle clod' at any wandering sheep with the hollow iron or horn that the crook normally bore at the opposite end from the hook;[3] but scarcely a single sheep makes an appearance, and they are certainly never important. The realistic herdsman with his realistic duties belongs to a different world; and this may be the reason why Sidney did not include in his revised *Arcadia* a poem that he apparently wrote for it,[4] describing how Strephon and Klaius came to fall in love with Urania, and which is the closest in content to the *bergerie* tradition of anything he ever wrote. The poem is not altogether in tune with the art-controlled mode of his romance, nor with the neoplatonic elevation of Urania in the opening pages. The poem starts with lines that place it artistically:

> A Shepheards tale no height of stile desires
> To raise in words what in effect is low;

and although the poem that follows betrays the double-edged attitude to decorum typical of Sidney, it does not strive for the elevation of content or form that many of the other eclogues in the *Arcadia* display. The tendency for Sidney to divide his shepherds into clowns and art-shepherds has already been noted;[5] Strephon and Klaius, as they appear in the *New Arcadia*, are definitely of the second kind, to the point where Sidney finds it necessary both for them to explain their superiority to the reader – that the love of Urania has made them '(being silly ignorant shepheards) raise up our thoughts above the ordinary levell of the worlde, so as great clearkes do not disdaine our conference' – and for Kalander to explain it again to Musidorus.[6] There is the occasional comic poem in the course of the interludes of eclogues in the *Arcadia*, but no shepherd who himself occupies the middle ground between the crude and the artificial. The Strephon and Klaius of 'A Shepheards tale', however, do just this. They are herdsmen who have to spend their time looking after their flocks, and when they are not busy with that they are occupied not in composing eclogues but in the *bergerie* pastimes of studying herbs for healing, hunting birds and squirrels, playing with their sheepdogs, piping, Maying or playing games – barley-break, 'keels' (a kind of ninepins), and running at the quintain (often a country sport, as distinct from the courtly version on horseback). Some details of their activities are unusually precise: Sidney tells of catching larks by attracting them to mirrors; and he describes Klaius marking his sheep with the sign of a pillar in ochre. Even the metonymy he uses for the occupation of the shepherd shows the same sharp focus:

> the life which on short-bitten grasse
> In shine or storme must sett the clowted shoe. (19–20)

The contrast of such a life with the court, and the comparison of shepherd and monarch, are also derived from the *bergerie* tradition:

> With nature pleas'd, content with present case,
> Free of proud feares, brave begg'ry, smiling strife
> Of clime-fall Court, the envy-hatching place:
> While those restles desires in great men rife
> To visite so low folkes did much disdaine,
> This while, though poore, they in themselves did raigne. (59–64)

The idea is commonplace, but it is given strength by the precision of his description of the shepherd life – a life that involves responsibility as well as pleasure. The pea under the mattress in all this is of course Love – not the joyful fulfilment of some of the pastourelles, but agonizing Renaissance love-melancholy that makes Strephon break his pipe, disown his sheep and drive away his dog; and by the end of the poem he has changed nature, from the herdsman whose thoughts are on his sheep to the poet who will use his sheep as images for his thoughts.

Even this kind of *bergerie* naturalism can be made to contain higher things, however. The game of barley-break is described with abundant detail, but not merely for its interest as a country pastime: it takes on a quietly neo-platonic element as well. The object of the game was for two couples at either end of the playing area to exchange partners without being caught by the couple in the middle, in 'Hell'; if they were caught, they in turn became the couple in Hell. The three shepherdesses taking part in the game are called Cosma (κόσμος, the world), Nous (νοῦς, mind) and Urania herself, commonly identified in the neoplatonic thought of the Renaissance with the 'heauenlie light of knowledge'.[7] Strephon has to partner each of the three shepherdesses in turn, though his mind is always set on Urania; and so the game becomes an image of the ascent of man's mind from the earthly through the intellectual to the heavenly. The naturalistic detail prevents it from being an allegory – Strephon is obviously not a *Faerie-Queene*-type character actually experiencing these phases: it is almost the reverse, a witty analogy for neoplatonic theory in a peasants' game of tag. There is nothing in it of the elevation of tone of the lovers' account of Urania in the *Arcadia*. The passage also makes an interesting gloss on the declaration of pastoral decorum that opens the poem: the low subject-matter of the shepherd's tale does not exclude intellectualism of this kind.

May revels are given a central place in 'A Shepheards tale'. Strephon is made 'village-Lord': with two heroes and one supremely beautiful heroine, it might seem that Urania ought to appear as the May Lady instead, but Sidney is probably representing actual folk practice – the May Queen apparently only existed at this date as the consort of the more important King.[8] It may be that 'the Lady of the whole moneth of May' who is the central figure in Sidney's earliest pastoral, the *Lady of May*, was made a queen regnant in honour of Elizabeth. This is the first English pastoral to make

May revels its setting; and it is also the first, and one of the best, of the many pastorals addressed to the Queen. The form is original – half masque, half play, and a mixture of eclogue and pastoral pageant – but the content is in many ways traditional. Sidney's concern that his pastoral should relate directly to life is expressed in the *Arcadia* through its broad moral structures; the *Lady of May* employs the mediaeval method of the hidden meaning, 'parabole couverte' – not quite a full allegory, but not so far distinct. It is a particularly fine example of the way the pastoral mode could be used to comment very closely on a particular personal and political situation without having to break through the confines of the shepherd world. Unlike the Petrarchan allegory, however, it does not depend on a precise interpretation; the piece is delightful in itself. The allusiveness is beside the point as far as the poetry is concerned, and it can be read simply as an interlude; but although outsiders may see a pleasant *divertissement*, those most closely involved with the piece certainly saw more in it than that.

The *Lady of May* was written to entertain 'her most excellent Majestie walking in Wansteed garden',[9] which she visited in the May of 1578. Wanstead was one of Leicester's properties, and Sidney, presumably with the Earl's knowledge if not at his instigation, designed his entertainment, pleasant enough in itself on the narrative and dramatic level, to have a bearing on Leicester's relationship with the Queen. The principal character of the piece is the May Lady, who is troubled by two suitors, the forester Therion and the shepherd Espilus. They are each accompanied by a group of their companions complete with appropriate musical instruments, cornets and recorders; and their rivalry provides the opportunity for a singing-match between them, taking the form of a *conflictus* as to the relative merits of their occupations and therefore of themselves. The debate between different forms of 'pastoral' life was new in English, as was the singing-match itself at this date; but forester eclogues were recognized as a legitimate form of bucolic,[10] and the same debate reappears later in England, most strikingly in *The Maydes Metamorphosis* and in Drayton's *Muses Elizium*.[11] The history of the forester eclogue is obscure: it could have its origins in *Franc Gontier* and its Latin translation. As far as England was concerned the slight literary background for foresters tended to show them principally as a danger to young women travelling alone;[12] and given the herdsman's traditional association with both responsibility and content it is perhaps not surprising that Elizabeth, called on to judge the argument, declared in favour of the shepherd. S. K. Orgel, however, has argued convincingly that the play was designed to favour Therion, and that Espilus, Elizabeth notwithstanding, is beaten in the debate.[13] The Queen was not the one to commit a blunder, and innocent as the piece looks she would know well enough that neither pastoral nor royal entertainments were designed for amusement only; and the May Lady tells her as much – 'in judging me, you judge more then me in it'. Various suggestions have been made as to its inner meaning – that it represents the policies of war and peace, or the courtship of the duke of Anjou;[14] but there is another possibility, that it represents the rivalry between Leicester and Sir Christopher Hatton. The name θηρίον, 'wild beast', for the forester, would match Leicester's badge of the bear and ragged staff; and he occasionally also used the oak, appropriate for the forester, as his symbol, from the similarity of *Robert* to *robur*.[15] 'Espilus' is derived from εἰς πῖλος, 'felt presser',[16] a reasonable Greek approximation to 'hatter' and hence 'Hatton'; and the shepherd disguise would also be appropriate for him, as Elizabeth called him her 'mutton', 'sheep' or 'bell-wether'.[17] The identification is confirmed by a letter from Leicester to Hatton in which he apparently discusses the piece.[18] A recently discovered manuscript, the Helmingham Hall MS, contains a conclusion that was omitted when the play was printed: the pedantic schoolmaster Rombus, one of the incidental characters of the piece, speaks of 'mr. Roberte of wansteed, he is counted an honeste man', and of how he has been wrongly accused of Catholicism – a typical extension of pastoral into religious controversy. Rombus presents the Queen with 'a chayne of Round Aggates somethinge like beades...*cum quos* with the which *omne dierum* every daie nexte after his pater noster he *semper* saith an Elizabeth as many times as theare be beades on this stringe';[19] in other words, Leicester will substitute in his prayers an 'Elizabeth' for the *Ave Maria*. It seems to be to this passage that Leicester refers in his letter to Hatton, which he wrote after the Queen had made another visit later in the year while he himself was absent.

> One thing hath troubled me not a little, to hear that her Majesty should come to Wanstead and her .=. [i.e. eyes, her nickname for Leicester] not there to receive her. I fear that little liking to it she had before will through too, too many more faults, breed her less love hereafter...But God grant I may hear that her Majesty doth both well rest, and find all things else there to her good contentment; and that the goodman Robert, she last heard of there, were found at his beads, with all his *aves*, in his solitary walk.[20]

The letter concludes with a request to Hatton to further Sidney's interests in a particular matter. The most curious thing about it is the implication that Hatton was himself familiar with the pageant, perhaps even that there was some kind of collaboration over the contents, that the question put to Elizabeth through Sidney was one to which both Leicester and Hatton wanted to know the answer. One matter that may well have been at the back of Leicester's mind when the pageant was designed was the prospect of his marriage to Lettice Knollys, the widowed countess of Essex, and of how the Queen would take it. The formal ceremony took place in September 1578; and Hatton certainly knew it was in the offing, for in June he wrote to the Earl that Elizabeth was in 'continual and great melancholy':

> She dreameth of marriage that might seem injurious to her; making myself to be either the man or a pattern of the matter...But, my lord, I am not the man that should thus suddenly marry.[21]

Perhaps the matter had been decided when she refused to favour Therion above Espilus, to guarantee Leicester an exclusive primacy in her affection.

Sidney made heavy demands on the pastoral mode, and in his hands it met them all – from hidden allusion to moral guidance, from neoplatonism in a game of barley-break or in love to comedy, from critical comment on his own art to an expression of his idea of himself as shepherd and knight. Apart from his letters and his specifically non-fictional or religious writing, his only work of any importance that is not set principally within the pastoral world is *Astrophel and Stella*, and even that becomes pastoral for brief moments. Astrophel was Sidney's second *persona*, alongside Philisides; and although he is usually a chivalric figure, he has something of the same double nature of shepherd-knight as Philisides. The shepherd here is the lover – this time the despairing lover: in one neat variation on an old commonplace he advises his sheep to protect themselves from the bad weather actually caused by their shepherd:

Go my flocke, go get you hence,
Seeke a better place of feeding,
Where you may have some defence
From the stormes in my breast breeding,
And showers from mine eyes proceeding.[22]

The fusion in Sidney of the rôles of poet, lover, knight and shepherd was recognized by his contemporaries; and although he died in battle, poet after poet who wrote in his memory – sometimes in formal elegies, sometimes in reminiscences slipped into works on other subjects – celebrated him as the shepherd as much as the martial hero. Spenser describes him as 'far passing all the pastors of his daies', the best at 'all the sports that shepheards are emong', who

> could pipe and daunce, and caroll sweet,
> Emongst the shepheards in their shearing feast.[23]

Sidney's sister, Mary, countess of Pembroke, probably wrote the lay of Clorinda that Spenser includes in his *Astrophel*, and she too calls on the shepherds and shepherdesses to mourn, to break their garlands and to cease from singing his poems. Lodowick Bryskett, Sidney's companion on his tour of the Continent, wrote a 'pastorall Aeglogue' on his death; so did an anonymous poet whose piece was collected by Davison for his *Poetical Rhapsody*, and so did Drayton.[24] To Drayton Sidney was Elphin, 'sweet Child of Pan', 'immortall morror of all Poesie', whose death has left the earth wintry and desolate; but he finishes his elegy on a different note – on a note of rejoicing, on the familiar Classical model, but with an even more familiar image for Elphin in heaven:

> Come and behold yon lovely shepheards swayne,
>   piping his fill,
>   on yonder hill.

Other poets took up different aspects of Sidney's multiple nature. Nicholas Breton, in his *Amoris Lachrimae*, describes how the herdsmen mourn and the earth fades; and also how

> Nature and Arte are gott about his grave
> And there sitt waylinge of eche others losse.[25]

His death may produce more sinister results too:

> Looke how the flocke begins to leave there feeding,
> While cruell beastes breake in among the sheepe.   (277–8)

Sidney as shepherd was the protector of England as well as poet and lover: his pastoral rôle becomes the image of his nature as warrior. Peele, in his *Eclogue Gratulatory* to Essex, recalls him in the same terms, as 'that great shepherd good Philisides', who

> watcht and waited late
> To keepe the grim Wolfe from Elizaes gate;   (66–7)

and he is also, in a phrase from a homelier tradition, 'that jolly groome'. Sidney was almost the only man of rank to be killed in action in Elizabeth's reign; he was also the man who had worked the hardest to create the new poetry, even more by his interest and inspiration than by his example. If the poets who wrote in his memory do not visualize the demise of poetry itself along with the renewed attacks of the wolf, it is because they knew too well that his work would not die, and by their very act of writing they can prove as much.

II. *Spenser*

Marot had indicated his dual allegiance to French and Classical traditions by giving himself the name of Robin in his eclogue; Spenser makes the same point even more strongly in more than one way. It is apparent in his choice of title for his first major poem: *The Shepheardes Calender*, 'applying an old name to a new worke'. The contents have little to do with the traditional calendar, with its encyclopaedic array of miscellaneous information, but the idea is none the less important: Spenser is declaring himself to be the mouthpiece of moral wisdom, and declaring too the relationship of man's life with the seasons – not merely, as the Italians or even to some extent Marot would have it, in terms of pathetic fallacy, but seeing both *sub specie aeternitatis*. The fact that the separate poems are eclogues, however, asserts his ambition as a poet: this is a Classical form, artistically demanding, and moreover, as E. K. points out, an implicit promise of greater things to come. The double allegiance, to the great poetic tradition of the Classics revived in the continental Renaissance and to the less sophisticated but no less vital traditions of English poetry, is repeated throughout the *Calender*, overtly as well as in the choice of theme and treatment. Spenser declares that his model is Chaucer, but he refers to him as Tityrus: his highest authority, in fact, is English, but the highest compliment he can pay him is to give him the name of the Classical master-poet. The explicit emphasis on the Chaucerian tradition is all the more necessary since it is the least manifest in the work itself: apart from the lines on the herdgrooms with their corn-pipes in 'February', there is scarcely any direct borrowing of either phrase or theme. It is likely that Spenser thought his rougher rhythms to be close to Chaucer's verse as it was mangled by the combined effects of the sixteenth-century press and linguistic changes; but there is no more proof of this than that he believed his assertion that the fable of the Oak and the Briar was Chaucerian in style, and this even E. K. can see to be wrong: 'this tale…he telleth as learned of Chaucer, but it is cleane in another kind'. It does bear something of the same ironic relationship to the rest of the eclogue as the *Canterbury Tales* do to each other – indeed, the whole *Calender* can be regarded in this way; but whether Spenser was at all aware of this as a Chaucerian scheme is very doubtful. In any case, Spenser is quite prepared to acknowledge himself as the heir to much cruder poetic traditions than those exemplified by the courtly master of English poetry. The old shepherds' calendars are of negligible literary merit; and his choice of name for himself, Colin Clout, establishes him as being not only in the tradition of Marot's most accomplished shepherd-poet, who sings the elegy on Loyse de Savoie, but also of Skelton, who made it his *persona* as the moralist of society and church, indicting both in words as rough and plain as Spenser's moral pastoral:

> For though my ryme be ragged,
> Tattered and jagged,
> Rudely rayne beaten,
> Rusty and moth-eaten,
> Yf ye take well therwith
> It hath in it some pyth.
> For, as farre as I can see,
> It is wronge with eche degre.[26]

Colin may have been one of the traditional English names for the peasant herdsman too: there is a Coll in one of the Wakefield plays, and the chief shepherd in the Scots *Colkelbie Sow* is called 'colyne cuckowe'.[27] Spenser as Colin is both the idyllic poet and the satirist, the shepherd-singer and the common man. The name itself embraces both traditions of pastoral.

Spenser's pastoral is the supreme example of the fusion of the mediaeval and Renaissance forms. Not only the *Calender* but also the shepherd interlude of Book VI of the *Faerie Queene*, *Colin Clouts Come Home Againe*, the occasional pastoral pieces and also *Mother Hubberds Tale* exemplify at one point or another almost all the ways the mode had been used over the preceding thousand years. He was a voracious reader, and the *Calender* bears abundant witness to his knowledge of the leading earlier pastoralists, Mantuan and Marot in particular, Virgil rather less obviously; but it is very difficult to be certain what else he had read. His frequent acknowledgement of Chaucer as his master in the *Calender* is backed by fewer echoes than even Barclay's work contains, and whether general similarities to other poets are the result of imitation or coincidence – pastoral is, after all, a strictly limited mode – is often impossible to tell.[28] He almost certainly knew the *Plowman's Tale*, with its ecclesiastical satire in pastoral form; if he did ascribe it to Chaucer he could believe his master to be behind him in his satirical eclogues, where many of the points at issue are the same. In addition to his possible reference to this work in the epilogue to the *Calender* – 'the Pilgrim that the Ploughman playde a whyle'[29] – there is one phrase that he might have taken from it, 'forswonck and forswatt', an expression that is not as commonplace as it may sound.[30] He probably did not know Theocritus directly; there is no proof that he had read Theodulus, or Petrarch's eclogues, or even Barclay or Googe, though some of these authors must have come his way, and he is often clearly using pastoral in the same ways and for the same ends as they do. Generally, however, he seems to work more from the associations the pastoral mode had collected – associations apparent from earlier English works such as 'Kepe well the shepe' or *Jolly Wat* or *Harpelus and Phillida* – than from specific sources. E. K.'s listing of the major pastoral poets in his introductory epistle proves little about his own reading and less about Spenser's: he too shows little or no firsthand knowledge of Theocritus; even a passing acquaintance with Petrarch would have assured him that he had not written his *Bucolicum Carmen* 'as not yet well feeling his winges'; and the often-cited similarity to the list of authorities in Barclay's *Prologe* may be no more than the result of the convention of giving a history of the eclogue to explain your own, as Boccaccio had done and as Drayton was to do. Since Barclay alludes to Theodulus but omits Boccaccio, E. K. obviously had at least some other source of information. Barclay was certainly known to Drayton, who includes him in his own history of pastoral.[31] What is clear is that Elizabethan scholars and poets were deeply interested in the pastoral mode in all its aspects, and that Spenser himself found a particular inspiration in the same things that had attracted mediaeval writers to pastoral – perhaps by his sensitivity to the mediaeval elements in Mantuan and Marot, perhaps by working directly from other earlier writers, perhaps just by seeing the same relationship between the shepherd world and the real as the Middle Ages had seen. He never forgets for a single line, however, that he is a Renaissance poet, and it is this artistic consciousness that gives the *Shepheardes Calender* its power and its importance.

These qualities were recognized as soon as the poem appeared. Several critics have recently attempted to explain the difference between the significance the work was felt to have, and is still felt to have, and the comparative dullness of the text on the page, by reference to its close allegory of contemporary events, to number symbolism and so on;[32] but these attempts, however illuminating they may be for some aspects of Spenser's technique, tend to abandon the poetry altogether, and the *Calender* begins to appear to justify the accusations of dullness as a result. But if the work is read against the background of varying poetic traditions, of the struggle for expression of the artistic consciousness of an English poet, then the poetry itself comes alive and its inherent excitement becomes clear. For the *Shepheardes Calender* is an exciting work: and that is because it is not simply a literary experiment or a programme for poetic reform but an achieved embodiment of a new poetry. The traditions of pastoral are imitated not in order to be preserved, nor even to show that Spenser is capable of imitating them, but because they offer the perfect medium for conveying his own excitement in the idea of his art. This kind of poetic self-consciousness is a typically Renaissance phenomenon – certainly not mediaeval, nor even Classical, though Spenser embraces the poetic of all three ages in the *Calender*. Virgil may make a personal appearance in the *Bucolics*, but Tityrus does not have the significance that Colin bears: he may sing, but he does not talk about his music. In several of his eclogues Spenser makes the most of the great Renaissance discovery that the whole countryside of pastoral could be a projection of the poet's own mind: in 'January', as Colin declares,

> Thou barrein ground, whome winters wrath hath wasted,
> Art made a myrrhour, to behold my plight; (19–20)

in 'August', the sympathy of the woods, the birds and the streams with his laments; in 'December', the cycle of the seasons as an image of his innocence and experience. This is less the poet in the landscape than the landscape in the poet, just as in 'June' Hobbinol is living in an idyllic place that calls from Colin the comment,

> O happy Hobbinoll, I blesse thy state,
> That Paradise hast found, whych Adam lost; (9–10)

but Colin himself cannot join him in that paradise. Such a return to delight and innocence is impossible for one who is suffering Colin's own bitter experience. The pattern of the lines, with one shepherd at ease in the shade, the other searching hopelessly for a refuge, is modelled on Virgil's first eclogue, with Tityrus under the beeches and the exiled Meliboeus; but the subject is not physical or economic but internal, about the state of mind of the shepherd-poet, not the state of his body. The Classical themes of pleasure and exile, the mediaeval image of the pastoral paradise, the Renaissance concern with poetic inspiration, are interwoven to make a statement on poetry at a deeper level than could have been possible before.

Rich in meaning as such passages are, they are not in the strict sense allegorical; and given the enormous influence that Petrarch's idea of the bucolic still exerted, and which shows itself repeatedly in Spenser's ecclesiastical eclogues in particular, it is significant just how far the general conception of the *Shepheardes Calender* is from such an interpretation. The detailed historical allegory of the poem has been frequently studied, most notably by Paul McLane; but even more important is the fact that, unlike Petrarch,

Spenser never depends on any such precise exegesis to be understood. The significance is certainly there, but it is contained in the poetry, not opposed to it. To make too immediate equation, for instance, of Pan and Syrinx in 'April' with Henry VIII and Ann Boleyn, is to destroy the magic of Eliza's mythological birth:

> Shee is Syrinx daughter without spotte,
> Which Pan the shepheards God of her begot.   (50–1)

This is not an historical statement, and the use by Marot and others of 'Pan' for the French king is beside the point. Eliza's parentage confirms her pride of place in the pastoral world, makes her seem sprung from music and from the harmony of the universe that the seven tubes of the panpipe symbolize. The lament for Dido in 'November' is an even more striking example of the irrelevance of allegorical detail for a first reading: not to know whether Dido is meant to represent Elizabeth, or indeed anybody particular at all, does not detract from the poetry in the least, nor from the fitting place of the lament in the month when, as the old *Kalender of Shepherdes* put it,

> the blastes of the wynde
> Abateth leues, and shedeth theyr verdure
> Wherfore euery prudent creature
> Ought for to lyue ryght as they wolde dye
> For all thynge taketh end naturally.[33]

The poetry itself, and the themes of death and immortality, are sufficient. In the same way, E. K. declares that Thomalin in 'March' and Perigot in 'August' represent 'some secret freend' or 'who is supposed'; but while such precise hidden interpretations are in accordance with the Petrarchan tradition of pastoral, they are of little importance in the *Calender* as a whole. Spenser uses the allegorical tradition persistently, but he fashions it to his own poetic ends. Allegory is something of a straitjacket: Petrarch himself had finished up shackled, and every ecloguist who had tried to follow him had found it a constraint, a limiting scheme into which the poetry had to be fitted. The recent emphasis on the importance of inner meanings in the *Shepheardes Calender* has perhaps obscured one of Spenser's most remarkable achievements: to make allegory subservient to poetry.

Spenser never set out his views on the pastoral mode in the abstract. There can be no doubt that he shared the same basic opinions as Puttenham, Sidney, E. K. himself or any of the other Elizabethan theorists, but the *Calender* none the less modifies these standard ideas in some important ways. It was generally agreed that pastoral was a humble yet significant mode: Spenser applies this to the poetry itself, so that he uses pastoral both to proclaim his own high mission and to present himself as the simple shepherd-singer. The style should preserve the decorum appropriate to the shepherd: Spenser will not follow Mantuan in providing occasional crudities, but creates a whole new language and incorporates a range of poetry such as would have been unthinkable in earlier serious art. Pastoral was to be seen in its historical context, as a variation on the greater master Virgil: Spenser looks even more to English poetic tradition. So it comes about that Spenser's pastoral can embrace not only Mantuan but also Chaucer and the folksong 'Hey ho hollidaye', the Italian sestina and the tail-rhyme stanza, panpipes and the bagpipe.

It is crucial to the *Shepheardes Calender* that it should contain both halves of all these pairs. Every aspect of pastoral, whether artificial or naturalistic, is subordinate to the poetry of the whole work. Earlier poets can be assigned to particular forms of the pastoral tradition – the idyllic, the satiric, the naturalistic: individual months in Spenser may tend more towards one than another, as E. K.'s classification indicates, but there are no absolute divisions. His language may keep decorum in so far as it rejects perfect art as unsuitable for shepherds, but it is certainly not 'a selection of language really used by men', and neither did he intend it to be – it was indeed its artificiality, and its lack of authority,[34] that was most held against it. He abandons the stereo-typed Classical names for his shepherds, but Perigot, Hobbinol and Palinode never inhabited the English countryside. Rural celebrations of spring are not described for their own sake; they are converted to serve the cause of political panegyric ('April') or ecclesiastical satire ('May'), or to make a general moral statement ('February'). This last instance illustrates par-ticularly well Spenser's handling of the various traditions, and the way he combines them to make a single moral and poetic statement. The old shepherd Thenot is attacking his young companion Cuddie's carefree attitude to life:

> So loytring liue you little heardgroomes,
> Keeping your beastes in the budded broomes;
> And when the shining sun laugheth once,
> You deemen, the Spring is come attonce.
> Tho gynne you, fond flyes, the cold to scorne,
> And crowing in pypes made of greene corne,
> You thinken to be Lords of the yeare.
> But eft, when ye count you freed from feare,
> Comes the breme winter with chamfred browes,
> Full of wrinckles and frostie furrowes:
> Drerily shooting his stormy darte,
> Which cruddles the blood, and pricks the harte.   (35–46)

The principal source for this is a passage in Mantuan's sixth eclogue, again about the improvidence of youth being shown up by the miseries of winter. In Mantuan, two shepherds are lying indoors, curled up in the straw for warmth; Cornix appears to be the senior – he gives orders to Fulica, his companion – but it is Fulica who is given the lines in question:

> Pauperiem declarat hiems. improvida certe
> turba sumus iuvenes; securi aestate vagamur
> immemores hiemis, nostrum aes tibicinis omne est;
> ut redit e Scythia Boreas nidosque volucrum
> frondibus ostendit nudata cadentibus arbor,
> frigemus nudi scapulas, dorsum, ilia, plantas.   (VI.19–25)

In Turberville's translation the lines run:

> The Winter doth forshew
>   the poore and needefull plight.
> We youthes are such a retchlesse route
>   as do not wey a white
> The aftertime to come:
>   In Sommer carelesse we
> Do lead our lives. not minding what
>   the Winter is wont to bee,
> And all our pence the Piper hath
>   for making merry glee.
> When Borias makes retourne
>   from Scythian frosty bounde

And bared trees with battred boughes
  and leaues ylayde in grounde
Bewray where byrds haue bredde
  and hatcht their chickens earst:
Poore naked soules our shoulders, back,
  ribbs, feete with colde are pierst.

Spenser's lines are designed to serve a much more vital function both in the eclogue and the whole *Calender*. His purpose throughout the passage is to emphasise the contrast between youth and age and all that that represents. Fulica and Cornix are both 'iuvenes' and their thoughtlessness is a fact of life of moral concern but of no final significance, while the distinction between Thenot and Cuddie is typical of the whole basis of the *Shepheardes Calender* as a representation of the life of man embodied in the changing seasons. Cuddie's youth is associated with the spring, the 'greene corne', and he thinks of nothing else; Thenot, with the wisdom of age and experience, knows that winter is equally a part of life, and winter itself, with its furrowed brow, is an image of age. Spenser is not interested in Mantuan's vivid naturalistic detail of the nests showing in the trees: he substitutes an iconographic picture of the season, more like the set-piece allegories of the *Faerie Queene*, which will convey his thematic concern more strongly. The Classical references (*e Scythia Boreas*) have to go too: there is no room here for such indecorous phrases, and, more importantly, Spenser's winter has never retreated to the ends of the earth–it is a constant threat. His shepherds have nothing Classical about them either: they are drawn not from life but from the Chaucerian tradition, the herdgrooms with their pipes of green corn, for it is they who can distil the image of careless merriment that Spenser wants. The result of all these changes is to make the 'February' passage significant in a way that Mantuan's cannot be. Mantuan tosses it off as a moral commonplace with no further thought; Spenser makes it a deeply significant passage for his whole poem. There is again no allegorical sense in the usual meaning of the term: it is a significance that is there to be noticed, but it is contained in the poetry and so cannot be separated from it. It stands on its own terms without any outside frame of reference; and for immediate comparison Spenser provides not an external historical event nor a general psychological state, but two analogues within the *Calender* itself: the winter world within Colin, as against Cuddie in the world of winter; and the fable of the Oak and the Briar, which follows immediately on the debate between Cuddie and Thenot and which shows their positions taken to an unacceptable extreme.[35] Here again, allegory is a secondary consideration, and whatever meanings the fable may have are carried by the story itself. If it is an allegory of the history of the Church, then Spenser gives all the clues for such an interpretation without forcing it on his reader; it works first of all poetically, on the first, the narrative, level of meaning, and it acts metaphorically as an illustration of the themes of time, authority, age and winter.

    Cuddie and Thenot, the Oak and the Briar, represent opposing attitudes, like the characters of the mediaeval debate eclogues – a tradition that started with a personified conflict of spring and winter; but Spenser is making his poem into something richer and deeper than the polemic that most debate poems embody. The debates most often contain a victory and a judgement: the shepherds of the *Conflictus Veris et Hiemis* declare for Spring, the pagan Pseustis concedes total defeat, Mantuan has the Observant faction of the

Carmelites win hands down. The polemical eclogues of John of Garland or Petrarch or Barclay or Googe may not have this decisive formal framework but their moral standpoint is if anything even clearer. Spenser will not be so absolute, however concerned he may be with moral issues. Thenot and Cuddie, or Piers and Palinode in 'May' and Thomalin and Morell in 'July', represent not simply a right and a wrong but different attitudes to life; as Patrick Cullen puts it, 'The debates are debates between personalities as well as perspectives' (p. 34), and in the final account the disputants may well be concerned with the same core of truth – a very different treatment from Theodulus' or Petrarch's before him, or from Fairfax's or Quarles' later ecclesiastical eclogues. In the bitterest of Spenser's poems, 'September', there is no debate at all: the shepherds are both essentially on the same side, united in condemnation of bad herdsmen, however differently they may wish to express it. In the other ecclesiastical eclogues, where the debate pattern is more important, the shepherd who finally comes off worse stands for nothing so evil as this. Palinode in 'May', with his delight in the country-side rites of spring, is bound to arouse some sympathy, and rightly so: he is not presented as resembling the wolves that Diggon Davie describes later, nor even the Fox in the fable that follows immediately. Instead he and Piers represent different aspects of the pastoral tradition, both drawn from *bergerie* – Palinode, the May revels, with their music and dancing; Piers, the Good Shepherd who cares for his flock above all else. It is the revellers' lack of care for their sheep that Piers condemns:

> Those faytours little regarden their charge,
> While they letting their sheepe runne at large,
> Passen their time. (39–41)

He then goes on to play on the double significance of the hireling, the *mercenarius*, who as in the Bible has no genuine concern for the flock, but as in *bergerie* must none the less ultimately answer to the Master Shepherd for his charge.

> Well is it seene, theyr sheepe bene not their owne,
> That letten them runne at randon alone.
> But they bene hyred for little pay
> Of other, that caren as little as they,
> What fallen the flocke, so they han the fleece,
> And get all the gayne, paying but a peece.
> I muse, what account both these will make,
> The one for the hire, which he doth take,
> And thother for leauing his Lords taske,
> When great Pan account of shepherdes shall aske. (45–54)

The master shepherds on earth, the prelates, and those to whom they commit their flocks will both have to justify themselves, not by their interest in the fleece but in the sheep. These same corrupt herdsmen have gone even further, through carelessness rather than positive evil, in letting in wolves 'vnder colour of shepeheards' who devour the sheep. The flocks are neglected, fleeced, butchered: the metaphors are all familiar from Langland, Gower and the Wakefield plays, Skelton, 'Kepe well the shepe', Petrarch, the French Reformation eclogues; and they are delivered in even more trenchant terms in 'September' – not now as possible events but as ones that Diggon, in the harsh experience traditionally acquired by the shepherd when he leaves his own environment, has actually seen, and that have destroyed his own flock.

The complaint of the mediaeval shepherds against the irruption of 'robbers and theefys' into their world has turned into an unholy alliance of shepherd and thief, where the two are indistinguishable, even synonymous:

> The shepheards there robben one another.
> And layen baytes to beguile her brother. (Sept. 38–9)

The 'beguiling' itself is a total inversion of pastoral 'faith and troth', and an activity that has so far in the *Calender* only been presented as a characteristic of wolves, not shepherds ('May' 127). The distinguishing humility of the herdsman and his concern for nothing more exalted than his own flock are also abandoned: these shepherds are 'Louers of Lordship and troublers of states' ('May' 123), and

> The shepheards swayne you cannot wel ken,
> But it be by his pryde, from other men. (Sept. 42–3)

The Good Shepherd tradition had exalted the office of the herdsman to a clearly recognized ideal; the distortion of that ideal is all the more clearly recognizable. The lines where Spenser spells out the difference between the two are hardly necessary to drive home the point – the lines in 'July' when Thomalin contrasts Abel, who was

>   the first shepheard
>   and liued with little gayne:
> As meeke he was, as meeke mought be,
>   simple, as simple sheepe,
> Humble, and like in each degree
>   the flocke, which he did keepe, (127–32)

with Paris,

> For he was proude, that ill was payd,
>   (no such mought shepheards bee)
> And with lewde lust was ouerlayd:
>   tway things doen ill agree. (149–52)

The 'tway things' cannot be lust and pride – as any handbook on the sins confirms, those two agree very well – but vice and the shepherd: pride cannot be accommodated to the idea of humility, nor lust to pastoral innocence.

Spenser makes it unequivocally obvious just what constitutes a bad shepherd. It is not quite so clear how a latter-day herdsman attains to the ideal of goodness. Abel, the Patriarchs and Moses are all models; Paris – in a typically Spenserian critical reinterpretation of the conventional list of great shepherds – is not, and it is clear why. But the shepherds who actually speak in the eclogues are never so clear-cut. Thomalin is obviously more in the right than Morrell, as his rôle as pastoral instructor indicates as well as his emphasis on humility, but they find plenty of points of agreement. The opposition of hill and dale had already been used by Mantuan, but the English shepherd had never before been indicted for sitting on a hill, and neither is Algrin within the poem. The moral doubtfulness of Morrell's position is carried more through his rejection of the traditional ideal: his motto, *In summo foelicitas*, may not be untrue, but it is dangerously suggestive of the aspiring mind; and his equation of riches with health is an explicit compromise with the evils that Diggon Davie experiences. It is as if he will not recognize evil, and so cannot admit to there being a good. Palinode in 'May' is in much the same position: to him, Piers' talk is foolish; and to

Piers' exposition of a kind of Good-Shepherd golden age, in which virtuous pastors are fed on 'butter enough, honye, milke, and whay' (115), he opposes a worldly practicality, that shepherds have to live and a divergence from the ideal is the easiest way of doing it. Piers couples his vision of a golden past with an insistence on present virtuous austerity; Palinode believes in making the most of God's abundance – in the way of spring, or wealth, or pleasure – here on this earth. Piers wants to see the impossible; but as Hobbinoll reminds Diggon when he spells out his programme of ceaseless vigil for the shepherd,

> We bene of fleshe, men as other bee.   (Sept. 328)

There is no solution possible in the 'moral' eclogues any more than in the others: Colin too is fallible in both human and pastoral terms, and Hobbinol, the shepherd who for a moment seems to have regained paradise, can do no more than sympathize unhelpfully with the struggling poet of 'June'; and in 'September' (in so far as he is the same character) he has already had to abandon his temperate ideal landscape for the cold of autumn, and he can only offer Diggon shelter from the worst of Fortune, and the plain man's compromising rejection of the other's ethic of harsh austerity.

The setting of the *Shepheardes Calender* is the fallen world: the calendar form itself, with its insistence on the changing seasons and so on mutability and mortality, emphasises that, and the corruption of the pastoral ideal that is described in 'May' and 'September' underlines it. Mutability was one of the great themes of pastoral in the Middle Ages, in Petrarch and Boccaccio, Bucarius, the Hundred Years' War moralities or the mystery plays; and it is Spenser's supreme concern in all his poetry. His choice of the calendar framework for his eclogues provides him with a splendid means of exploring the theme. Mortality is a constant pressure within the *Shepheardes Calender*; yet it can be overcome in immortality, as Dido goes to Heaven, as the poem itself 'time in durance shall outweare'. The calendar is an epitome of the cyclical movement of the seasons and man's life that is the subject of the *Mutability Cantos*; and its implication of immortality is a guarantee of the value of the poem, humble in subject as it may be. The nature of the shepherds' calendars themselves reinforces these ideas, with their stress on the ages of man in parallel to the months and seasons. They are handbooks of morality as well as husbandry; Spenser's aim likewise is

> To teach the ruder shepheard how to feede his sheepe.

The calendars are concerned with teaching how to live and how to die; in Spenser conflicting views of life and death, of poetry and fame, of love, of the shepherd's duties, of celebration and mourning and eternal life, are brought together in every eclogue. Even the astrological themes of the calendars have their place. 'Skill in starres,' as E. K. notes, is 'conuenient for shepheardes to knowe, as Theocritus and the rest vse.' The Master Shepherd of the calendars or the *Complaynt of Scotlande* can explain the whole course of the heavens; Colin too 'learned als the signes of heauen to ken' ('December' 83), and so he has authority for his claim of poetic immortality:

> If I marked well the starres reuolution,
> It shall continewe till the worlds dissolution.

Man's fate is written in the stars and embodied in the poem. Spenser has used the different perspectives and traditions of pastoral to state problems, not give answers; but his poetic presentation of the life of man, worked out of the interwoven strands of all the themes of pastoral, is the work of a consummate poet. He takes his farewell of his readers, appropriately enough, by putting side by side the paradox of high poetry and humble pastoral. His calendar will outwear time itself: but it will 'goe but a lowly gate'. It may be the harbinger of the New Poetry, but there are still greater things to come.

The *Bucolics* to the *Aeneid*, the *Shepheardes Calender* to the *Faerie Queene*: the progression was deliberate, but in Spenser's case not final. Pastoral exercized an extraordinary fascination for him, and he returned to it time and again. For all his disclaimers, he had given the mode a depth and range such as he could not simply leave behind. He never again explored the mode for its own sake, setting up and contrasting different aspects of the tradition and searching for a common ground that could unite human experience; but he will take one part of it at a time and use it as the setting for different kinds of meditation or activity. Colin's laments, over his own state or over Dido's death, and the irruption of death into an ideal pastoral world, turn into *Daphnaida* or *Astrophell*. The shepherd's experience outside his own sphere, the corruption of a society that has lost its roots in the 'troth' of the country-side, the elaborate praise of Elizabeth, Colin's view of himself as poet, combine to make *Colin Clouts Come Home Againe*. Spenser's first return to pastoral after the *Calender*, however, was to one small part of it: to the beast-fable of sheep and their predators. *Mother Hubberds Tale* is not usually classified as pastoral: the poem is very close to the fables enclosed within some of the eclogues of the *Calender*, but here there is no shepherd framework. The final point at issue, however, and the standard of judgement throughout the poem, is the welfare of the sheep – the theme that mediaeval pastoral had made its own. The various exploits of the Fox and the Ape are continually criticized by this standard, and the various rôles they assume in the course of the poem – as shepherd, pastor, prince – are all aspects of the single pastoral metaphor. Spenser set out to write in the simple, direct style of his moral eclogues:

> Base is the style, and matter meane withall. (44)

The pastoral beast-fable, as Sidney acknowledged, is a disguise for high matters, though the disguise cannot have been sufficiently thick since the poem was apparently called in on publication. It seems to have been written in two parts: the first part, of more general satire, probably soon after the *Calender*, the second, apparently a direct attack on Burghley, in about 1590.[36] Spenser sets the whole poem firmly in the fallen world: Mother Hubberd may be noted for her 'honest mirth', but she tells her tale in August, in

> the month, in which the righteous Maide,
> That for disdaine of sinfull worlds vpbraide,
> Fled back to heauen. (1–3)

Astraea has departed, leaving behind a social order devoid of justice; and the fable itself drives the point home. The pastoral ideal has gone: Nature no longer spreads her blessings equally,

> That there might be no difference nor strife,
> Nor ought cald mine or thine: thrice happie then
> Was the condition of mortall men.
> That was the golden age of Saturne old,
> But this might better be the world of gold:
> For without golde now nothing wilbe got. (148–53)

The Fox sees nothing of ethical instruction in these facts, however: the only moral he draws is that he and the Ape are entitled to as much share in the world's riches as anybody, so they may as well go out and claim it. They set off to seek their fortune and meet 'a simple husbandman in garments gray' (228) who offers them various jobs, and they accept sheepkeeping as being the easiest: the Ape will be the shepherd, the Fox his dog. They make the most of the months before they have to give an account of their charge:

> For not a lambe of all their flockes supply
> Had they to shew: but euer as they bred,
> They slve them, and vpon their fleshes fed. (316–8)

After such a generous diet of fresh lamb they find themselves in something of a quandary; they ask for an extra day's grace to prepare their reckoning, kill the remaining sheep and hastily leave. They are still determined to find some sort of advancement in the world – their experience of sheepkeeping has taught them nothing of the value of the contented mind – and the next route they try is through the Church. This is specifically linked with what has just passed: Christ

> is the Shepheard, and the Priest is hee;
> We but his shepheard swaines ordain'd to bee. (433–4)

The lines are spoken by a priest who has been portrayed with sharp satire: he takes the low position of the priest compared to God to mean that the flock are Christ's responsibility, not his, but the adventure that has just passed gives him the lie just as much as the tradition of the Good Shepherd. The Fox's activities in his benefice, with the Ape as his parish clerk, are a parallel to their career as shepherd, and end the same way: when the bishop threatens to come on a visitation they clear out. Their next adventure, at court, is an epitome of everything any pastoralist ever had to say about it: 'newfanglenesse', disdain of 'low degree', stealing, flattery, 'lewde speach', 'costly riotize' and all kinds of hypocrisy and sharp practice make up their life. In the final section of the poem the Ape steals the Lion's skin and usurps the throne; and even here the pastoral frame of reference is still maintained. The first beasts the animals meet after they have assumed their new rôles are the Sheep and the Ass, and the Fox assures them of protection and favour; but later, when the Sheep comes to complain of the murder of her lamb by the wolf, the Fox's cousin, she is refused justice. Shepherd, pastor and prince are judged by the same measure and found wanting.

Colin Clouts Come Home Againe also has as one of its principal subjects the contrast of court and country, seen in a double perspective: country innocence against courtly corruption, and crude ignorance against nobility and courtesy. Much of the poem consists of the playing off of these perspectives against each other, with Colin, the humble shepherd-singer whose songs please shepherds and court alike, as the focus of the opposed sides, the poet whose experience can embrace them all. The shepherd who returns to the country to recount his experiences at court is familiar from the long tradition of Deschamps, Mantuan, Barclay, more recently Tasso; Colin describes not only the 'enormities' of the court (665), the malice and strife and ruthless ambition, but Cynthia, the supreme shepherdess who, like the Eliza of 'April', belongs to the pastoral world of spring, of faithfulness, the same harmony of nature as was expressed by the union of Pan and Syrinx:

> I would her lyken to a crowne of lillies,
> Vpon a virgin brydes adorned head,
> With Roses dight and Goolds and Daffadillies;
> Or like the circlet of a Turtle true,
> In which all colours of the rainbow bee. (337–41)

She may be a shepherdess, but of a glory that lifts her beyond humble pastoral, and Cuddy objects to Colin's description of her as an angel on the grounds that

> Such loftie flight, base shepherd seemeth not,
> From flocks and fields, to Angels and to skie.
>   True (answered he) but her great excellence
> Lifts me aboue the measure of my might. (618–21)

Colin's justification goes beyond Elizabeth herself: after all, pastoral poetry had once before been lifted 'to Angels and to skie'. *Colin Clouts Come Home Againe* uses the paradox of decorum with a directness that is rarely found in the *Calender*. Colin's songs have been approved by Cynthia herself, and he will make her the subject of his poetry; but the form Spenser gives the poem, the careful explanation by the enlightened shepherd to his ignorant companions of the wonders they cannot imagine – the sea, Cynthia's power, Cynthia herself – are a means of heightening the compliment to the Queen. The pastoral metaphors are none the less all-important: Cynthia's servants and ladies are all shepherds and shepherdesses, though of a superior kind; and the country has a value of the sort Colin bitterly disclaims for the court. His own rhymes are 'rude and roughly dight', but the court provides

> A filed toung furnisht with tearmes of art,

guile opposed to humbleness in the way Sidney contrasts them in *Disprayse of a Courtly Life*; and true love is only to be found among the shepherds, for at court it has become a frivolous but obsessive game, 'a complement for courting vaine' (790) that ignores the divinity and mystery of the greatest of the gods, the mighty Cupid. Cynthia and her followers are not touched by the corruption around them; and so Colin's companions, for all their distance below her, are yet united with her in an ideal of pastoral that is contrasted with the evil, and the art, of the court.

The shepherd of *bergerie* could be presented as the Chaucerian herdgroom, as a music-maker, as true lover, as moralist, priest or prince. Spenser preserves all these rôles for his shepherds, even though Colin himself represents other traditions as well – the lover lamenting his unhappiness, or the Virgilian shepherd-poet: he has more of Mantuan's Amyntas than of the pastourelle Robin, more of Tityrus than of Willie and Perigot. For what was probably his last excursion into pastoral, in Book VI of the *Faerie Queene*, Spenser uses the vernacular traditions with a directness and simplicity such as he had never tried before. None of his other pastorals is so free from specific allusiveness: the allegory here is of a different kind altogether – a statement about the nature of courtesy embodied in the pastoral vision. The Arcadian themes of idealized shepherd-poets and love-melancholy are abandoned for the older traditions of carefree revels and joyous and fulfilled love. The country of the shepherds into which Sir Calidore rides is the world of Robin and Marion, of Franc Gontier, of Christine de Pisan's Marotele.[37] Calidore comes upon the herdsmen as suddenly as the knight of the pastourelles:

> There on a day as he pursew'd the chace,
> He chaunst to spy a sort of shepheard groomes,
> Playing on pypes, and caroling apace... (VI.ix.5)

The *bergerie* setting is painted in greater detail later, in the giving of garlands, the round-dancing and the shepherd pastimes. Pastorella herself and her companion shepherdesses come, as her name indicates, from the world of the pastourelle, not from anything more Arcadian: these girls could never be referred to as nymphs. The rival lover, the shepherd who could prove the barrier to the knight's wooing, is also a figure from the pastourelle. The significance of the pastoral interlude, however, is a much more complex thing than the simplicity of the story would suggest, and Spenser's attitude is strangely double-edged. The overwhelming value of the simple life is stressed time and again: it has none of the corruption of the court; nothing is known of the Blatant Beast. The shepherd world appears to be the natural home of Courtesy, a parallel in the thematic structure of the book to the House of Holiness or Alma's castle.[38] As in mediaeval pastoral lyric, true and faithful love is fulfilled:

> At the last vnto his will he brought her...
> And ioyed long in close felicity; (VI.ix.38)

and the scene on Mount Acidale, with Colin piping for his own true love to dance, reads like a neoplatonic perfection of the pastourelle idea. But yet, as in the *Dit de la Pastoure*, rusticity is not enough. Marotele too finds that her lord's courtesy makes the shepherd world seem inadequate. It is of courts that men Courtesie do call, and however genuinely beautiful the pastoral life may be Calidore has something that the real shepherds lack – something that Pastorella immediately recognizes. Her suitor Coridon appears boorish beside him, his attempts at winning her favour crude; and like the peasants of Sidney's *Arcadia* he scarcely even qualifies as a shepherd – he is a 'cowherd', a coward, in an unusual and possibly deliberately ambiguous spelling. Meliboee himself, the most courteous of the shepherds, has spent ten years at court, even though in the humble capacity of gardener; and the crucial character, Pastorella, is, like Perdita or the first version of Urania, high-born. The mediaeval knights had flattered their shepherdesses by claiming that their beauty was too great for their station; Calidore's impression that her 'rare demeanure' excelled 'the meane of shepheards' turns out to be fully justified. The pastourelle had provided one of the few genres of mediaeval literature where the low-born girl could be beautiful, but courtly Renaissance romance almost invariably rejected the idea. By tradition the shepherd world was of supreme value, but beauty, courtesy and high birth also belonged together in a kind of symbolic decorum. The union of Calidore and Pastorella is never finally achieved within the poem, but it is at least a possibility – there does not have to be a break, as there is in Christine's *Dit*; and, as in *The Winter's Tale*, it represents a fusion of the worlds of pastoral and the court.

The love of knight and shepherdess is still only one part of Spenser's final statement on pastoral. There are two other episodes of equal, if not ultimately greater, importance: the dance on Mount Acidale, and the brigands' destruction of the shepherd world. They appear at first to be absolutely opposed in tone – the poet's attainment of grace against the wrecking of the beautiful – but both episodes are deeply concerned with Spenser's great preoccupation, mutability. Whoever the lady at the centre of the dance may be – his wife Elizabeth, the symbol of his inspiration, his own poetry – she and all her companions are too precious for the earth, and the interruption even of Courtesy will make them disappear. This is one reason why the dance is so reminiscent of fairy dances: they belong to another world, and cannot endure human contact – unless through the medium of poetry itself. The imagery that Spenser uses, of Ariadne's crown encircled by the stars,

> Which round about her moue in order excellent, (VI.x.13)

confirms the exaltation of his vision. But the narrative that carries all this is far from the usual Renaissance style of conveying the idea of poetry in pastoral. There is nothing Arcadian or Classical about Colin; Calidore comes on him as Moniot de Paris' knight comes upon his Robin,[39] as an outsider who cannot share his joy and his fulfilment in love, and who can only watch, and envy, the 'iolly shepheard' and his 'lasse',

> she to whom that shepheard pypt alone,
> That made him pipe so merrily, as neuer none. (VI.x.15)

The phrasing is intentionally reminiscent of folksong, the jolly shepherd merrily piping on the hill, and of so many of the French pastourelles, still current in songbooks and anthologies; and Colin's instrument is appropriately the bagpipe (x.18). The equation of pastoral with poetry was a commonplace by this date – one suspects that Spenser could not have written these cantos without introducing Colin; but it is a new and daring act to look not to art-pastoral but to the humbler traditions of folksong, and still to raise them to the heights of Acidale. The mediaeval shepherd-lovers could instruct the knights in love; Colin's instruction of Calidore includes the nature of virtue, of the Graces, of poetry itself.

Acidale is an ideal place, released from the normal cycle of the seasons: the trees 'all winter as in sommer bud' (x.6), and the fragility of the dance is less a symbol of mortality than of human fallibility. The dance, one feels, continues, even if mortals can no longer apprehend it. The beauty of the shepherd country feels much more solid, but it is much more liable to destruction. That there are tigers among these fields and folds is bad enough, and already a denial of the illusory safety the shepherds had seemed to enjoy from such nasty creatures as the Blatant Beast; but at least Calidore can overcome the tiger, even if the herdsmen are not capable of it. The attack by the brigands is devastatingly final. That war and violence were a perversion of pastoral peace and content was a commonplace of *bergerie* and eclogue alike, but the idyll had seldom been so brutally shattered: Meliboeus may be a refugee, but Tityrus is secure in his ideal landscape; even the sacking of Compiègne in the *Pastoralet* is followed by the restoration of order and the pastoral vision of Heaven. Spenser is too conscious of the conditions of the fallen world to rest in his idyllic creation. Evil destroys every paradise; to maintain the good demands a constant effort – Calidore must resume his quest, and even that will never be complete. The epic must succeed the pastoral, not just because it is a more demanding form, but because the world itself requires more. The pastoral vision embraces both the ideal of the golden world, of Eden, and its destruction; it is the fallen Adam's comparison of his past state and the present. The way back must be achieved through different means.

III. *Drayton*

Drayton's poetic career began and ended in pastoral poetry. At the age of 'scarse ten yeares' he came to his tutor to entreat,

Make me a Poet, doe it; if you can,
And you shall see, Ile quickly be a man,
Who me thus answered smiling, boy quoth he,
If you'le not play the wag, but I may see
You ply your learning, I will shortly read
Some Poets to you; Phoebus be my speed,
Too't hard went I, when shortly he began,
And first read to me honest Mantuan,
Then Virgils Eglogues, being entred thus,
Me thought I straight had mounted Pegasus.[40]

The enchantment pastoral held for him never left him: his own series of eclogues, *Idea: The Shepheards Garland*, was published in 1593, to be extensively revised in 1606 as *Pastorals*; and he kept returning to the mode, for *Endimion and Phoebe, The Shepheards Sirena, The Muses Elizium* and many slighter works or passages. His first model was not Virgil or Mantuan but 'the prime pastoralist of England',[41] Spenser, and his own intense love of his country makes his poems vibrant with English life in a way that Spenser's are not. The realism of mediaeval pastoral was now only one of a series of artistic conventions; but when Drayton surveyed England, he saw Arcadia. He invites the reader of *Poly-Olbion* 'to walke forth with the Muses',

convaying thee downe by a soule-pleasing Descent through delicate embrodered Meadows, often veined with gentle gliding Brooks; in which thou maist fully view the dainty Nymphes in their simple naked bewties, bathing them in Crystalline streames; which shall lead thee, to most pleasant Downes, where harmlesse Shepheards are, some exercising their pipes, some singing roundelaies, to their gazing flocks.[42]

The shepherd of the English countryside, of Drayton's own hills, the Cotswolds, becomes the typical figure of the pastoral landscape.

There is plenty of evidence that this aspect of Drayton's pastoral was a conscious part of his use of older traditions. The tale of Dowsabell and its placing in the context of a discussion of style illustrates his thorough familiarity with mediaeval pastoral conventions and his sensitivity to the contrasting potentialities within the mode. He himself is as rigorous a theorist as Spenser, with the same results in pastoral poetry of immense range and richness. His fullest statement of pastoral theory is contained in the epistle 'To the Reader of his Pastorals' prefaced to the 1619 edition (II.517–8). He describes the nature of pastorals, 'by way of general preparative', and summarizes their history; by this date such an introduction might seem superfluous, but Drayton's comments are not merely the standard commonplaces. He describes eclogues as 'fained Dialogues, or other speeches in Verse, fathered upon Heardsmen...worthily therefore to be called base, or low'. He lays stress both on the high matters that can be contained in the pastoral mode and on 'the chiefe Law of Pastorals...DECORUM'. His poems will be laden with significance:

He who hath almost nothing Pastorall in his Pastorals, but the name (which is my Case) deales more plainly, because *detracto velamine*, he speakes of most weightie things.

This is especially true of the revised version of his eclogues: the most striking overall difference between *Idea: The Shepheards Garland* and the *Pastorals* is that the emphasis has shifted from the manner to the matter. Like the poets of the Middle Ages, Drayton also sees a still higher justification for the mode:

> The Blessing which came in [the *Bucolics*] to the testimoniall Majestie of the Christian Name, out of Sibyls Moniments, cited before Christ's Birth, must ever make Virgil venerable with me: and in the Angels Song to Shepheards at our Saviours Nativitie Pastorall Poesie seemes consecrated.

His own pastoral is as wide-ranging as this summary of the theory could suggest: lyricism and satire, Cotswold revels and nymphs, Arcadia and the grim world of the Petrarchan eclogue all have their places.

Many of the themes of *Idea: The Shepheards Garland* are imitated from Spenser: youth and age, unhappy love, the poet in a hostile world, the elegy and the panegyric. The imitation itself is a means of confirming Spenser's pride of place in English poetry: Virgil too had been the principal influence and inspiration of his successors. The revision removed some of the closer imitations of Spenser, especially in rustic language, and it also loosened the poems' contacts with the shepherd world; but Drayton added a completely new eclogue, owing nothing to Spenser, which ties the series to the life of the countryside as nothing in the *Shepheardes Calender* does. The Ninth Eglogue is an account of a Cotswold shearing-feast, taking place in late June. Each shepherd has 'greaz'd his start-ups blacke as Autumns sloe' for the occasion; they wear posies and garlands, concealing messages of love but revealing their hearts –

> For Countrey toyes become the Countrey best,
> And please poore Shepheards, and become them well.   (27–8)

The ram and the bell-wether lead the flock, their horns decked with flowers, driven by shepherds blowing their bagpipes. Rowland himself 'by the ancient Statutes of the Field' has been declared the 'Shepheards King', as his flock produced the first lamb. The company sit down to a splendid feast:

> New Whig, with Water from the cleerest streame,
> Greene Plummes, and Wildings, Cherries chiefe of Feast,
> Fresh Cheese, and Dowsets, Curds and clowted Creame,
> Spic'd Syllibubs, and Sider of the best.   (45–8)

They are joined by a number of 'shepherdesses', including Spenser's own Rosalinde; and Rowland, as King, commands the others to sing. Finally Idea herself approaches, leading instead of driving her flock in a neat pastoral conceit, and the company all sing in her honour, hailing her as the 'Shepheards Queene'. The poetic development of the eclogue and the pastorally-disguised ladies are artificial; but the revel itself, idyllic as it appears, is drawn from life, and the intense attraction of the occasion for Drayton is indicated by the number of times he brings it into his poetry. The fullest account comes in the description of the Cotswolds in *Poly-Olbion*. The map draws the scene – the decorated bell-wether, shepherds feasting at a tablecloth spread on the ground, another group dancing around a pole topped by a flag inscribed 'Heigh for Cotswold'. Drayton describes in loving detail

> The faire and goodly Flock, the Shepheards onely pride,
> As white as Winters snowe, when from the Riuers side
> He drives his new-washt Sheepe; or on the Sheering day,
> When as the lusty Ram, with those rich spoyles of May
> His crooked hornes hath crown'd; the Bell-weather, so brave
> As none in all the Flock they like themselves would have.

> But Muse, returne to tell, how there the Sheepheards King,
> Whose Flock hath chanc't that yeere the earliest Lambe to bring,
> In his gay Bauldrick sits at his lowe grassie Bord,
> With Flawns, Curds, Clowted-creame, and Country dainties stor'd:
> And whilst the Bag-pipe playes, each lustie jocund Swaine
> Quaffes Sillibubs in Kans, to all upon the Plaine,
> And to their Country-Girles, whose Nosegayes they doe weare,
> Some Roundelayes doe sing: the rest, the burthen beare.   (XIV.265–78)

On Latmus itself, Phoebe offers Endimion a life of pastoral delight in the same terms:

> Ile deck thy Ram with bells, and wreathes of Bay,
> And gild his hornes upon the sheering day;
> And with a garlond crown thee Shepheards king,
> And thou shalt lead the gay Girls in a ring.   (209–12)

Melanthus, the shepherd who makes his appearance in the Sixth Nimphall of the *Muses Elizium*, leads the same life; and if the Elizian setting is as idyllic as that of Latmus, he himself is realistic in the mediaeval tradition, with care for his flocks as important a part of his life as music-making or feasting:

> Survaying of my sheepe if Ewe or Wether looke
> As though it were amisse, or with my Curre, or Crooke,
> I take it, and when once I finde what it doth ayle,
> It hardly hath that hurt, but that my skill can heale.   (203–6)

He has the good shepherd's uprightness of character – he and his companions will play quoits or nine-men's morris but no 'false and cheating Games'(202); and in appearance too he belongs to the tradition of Jehan de Brie or Jolly Wat, with his tarbox, scrip, bagpipe and crook. The clothing and equipment of Dowsabell's shepherd is described in even fuller detail. The shepherds 'that kept Revells on the Plaine' in the *Shepheards Sirena* dance and sing to the music of pipe, tabor, gittern and shawm; and the piper playing for the morris-dancers makes his appearance in the eclogues.[43] In *Poly-Olbion* Drayton makes use of yet another mediaeval convention, the association of herdsman and hill. The maps show almost every mountain or upland marked by a shepherd, as the rivers are by nymphs, from St. Michael's Mount in the south to Skiddaw in the north; and the Cotswolds themselves are described as 'that great King of Shepheards' (XIV.219).

The pastorals Drayton wrote during the reign of James I take on an increasingly bitter note. The revision of his eclogues included not only the Cotswold revel but an attack on Olcon, the King himself, who

> forsakes the Heard-groome and his Flocks,
> Nor of his Bag-pipes takes at all no keepe,
> But to the sterne Wolfe and deceitfull Fox
> Leaves the poore Shepheard and his harmelesse Sheepe.[44]

There is a similar passage in the *Shepheards Sirena* (356–71), where Olcon is accused of inciting the swineherds to bring their hogs to root up the sheep-walks. Drayton's precise reference is not known, but the theme of dangerous satire in beast-fable form is of many centuries' standing. In the 1606 edition of his *Pastorals* Drayton also published an entirely reworked version of *Endimion and Phoebe* entitled *The Man in the Moone*, and here the emphasis has moved completely from idyll to satire. The form of the poem is a shepherd's tale, and the whole work is a kind of inverted eclogue in the mediaeval tradition. The setting is a revel, but a night-time one, and the shepherds break up not at nightfall but at dawn; their enemy is not the wolf but the werewolf. The tone of the poem is bitter, and Endimion's study of the moon has become astronomical in the calendar tradition. The shepherd's traditional knowledge of the heavenly bodies has assumed sinister overtones, as they can see grim portents as well as simple weather signs:

> Inly they were sad,
> For some amongst them perfectly there knew
> That the sad tymes were shortly to ensue,
> When they of all the sorts of men neglected,
> In barren Fields should wander unrespected.
> For carefull shepheards that doe watch by Night,
> In the vast Ayre see many a fearefull sight:
> From whose observance they doe wisely gather
> The change of Times, as well as of the weather. (22–30)

Drayton foresees the death of poetry in the dark times ahead as clearly as the shepherd of the calendar could foresee storms.

His poetic career did not end on this note. *The Muses Elizium*, published in 1630, the year before his death, sets an entirely new tone for pastoral poetry. Elizium itself is a place like the *sedes Naturae* or Olympia's Heaven:

> A Paradice on earth is found,
> Though farre from vulgar sight,
> Which with those pleasures doth abound
> That it *Elizium* hight.

It is a land of eternal blossom and birdsong, free from storm or snow:

> The winter here a Summer is,
> No waste is made by time,
> Nor doth the Autumne ever misse
> The blossomes of the Prime. (37–40)

Above all, it is 'the Poets Paradice', and poetry is almost the one theme of the Nimphalls: Drayton turns his back on the typically Jacobean pastoral of his own middle years, of Browne, Wither and Brooke, and re-creates an Elizabethan age of lyric poetry. The poet whose voice is most often heard is Marlowe – the Marlowe of Tamburlaine's speeches to Zenocrate or the shepherd's appeal to the nymph. Raleigh's sterner reply has no place in this winterless, ageless world. The sad old satyr of the last poem is able to find a refuge from Felicia in a paradise of poetry. Melanthus himself, for all his realism, is set in an idyllic world of nymphs and fairies. The pastoral themes of the decades since Elizabeth's death are abandoned: satire is touched on only to be symbolically withdrawn as the satyr escapes to Elizium; love is explicitly banished. Drayton was the last of the Elizabethan poets, and he found in pastoral the heart of the golden age of poetry.

IV. *Shakespeare*

Shakespeare was not fascinated by pastoral for its own sake in the way that Spenser was. None of his plays is set exclusively in the shepherd world, though *As You Like It* is predominantly pastoral, and the single pastoral act of *The Winter's Tale* has an importance out of proportion to its size. The plots of each of these plays are drawn from pastoral romances, Lodge's *Rosalynde* and Greene's *Pandosto*, but it was not the romance form, nor any of the other Renaissance movements in pastoral, that most profoundly affect Shakespeare's use of the mode. Pastoral in his work is as dependent on tradition as in any other author, although he also extends and develops that tradition more than anyone; but the aspects of the tradition that he draws on most are the same as had been explored in the mediaeval vernacular conventions of *bergerie*. This is not because of what Lodge and Greene had done: there is, for instance, no parallel to the shearing-feast in Greene, and in any case Shakespeare's whole use of the pastoral metaphor is very different from theirs. But in these plays, and in references to the shepherd world elsewhere in his works, he demonstrates his interest in the themes that *bergerie* had made its own: themes of fulfilled love, criticism of the court, political comment, indictments of war, the shading from rustic ignorance to pastoral innocence, 'faith and troth'. His shepherds sing and dance, revel and feast, watch the stars and the passage of the year. There is nothing of the eclogue, nothing of Sannazaro's Arcadian haven for poetic melancholy, no nymphs or satyrs; and given this weighting of interest, it is all but inevitable that the plays containing the most pervasive pastoral reference, after the two romances themselves, should be the plays most concerned with war: the *Henry VI* group. It is also no surprise that Shakespeare's use of pastoral conventions should become increasingly complex, and increasingly unconventional, as his style developed.

The three parts of *Henry VI*, with their subject-matter of perpetual conflict abroad and at home, exploit the pastoral metaphor in the same way as the *Pastoralet* or the *bergeries moralisées* had done in the same context: as a foil to suggest peace and goodness, and as an image of the ideal prince. Duke Humphrey in *2 Henry VI* is the shepherd beaten from Henry's side by the wolves 'gnarling who shall gnaw [him] first'; it is Shakespeare's first use of an image of a kind that was to recur a number of times in later plays.[45] Henry's own persistent refusal to see himself as the shepherd-prince is perhaps itself a comment on his own weakness: he is more the sheep, the one who needs protection – from the Yorkist wolves, or at his death from the butcher Richard of Gloucester. When Gloucester comes to murder him and dismisses the Lieutenant of the Tower, Henry comments,

> So flies the reckless shepherd from the wolf;
> So first the harmless sheep doth yield his fleece,
> And next his throat unto the butcher's knife.　　　　(*3 HVI* V.vi.7–9)

The one time when he does imagine the life of the shepherd it is as the opposite of his own, not as the image of the kingship he bears. He dreams of the shepherd sitting on his hill, ordering time as the shepherds of the calendars could do rather than being its slave, filling it with the simple occupations of sheepkeeping, contemplation and shepherd pastimes, understanding the scope of man's mortal span.

> O God! methinks it were a happy life
> To be no better than a homely swain;
> To sit upon a hill, as I do now,
> To carve out dials quaintly, point by point,
> Thereby to see the minutes how they run,
> How many make the hour full complete,
> How many hours bring about the day,
> How many days will finish up the year,
> How many years a mortal man may live.
> When this is known, then to divide the times:
> So many hours must I tend my flock,
> So many hours must I take my rest,

So many hours must I contemplate,
So many hours must I sport myself,
So many days my ewes have been with young;
So many weeks ere the poor fools will ean,
So many years ere I shall shear the fleece:
So minutes, hours, days, weeks, months and years,
Passed over to the end they were created,
Would bring white hairs unto a quiet grave.
Ah, what a life were this! how sweet! how lovely!   (*3 HVI* II.v.21–41)

He concludes with a more specific contrast of the shepherd's state with his own – a contrast commonplace since the fourteenth century at least, but given an entirely new force here from the fact that the man who says it is not the shepherd secure in his content but the king sickened and despairing from the troubles of civil war:

Gives not the hawthorn bush a sweeter shade
To shepherds looking on their silly sheep,
Than doth a rich embroidered canopy
To kings that fear their subjects' treachery?
O yes, it doth; a thousand-fold it doth.
And to conclude, the shepherd's homely curds,
His cold thin drink out of his leather bottle,
His wonted sleep under a fresh tree's shade,
All which secure and sweetly he enjoys,
Is far beyond a prince's delicates,
His viands sparkling in a golden cup,
His body couched in a curious bed,
When care, mistrust and treason waits on him.

Alarum. Enter a son that hath killed his father ... Enter on the other side a Father
that hath killed his son.   (42–54)

The stage directions are the final, and the most devastating, comment on Henry's speech, on the irrelevance of his dream and its total perversion in life. He sees these people as 'poor harmless lambs' at the mercy of lions; he still will not recognize his own responsibility as shepherd. But although his vision of the shepherd life is inadequate in all kinds of ways, it does none the less provide the image of an ideal of which the slaughter of son by father and father by son is the total denial: an ideal that was abundantly recognized in the Elizabethan age in the political pastoral addressed to the Queen.

The *Pastoralet* had given a contemporary pastoral comment on civil war, the *bergeries moralisées* on the Hundred Years' War; in England both had to wait for Shakespeare. Joan of Arc's status as literal shepherdess had led to her appearance in one of the shepherd moralities, and Shakespeare too uses her peasant origins in a way that relates specifically to the whole pastoral tradition – not to indicate a return to idyllic peace in the countryside, as happens in *Mieulx-que-Devant*, but to measure her fall from at least an appearance of innocence to open witchcraft and fraud. Her initial speech to the Dauphin defines her as a mere peasant, of 'base vocation', but whose very simplicity and humility have made her favoured by the Virgin, chosen to save her country and at the same time endowed with beauty in place of the hardened sunburn of the labourer.

Dauphin, I am by birth a shepherd's daughter,
My wit untrain'd in any kind of art.
Heaven and our Lady gracious hath it pleased
To shine on my contemptible estate.   (*1 HVI* I.ii.72–5)

She is not yet presented as the evil witch: misguided perhaps, from the Protestant – and the English – point of view, not altogether reverenced by the French either, but her fall is yet to come. At this stage Shakespeare seems to be making her a much more sympathetic character than did the chronicles from which he worked. There are several hints of worse qualities about her, but so far they do not involve her directly,[46] and she does come across as being what she claims: the shepherdess who will be the saviour of France. The means she uses to attain this, the 'familiar spirits' whom she has fed with her blood and to whom she is ready to give her soul, only appear at the very end; and the final stage of her corruption is marked, significantly enough, by her furious rejection of her shepherd origins. When she is brought face to face with her father she accuses the English,

> You have suborned this man
> Of purpose to obscure my noble birth. (V.iv.21–2)

He replies, in bewilderment,

> 'Tis true, I gave a noble to the priest
> The morn that I was wedded to her mother.

The comic ignorance underlying that remark is more than comic relief: it represents all the innocence that Joan has rejected. She refuses to receive his blessing, and instead he curses her – the final mark of her damnation.

Simple as the old shepherd may be, he does represent a good of which her evil is the total corruption. There is perhaps something of the same kind of moral ideal underlying even so simple a passage as Tom's song in *King Lear* – lines that, whether genuinely traditional or not, belong with the history of the shepherd folksong:

> Sleepest or wakest thou, jolly shepherd?
>   Thy sheep be in the corn;
> And for one blast of thy minikin mouth,
>   Thy sheep shall take no harm. (III.vi.41–4)

The verse is placed at the beginning of the 'trial scene', as the mad King, the Fool and the disguised Tom o' Bedlam assemble to arraign the world for injustice; and Edgar introduces the lines with the words,

> Let us deal justly.

It is part of his rôle as madman to show no consistent line of thought, but there is often none the less a kind of wild association, and there may be here: the shepherd negligent of his charge, who could control his sheep if he would, is not so far from the 'man of justice' who achieves nothing.

If these lines indicate Shakespeare's familiarity with the folksong tradition of the 'jolly shepherd', he was even more alive to the lyrical possibilities of pastoral, its association with music-making, with the seasons and especially with spring. It is *bergerie* that ultimately lies behind the simplicity of the spring song in *Love's Labours Lost*,

> When shepherds pipe on oaten straws, (V.ii.899)

not the formalized poetic images of Arcadian pastoral; and the song itself is only half of the diptych, for against it is set the winter scene,

> When icicles hang by the wall,
> And Dick the shepherd blows his nail. (908–9)

There is the same concern in the pastoral plays with the changing of the seasons, with 'the year growing ancient', the 'winter wind', or, most persistently, with the moment of the unfolding of spring that in *A Midsummer Night's Dream* provides one of the most evocative, and briefest, descriptions of the shepherd world ever written:

> Your eyes are lode-stars, and your tongue's sweet air
> More tuneable than lark to shepherd's ear,
> When wheat is green, when hawthorn-buds appear. (I.i.183–5)

The sense of fulfilled love to which Helena is referring and the lode-star itself are as much a part of the pastoral image as the lark or the hawthorn. Shakespeare's shepherds, like those of the calendars, measure their lives by the skies: there is the traditional nightfall:

> Look, th'unfolding star calls up the shepherd; (*M for M* IV.ii.199–200)

or Henry VI on the edge of the battlefield, watching the dawn break:

> This battle fares like to the morning's war,
> When dying clouds contend with growing light,
> What time the shepherd, blowing of his nails,
> Can neither call it perfect day nor night (*3 HVI* II.v.1–4)

– lines that lead him on to his meditation on the shepherd's life; or the reference to the passing of the year that opens the first major scene of *The Winter's Tale*,

> Nine changes of the wat'ry star hath been
> The shepherd's note, since we have left our throne
> Without a burthen (I.ii.1–3)

– perhaps, like the song in *Lear*, an implied comment by Polixenes on his own negligence.

The total effect of images such as these is to present the shepherd as being in touch with the course of nature – spring and winter, day and night, work and rest. The extension of this natural life to moral simplicity, to an image of something that if not presented as an actual ideal of goodness (as Franc Gontier, for instance, is explicitly an ideal) none the less has many virtues that the outside world has temporarily lost, is developed in the two pastoral plays. The purity of country life is one of the oldest and most persistent pastoral themes; and its explicit use for commentary on the corruption of court or city was one of the principal mediaeval uses of the mode. The pastoral romance does not usually make much of this particular aspect: Sincero's past, or the civilization that Montemayor's lover-knights have abandoned, are kept far in the distance, never allowed to enter into any significant relationship with the shepherd world. It was in the romance that pastoral first became really escapist, where the hero could abandon his more demanding and more painful existence (if he ever had one) for the saccharine sweets of an idyllic Arcadia; and it was from this kind of idea that the eighteenth century derived its artificial scenario of nymphs and love-sick swains. Shakespeare's use of the romance, however, leads him in the opposite direction. We are shown clearly enough in *As You Like It* the hatred and treachery that compel the Duke, Orlando and Rosalind to flee to the forest of Arden; and it is in the forest that the final resolution, the replacement of hatred by love and treachery by faith, is brought about, not only in the lovers' marriages but in the restoration of right to the Duke and Orlando. The actual means may be

totally non-realistic – the very brevity of the report of Duke Frederick's conversion 'from his enterprise and from the world' underlines Shakespeare's
refusal to make anything but a romance convenience of it – but none the less
it is the country that is restoring wholeness to the court. The pattern is even
more sharply defined in *The Winter's Tale*, where the pastoral scenes occupy a
single act, the court they affect the other four. The first three acts demonstrate
the breakdown of positive human values at the court, and its inability to heal
itself; the final scenes show the healing, the reconciliation, that only Perdita
– courtly by nature, pastoral by nurture – can inspire.

If the plot of *As You Like It* is typical of the pastoral romance, with its chain
of unrequited lovers – Silvius loves Phebe, who loves 'Ganimede', who loves
Orlando, who loves Rosalind and doesn't realize he has got her – the texture
of the pastoral fabric is rather richer. The forest of Arden sounds delightful,
in many ways, from the moment of its first being mentioned as the place
where the banished Duke and his men 'fleet the time carelessly, as they did
in the golden world' (I.i.112–3). But such places always look better from a
safe distance. To Rosalind and Orlando it appears as a 'desert', where
Orlando assumes every living thing must be savage, and where there are
indeed snakes and lions. The idyllic content of the place, its conventional
freedom from envy and ambition, is countered – though not outweighed –
by the men's exposure to the winter; and even the Duke admits that the
bareness of the life takes some getting used to ('old custom'):

> Hath not old custom made this life more sweet
> Than that of painted pomp? Are not these woods
> More free from peril than the envious court?
> Here feel we but the penalty of Adam,
> The seasons' difference, – as the icy fang
> And churlish chiding of the winter's wind,
> Which, when it bites and blows upon my body,
> Even till I shrink with cold, I smile and say,
> 'This is no flattery: these are counsellors
> That feelingly persuade me what I am.'   (II.i.2–11)

Hypocrisy, in the form of 'painted pomp' or flattery, is stripped away by the
wind. But this is romance, not Lear on the heath; the stripping carries no
dynamic moral force, but is relegated to the sweetness of song, to 'Under
the greenwood tree' and 'Blow, blow, thou winter wind'.

There is little in these ideas more than convention; but Shakespeare will
not stop there, and Touchstone gives a much more complete picture when
Corin asks him how he likes a shepherd's life.

> Truly, shepherd, in respect of itself, it is a good life; but in respect that it is a
> shepherd's life, it is naught. In respect that it is solitary, I like it very well;
> but in respect that it is private, it is a very vile life. Now in respect it is in the
> fields, it pleaseth me well; but in respect it is not in the court, it is tedious. As
> it is a spare life, look you, it fits my humour well; but as there is no more
> plenty in it, it goes much against my stomach.   (III.ii.13–20)

The two views of pastoral had never been so bluntly stated, and if the
attitude were allowed to spread it would be the end of pastoral altogether.
But there is plenty of truth in it especially where the romances are concerned,
this play included: the Duke and Rosalind are happy enough to return to
civilization, painted pomp or not, when the opportunity offers. Rosalind
never in fact compromises herself with regard to her surroundings in the way
her father does: she has an integrity of her own that does not need to pretend

to identify with them too completely, and the physical disguise is enough for her. Arden is not in any case, as Touchstone points out, Arcadia. It is affected not only by winter and savage beasts, but by economic hardship, the absentee landlord who will sell the cottage over the tenant's head; it contains not only the shepherdess Phebe, but Audrey and her goats. Corin shows a genuinely charitable hospitality to the weary travellers, and he sets out the pastoral ethic clearly enough:

> I am a true labourer. I earn that I eat, get that I wear, owe no man hate, envy no man's happiness, glad of other men's good, content with my harm; and the greatest of my pride is to see my ewes graze and my lambs suck
> (III.ii.71–5)

– but this is his last and desperate attempt to counter Touchstone's superior 'philosophy', and the lines are coloured by the clown's absolute refusal to be impressed. The pastoral world can perhaps instruct the court, but the shepherd is not the master. It is Rosalind herself – from the court, and yet strangely independent of it – who is able to control and guide at least some of the events of the pastoral world: the events of the sunnier side, perhaps, of the 'sheep-cote fenced about with olive trees' beside the stream, rather than of the thicker woods where the hunters and the lioness live, and where the winter wind is always close to men's minds. There is no geographically defined pastoral oasis[47] within the forest, but Rosalind almost personifies something of the kind. Her greatest strength is her control over the dream of pastoral – over Orlando's game of a happy courtship; and when he declares, 'I can live no longer by thinking,' she is wise enough to know that the dream must end.

The forest of Arden is the place of retreat where the human virtues, true love and loyalty and generosity, can be maintained unsullied by the corruption of the outside world, and can ultimately return to be restored to the world: the basic idea is not so far different from the *Moralité de l'Alliance de Foy et Loyalté*. In *The Winter's Tale* the process is made part of a larger pattern, where we are shown the progress of corruption in Leontes, from the description of his boyhood innocence in a kind of unfallen Eden to the senseless jealousy that destroys everything around him, and where the restoration of Perdita and Hermione's return are the culmination of the play – events that happen once again at court, and that in a sense happen 'to' Leontes. It is he who is the protagonist of the play – who looks, as the catastrophic events of the first three acts unfold, as if he is going to be its tragic hero. He has no direct part in the pastoral scenes – they are even set in a different country; yet they are made part of his own history. They are not in any sense the landscape of his mind, in the typical Renaissance poetic metaphor: pastoral has become the expression of 'great creating Nature', the force that Leontes can deny but cannot overcome, and that is the ground of all true harmony in the world and in himself.

To say even this much indicates the extraordinary richness of Shakespeare's use of the pastoral mode in this play: *The Winter's Tale* gives the metaphor a depth of meaning that it had never attained before, and never reached again. The scene of the sheep-shearing feast is the culmination of the whole pastoral tradition, its symbolism going beyond anything that had been expressed before; but it still starts from conventional ideas. Nature itself is the most significant of these. The modern association of pastoral with the beauty of the natural world is given almost its first expression here – the first that goes significantly beyond the conventional idyllic landscape with its fountain or its beech-tree shade, to the

> daffodils
> That come before the swallow dares, and take
> The winds of March with beauty,   (IV.iv.118–20)

or the eternally dancing wave of the sea. This is beautiful enough, but it is still not all: Shakespeare is concerned too with the 'seeds' of Nature, its secret operations beyond man's knowledge – with

> all the sun sees, or
> The close earth wombs, or the profound seas hide
> In unknown fathoms.   (IV.iv.486–8)

Nature in earlier pastoral had been analysed principally in terms of an artistic problem – the problem of decorum – and, proceeding from that, in terms of morals, a 'natural' unadorned ethic of faith and troth. Both of these are important in *The Winter's Tale*, in the straightforward stylistic contrasts of the peasant and the high-born, the discussion on the grafting of plants, the truth of Perdita's love; the great innovation is to see Nature as so much more than any of these, as a life force to which they may all be related in different ways but which in its completeness can only be glimpsed through them all.

It is 'by law and process of great nature' that Perdita is born, at the moment when tragedy is most imminent. She is nurtured in the pastoral world – the world of comedy. The materials from which Shakespeare constructs his shepherd world are again almost all traditional, but given a new turn: principally, as far as the shepherds themselves are concerned, by Autolycus. Autolycus is an ex-courtier – or an ex-would-be-courtier – and his experience of the world enables him to wrap the peasants around his little finger. His life at court has not made him retreat to the country to bore the younger generation with stories of how well off they are (as Belarius does in *Cymbeline*); the court, in fact, had the sense to turn him out, and it is only in the simplicity of the country that he can cut purses to his heart's content. 'What a fool Honesty is!' he declares, 'and Trust, his sworn brother, a very simple gentleman!' (IV.iv.592–3). The young shepherd's good-heartedness makes him lose all the money for buying provisions; and the peasants' simple-mindedness puts the innuendos of the ballad refrains quite beyond them. The limitations of their virtues are made abundantly clear. A portrayal of shepherd ignorance had long been used as a measure of their distance from sophisticated society; here it is also a measure of a kind of inadequacy. It is one thing to know nothing of guile and thievery and obscenity, but another to be at their mercy. Nature, at this level, is not enough: an awareness is needed too – an intelligence, a sensibility, that can understand experience without losing its innocence. Innocence alone, as the shepherds demonstrate, is too vulnerable, and in Leontes experience has shattered the innocence of the past (it is Shakespeare's one comment, and a final one, on the idea of the pastoral of childhood.) Perdita can encompass both innocence and experience, and through her the fruits of the past can be restored to Leontes: Hermione, peace of mind, herself as the lost heir.

Perdita herself has the biography of a romance heroine: cast away at birth, rediscovered as a young woman when she has fallen in love with her prince. The shepherds, on the other hand, are markedly different from the usual romance variety. In *Rosalynde* they have a tendency to break out into eclogues at the slightest excuse, and Shakespeare's love-sick Silvius still has more than a touch of Arcadian melancholy about him; Corin lapses towards clownishness occasionally, but he is still an 'art-shepherd'. The shepherds of *The Winter's Tale* belong more with the comparative realism of much *bergerie*. The setting of the principal pastoral scene, which is Shakespeare's own invention, is the English shearing-feast – the kind Drayton was describing with such loving detail in his *Pastorals* and *Poly-Olbion*; the shepherd revels have at last earned a proud place in English literature. The peasants themselves feast, dance and sing in traditional style, but they eat not what a court poet imagines country cates to be but sugar and currants and rice that have to be bought from the market, they sing not eclogues but ballads acquired from the pedlar, and although there is a dance of twelve satyrs we know that they are men dressed up with real occupations of their own. The point may be obvious, but it does show how far these revels are from the Italianate pastoral drama where satyrs are a normal feature of the cast-list; they would be unthinkable here. 'Satyr' itself is probably a Jacobean standardization of the 'salvage man', the wild man or wodwose who had figured in pageants in the country and at court for centuries, long before the satyr proper and his accompanying nymphs and shepherds became fashionable. The shearers themselves are, like the Wakefield shepherds before them, 'three-man song-men all', and even Mopsa and Dorcas can sing a simple three-part song with Autolycus. The closest artistic parallel is probably Bruegel, with his scenes of indoor feasting and outdoor revelry, and the comparison helps to define their treatment: it is a kind of realism with the balance tilted towards rustic decorum (Dorcas' unkind joke about Mopsa's bad breath, and so on), given a vigour that is too strong for literal nature. Where Shakespeare departs from this kind of presentation is in Perdita and all she stands for. Like Pastorella, she stands out as being of a different strain:

> Nothing she does or seems
> But smacks of something greater than herself,
> Too noble for this place. (IV.iv.157–9)

She is not one of Bruegel's peasant wenches; the nature she represents is of a different kind – but again, one that has at least some of its origins in *bergerie*, in its spontaneous and fulfilled love. The love she imagines is open, joyous and unashamed, as she speaks about strewing Florizel with flowers,

> Like a bank for love to lie and play on,
> Not like a corse: or if, not to be buried,
> But quick, and in mine arms. (IV.iv.130–2)

Her associations are all with life, fertility, 'creating Nature'; associations of the shepherd world that are to some degree implicit in a few of the pastourelles and are made explicit in the *Roman de la Rose*, but which had never had the force and symbolic power they are given here. Perdita can encompass all this, however, because she is more than just a shepherdess; but the discovery of her birth does not mean simply abandoning all her past life. Court and country are linked, and the connection is acknowledged: as the Clown puts it,

> The King's son took me by the hand and called me brother; and then the
> two kings called my father brother; and then the Prince (my brother) and
> the Princess (my sister) called my father father; and so we wept; and there
> was the first gentlemanlike tears that ever we shed. (V.ii.135–40)

The gulf between prince and peasant is ludicrous and delightful, but their common emotion is genuine. Nothing quite like this had ever happened in pastoral before; but then that is characteristic of this play.

The twenty years or so that separate the *Henry VI* plays from *The Winter's Tale* show as great a change in Shakespeare's handling of pastoral as in any other aspect of his art. The change is not simply a development from convention to originality: there is nothing quite like Henry's great speech to be found elsewhere, and the shearing-feast is thoroughly grounded in convention. The process is more one of enlargement – from the accepted metaphors of the *Henry VI* trilogy to their deeper exploration and criticism in *As You Like It*, and from there to the rich symbolism of *The Winter's Tale*. The metaphors themselves have not changed, but they have been analysed, mocked, turned inside out, and a new energy and meaning found in them. The foundation for all these ideas, however, had been laid in the mediaeval vernacular explorations of the shepherd world. It is there that the consciously paradoxical association of pastoral and war was exploited; and because of that association it is there that pastoral peace acquires its fullest meaning. Pastoral indeed implies peace, the 'Pax in terra' of the royal entries; and Shakespeare's two pastoral plays portray the shepherd world as a source of harmony on which the outside world can draw. It is not Paradise, but at least the worst of human corruption is first excluded, then outweighed: the Duke feels 'the penalty of Adam,/The seasons' difference', but nothing worse; the untested ideal of the twinned lambs exchanging innocence for innocence gives way to a moral vision of good based on experience, an ideal even within the fallen world. Shakespeare shares his vision of pastoral with the poets of the Middle Ages; in a way he fulfils their work. There is a sense of a struggle for final expression in some of their poems, or of an ultimate frustration in having at last to withdraw from their ideal – Marotele abandoned by her lord; the narrator retreating baffled from the scenes of joyous love; the destruction of pastoral peace; the confinement of Nature to a localized beauty-spot, a moral attitude or a poetic rule. *The Winter's Tale* concerns itself with all these issues, and transcends them. Pastoral had been, and continued to be, a problem in a very real sense; *The Winter's Tale* comes closest to being the answer. It is an affirmation of the golden world within the fallen, presented not as a piece of romantic optimism but as a counterweight to a tragic view of the human condition.

V. *Minor Pastoral*

The minor pastoralists of the Elizabethan and early Stuart age can be counted as less important not simply because they wrote less pastoral than the great figures – some indeed far outweigh at least Shakespeare in sheer quantity – nor because what they wrote is necessarily less beautiful, for lyric beauty is the outstanding characteristic of much of their verse. The feature that most persistently distinguishes them from figures such as Spenser or Sidney or Shakespeare is that they deal in the commonplaces without transforming them; they mix traditions rather than fusing them, and the result is not just a lack of control but a lack of a consistent moral vision. The problem tends to become the more acute the more lyrical the poet: Richard Barnfield maintains a delightful sweetness of tone but his poems are undercut by a blatant desire to have the best of every pastoral world; Nicholas Breton repeats again and again a few highly attractive themes in words that are often barely altered. This limitation is less apparent than it might be simply because it is the lyric that is one of the commonest forms of pastoral, and that is generally sufficiently short to be at least consistent with itself: *Englands Helicon*, the first anthology of English pastoral, presents almost as many attitudes to the mode as poems, but at least not more. Even writers whose main composition of pastoral was not lyrical – men such as Greene and Lodge – are very conscious of its connection with the lyric and easily slip into song. One of the things that seems to have attracted many of these writers to the mode, in fact, is its distance from the real world; they use it not to reflect back onto life but as a kind of escapism, for writing introspective poems of love-melancholy, for drawing irrelevant pictures of the bliss and contentment of the shepherd's life, or just as a means of practising their art. The results may be beautiful, as the most famous of the poems in *Englands Helicon*, Marlowe's 'Come live with me and be my love', proves, and the mere presence of a sterner moral element certainly does not make Raleigh's reply greater as poetry; but it is just such a commitment to a serious view of life that makes Spenser greater than Mantuan, Sidney than Sannazaro or Montemayor, and that can make the anthology disturbing through its general absence. Mediaeval poets, especially the authors of the pastourelles, had played with just such lyrical fantasies, and the influence from this genre can be seen just occasionally beside the more Italianate nymphs – in Phyllis's fear of being caught with her lover by her mother, for instance;[48] but the use of the shepherd world as a perspective on society such as characterizes most mediaeval pastoral, and which the great Elizabethans inherited, rarely finds expression in the lyric. It emerges most often in the weightier poetic forms – in the eclogue in particular – and the poets who exploit it, men such as Lodge or Fairfax, are not primarily concerned with making their poetry attractive. It is the distinction between the Italianate shepherd, the poet-lover, of

> What shepheard can expresse
> The favour of her face?
> To whom in this distresse
> I doo appeale for grace,[49]

and the shepherd as moralist, as when Lodge rejects art in his eclogues,

> Who waites for words, may get him hence,
> For shepheards onely sing for sence.[50]

The context of these lines makes the declaration a specific rejection of the new styles of poetry, 'moderne and newfangled laies', in favour of older traditions. The two branches of pastoral, lyric and moral, are made to support each other in Spenser and Sidney; in the lesser poets, or even in Milton's few passages of pastoral, they tend to lead separate existences.

The contribution made by mediaeval pastoral traditions over the whole range of late sixteenth and early seventeenth century literature can best be seen through a concentration on theme and treatment rather than on individual writers, for it is through the constant repetition of ideas that the magnitude of the heritage becomes clear. The kind of thing they inherited covers every variation of the mediaeval usages of the mode, from tiny details of dress or food to the whole tendency to use the pastoral metaphor as a criticism of life or society or to comment on the intellectual movements of the age. The borrowings from the Italian tradition may be more immediately striking, but they refer to a much narrower range of experience and idea, and by themselves they account for little of the best work. England never produced a poet like the Tasso of the *Aminta*, who could write with a joyful and unfettered paganism in verse of a strength that was able to carry triviality of plot and fantasy of 'moral'. The aspect of Renaissance culture that the *Aminta* represents was never successfully transplanted in England; and the power of English Renaissance pastoral comes from a different source – ultimately, from the Middle Ages.

The realism at the base of *bergerie* is usually missing in this period. There will be realistic details, of dress or food, but except in a few cases poets use these as artistic properties – a 'particularity, of what we may call the "curds and clouted cream" variety', as Joan Grundy puts it.[51] Elizabethan shepherd descriptions are accordingly shorter and more directly aimed at lyrical development than their earlier counterparts, though the tradition is basically the same. Drayton's shepherd in the song of Dowsabell, with his grey cloak, mittens, cockers, hood and equipment hanging from his belt is more detailed than most but certainly not unique. Watson's lamenting Amyntas – a shepherd who seems on first acquaintance much too limited to his rôle as lover ever to have known such shepherdly equipment – reports losing his leather bottle and his shoes and mittens, breaking the tarbox at his side, throwing away his sheephook and abandoning his dog Lightfoot.[52] The 'grey russet coat' is the typical garment of the Elizabethan shepherd ('russet' being in its primary meaning a homespun woollen cloth); Adam in *King Edward and the Shepherd* also wore russet. Greene's Coridon, who appears in a song sung by other shepherds in *Tullies Loue*, has

> A russet Iacket, sleeues red,
> A blew bonnet on his hed:
> A cloake of gray fencst the raine,
> Thus tyred was this louely swaine.
> A shepheards hooke his dog tide,
> Bag and bottle by his side.[53]

Another Coridon in a song in *Greenes Mourning Garment* is equally carefully described, in a green coat this time with russet cape, leather scrip fastening with a button, bottle, and dog alongside.[54] The context of both these descriptions is significant: the realistic detail is kept at one remove by being embodied in octosyllabics in the middle of prose romances, so that it seems even more artificial than the elaborate stories in which it is set.

Shepherds sing and make music as readily in the Renaissance as in the Middle Ages; that is one reason why they figure so frequently in the song-books. Many of these appearances are derived from neo-Latin or Italianate pastoral, but the influence from *bergerie* can often be traced alongside. The bagpipe is still a common instrument: it is a bagpipe that Colin plays in Book VI of the *Faerie Queene* and that the 'January' woodcut shows him as breaking, and the pipe that Strephon 'bursts' in Sidney's 'A Shepheards tale' is presumably also a bagpipe. Many poets who give their shepherds pipes of unspecified type may well have had the bagpipe in mind in this way. A number of other instruments receive an occasional mention, especially in descriptions of shepherd revels. Festivities are marked by dancing, games and feasting as well as music. The food tends to be strictly conventional – butter, cheese, cracknels and the inevitable curds and clouted cream are typical; Warner adds whig, brown bread and fruit, Drayton green cheese, custards, cider and so on. The principal season for revels is still spring, and specifically May, and the close association of pastoral with maygames is indicated not only by how often May revels occur as a subject but by statements that suggest that the two could almost be taken as synonymous. The original billing of *The Faithful Shepherdess* as a 'pastoral tragi-comedy' led the audience to expect 'Whitsun-ales, cream, wassail, and morris-dances', and they were duly angry when they discovered the Arcadian fantasy that Fletcher had in store for them. Whitsun was one of the principal occasions for maygames – Stubbes describes them as taking place 'against May, Whitsonday or other time',[55] and Warner lists the annual country feasts,

> At Paske begun our Morrise, and ere Penticost our May,
> Tho Roben Hood, liell John, Frier Tucke, and Marian deftly play. (V.xxv)

Perdita's reference to 'Whitsun pastorals', seen in this context, need mean no more than maygames. Robin Hood, as a figure from the games, accordingly becomes associated with pastoral: there is an entry in the Stationers' Register for 14 May, 1594, for a 'Pastoral Pleasant Comedie of Robin Hood and Little John'; and Jonson's play *The Sad Shepherd*,[56] which has Robin Hood as one of its central characters, shows how the association was acknowledged by even the rigorous scholar. Barclay's Codrus asks the shepherd-poet Minalcas to sing not a song in the high style he can achieve but

> some mery fit
> Of mayde Marion, or els of Robin hood. (IV.720–1)

This is the first known mention of Maid Marian; Robin was a figure from the ballads as much as the maygame, but Marian is mentioned elsewhere in the sixteenth century only in the context of maygames or morris-dances, and Barclay's reference to them is part of his attempt to naturalize pastoral. Breton's Phillis strikes the nightingale silent by singing of Robin Hood,[57] and he obviously felt the conceit to be a neat pastoral paradox. The commonest form of May celebration to be described within pastoral poetry is dancing round the Maypole; there are also plenty of references to shepherds' singing and dancing and feasting, or to their going to the woods to 'fetch in May', to bring hawthorn and green boughs to decorate the houses and the church, a custom that seems to have been universal among all social classes. The shearing feast provides an alternative occasion for revelling, and Drayton and Shakespeare provide particularly striking examples. The games played by the shepherds on all these occasions are again part of the traditional pastoral convention: games such as nine-men's morris, quoits, throwing the bar or the sledge-hammer, or, in the entertainment given for Elizabeth at Sudeley in 1592, the same game of Kings and Queens as the shepherds of the *Jeu de Robin et Marion* had played.[58]

The everyday occupations of the shepherds generally receive rather less attention from the Renaissance poets. Watson's Amyntas did at least spend some time looking after his sheep, and as a boy he learned the whole range of essential shepherd crafts from music to shearing:

> The friendly shepards route
> Admitted me, and countrie secrets taught
> To heale my flocks, to fould them round about.
> In threatned stormes, to lead them to the lee,
> To sheare in time, to driue the wolfe awaie,
> To knowe the course, of starres that fixed bee;
> To pipe on meadow reeds, each holy-daie.

> To sing in rime, as sometimes shepards vse,
> To daunce our Iiggs on pasture grac't with flowrs.[59]

The emphasis on teaching is again mediaeval. Colin Clout refers to the same kind of range of activities, though neither he nor Amyntas is ever shown actually doing them. Amyntas' love Phillis had also led an active life, milking the goats, making clouted cream or cakes and weaving baskets as well as dancing.[60] Drayton's Melanthus takes particular care of the health of his sheep, and the early Stuart poet William Basse describes the custom of covering an orphaned lamb with a dead lamb's skin to make the living mother willing to foster it;[61] but generally the flocks are of minimal importance. Hunting, fishing and fowling are given more attention than sheep-keeping by many poets; Francis Sabie gives a particularly fine description of fowling in *Pans Pipe*:

> With milk-white snow when th'earth was al hidden
> Forth with a fouler he was, to the welsprings and to the fountains
> And to the running lakes, whose euer mooueable waters
> Frost neuer alter could, there for the long-billed hernshue,
> And little Snype did he set snares.　　　　　　　　　(II.59–63)

Looking for herbs (which could be endowed with magical properties, so making the occupation appropriate for Italianate pastoral romances, plays or masques), and, inevitably, studying the stars, complete the shepherd's activities.

The value of this kind of life is perpetually stressed. The shepherd is still king in his own realm, or better even than a king; and princes – even gods – have been happy to become shepherds.

> You Sheepheards which on hillocks sit
>   like Princes in their throanes:
> And guide your flocks, which else would flit,
>   your flocks of little ones:
> Good Kings have not disdained it,
>   but Sheepheards have been named:
> A sheepe-hooke is a Scepter fit,
>   for people well reclaimed.
> The Sheepheards life so honour'd is and praised:
> That Kings lesse happy seeme, though higher raised.[62]

Poets are only too ready to cite Apollo, Jove, Pan, Paris, the Patriarchs, the Bethlehem shepherds and any other relevant examples to justify the high calling of the herdsman.[63] Christ Himself is usually cited only when the subject is specifically religious, as for instance in Spenser's ecclesiastical eclogues; He is only referred to once in *Englands Helicon*, in a poem by Edmund Bolton on the Bethlehem shepherds, where He is named as 'the worlds great Sheepheard' (p. 136). Despite the still scarcely extinct tradition of the mystery plays, Elizabethan poets tended to abandon any *bergerie* elements in the treatment of the Annunciation to the Shepherds: if a writer goes beyond the Gospel account at all, it is more likely to be in the direction of poetic elevation (as it is with Bolton) than homeliness or realism or symbolism arising directly out of the pastoral metaphor. Milton's shepherds in the *Hymn on the Morning of Christ's Nativity* are more 'mediaeval' in this respect.

The main subject in Elizabethan pastoral is not religion but love; and although Arcadian love-sickness and *bergerie* fulfilment are often found jumbled together, there is still a strong theme of true love simply given, echoed in closely similar words from poet to poet – Lodge's 'only faith and troth, thats shepheards wooing' or 'love and faith is Sheepheards treasure', Breton's 'yea and nay, and faith and troth'.[64] Greene's Phillis and Coridon also swear faith and troth, and exchange the love-gifts that are at least as old as the *Jeu de Robin et Marion*:

> The swaine gaue a girdle red,
> Shee set garlands on his hed.[65]

Love of this kind is several times contrasted in detail with the kind of love found at court – at length in *Colin Clouts Come Home Againe*, more briefly in Lyly's, 'Heere is flat faith *amo amas*; where you crie, *ô utinam amarent vel non amassem*': 'Would that they would love, or that I had not loued!'[66] The idea of true and simple wooing was, not surprisingly, beginning to turn stale by the turn of the century, and the two heroes of John Day's *Humour out of Breath* get nowhere with the heroines when they try to court them in this style while they are disguised as shepherds.[67] It was possible to turn the theme into something more significant in two ways: through its connection with moral decorum and the rejection of art; or by elaborating the whole idea of love into a neoplatonic statement on the nature of existence. Neither of these developments had occurred – or could have occurred – in the Middle Ages, but both were made possible by mediaeval traditions: the idea of moral decorum through the existence of a simple ideal, the neoplatonic movement through the belief in the high mission and essentially allegorical nature of pastoral.

This particular kind of allegory is seldom strained: as in Sidney's 'A Shepheards tale', it is held in the poetry and develops out of it, and it is possible to read it on a literal level with plenty of enjoyment. Breton just touches on this higher idea of pastoral love in his *Passionate Shepherd*: Aglaia may be beauty personified, but she exists in a countryside where her shepherd can pipe for her, provide a feast for her from his scrip or spread his cloak on the ground for her to sit on, and where they can see

> The little blacke-haird Cony
> On a banke for Sunny place,
> With her fore-feete wash her face.

He moves to an overtly higher idea only for a few lines, as he rejects not only the conventional evils of civilization in favour of the country but earthly considerations for heavenly contemplation:

> I wil leaue Court, Cittie, towne and fielde,
> Warres, Lawe and traffique, pollycie and paine:
> And see what life the country loue will yeelde,
> Where Shepheards keepe the flockes vpon the plaine.

> There will I sit and in the sacred sence,
> Of heauenly vertues high instructions:
> Learn in Aglaias natures excellence,
> Of Loues conceites, to make the best constructions.
> Where God alone shall in my soule be loued,
> And faithes affection in true fancy proued.[68]

Drayton occasionally makes the same kind of transition from earthly love to heavenly – Rowland's love, Idea, is obviously particularly well named for the purpose; and *Endimion and Phoebe* turns from the mythological-erotic kind of poem, where Phoebe can none the less promise to make her lover 'shepheards king' on shearing-day, to the explicitly Platonic, where the music of the spheres is echoed in the soul. Nothing so elaborate is necessary, however: Bolton's Theorello ('contemplative'), in *Englands Helicon*, is in love with a shepherdess named Cosma, and through the description of her body and clothing her true nature gradually emerges:

> Her mantle dooth the formes expresse,
> of all which may be seene. (p. 5)

She is the world ('Yet hath the world no better name then she') in its function of leading the mind through its beauty to contemplate the intellectual sphere of existence – κόσμος means both 'world' and 'ornament'; and Theorello ends the poem with a promise to look on her in just these terms.

> On thee (o Cosma) will I gaze,
> and reade thy beauties ever:
> Delighting in the blessed maze,
> which can be ended never.
> For in the luster of thy rayes,
> appeares thy parents brightnes:
> Who himself infinite displaies
> in thee his proper greatnes.
> My song must end, but never my desire:
> For Cosmas face is Theorellos fire. (p. 6)

In form and genre the poem never moves beyond the blazon of the shepherdess's beauty; it is like Botticelli's *Primavera* (to compare small things with great), a beautiful picture from a kind of Arcadian dream-world to the careless sight, a revelation of the nature of things to the initiate. Sidney's fusion of neoplatonism and pastoral in 'A Shepheards tale' is in some ways the opposite of this: the game of barley-break seems to become allegorical in despite of the shepherds themselves, and the intellective patterns that their steps form as they run are a kind of joke shared between the Form of Forms and his co-creator, the poet. What Sidney and Bolton have in common is the typically Petrarchan assumption that a complete understanding of pastoral is only for the chosen few.

Since it was so easy for the shepherd to carry connotations of this kind it is no surprise that he continues to fill his mediaeval rôle as teacher – the rôle Languet assumes in Sidney, or Colin in the epilogue to the *Calender*. Lodge gives the strongest expression to this function in the austerely moral eclogues of *A Fig for Momus*, with Damian's categorical rejection of the identification of shepherd and poet in favour of shepherd and moralist. Just what their teaching consists of varies from poet to poet. Barnfield's Daphnis, in his *Affectionate Shepheard*, slides imperceptibly from an appeal to Ganymede to love him to a disquisition on the works of mercy and the way to Heaven. Nathaniel Baxter, who had been one of Sidney's tutors and whose poetic style never really caught up with the new generation, wrote in 1606 a work entitled *Sir Philip Sydneys Ourania* which he declares contains 'all Philosophie' – a complete summary of natural science, from the structure of the universe down to lice, spoken by himself in the guise of the shepherd Endymion. The encyclopaedic nature of the work is reminiscent of the *Kalender of Shepherdes*, and so is the style, both in its metrical roughness, its repeated 'Shepheards sayne –' or 'Lysten you Shepheards –', and its moral emphasis:

The Storke may teach children with reuerence,
To yeeld their parents due obedience.

His listing of the metals gives him the opportunity for a long digression on gold, which is the cause of war, corrupts society and the Church, and is responsible for the rise of the Puritans, to whom

The Booke of Common-prayer is tittle tattle,
Much like to a Babies playing rattle.

The poem ends with the appearance of Sidney's ghost, who tells Cynthia (representing Mary, countess of Pembroke) to give Endymion a pension, and Baxter imagines him spending his time after that 'expounding Oracles of Theologie'. The idea of the shepherd's teaching is usually rather better assimilated, though the purpose may be just as didactic. William Basse devotes each of his nine eclogues to the praise of a different virtue, including the characteristically pastoral ones of Contentment (Eglogue 3), Temperance (5) and Humility (9), and his typical method is to make one shepherd expound the virtue in question to his companion. Praise of the good life is a perpetually popular theme: *Greenes Mourning Garment* closes with a song about a shepherd whose 'lofty thoughts' led him to abandon the country for the town, and whose bitter experience there brought him back to the sweetness and purity of the country; and Lodge's Old Damon, in a poem in *Englands Helicon*, insists on the same contrast of court and country as Franc Gontier:

Envie of a forraigne Tyrant
    threatneth Kings, not Sheepheards humble:
Age makes silly Swaines delirant,
    thirst of rule garres great men stumble.
What to other seemeth sorrie,
    abject state and humble biding:
Is our joy and Country glorie,
    highest states have worse betiding.
Golden cups doo harbour poyson,
    and the greatest pompe, dissembling:
Court of seasoned words hath foyson,
    treason haunts in most assembling.   (p. 19)

There are plenty of other examples of the same kind of thing, and the shepherds of the romances are particularly fond of discoursing on the value of country life. It is only a short step from this to more explicit condemnations of court life, such as occur in *Colin Clouts Come Home Againe* or with more specific reference in Drayton; and the bitterly satirical tone of some of the Jacobean eclogues as they attack social abuse, and particularly the neglect or ill-treatment of poets – George Wither wrote an entire eclogue cycle on his imprisonment in the Marshalsea[69] – is an extension of this. The collection entitled *The Shepherd's Pipe*, published in 1614 and containing poems by Browne, Brooke, Wither and Davies, perpetually returns to this theme; the very first eclogue tells how the good shepherds are being attacked by 'wicked swains' to the point where there is a risk that nobody will dare to

            take in task
Any wrong, nor once unmask
Such as do with vices rife
Soil the shepherd's happy life.[70]

The morally upright shepherd, the didactic poet, is threatened with being overwhelmed and silenced. The tone of this pastoral is markedly different from most Elizabethan poetry: they are more interested in the 'satiric reed' than in the *tenuis avena*, which was always first and foremost the medium of art. Satiric comment can intrude in the most unlikely places: Daniel's elaborate and Italianate love-comedy, *The Queenes Arcadia*, contains an attack on tobacco – one of several pastoral references to the new fashion. The shepherds who had been accustomed

> At all their meetings, and their festiualls,
> To passe the time in telling witty tales,
> In questions, riddles and in purposes,
> Now doe they nothing else, but sit and sucke,
> And spit, and slauer.[71]

Getting the shepherds to smoke is the villains' crowning success in their policy of destroying the traditional virtues of Arcadia.

The astrological emphasis of the calendar tradition played its part in endorsing the shepherd's rôle as teacher. The *Kalender of Shepherdes* itself was frequently used as a means of divination; when Francis Quarles, in an eclogue composed apparently in 1632, speaks of

> the kalender, whereby
> We rurall Shepheards calculate and forespy
> Things future, Good or Evill,[72]

he is referring to a common practice that may be especially appropriate to bring into an eclogue but was certainly not limited to the countryside. John Harvey's *Discoursive Probleme concerning Prophesies* was 'deuised especially in abatement of the terrible threatenings, and menaces, peremptorily de-nounced against the kingdoms, and states of the world, this present famous yeere, 1588', and one of the sources of prophecy that he singles out for particular attack is 'the old shepherds Kalender'. The work was believed to be full of concealed prognostications (it is not insignificant that Dr. John Dee, Elizabeth's favourite astrologer, owned a copy), giving the shepherd (like Virgil before him) something of the status of a magician. What particularly annoys Harvey about this use of the work is not that omens are not genuine or cannot be found in this kind of way, but that the shepherd is, after all, not a wise teacher but an ignorant peasant.

> Must we resort to wizards, or southsaiers, or sorcerers, or cuniurers, or witches, or gypsies, or shepheards, or any like priuate prophets of basest condition, and silliest intelligence, in highest occurrences of state?   (p. 64)

The herdsman is no longer the voice of truth but the author of 'shepheardly soothsayings, which are not any farther to be dreamed vpon'.

Harvey's wizards and gypsies are the strangest bedfellows the shepherd ever found himself with in the Middle Ages or the Renaissance, and this use of an old-fashioned didactic almanac for prophecy at first appears a long distance from pastoral; but several poets did make the connection, and not only, like Quarles, by reference to the custom in an eclogue. This whole poem of his is in fact a political 'prophecy' on the coming of Gustavus Adolphus, and which concludes with a report of his death; and the shepherds' under-standing of the stars becomes the means whereby their knowledge of political events in Europe can be made decorous. The astrological tradition, the fact that shepherds watch the stars that is basic to the *Kalender* and is noted in the Bible and many pastoral works, is made the link between the shepherd him-self and the mediaeval use of pastoral for political comment. The same idea seems to be at work behind one of the oddest Elizabethan pastorals, published in 1591, Thomas Bradshaw's 'Shepherds Starre, Now of late seene, and at this hower to be obserued merueilous orient in the East: which bringeth glad tydings to all that may behold her brightnes, hauing the foure elements with the foure Capitall vertues in her, which makes her Elementall and a vanquishor of all earthly humors'. In case this should seem to possess nothing pastoral but the name of shepherd, Bradshaw adds that the work is a 'paraphrase' of the third idyll of Theocritus – a debt that we would almost certainly overlook if he did not tell us, as the similarities are, to put it mildly, slight. Theocritus' short love-song becomes a long disquisition, in prose with inset songs, on a wide variety of subjects including the European political situation, the right of a country to decree its own religion, weather signs, and the science of physiognomy, which is traced back to 'Iacob the father of all shepherdes' (sig. E4ª). Just what the significance of all this is meant to be is not at all clear; but the very use of the pastoral guise for such esoteric verbiage is an indication of how persistent the tradition of arcane pastoral allegory was.

Allegory in Renaissance pastoral, as in mediaeval, was concerned with two principal subjects: politics and religion. Political pastoral in the Elizabethan age – with a few notable exceptions such as *Mother Hubberds Tale* – concentrated on panegyric of the Queen herself, and constitutes such a large and autonomous literary genre that it requires a chapter to itself. Some religious allegory was also attracted into this field by virtue of Elizabeth's position as Head of the Church, and also because of the association of both Elizabeth and religious satire with May festivities; but there is a certain amount written without reference to her, and even more from the early Stuart era when religious issues were becoming increasingly pressing. The concern of pastoral with religion had been persistent throughout the sixteenth century, in Skelton, in 'Kepe well the shepe', in Googe's eclogues, in Sidney's epilogue to *The Lady of May*, the *Shepheardes Calender* and so on; and, like tobacco, religion can crop up in the most unexpected places – unexpected except for the constant pull of the mode towards satire. William Browne breaks off in the middle of Marina's exotic adventures in *Britannia's Pastorals* to describe the prevailing ills of society, including

> The prelate in pluralities asleep
> Whilst that the wolf lies preying on his sheep; (II.i.869–70)

Baxter squeezes his attack on the Puritans into his treatise on the sciences; and Warner introduces into the 1612 edition of *Albions England* the curious incident of a shepherd (complete with bagpipe, crook, scrip, bottle and dog Patch) who tells the world of a speech uttered by a 'bare-breecht' Robin Goodfellow who came and sat on his face while he slept and denounced the state of the Church – a denunciation that extends to various other social ills, including tobacco (ch. 91). More complete allegories are found in genres that had a conventional association with inner meanings: the dream poem proper, and the eclogue. A number of eclogues of the late sixteenth and early seventeenth centuries take religious matters as their exclusive subject, but even when they claim to be about something else poets kept finding the form too well suited to ecclesiastical satire to let the opportunity pass; *Lycidas* is the most famous instance, where the Classically structured lament for Edward King is interrupted by the imposing figure of St. Peter, portrayed, as Petrarch

had also imagined him in his own eclogues, with his 'massy Keyes', who
speaks the indictment of all those shepherds who

> for their bellies sake,
> Creep and intrude, and climb into the fold.
> Of other care they little reck'ning make,
> Then how to scramble at the shearers feast,
> And shove away the worthy bidden guest;
> Blind mouthes! that scarce themselves know how to hold
> A sheep-hook, or have learn'd ought els the least
> That to the faithfull Herdmans art belongs!
> What recks it them? What need they? They are sped;
> And when they list, their lean and flashy songs
> Grate on their scrannel Pipes of wretched straw,
> The hungry sheep look up, and are not fed,
> But swoln with wind, and the rank mist they draw,
> Rot inwardly, and foul contagion spread.
> Besides what the grim Woolf with privy paw
> Daily devours apace.   (114–29)

The artistic impetus for the attack on bad shepherds comes from the Petrarchan tradition; the details are from *bergerie* – their ignorance of the arts of
sheepkeeping, of healing and not least of music, their greed at the shearing-
feast, their total irresponsibility towards their flocks. This, for Milton, is as
central to the pastoral tradition as the dancing satyrs or Amaryllis in the
shade, as driving the flocks afield or the vision of Heaven.

One of the most detailed satires in pastoral form on a precise ecclesiastical
situation occurs in James Melville's dream poem *The Black Bastel*, which he
wrote while he was in prison in Berwick in 1611.[73] The poem is an attack on
James I's establishment of bishops in the Kirk of Scotland. The poet-dreamer
falls asleep in a cave in the course of a winter walk, and dreams of how a
woman – the Kirk itself – has been forced to dress gaudily; thirteen wolves
('now 14', as a marginal note adds), representing the bishops, have been put
in charge of her sheep; her shepherds, complete with 'dog and staff', have
become 'carelesse' of their charge; and the sheep themselves have been
'well pluck'd and clipped bare'. The church is staffed entirely by 'bite-sheep
Bishops' and hired shepherds, and the only way Melville can devise a happy
ending is through the intervention of St. Michael and all the angels.

The dream poem, with its possibilities of narrative development, is
particularly well suited to this kind of detailed allegory (another of Sidney's
'tales of wolues and sheep'); the eclogue, with its usual subject of meditation
on a situation rather than actual plot, and its long association with polemic,
was used several times not just for attacks on the state of the Church but for
actual doctrinal debate. The shepherds in Spenser's 'May' are concerned
with just such a conflict of belief; and three ecloguists in particular of the late
Elizabethan and early Stuart age took up the idea: Edward Fairfax, Thomas
Randolph and Francis Quarles. Randolph and Quarles, as might be expected
from their later date – they were both writing in the reign of Charles I – are
concerned principally with the comparatively minor differences that split
the Protestant church into so many sects; Fairfax is still concerned with the
first great division, between Protestant and Catholic, and directly with the
question of man's salvation.

Fairfax's series of twelve eclogues was written around 1603. He did not
publish them; one manuscript was burnt in 1619, and his own copy was

last heard of in 1789. The Fourth Eclogue had already been printed by then; two more have since been found in other manuscripts.[74] It is clear even from these three poems that Fairfax's understanding of the pastoral mode was typically Elizabethan in its generosity; nothing can be out of place – 'according to the Evidence of his Son, (who has written large Annotations on each) No Man's Reading, beside his own, was sufficient to explain his References effectually.'[75] The *Ecloga Octava* is a panegyric of contemporary explorers, from Columbus and Magellan to Drake, Frobisher, Sir Humphrey Gilbert and Willoughby. The other two poems are both theological allegories, but written with all the trappings of the Virgilian, rather than the Petrarchan, eclogue. The fourth eclogue, 'Eglon and Alexis', contains Eglon's story of how he has lost a beloved lamb,

> That in my Bosom its soft Lodging made,
> And cherisht was, and fed as I was able,
> It was my child, my Darling and my Queen,
> And might for shape a Passover have been!
>
> I kept it for an Off'ring 'gainst the Day
> That the great God of Shepherds Pan shall come. (p. 366)

The poem, like Spenser's 'May', turns into an allegorical beast-fable, but the subject this time is not the battle for man's soul viewed from outside, by a member of one sect or party as opposed to another, but from inside: the lamb is man's own innocence. Eglon describes how it broke away from its shed and was enticed by the fox Malpardus, dressed in a kid's skin, to his den, by the temptations of a life of ease and revelling: he offers to deck its horns with roses, and invites it,

> Come, be thou Lady of our May, and Mirth! (p. 368)

The Lamb sees through the fox's disguise, but it yields none the less and lets itself be bound in a chain forged of the links of deadly sin. Its wool is cut off and it is given a many-coloured coat instead; it is feasted, given brittle honours, poisoned by the fox's embraces. Alexis can none the less comfort his companion:

> That Shepherd, who our Flocks and us doth keep,
> To remedy this Sickness long before,
> Killed a holy Lamb, clear, spotless, pure;
> Whose Blood the Salve is all our Hurts to cure! (p. 373)

Man's only justification, in other words, is the Lamb of God, his only hope the Good Shepherd. This is pastoral in the tradition of Sedulius Scotus, with his description of the spotless sheep, or Jean de Meung, with his portrait of the Good Shepherd; and the basis of the interpretation of the mode is the same – that pastoral offers an image both of the corrupt world and the way to transcend it.

It is not impossible that Fairfax, voracious reader as he was, knew these authors; he certainly knew both Petrarch's eclogues and the *Ecloga Theoduli*, and he wrote his own Reformation version of Theodulus as a singing-match of Catholic versus Protestant. The setting is purely mythological, with nymphs and 'half-gods', satyrs and fauns, listening to the singing; there is no adjudication, but the eclogue is none the less at the centre of the *conflictus* tradition. Hermes is a shepherd, and he sings of his beloved Psyche; Lycaon, significantly, is a goatherd, and his mistress is named Flora – to Fairfax as to E. K., 'a famous harlot, which with the abuse of her body hauing gotten great riches, made the people of Rome her heyre'.[76] She is a goatherdess, Lycaon sings, who has been loved by ten kings and slept with them; she received from them a triple crown; she rides on a scarlet beast. Psyche is at once the soul and the true Church, the spouse of Christ figured in the Song of Songs – Hermes prays,

> O comfort me for I am sick of loue   (MS p. 649)

– and the woman crowned with twelve stars of the Apocalypse. Flora's scarlet beast is balanced by the four beasts of the Evangelists in the same way that Theodulus matched his protagonists' arguments. Flora has made Lycaon

> maister of her flocks and fould
> Her goats to keepe or kill or sell for gold;   (p. 651)

Psyche has crowned Hermes with the blood of a 'lamb new slain', and his concerns are not with earthly wealth but with eternal bliss:

> Her sheepe my playfelowes, heauen our fould
> Her spouse the doore.   (p. 651)

Flora is as criminally careless of her herds as the Avignon papacy was in Petrarch's eyes; Hermes warns,

> Shepards beware;
> Wach, feed, defend your sheep, charge asketh care.
> All that is stolne or slaine you must make good.   (p. 653)

Each singer ends by threatening that the other's lady will be destroyed, and the eclogue closes with the beasts standing silent to listen to the music. Pastoral of this kind may seem to be set in Arcadia, but its place is in contemporary controversy or in man's soul.

Randolph's ecclesiastical eclogue concentrates on a single doctrinal point – it is entitled 'An Eglogue occasion'd by two Doctors disputing upon predestination'[77] – though its conclusion is Christian in a wider sense than the theological hair-splitting of the debate itself would allow for. 'Hermes and Lycaon' lacks an explicit judgement within the poem, but the issue is absolutely clear; Randolph uses she *conflictus* eclogue to emphasise that debate and Christian pastoral will not, ultimately, mix. The dispute springs from Tityrus' bewilderment over the fact that one of his ewes has borne twin lambs, one black, one white. Alexis tells him to trust in God's providence; and when the argument is becoming heated it is interrupted by Thyrsis, who points out that while they are quarrelling the wolf can creep up on the flock. He urges them to sing of Love instead – of divine love; and the pastoral imagery is infused with a new meaning. The lover's garland is replaced by the crown of thorns; and faith and humility are given a new significance:

> His cradle was a manger; Shepheards see
> True faith delights in poore simplicitie.

The conventional nightfall close of the eclogue, the judgement of the singing-match and the shepherd revels take on an apocalyptic meaning:

> The great night is come.
> Flocks to your folds, and Shepheards hye you home.
> Tomorrow morning, when we all have slept,
> Pan's Cornet's blowne, and the great Sheepshears kept.

The shepherd must be responsible for his flock before God; and it is to Him that judgement belongs.

Quarles' cycle of eleven eclogues is, by contrast, constructed purely as a polemic in favour of Elizabethan-style Anglicanism against all its rivals, whether Puritan (in any form), Catholic, atheist or Arminian; and also against the present corruption of the Church, where the 'good shepheards' of the past are 'growne Plough-men all', and neglect their sheep to pursue material wealth. The work was published posthumously, in 1646, with an epistle to the reader, probably by Izaak Walton, in which it is said that Quarles had left a blank page as for a preface, which would perhaps have included 'some Allegorical exposition of the Shepheards names, of their Eglogues'; but the absence of such an explanation is no barrier to interpretation, for the true nature of shepherds named Nullifidius, Pseudo-Catholicus or Schismaticus could hardly be mistaken. The frontispiece of the original edition, which shows the tree of religion protected by Charles I and watered by Anglican divines while Puritans up in the branches lop off boughs labelled Obedience and Good Works, serves to indicate the subject-matter before the reader has even reached the eclogues themselves. As pastoral poetry, the collection is much better than it might sound: ecclesiastical pastoral offered a wide range of traditional metaphors, from the simple content of the true pastor to different shepherds' attitudes to revels or the activities of the wolf, and as well as drawing on all these Quarles invents a lot more that work equally well – that Arminius hesitates to look for his lost sheep in the Roman fold because the brands are too alike to make recognition easy, or that a particular kind of grass called Opinion bloats the sheep without really fattening them – 'swoln with wind', in Milton's phrase. The poems, obviously, exist only half in the shepherd world, and the pastoral metaphor is sometimes dropped for quite long sections; but the principle is always the same, to give a new perspective that ignores irrelevant complexities and focuses on a single issue in a new light. The especial virtue of the work lies in Quarles' sense of humour – a virtue all too often lacking in this kind of pastoral – and the Brownist Anarchus' song, with its increasingly improper refrain of

> Hey! then up go we,

is one of the liveliest pieces of religious satire of the period and enjoyed a well-deserved popularity outside its eclogue context. Just one of Quarles' eclogues is concerned not with religious polemic but with religion itself: the fifth poem is a Nativity eclogue, and its place in the middle of the work provides a foil for the rest – a presentation of the good shepherds who are instructed directly by an angel, and who go to see the Good Shepherd face to face.

Quarles and Walton were writing in a dying age of pastoral, and they knew it: the nostalgia for a lost golden age that characterizes so much pastoral from the earliest times now becomes more specific, as a longing for the lost days of Elizabeth, when England had approached Arcadia in peacefulness and religious harmony. So it seemed looking back; and although the picture may appear hopelessly distorted in the light of the persecution of the Jesuit priests, the battles fought by the Puritans in Parliament, the bad harvests and the incurable inflation of the later years of the reign, it was still the picture that the Elizabethan poets themselves saw when they looked at their country. The most marked change between Elizabethan and Jacobean pastoral is the sudden onset of disillusionment. Elizabethan pastoral is almost unique in its refusal to be nostalgic: the pastoral dream is fulfilled, and it is the Queen herself who holds it in being.

VI

THE SHEPHERDS' QUEEN

Elizabeth herself was the focal point, the inspiration and the subject of much of the literature of her age, not least of its pastoral; and the pastoral celebrations of her together form a summary of all the themes and forms the mode had drawn to itself in the course of the Middle Ages and the Renaissance. The long-established uses of the mode for panegyric and political and religious comment could all be turned to her service. The rhetorical paradox of celebrating the Queen in pastoral terms could become a compliment, and, more importantly, it allowed poets and dramatists to write of her with greater vividness and intimacy, to overcome the distance between prince and subject. She was herself fully alive to the possibilities of reversing the procedure and comparing herself to that most English of pastoral figures, the milkmaid. The milkmaid, like the shepherdess, could be not only the heroine of a love-adventure (a rôle she was assigned increasingly often with the growth of ballad and broadside literature), but the type of idyllic content: Overbury and Brathwaite both exalt her in these terms in their books of characters, and Izaak Walton's milkmaid Maudlin even sings Marlowe's *Passionate Shepherd*. When Elizabeth, as the princess held captive at Woodstock, wished herself a milkmaid, she was simply reversing the usual convention: not the contented shepherd rejecting kingship, but the unhappy princess longing for pastoral bliss. Also like the shepherdess, the milkmaid could be an instance of base simplicity; and this too the Queen knew, as she stated in her speech to Parliament in 1576 declaring her intention of remaining single:

> If I were a milkmaid with a pail on my arm, whereby my private person might be little set by, I would not forsake that poor and single state to match with the greatest monarch.[1]

Such a humble comparison could only come from herself, however; her poets chose a more exalted rôle for her within the pastoral world – the rôle of the Spring or Summer Queen. It was a theme that was established in the first major pastorals of the reign, the *Lady of May* and the *Shepheardes Calender*, and that came to govern all the pastoral addressed to her. Her most obvious function in this rôle was as mistress of the shepherd revels, but it has other equally important associations: with the themes of time, eternity and the seasons that the pastoral tradition had drawn in, with the ideas of peace and plenty, and, less obvious but no less significant, with religious controversy.

The two traditions of religious comment in the scholarly eclogue and in popular maygames were originally quite distinct; it was part of the great Elizabethan synthesis of pastoral to identify the two, and the association of maygames with pastoral was strengthened by this common satirical element.

There had been a marked tendency from at least early in the century for maygames to have a political or satirical content. In 1537 a maygame was played in Suffolk '"of a king how he should rule his realm"; in which one played husbandry and said many things against gentlemen more than was in the book of the play'.[2] The duke of Suffolk made efforts to have the man traced, but did not apparently succeed; he promised, however, that he would 'do his best...for staying of the games'.[3] The government clearly disapproved strongly of this kind of thing; they were considerably more tolerant of games that supported their policies, and there is certainly no evidence of any attempt to suppress the outburst of anti-papal maygames that the French ambassador reported in 1539:

> As to the sports and follies against the Pope made on land; there is not a village feast nor pastime anywhere in which there is not something inserted in derision of the Holy Father; and it seems, under correction, superfluous to write of them.[4]

He gives no information as to what form these games took; the only surviving example that suggests what they may have been like is the play of Robin Hood and Friar Tuck, 'verye proper to be played in Maye games', published by Copland in 1560, in which the friar is the epitome of the non-ideal religious, with a zestful addiction to the lusts of the flesh.[5] At least one man, probably Sir Richard Morison, had the idea of putting this potential of maygames to official use, and at about the same time as the French ambassador was making his complaint he drew up a plan for turning them into occasions of anti-papal propaganda in a splendid annual national Protestant triumph.[6] He addresses the King,

> In somer comenly upon the holy daies in most places of your realm, ther be playes of Robyn Hoode, mayde Marian, freer Tuck, wherin besides the lewdenes and rebawdry that ther is opened to the people, disobedience also to your officers, is tought, whilest these good bloodes go about to take from the shiref of Notyngham one that for offendyng the lawes shulde have suffered execution. Howmoche better is it that those plaies shulde be forbodden and deleted and others dyvysed to set forthe and declare lyvely before the peoples eies the abhomynation and wickednes of the bisshop of Rome, monkes, ffrees, nonnes, and such like, and to declare and open to them thobedience that your subiectes by goddes and mans lawes owe unto your magestie.

Nobody ever really managed to control the satirical side of the maygames, however, whether it bore a political, religious or personal aspect. The approach of the Civil War was still giving rise to similar outbursts, and a pamphlet of 1642 describes how an image of a particular Puritan – 'a godly honest man, having repetition of sermons in his house' – was set up on a maypole in Oxford and shot at with muskets by the onlookers.[7] Maygames were also a weapon in the religious controversies of Elizabeth's reign, and the theme made its way into the eclogue through the double connection of pastoral with both the games themselves and ecclesiastical satire.

The association may have been in Sidney's mind in the epilogue to the *Lady of May*, in which he denies Leicester's Catholic sympathies; but it was Spenser, with his characteristic stress on the native English element in his work, who first combined the two traditions of politico-religious comment. In his 'May' eclogue the licence of the games, the pastoral disguise and the appropriateness of the month to religious controversy and propaganda are brought together; and the discussion on the shepherd-pastor's responsibility for his flock is as appropriate to the season as the Maying itself. Maygames were continually associated by the Puritans with popish idolatry, and this connection extends into both the debate and the fable of the Fox and the Kid, with its theme of ecclesiastical conflict whether of Romish versus Protestant or of High versus Low Church.[8] The maygame theme was taken up again by various pamphleteers on both sides of the Marprelate controversy, the pamphlet war on the question of the institution of bishops that raged with immense vitality in the late 1580's. 'Martin Marprelate' himself tells of one parish priest who broke off the service to join the maygames, and of another who 'bare the Potters part' in a Robin Hood play.[9] The anti-Martinists frequently used the maygame theme as a means of mocking their opponents, and Nashe declares that he has in hand a new work entitled ' *The May-game of Martinisme*. Verie defflie set out, with Pompes, Pagents, Motions, Maskes, Scutchions, Emblems, Impreases, strange trickes, and deuises...', and with Martin himself as the Maid Marian.[10] If Spenser was the first poet to perceive that the relationship between May revels and pastoral went beyond the popular equation of the mode with Whitsun-ales and Robin Hood, he had an anonymous follower in the author of the fragmentary eclogue *A Tale of Robin Hood*, apparently written during the course of the Marprelate controversy.[11]

'A tale of Robin hoode, dialouge wise betweene Watt and Ieffry,' reads the heading. 'The morall is the overthrowe of the Abbyes, the like being attempted by the puritane, which is the wolfe; and the politician, which is the ffox, agaynst the bushops.' The poet once again associates maygames with the High Church party, but this time sympathetically: Robin Hood represents the bishops themselves. The maygame connection, however, ends with the name: the work is an eclogue, written by a poet well versed in Mantuan, and not a revel. The opening has a trace of Mantuan's irony, as Jeffry describes the fight of

> Two fatt ramms, for one leane ewe:
> With sucth force each other battred
> That their heads were both beemattred;
> So all three were in one plighte,
> She with leanesse, they with fight. (8–12)

Watt invites his companion to sit in the shade and tell his 'loves storye', but Jeffry, like Barclay's Codrus, demands instead either a popular romance or a 'tale of Robin hoode'. Watt accordingly proceeds to give an allegorical account of the rise of the bishops, of Robin, capable of hurting even Leviathan with his arrows. Robin then founds the monasteries, with Adam Bell at their head; and finally he establishes the 'Colleauge or the vniuersity', alias Little John:

> On two mounteynes hee thee planted,
> ffull of springs which never scanted...
> ffull of pretious stones and goold (67–8, 72)

– lines that recall not 'July' and the rising of the Medway in the hills but the eclogue from which that derives, Mantuan's eighth:

> unde fluunt amnes?...
> fulgens ubi nascitur aurum?[12]

In the course of time the monasteries decline from their first perfection:

Adam Bell was ware and wise
when hee firste beegann to rise,
till with fatnes of his fare
hee grew iolly, past all care,
As the bee in sommers prime
Sucks the marigoolde and thyme,
Sucks the rose and daffodill,
Leavinge, takinge, what hee will;
And from flowre to flowre doth glyde
Sweetly by the rivers side,
Where christall streames delightfull ronninges
Ar ever sweetned with his hummings.   (75–86)

He carelessly falls asleep; and the lion, Henry VIII, comes upon him and tears him to pieces. It is at this point that the poem begins to move into contemporary matters: the wolves and foxes see Adam 'in the lyons pawe', and immediately prepare to set on Robin. At this point, however, the single manuscript sheet preserving the poem breaks off, with the catchword 'thus –'. The allegory of the poem may be awkward, but at its best it works splendidly because of the clarity of the poetry. The author may owe some things to Mantuan, but the poem itself is thoroughly English. The shepherds' names, Watt and Jeffry, are at last realistic rather than poetic.[13] It is the only eclogue that actually does 'tell a tale of Robin Hood', but it uses more serious traditions of satire than maygame mockery – the traditions of the pastoral beast-fable and of the Petrarchan eclogue.

This theme of religious polemic forms half – the smaller half – of the background of the celebrations of Elizabeth as the May Lady or the Summer Queen. The other half is more directly concerned with the movement of the seasons; it is a theme that depends on the long association of pastoral, whether bucolic or *bergerie*, with spring, so that winter itself, or the changing course of the year, takes on an almost ironic significance. The pastoral exploitation of the contrast between the seasons goes back at least as far as the *Conflictus Veris et Hiemis* – it is typically a post-Classical phenomenon, and most emphasised in northern Europe where spring is so much more welcome than in Theocritus' Sicily or Virgil's derivative Arcadia – and poets of the Middle Ages and the Renaissance continually return to the theme: Marcabru's winter pastourelle of the girl who prefers honesty and exposure to the weather to protection and prostitution, the playwrights who saw in the Annunciation the shepherds' release from winter hardship to unchanging bliss, Boccaccio's sense of approaching winter and death, Bucarius' image of man's life as a flower beaten down in a storm and Strozzi's celebration of the seasons are just a few examples. The Elizabethans found the theme particularly fascinating, at various levels of seriousness. Bolton's 'Sheepheards Song: a Caroll or Himne for Christmas' sees Christ as transcending seasonal change:

Sprung is the mirthfull May,
Which Winter cannot marre;   (*EH* p. 136)

and the subjection of the world of the pastoral love-lyric to the seasons is echoed from poem to poem, supremely in Raleigh's reply to Marlowe's *Passionate Shepherd*. Marlowe's shepherdess may need 'fayre lined slippers for the cold', but otherwise she will live in a world where every day is a May-morning; Raleigh's reply is an acknowledgement of the harsh reality of the world, and of the intense attraction of the dream.

Time drives the flocks from field to fold...

The flowers doe fade, and wanton fieldes,
To wayward winter reckoning yeeldes...

But could youth last, and love still breede,
Had joyes no date, nor age no neede,
Then these delights my minde might move,
To live with thee, and be thy love.   (*EH* p. 193)

It is the opposition of the fantasy world of idyllic *bergerie*, with its spring setting, its rustic gifts and its shepherdess inclined to love, and the brazen world with all its hard conditions; and Raleigh admits his longing for the golden. The central import of the theme of the contrast of the seasons is always mutability and mortality: man in Paradise knew no seasonal change until death came into the world. Spenser worked his way through the calendar form to the declaration of eternity within mutability; and the pastoral addressed to the Queen is perpetually pressing towards the same kind of statement. Her motto was *Semper eadem*, 'ever the same'; her birthday was 7 September, at the end of the summer, and her Accession Day 17 November, at the beginning of winter, yet her poets found in her a symbol of a perpetual May. Extravagant as the idea may be in literal terms, it cannot be dismissed as mere flattery. The number of poets who took up the theme and the multiplicity of forms it assumed show that it fulfilled a genuine need of expression – a belief that England was a good country to live in, that the Elizabethan age was a great one, that the arts were flourishing as they had never done before, and that all these things were in some way embodied in the person of the Queen herself.

It was Spenser's 'April' that guaranteed the popularity of the theme of Eliza as 'Queene of shepheardes all', as the Spring Queen. She is attended by the Graces, the Muses and the ladies of the lake, but the 'shepheards daughters, that dwell on the greene' have their own right and duty to pay her homage. She is crowned with an abundance of flowers, like a goddess of spring – or like a shepherdess – but some have special meanings: the red and white roses, the olive branches. Spenser reserved his May eclogue for a theological discussion on maygames, but to Eliza is given the first eclogue of the spring, the declaration of blossoming abundance after the 'bitter blast' and 'winters sorrow' of the preceding months. Echoes of this poem recur throughout the Elizabethan age in pastoral celebrations of the Queen. The closest imitation is Rowland's song in praise of Beta, 'the shepheards Goddesse', in Drayton's third eclogue. Drayton does not give his eclogues Spenser's framework of the seasons, but this song, 'which once thou sangst to me in Janeveer' (38), is an evocation of spring made in winter: the earth is in full bloom, the nightingale and thrush, 'chief musick of our maye', provide the accompaniment to the shepherds' songs of praise. The panegyric quality of the piece is emphasised by Rowland's preliminary declaration of pastoral insufficiency:

Fair Betas praise beyond our straine doth stretch,
Her notes too hie for my poore pipe to reach,
   poore oten reede   (18–20)

– the humble *tenuis avena* can only be a paradoxical means of honouring the Queen. Spenser turns a compliment in the same way in *Colin Clouts Come Home Againe*, when Cuddy objects to Colin's description of Cynthia as an angel on the grounds of decorum; the panegyric of Cynthia in the whole poem has a double emphasis, on the lyrically compelling portrait of her as the Spring

Queen, and on the idea of her as shepherdess of her people, ruling a land of pastoral peace and content.

> There all happie peace and plenteous store
> Conspire in one to make contented blisse...
> The shepheards there abroad may safely lie,
> On hills and downes, withouten dread or daunger:
> No rauenous wolues the good mans hope destroy,
> Nor outlawes fell affray the forest raunger.
> There learned arts do florish in great honor,
> And Poets wits are had in peerlesse price:
> Religion hath lay powre to rest vpon her,
> Aduancing vertue and suppressing vice. (310–11, 316–23)

In case this sounds too good to be true, Colin adds a footnote that 'graceless men' abuse these virtues, but the lines still express forcefully the ideal that the Elizabethans felt the Queen to embody: true poetry and true religion in an ambience of pastoral peace.

The first work to show any direct influence from the *Shepheardes Calender* was Thomas Blenerhasset's *Revelation of the True Minerva*, published in 1582,[14] and it is 'April' that the author echoes. The 'true Minerva' of the title is of course Elizabeth, chosen by the gods to become the new goddess of wisdom. Mercury, who has been sent out to survey the earth for a mortal worthy to be deified, comes back and reports the general desolation of the world: Troy is razed without trace, Parnassus overgrown with brambles, 'Barbarye doth Christendom deuoure'. Only in England are the splendours of the ancient world preserved under Minerva's reign, where peace has brought prosperity to Troynovaunt. There follows a strange interlude apparently designed to show what such a reign was like, in terms of the common man rather than myth. Pan makes his appearance with three shepherds, and as he pipes one sings, one sighs and one groans. First Bembus, then Colon and his wife, tell of how their rustic wealth has come to nothing through war and pillage, the crops have been destroyed, towns burnt, flocks stolen. Colon declares,

> The people for the princes pride are plagde; (Bi^a)

it is the commons who suffer from the effects of high politics, who have to endure the destruction of the countryside and see the produce of their labour consumed by soldiers. The shepherd speaks for the suffering common man, just as in the *bergeries moralisées* of the fifteenth century. In *Mieulx-que-Devant* two shepherds had lamented the same conditions that Bembus and Colon now suffer: the hedges are fired or trodden down; sheep and cattle are taken; the country is ruled by armed men; shepherds' singing and piping has ceased. But Elizabeth has maintained a world of pastoral peace in England. Bembus and Colon are victims of the European wars, of France or the Low Countries. The third shepherd, their servant Epizenes who had set out on his travels through aspiring ambition, comes from the land of 'godesse great Elizabeth',

> where want of warre and quiet rest
> Doth plainely proue Brittaine to be the best. (Bi^b)

When the Queen stayed at Bisham in the course of her progress in 1592, the entertainment – probably written by Lyly – repeats the theme, as the shepherdess Sybilla speaks, like Epizenes, of the blessed state of England compared with the rest of Europe:

By her it is (Pan) that all our cartes that thou seest are laden with corne, when in other countries they are filled with harneys; that our horses are ledde with a whip, theirs with a launce; that our rivers flow with fish, theirs with bloode; our cattel feede on pastures, they feed on pastures like cattel. One hand she stretcheth to Fraunce, to weaken Rebels; the other to Flaunders, to strengthen Religion... We, upon our knees, wil entreat her to come into the valley, that our houses may be blessed with her presence, whose hartes are filled with quietnes by her government.[15]

Pan blesses the Queen in words that emphasise anew the contrast between the abject misery of a country at war and the eternal fertile spring of her own land.

Here I yeelde all the flockes of these fields to your Highnes: greene be the grasse where you treade: calme the water where you rowe: sweete the aire where you breathe: long the life that you live, happy the people that you love: this is all I can wish. During your abode, no theft shall be in the woods; in the fields no noise, in the vallies no spies: myselfe will keepe all safe.

She is under the special protection of the shepherds' god, herself like a goddess of nature; and Ceres herself yields up her crown to her, acknowledging a greater cause of plenty in the land.

The emphasis on olives in the lists of flowers and branches brought to Eliza in various eclogues and songs springs from the same sentiment – they represent rather more than a formal compliment, as does the union of the red and white roses. Blenerhasset places them all side by side to stress further the internal peace of the country under Elizabeth:

From hiest top out of one stately stemme
Two royall Roses white and redde did growe,
The Oliue tree most brauely grew by them. (Ei[b])

He does make one change from Spenser in his account of the garlands and flowers promised to the new Minerva. Spenser, writing in 1579 when the possibility of the Queen's marriage to Alençon was still very much in the air, had included a cautiously obscure hint as to a 'match with the fayre flowre Delice'. By 1582 all prospect of the marriage was over, and the fleur-de-lis could resume its place as the symbol of war for England and so be rejected.

The Flower deluce though louely to beholde
In question these the wisest did it call,
And to refuse the same the gods were bolde:
It representes trouble and cruel thrall. (Dii[b])

It is not only the other gods who pay tribute to Eliza: as in the *Shepheardes Calender*, the country people have their opportunity to show their own service to the Queen.

Then might you see the rurall dames come in,
The youth like frie, olde folke like foules did flocke:
With bags and baskits filde vp to the brimme,
For Fauni did the Forrest gates vnlocke:
And simple Cate clad in a russet frocke
Brought branches thence, and flowers aprone full,
The waies were woods made by the gadding scull. (Eii[a])

They go to the woods to fetch branches and flowers: it is the same form of celebration as for a Maying. The deified Eliza is still the queen of the country revels.

The *Lady of May* was the first work to place the Queen in the pastoral world in the setting of spring; and its great achievement lies in Sidney's imaginative creation of Elizabeth as the May Lady, the spring or summer queen of the shepherd revels. 'No estate can be compared to be the Lady of the whole moneth of May as I am,' the May Lady declares on her first entry; she is the sovereign of the year's festivities at the time of growth and abundance. Yet it is the Queen herself who possesses the highest estate, and at the end the May Lady hands over the qualities of her office: 'I will wish you good night, praying to God according to the title I possesse, that as hitherto it hath excellently done, so hence forward the florishing of May, may long remaine in you and with you'.[16] 'In you and with you': Elizabeth is the bearer of spring, the incarnation of a perpetual May. The motif gained an increasingly strong hold over the imagination of the country in the succeeding years. The autumn dates of Elizabeth's two annual festivals, Accession Day and her birthday, emphasised rather than discouraged the May-like qualities of the celebrations: she is the sovereign of an everlasting spring, and the revels of her true subjects, the shepherds, can continue all the year through the reflection of her May. Throughout the country on Accession Day processions were held, bells rung and bonfires lit; at court the day was celebrated by tilts, held annually from 1581 (the year when Sidney made his appearance as Shepherd Knight) and probably before then. The festivals that were used to honour her sometimes consisted of panegyric alone, but propaganda and allegory often had a part in them too: very often the praise included the fact that she was the guarantee of Protestant Truth in the country. Sir Richard Morison, with his plans for making something more patriotically Protestant out of the maygames, would have seen his desire fulfilled in the promotion of Accession Day into a national holiday, and the government fully encouraged its development as a replacement of saints' days; it was itself made a feast day of the Established Church in 1576.

A pageant has been preserved in the so-called Ditchley Manuscript that shows how Protestant pastoral and rustic revels could be combined to honour the Queen.[17] The central character is a knight who has sworn to fight for the Queen each year on Accession Day and now comes before her to fulfil his vow; he is presented, 'clownishly clad', to the Queen the day before the tilts, by a hermit whose speech of introduction makes up the piece. The knight is accompanied by a 'homely rude Companye' of peasants singing and dancing, 'no better then Shepards, and heardmen, breaders of Cattell, and followers of the plough'. Wild men were all but inevitable as part of the pageantry staged to welcome Elizabeth on her progresses; peasants were a new feature. They made their only appearance in the pageantry of the 1570's in the rustic wedding at Kenilworth, and that apparently was a burlesque, a comic interlude; the pageant here presents something much more closely in touch with the pastoral tradition. The knight has left the court in despair, and in the course of his wanderings has met the hermit, who has suffered, like himself, from the serpent Wrong. The knight decides to take up a solitary life, but then meets the peasants searching for their lost cattle. They are about to run away when he assures them that he is 'only foe to wronge'; whereupon they entreat him to go with them. They may be homely and rude, even comic, but they live in pastoral purity and uprightness, and the knight can find among them a life free from all the vices and abuses associated with courts. The conventionality of the theme removes too much personal application it might risk – it would scarcely be tactful to attack court vices too strongly in a pageant for the Queen; but Elizabeth is presented, as she is in

Colin Clouts Come Home Againe, not as the centre of the restless and evil court but as the sovereign of the good and the simple, through whom their state of pastoral happiness exists. In the country

> ther was no deuises or discorses of princes or stats, nor whisperinge of lies to breed or feed factions, to vptorne noble houses, and troble comon wealths,... no sarvants of Ambition, thatt intangle themselves oft in ther owne snares, but they loocke to ther Cattell, and followe ther plough, that doth reuerence the magistrate, and obaye the lawe, that loues to heare of no change, and goes no farther, but daylye thancks god for his benefitts, and prayes much for fayer weather; and more for that blessed fayer queene, by whose holy and happye gouernment, they enioye the gospell of grace, and the safe days of peace.

The new age of pastoral innocence and peace surpasses any other such state through its knowledge of the Truth, that is, Protestantism; at times the Golden Age sounds like the Anglican Church in its mood of homilist propaganda. Moreover, the peasants have just heard from their curate about a 'holidaye which passed all the popes holidayes', to be kept on 17 November. They all declare their intention of following the knight as he comes to joust before the Queen, not only in order to see her but to join in the tournament if they are allowed – indeed, whether they are allowed or not. Elizabeth, it is suggested, is adored by the simple country folk as the Virgin was, but for more immediate reasons. Not only is she the upholder of religious truth, she is also the guarantee of peace. The most genuine and faithful service of the Queen is found not at court but among the commons and those close to them in spirit, for whom simplicity and loyalty are one and the same. The knight himself comes to offer his strength in her service as their leader.

The pageant is intended for presentation by courtiers on a court occasion: it does not in itself give any evidence of popular expression of emotion for the Queen. But it does indicate how closely rustic merry-making, the 'homely melodye' the peasants have brought to honour her, was associated with the celebration of the national Protestant holiday. Angel Day went so far as to insert a special section describing 'a certain yearly feast' held in honour of the Queen's accession in his translation of Amyot's version of that most idyllic of pastoral romances, *Daphnis and Chloe*, and he considered it of sufficient importance to give his work the sub-title, 'The Shepheards Holidaie'.[18] In the same year, 1587, Maurice Kyffyn published *The Blessednes of Brytaine, or a Celebration of the Queenes Holyday*,[19] which plods through the achievements of the reign – currency reform, the improvement of the royal armoury and so on – and culminates in an account of Accession Day, 'more fit to be solemniz'd', as the marginal note affirms, 'than many other dayes noted in the Kalender'. Kyffyn calls on the knights to do their best in the tilts, then turns to the peasants:

> Ye Cuntry folke, foorth stalking in your feelds,
> Lowd Carols sing, to celebrat this Tyme;
> Show Signes of ioy (as Cuntry manner yeldes,)
> In Sporting Games, with Daunce, and rurall Ryme:
>   Ech Swayne, and Sheppard, sound his piping Reede,
>   For ioy, enioying Feelds, and Flocks to feede.

The style is rhetorical, and the contrast between the heroic and the pastoral is poetically useful; but in view of Kyffyn's persistent clinging to fact, it is at least possible that he is drawing from life as well as literary traditions.

Shepherd revels proved an admirable setting for celebrating Elizabeth, especially the springtime Cotswold feasts such as Drayton describes. The entertainments provided for her in 1592 at the Cotswold castle of Sudeley were all variations on the pastoral mode, with greetings delivered by a shepherd and a pastoral interlude about Apollo and Daphne. The last of them, which was in fact never presented because of bad weather, was to have been a mimic revel with its shepherd king and queen. The introduction consisted of a man disguised as a ram and, since he could only say 'Bea', an interpreter, who welcomes Elizabeth as

> such a one...by whome all the shepheards should have their flocks in safety, and their own lives, all the country quietness, and the whole world astonishment.[20]

As in the Ditchley pageant, she is sovereign of the pastoral world in more than a metaphorical sense. The interpreter goes on to tell her that the Constable has ordered the day to be 'kept holliday', and invites her to watch the shepherds' pastimes. The three taking part in the holiday revels are named Melibeus, the Cutter of Cotsolde and a shepherdess Nisa – a good mixture of Classical pastoral and local colour. They choose a king and queen who then have the right to ask questions and issue commands – the same game as is played by the shepherds of the *Jeu de Robin et Marion*. They finally call for an almanac, which is filled with references to Elizabeth; then they at last realize she is present, kneel to her and acknowledge her as the true sovereign in the pastoral world and their own titles for the games they are.

The entertainment uses themes that are centuries old, but it has a significance beyond summer pastimes. Melibeus reads from the almanac,

> The seventh of September Happiness was born into the world. It may be the eleventh is some wonder; the Moone at the ful, tis true, for Cynthia never shined so bright. The twelfth, the weather inclined to moisture, and shepheards devises to drynes. The thirteenth, Sommer goeth from hence; the signe in Virgo; Vivat clarissima Virgo.

September 7 was the Queen's birthday; she arrived at Sudeley on the eleventh, and was to depart that day, the thirteenth. And with the passing of the Summer Queen, summer itself would die. It is a conceit that was often used, but that was particularly rich in the pastoral context, the shepherd world that found its golden point in maygames and summer revels. Just as Elizabeth brought peace to this world, so she brought its other idyllic attributes of fertility, flowers, birdsong and sunshine. When she visited Elvetham in 1591 the landscape itself welcomed her:

> Te, te, dulcissima princeps,
> Terra, polus, fluvii, plantae, pecudesque salutant,[21]
>
> *Sweet princess, the earth, the heavens, the rivers, plants and herds greet thee;*

but when she departs the fertile season goes with her, leaving behind nothing but winter and dreariness,

> For how can Sommer stay, when Sunne departs?[22]

The conceit has its other side: because Elizabeth is summer, because she is 'semper eadem' in the changing cycle of the seasons and among the troubles of the world, the country never knows winter. Edmund Bolton's *Canzon Pastorall in honour of her Majestie*[23] is a winter poem proclaiming England's eternal spring:

Naked the fields are, bloomelesse are the briers,
  Yet we a Sommer have,
Who in our clime kindleth these living fires,
  Which bloomes can on the briers save...
    Winter though every where
    Hath no abiding heere:
On Brooks and Briers she doth rule alone,
The Sunne which lights our world is alwayes one.

Nashe describes the same imaginative aura surrounding her in *Summer's Last Will and Testament*: she is the perfection of the year's cycle, and the peace of her reign is an extension of her image as the Queen of perpetual summer.[24]
  If summer was her season, May was her month:

This sweet and merry month of May,
While Nature wantons in her prime,
And birds do sing, and beasts do play,
For pleasure of the joyful time,
I choose the first for holiday,
And greet Eliza with a rhyme.
O beauteous queen of second Troy,
Take well in worth a simple toy.[25]

Eliza was above all the Queen's pastoral name, but just as Spenser gives her divine parentage, so she herself becomes almost a goddess, and the earth springs at her approach. This is the feeling Watson expressed for her visit to Elvetham:

Now birds record new harmonie,
And trees do whistle melodie;
Now everie thing that nature breeds
Doth clad itself in pleasant weeds.[26]

When the poem was reprinted in *Englands Helicon* it was given a significant heading – 'The Nimphes meeting their *May Queene*, entertaine her with this Dittie'. *The Triumphs of Oriana*, perhaps compiled to celebrate the Queen's birthday,[27] works through the same conventions, honouring Elizabeth as the queen of the springing earth and of shepherds homely or Arcadian. She comes like Flora herself, garland-crowned in the manner not only of Primavera but of shepherdesses down the centuries; the crown of flowers is the highest honour the pastoral world can offer. Her birthday may have been in September, but still there is one setting, picked out by Morley, that is most appropriate for her:

Lo where she comes in gaudy green arraying,
  A prince of beauty rich and rare
For her delight pretends to go a-maying.   (XIII)

'With us as May, September hath a prime,' as Bolton expressed it. Other songs in the *Triumphs* select equally popular themes: in Richard Carlton's madrigal she is the shepherds' 'sovereign mistress...that kept their flocks and them from fear' (VII). There may seem a vast gulf between the rustic pastoral of the game of Kings and Queens and Diana's nymphs strewing roses, but the two worlds meet in the person of Elizabeth. The shepherds of the *Triumphs* feast to celebrate the day, as shepherds had feasted in literature and perhaps in life since the time of the Chester play and before; and in one of Morley's canzonets their music is dedicated to her.

Blow, shepherds, blow your pipes with gladsome glee resounding.
See where the fair Eliza comes with love and grace abounding.[28]

It was only when the figure of Elizabeth came to provide an imaginative stimulus that idyllic shepherd revels really took hold as a literary motif among English court poets.

It may be in this context that two of the most puzzling poems in *Englands Helicon* should be placed, *Wodenfrides Song in Praise of Amargana* and the following poem, *Another of the Same.*[29]

> The pathes where Amargana treads,
> With flowrie tap'stries Flora spreads.
> And Nature cloathes the ground in greene:
> To glad our lovely Sommer Queene.
>
> . . . .
>
> Great Pan (our God) for her deere sake,
> This feast and meeting bids us make,
> Of Sheepheards, Lads, and Lasses sheene:
> To glad our lovely Sheepheards Queene.
>
> . . . .
>
> All happiness let Heaven her lend,
> And all the Graces her attend,
> Thus bid me pray the Muses nine,
> Long live our lovely Sommer Queene.

It would fit the context of a progress excellently. The second poem, in praise of Amargana's beauty, sounds equally as if it refers to Elizabeth. Much of the description of her looks is conventional, and the Queen was too close to the convention, with her golden hair and so on, for identification to be certain that way. But the opening lines leave less room for conjecture:

> Happy Sheepheards sit and see,
>   with joy,
>   The peerelesse wight:
> For whose sake Pan keepes from ye
>   annoy,
>   and gives delight.
> Blessing this pleasant Spring,
> Her praises must I sing.

If the poems do come from some lost romance of Wodenfride and Amargana, it still seems likely that the poet was drawing on the Eliza tradition to describe his lady, so choosing the highest terms he could. The echoes of 'April' – in the Graces and Muses, the rhythm of the second poem, phrases such as 'the peerelesse wight' – give proof of that.

Peele wrote his *Anglorum Feriae*[30] to commemorate the Accession Day of 1595, and the work again shows how closely the festivities were linked with the idea of pastoral revels and drawn into the imaginative setting of summer:

> Weare Eglantine
> And wreathes of Roses red and white put on
> In honor of that day yow Lovelie Nymphes,
> And paeans singe and sweete melodious songes:
> Alonge the chaulkie clyffes of Albion
> Leade Englandes Lovely Shepherdes in a daunce
> Ore hill and dale and downes and daysie plotts
> And bee that Day Englandes highe Hollyday
> And hollydayes and highe daies be they all
> High hollydaies, daies minutes monethes and howres
> That multyplie the number of hir yeares
> Yeares that for us begett this golden age
> Wherein we live in safety under hir.   (39–51)

Under her rule the golden age, the age of peace and plenty, is restored. She is not only Eliza, she is

> Englands Astraea, Albions shininge Sunne. (331)

The Virgin Queen takes Mary's place as the Virgo of Virgil's fourth eclogue. The celebration of Elizabeth as Astraea is closely linked with the presentation of her as Shepherd Queen or May Lady through the original myth of the Golden Age. The associations of Astraea could be more imperial than pastoral; but in Peele's pageant *Descensus Astraeae* she appears 'with hir sheephook' as if it was the most natural thing for her to carry.[31] That Astraea was herself a shepherdess is a new development of an old idea; Peele is taking Dupuys' idea of her residence among the shepherds to its logical conclusion. Her time on earth had been the age of pastoral innocence, and the connection follows naturally enough: if Apollo could be a shepherd, certainly Astraea must have been a shepherdess. The innocence and integrity of pastoral life was particularly closely associated with her. To celebrate any monarch as the bearer of a golden age was a commonplace of Renaissance flattery,[32] but in the figure of Elizabeth, the second Astraea, the compliment rang true in an exceptional way. The name implied something about the realm, about her second body, the state, more than about her own person: Astraea existed through her embodiment in the country, in its justice, its peace, its abundance, its perfect balance of the seasons. To call Elizabeth, the Summer Queen, Astraea, was to say that the land reflected her.

Even this representation of the Queen was rapidly drawn into the almost inevitable theological pastoral of the age. Astraea-Elizabeth's task in Peele's pageant is to defend her fountain from Superstitition, a friar, and Ignorance, a Catholic priest. The flock she tends are the pastor's flock as well as her subjects – Elizabeth is after all the Head of the Church – and the landscape they inhabit is the country of the Good Shepherd of Psalm 23.

> Feed on my flocke amóng the gladsome greene
> Where heavenly Nectar flowes above the banckes.
> Such pastures are not common to be seene,
> Pay to immortal Jove immortall thankes. (54–7)

She is the same ministering shepherdess in *Anglorum Feriae*, where Peele celebrates her as

> reserved for Englandes happines,
> And comforte of the longe afflicted flock
> That straide lyke skattered sheep skard fro the folde. (64–6)

She is portrayed again as a shepherdess protecting her flock from wolves in a presentation set of Latin poems written by boys of St. Paul's School, perhaps in 1573;[33] John of Garland once described the other Virgin in the same terms. The Astraea theme also links up with another pastoral motif, the concern with astronomy of the calendars, for Astraea was identified with the constellation Virgo. Astraea-Elizabeth is a 'radiant light' to England, a destructive comet to Spain.[34] The Queen is continually described in terms of the heavens: that she surpasses Phoebus and Cynthia is a common tribute paid to her. Perhaps Michael East makes the further association with the calendars as he describes her as the 'shepherds' star' in his contribution to the *Triumphs of Oriana* (1): in the calendar tradition the shepherds would have their eyes constantly turning to the heavens, and it would be fitting for them to see Eliza as their guiding light.

Astraea is a goddess both of plenty and of eternal spring; Elizabeth is the creator of prosperity and plenty, the ever-shining sun, the Spring Queen whose feast day lay at the beginning of winter. Many of the poems addressed to her as Astraea picture her in these terms. The countess of Pembroke wrote a *Dialogue between two shepherds Thenot and Piers, in praise of Astraea,*[35] which is a kind of singing-match *conflictus* in which each of Thenot's hyperbolic compliments is denied by Piers as being too mean. Thenot declares,

> Astraea may be justly said
> A field in flowery robe arrayed,
> In season freshly springing.

Piers replies with a reminder of the eternal spring of the Golden Age:

> That Spring endures but shortest time,
> This never leaves Astraea's clime.

Sir John Davies, in his *Hymnes of Astraea* (1599), a series of poems on the acrostic 'Elisabetha Regina', frequently writes of the Queen in this way, a theme reinforced by the fact that the book was written for presentation on Accession Day. The country flourishes with its sovereign, reflecting her constant spring, and it is to that season he appeals to crown her with garlands in the manner of the shepherd queen, with

> *E*ternall garlands of thy flowers,
> *G*reene garlands never wasting;
> *I*n her shall last our states faire spring,
> *N*ow and for ever flourishing,
> *A*s long as heaven is lasting.[36]

Flora herself, the goddess of the spring, goes a-Maying to the court (IX). Astraea may be exiled Justice returned to the earth, the contemplation of her mind may send Davies into mystical neoplatonic ecstasy, but it is as the May Queen that she is supreme.

> *E*ach day of thine, sweete moneth of May,
> *L*ove makes a solemne holy-day,
> *I* will perform like dutie,
> *S*ince thou resemblest every way
> *A*straea Queene of beautie.
> *B*oth you fresh beauties do partake,
> *E*ithers aspect doth Sommer make.   (IV)

Elizabeth is Flora, Astraea, Oriana with the flowers breaking into blossom at her feet; she is a goddess 'greater than Ceres'. She is also the new Augustus, whose reign brings again the peace and contentment that enables Tityrus to sing –

> Elizabetha Deus nobis haec otia fecit.[37]

Tityrus had become the poet of the *Aeneid*, who sang of the wars of Troy; but New Troy's epic was an epic of peace. The Judgement of Paris had brought war and destruction; Elizabeth outshines all three goddesses, Juno, Minerva and Venus, and her realm is 'Elizium', where the pastoral bliss that Paris destroyed is preserved. Blenerhasset touched on the theme, Peele elaborated it in his *Arraignment of Paris*; later in the reign the theme came to refer more specifically to poetry. Poetry, peace and prosperity go hand in hand; the quiet life of the fields, under its summer goddess, enables the shepherds to flourish, and specifically to pipe. Francis Sabie's third eclogue is

partly devoted to this idea. An old shepherd tells how he remembers a time
when the herdsmen

> Could not vse their pipes, could not as we do together
> Sit thus far fro the flocks,   (III.11–2)

for fear of the wolf's attacks; and in the final song of the singing-match that
makes up the main part of the eclogue, one of his younger companions
explains how the change has come about: through Elizabeth. It is she who
overgoes the rival goddesses, she who delivered the country from 'Romish
Pharaohs tyrannous bondage' (199) and protected it from 'Spanish armies',
and whose reign provides the conditions for a life of peaceful piping:

> The plowman now may reap his haruest in ioy,
> Each man may boldly lead a quiet life here,
> We shepherds may sit with our herd in field, and
>   merilie pipe here.   (216–9)

The shepherd merrily piping is only partially Classical: Tityrus and Jolly
Wat are scarcely distinguishable in this new Arcadia.

As 'shepherds' Queen', Elizabeth is the sovereign not only of her subjects
but specifically of her poets; and pastoral poetry depends on her not only for
much of its subject-matter but for its very existence. The withdrawal of her
favour could be mirrored in poetic sterility – a theme Raleigh takes up in his
winter pastoral *The Ocean's Love to Cynthia*. The sun of Elizabeth no longer
shines, and flocks and blossom and singing, all the attributes of Arcadia or
idyllic *bergerie*, are extinguished by storm and cold. Francis Davison, editor
of the *Poetical Rhapsody*, wrote an eclogue for the collection describing the
same winter of discontent as suffered by a shepherd named Eubulus, the
good counsellor;[38] the poem is in fact an account of the continuing disgrace
suffered by his father, William Davison, who as Secretary of the Council had
despatched the death warrant of Mary Queen of Scots. Eubulus used to
enjoy

>   the pleasant spring of her sweete grace,
> And then could sing and dance, and sporte and play;

now he is stricken with 'dreriment', with age and woe, and he asks,

> How long, alas, how long doth last
> My endlesse Winter without hope of Spring?

His sun has withdrawn, leaving him in darkness. Davison chooses the name
Astraea for the Queen: he will not accuse her of injustice, but at the same
time he suggests that justice ought to restore to the good counsellor a more
fruitful crop than grief and contempt.

The season for the celebration of Elizabeth as the incarnation of May, at
the onset of winter, was paralleled by the increasing number of these celebrations as her years advanced. By the 1590's she was herself in the winter of
her age, and it was obvious to everybody that her summer could not last for
ever. The many November–May celebrations of the decade are a tribute to
her personality and energy, and also a form of flattery; they are also an
invocation of peace and stability at a time when the sovereign through whom
such a state existed was moving towards death. There is a quality almost of
sympathetic magic about them as there is in so many of the entertainments
and masques of the period, as if the presentation of the desired good would

play its part in bringing it to pass. The *Hymnes of Astraea* are addressed not to the old woman but to her second body, the state, and to the spirit that had made the May image so appropriate for her; and they are almost a prayer for the continuation of the spring of the country reflected from her. It may be that the death of Essex cast its shadow over even this aspect of her reign, for in her last years these celebrations almost ceased;[39] but the tradition was not forgotten, and it gains a new poignancy in the elegies mourning her death. The pastoral themes of mutability, of lamentation, of heavenly bliss, even shepherd revels, acquire a new poetic dimension by contrast with it.

The first pastoral elegy for Elizabeth, describing winter closing in on the Spring Queen, was in fact written many years earlier: Spenser's 'November', on the death of Dido, of Elissa,[40] the Eliza of 'April'. Spenser's declared intention was to make 'a Calendar for euery yeare', to describe the whole life of man in terms of the months and seasons, and the inclusion of the elegy makes the work complete: even the death of the Queen must be taken into account. The identification must have been clear to his contemporaries: the name and the month would both bring Elizabeth to mind, and there are many other indications as well. One of Thenot's lines is ambiguous, but may none the less refer to the May Lady whose feast day lay in November:

> The fayrest May she was that ever went. (39)

If the phrase is a coincidence, it is a happy one, and it was taken up after her death. E. K. may declare his ignorance as to the identity of Dido, but this is coupled with his description of her as 'some mayden of greate bloud' and his reference to her father 'the greate shephearde' as not being 'as some vainely suppose the God Pan' – a gloss that recalls 'April' even while he denies the association. He clearly cannot state that the elegy is for Elizabeth, just as he pretends ignorance over Grindal. Spenser himself gives plenty of indications that he is speaking of the Queen. Colin's elegy abounds with echoes of his song from 'April', with the joyful celebrations turned to mourning. The ladies of the lake had brought a coronal of olive, the Muses bays; in 'November'

> The water Nymphs, that wont with her to sing and daunce,
> And for her girlond Oliue braunches beare,
> Now balefull boughes of Cypres doen aduaunce:
> The Muses, that were wont greene bayes to weare,
> Now bringen bitter Eldre braunches seare. (143–7)

The flowers, the meadows and the flocks fade in mourning. Eliza had out-shone Phoebus, she had appeared amid blossoming abundance; now all is changed.

> The sonne of all the world is dimme and darke... (67)
> The fayrest floure our gyrlond all emong,
> Is faded quite and into dust ygoe.
> Sing now ye shepheards daughters, sing no more
>   The songs that Colin made in her prayse. (75–8)
> The gaudie girlonds deck her graue,
> The faded flowres her corse embraue. (108–9)

She was the ruler of the shepherd revels who had given them cakes and cracknels and 'clouted Creame'; she was the 'shepherds wonted solace'. Besides all this, Dido is the shepherdess who had kept her flock safe from the wolves. The vision of Elizabeth as a saint, as a goddess, is presented as a reality:

> She raignes a goddesse now emong the saintes
> That whilome was the saynt of shepheards light:
> And is enstalled nowe in heauens hight.
> I see thee blessed soule, I see,
> Walke in Elisian fieldes so free. (175–9)

Elysium was her own land as well as Heaven; and Heaven itself becomes almost a mirror image of the peace and happiness she had given her country.

Elizabeth died on 24 March, 1603, at the very beginning of the spring. Among the first poets to lament her death was John Lane, with his *Elegie vpon the death of the high renowned Princesse, our late Soueraigne Elizabeth*. He describes his poem as an 'April-song': that was presumably the month when he wrote it, and the association of showers suggests the sorrow of his theme. Equally importantly, it is a lament for Eliza, for the Queen of Spenser's 'April'. The identification of Dido and Elizabeth could not be made too openly during her lifetime; after her death, its full appropriateness could be revealed. His elegy echoes both 'April' and 'November'

> Lament, lament, you Sheepeheards daughters all,
> And eke you Virgins chast, lament her fall:
> The Goddesse of your sports is lapt in lead,
> And fair Virginia's fairest Queene is dead,
> Oh, come, and do her corse with flowres embraue,
> And play some solemne musicke by her graue,
> Then sing her Requiem in some dolefull Verse,
> Or do the songs of Colin Clout rehearse.

Lane would not call on the shepherds' daughters to sing the joyful song to Eliza; Spenser was dead, but Colin had left behind the elegy for this occasion that demanded the greatest of poetic tributes. Lane goes on to take up other themes from later celebrations of Elizabeth: she is Drayton's Beta, she is the Phoenix, Astraea, Judith, and also the perpetual Spring Queen whose season is at last ended.

> Weepe, Flora, weepe, and doffe thy spangled gowne,
> And weare no more thy flower enameld crowne:
> Cast not thy Tapstry mantels at our feete,
> Nor fill the fragrant ayre with odours sweete;
> For loe, the Flower which was so fresh and gay,
> And made Nouember like another May,
> How daintily so ere it did compose
> The beautie of the white and crimson Rose,
> The Flower is parcht, the silken leafe is blasted,
> The Roote decay'd, and all the glory wasted.

Yet Lane, like Spenser, finds comfort in the thought of her new bliss as the highest of the saints, matching her position as God's favoured handmaid on earth.

> Raine euer there on that Elyzian greene:
> Eliza, well may be Elyziums Queene.

Lane's April-song was followed by Chettle's May lament. *Englands Mourning Garment*, 'wrought by plaine Shepheardes, for the death of that most excellent Empresse Elizabeth', reads like the consummation of all that had gone before in the reign. The form of the work is the mixed poetry and prose such as Sidney had used in the *Arcadia*; the shepherds' names are taken from 'November'. The piece opens as Thenot questions Collin on the cause of his grief – a grief that prevents him even from celebrating May. Collin breaks his pipe in despair and faints; but when the other shepherds gather round he recovers sufficiently to speak of the virtues of 'that sacred Nymph, that careful Shepheardesse Eliza'.

> Sweete Virgin, shee was borne on the Eue of that blessed Virgins Natiuitie, holy Mary, Christs mother: shee dyed on the Eue of the Anunciation of the same most holy Virgin; a blessed note of her endlesse blessednesse...Shee came vnto the Crowne after her royall sisters death, like a fresh Spring euen in the beginning of Winter, and brought vs comfort, as the cleare Sunne doth to storm-dressed Marriners; shee left the Crowne likewise in the winter of her Age, and the beginning of our Spring: as if the Ruler of heauen had ordained her coronation in our sharpest Winter to bring vs happinesse, and vncrowned her in our happiest Spring, to leaue vs in more felicitie by her Succeeder. (pp. 104–5)

She is the shepherds' queen, the spring queen, who had replaced the Catholic saints in their hearts as in the calendar. As Dekker noted in his *Wonderfull Yeare*, she left behind her a nation 'that neuer shouted any other Aue than for her name'; and at the season when 'Shepheards sat piping, country wenches singing', the death of the 'Shepheards Goddesse' cut off their joys. He, like Chettle, feels the full force of the seasonal paradox:

> Shee came in with the fall of the leafe, and went away in the Spring.[41]

Chettle's shepherds and shepherdesses join in a funeral song that repeats the theme; Summer cannot stay when Sun departs.

> Instead of Roses sweete,
> (For pleasant Spring-time meete)
> Strew all the paths with Yeugh,
> Night-shade and bitter Reugh,
> Bid Flora hide her Treasure,
> Say 'tis no time of pleasure. (p.106)

Oriana's triumphs are replaced by mourning obsequies. The shepherds' epitaphs for her are reminders of what they have lost: the Queen who was 'still the same' has gone; the Golden Age has passed with

> Eliza, Maiden Mirror of this Age,
> Earths true Astraea while she liu'de and raign'de. (p. 107)

The new Astraea, like the old, has left the earth for Heaven, leaving desolation and, by implication, worse to come. The lament is for more than the Queen herself: the Golden Age will not return again.

Neither Lane nor Chettle nor Dekker ends on this note. Chettle had written partly to blame other poets for not doing the same: Drayton won notoriety, and disfavour, for rushing in to welcome James before mourning Elizabeth's death. But congratulations were in order too, and the final section of all three works is a celebration of the 'more felicitie' that is to come from the new King. Chettle's shepherds greet him with a 'Spring Song' that celebrates him as Elizabeth's successor in the pastoral world. The earth flourishes before him as it did before Oriana; the nymphs strew his path with red and white roses. He, like Eliza, will keep the wolf from his flock. Yet the celebration itself recalls the shepherds' true sovereign, and the true source of inspiration for their revels.

Thus were yee wont to trip about the Greene,
And dance in ringlets, like to Fairie Elues,
Striuing in cunning to exceede your selues,
In honour of your late falne summer Queene. (p. 115)

At the moment of triumphant welcome to the new and untried king, there is the reminder that the shepherds' hearts are still with Eliza.

Chettle's Collin had expressed his fears for Elizabeth's poets, for she had been the 'Hellicon of all our best and quaint inuentions'; and only James' known poetical tendencies encourage him in the hope that 'Pastoricall song', as he calls it, may continue. But his fears were better justified than perhaps Chettle himself realized. The adoration of Elizabeth as the Summer Queen was far more than a commonplace of flattery. Chettle was prepared to present James as the new lord of the shepherd world, but such celebrations collapsed before his obvious inappropriateness for the rôle. Elizabeth had been the incarnation of England's eternal spring, *semper eadem*; the tradition died with her, and with it went something of the pastoral world itself. Many poets continued to take up the shepherd's pipe, but all too often the tone was different – either much sweeter, as it celebrated a fantasy world of sentimental love, or harsher, as the satyr rather than the shepherd played upon it –

The silly Satyre, by whose plainesse, they
Are taught the worlds enormities to trace.[42]

The Elizabethan note was still sometimes sounded by poets who had known the previous reign: by Shakespeare, in the shepherd revels of *The Winter's Tale* and the evocation of spring in the new mistress of the feast; by Drayton in his ninth eclogue. But perpetually throughout the early Stuart era, as both England's internal peace and the Anglican settlement became more and more unstable, pastoral would look back to the Elyzium of her reign as its poetic golden age.

She, while she was, (ah!) was the shepherds Queen;
Sure such a shepherds Queen was never any;

or she was

the sweetest May
That ever flowr'd in Albions regiment

– these from Phineas Fletcher's pastoral on Man, *The Purple Island*, published three decades after her death;[43] and Wither, in his Epithalamium on the marriage of James' daughter Elizabeth to Frederick, count Palatine, in 1612, can think of no higher compliment to the Princess than that with the other shepherds and shepherdesses he will,

When we drive our flocks afield to graze them,
So chant your praises, that it shall amaze them.
And think that Fate hath new recall'd from death
Their still-lamented, sweet Elizabeth.[44]

But if the shepherd-poets and the shepherd-princes missed their Queen, her absence was felt even more sorely in the homelier setting of the shepherd revels. The idyllic feasts of the Cotswold shepherds may seem a long way from the pressing of maygames into the service of religious controversy; but pastoralists of the early seventeenth century could look back to the days of Elizabeth and see in revels such as these the epitome of a Golden Age now crushed by Puritan zeal. Captain Robert Dover's revival of the Cotswold

Games was celebrated in a collection of commendatory poems and eclogues, written over a few years before its eventual publication in 1636,[45] in which several writers take up this theme. Thomas Randolph's *Eglogue on the Palilia* is the most striking: Collen and Thenot are comparing the shepherds' general lethargy with their previous energy, typified in maygames and sports of various kinds – music, dancing, wrestling and throwing the bar for the reward of a kiss or a garland. The decline, Collen declares, is due to the 'melancholy Swaines' who

> teach that dauncing is a Jezabell
> And Barley-brake the ready way to Hell;
> The Morrice, idols; Whitson-ales can bee
> But profane reliques of a Jubilee!
> These in a Zeale, t'expresse how much they doe
> The organs hate, have silenced bagg-pipes too;
> And harmless May-poles, all are railed upon,
> As if they were the Towers of Babilon. (p. 125)

The games alone will help to recover the Cotswolds' lost glory. Ben Jonson takes up the same theme in the *Sad Shepherd*, when Robin Hood calls on the shepherds to celebrate the end of their shearing with spring revels, to cut down boughs, to dance and sing;

> Such are the Rites, the youthfull Iune allow. (I.iv.17)

Clarion replies:

> They were, gay Robin, but the sowrer sort
> Of Shepherds now disclaime in all such sport:
> And say, our Flockes, the while, are poorely fed,
> When with such vanities the Swaines are led. (18–21)

It is the argument of Spenser in 'May', but seen from a different viewpoint. There is no question as to where Jonson's sympathy lies:

> I should thinke it still might be
> (As 'twas) a happy age, when on the Plaines,
> The Wood-men met the Damsells, and the Swaines,
> The Neat'ards, Plow-men, and the Pipers loud,
> And each did dance, some to the Kit, or Crowd,
> Some to the Bag-pipe, some the Tabret moved,
> And all did either love, or were belov'd. (41–7)

This is the very specific pastoral nostalgia of the troubled years preceding the Civil War: Jonson is looking back, not only to the never-never-land of a Golden Age always in the past and the legendary Merry England of Robin Hood, but to an actual time not so long before when the poets had found an imaginative ideal in shepherd revels and faithful and mutual love under their Summer Queen. This pastoral, Jonson declares in the Prologue, will bear comparison with the best Classical models, though it is made up of 'meere English flocks'. This is where he finds the heart of English pastoral, in a strange mixture of popular May revels and the Anglican church settlement. Walton's epistle to the reader prefixed to Quarles' *Shepheards Oracles* expresses the same kind of nostalgia in its prayer for

> love and peace, which Pan (for he onely can doe it) continue in Arcadia, and restore to the disturbed Island of Britannia, and grant that each honest Shepheard may again sit under his own Vine and Fig-tree, and feed his own flock, and with love enjoy the fruits of peace, and be more thankfull.

Elizabeth's own shepherds had been more thankful. 'By her it is (Pan) that all our cartes are laden with corne, when in other countries they are filled with harneys.' It is political as well as poetic disillusionment that makes Drayton, in his last poem, give England the ironic name of Felicia and set his pastoral dream in Elizium, the home of the Muses that no longer exists on earth. The land he creates is a perpetual Golden Age of pastoral poetry that recalls in more than name the lost golden days, before Eliza withdrew from the earth to Heaven.

LIST OF NOTES

INTRODUCTION

1. The main exceptions are Enrico Carrara's monumental *La Poesia Pastorale* (Storia dei Generi Letterari Italiani, Milan 1909); Mia Irene Gerhardt's more selective *Essai d'Analyse Littéraire de la Pastorale* (Netherlands 1950); and on the French tradition, Alice Hulubei's *L'Eglogue en France au XVIe Siècle* (Paris 1938). The only thematic study of mediaeval vernacular pastoral is the stimulating chapter on 'The Idyllic Vision of Life' in Jan Huizinga's *The Waning of the Middle Ages*, trans. F. Hopman (Penguin, Harmondsworth 1965).

2. S. K. Heninger, Jr., 'The Renaissance Perversion of Pastoral', *Journal of the History of Ideas* XXII (1961) pp. 254–61.

3. *Some Versions of Pastoral* (1935; Penguin, Harmondsworth 1966) p. 25.

4. There was one Hellenistic pastoral romance, Longus' *Daphnis and Chloe*, which was rediscovered at the Renaissance and had some influence on the romances of the age; but the first, and most influential, author to compose one, Sannazaro, did not know it, and the form effectively evolved independently of Longus. Shepherds appear occasionally in mediaeval romances, but apart from a couple of works by Boccaccio that contain very little true pastoral material nothing resembling the pastoral romance was written during the Middle Ages.

5. See Gordon Williams, *Tradition and Originality in Roman Poetry* (Oxford 1968) pp. 307–12.

6. *The Prose Works of Sir Philip Sidney* ed. Albert Feuillerat (4 vols., Cambridge 1912/1962) Vol. III p. 22.

7. *Five Pastoral Eclogues* (anonymous; 1745). They are printed as Warton's by Alexander Chalmers in his *Works of the English Poets* Vol. XVIII (1810) pp. 136–41.

8. The lines are listed by Caesar Giarratano, *Calpurnii et Nemesiani Bucolica* (Corpus Scriptorum Latinorum Paravianum, 1st ed., Turin 1924) p. xxix. For a full account of the diffusion of their work in the Middle Ages, see Luigi Castagna, *I Bucolici Latini Minori* (Letterature d'Oltralpe e d'Oltreoceano 5, Florence 1976), especially pp. 264–75.

CHAPTER I

1. *PLAC* Vol. I pp. 384–91.

2. I.42 in *Minor Latin Poets* ed. J. Wight Duff and Arnold M. Duff (Loeb, 1934) p. 218 ff.

3. Max Manitius, *Geschichte der lateinischen Literatur des Mittelalters* (3 vols., Munich 1911–31) Vol. I p. 550.

4. William Webbe, *A Discourse of English Poetrie*, in *Elizabethan Critical Essays* edited by G. Gregory Smith (1904/1967) Vol. I p. 262.

5. *PLAC* Vol. I pp. 360–3.

6. Ibid. pp. 269–70.

7. Ibid. p. 270.

8. 'Classical Eclogue and Mediaeval Debate', *Romanic Review* II (1911) pp. 16–31, 129–43.

9. Betty Nye Hedberg, 'The *Bucolics* and the Mediaeval Poetic Debate', *Transactions of the American Philological Assoc.* LXXV (1944) pp. 61, 67.

10. *In Vergilii Bucolica et Georgica Commentarii* ed. George Thilo (Leipzig 1887) p. 29: Transiit in eclogam plenam iurgii et conviciorum pastoralium...haec vero lites habet et altercationem.

11. *Accessus ad Auctores, Bernard d'Utrecht, Conrad d'Hirsau* ed. R. B. C. Huygens (Leiden 1970) p. 95 ll. 715–8: Nec ratione caret, quod in hac altercationis materia pastores introducuntur, quia genus illud semper est litigiosum, contraria contrariis iaculando et alterna malitia vel dolo rixas excitando.

12. Ibid., Bernard p. 61 ll. 266–8, and *Theoduli Eclogam* ed. Joannes Osternacher (Urfahr-Linz 1902) p. 10: Pastores sepius inter se litigant et plus quam alii.

13. *The Parisiana Poetria of John of Garland* ed. Traugott Lawler (1974) p. 102, V.368–9.

14. The ascription to Alcuin has been challenged on the grounds that the author knew Horace and Alcuin did not (F. J. E. Raby, *A History of Secular Latin Poetry in the Middle Ages* (2nd edition, Oxford 1957) p. 208). There is still the possibility that Alcuin could have picked up the odd line through personal contacts or through *florilegia*, or the similarity could easily be coincidental – pastoral vocabulary is necessarily limited.

15. Boccaccio, *Opere Latine Minori* ed. A. F. Massèra (SI, Bari 1928) pp. 62–6; *Comedia delle Ninfe Fiorentine (Ameto)* ed. Antonio Enzo Quaglio (Florence 1963) pp. 47–52.

16. *PLAC* Vol. III pp. 45–51.

17. For a collection of these see T. P. Harrison, *The Pastoral Elegy* (Austin, Texas, 1939/New York 1968). Paschasius' poem is also in this, pp. 55–64.

18. Paschasius l. 16, Virgil V.44.

19. See Erwin Panofsky, '*Et in Arcadia Ego*: Poussin and the Elegiac Tradition', reprinted in his *Meaning in the Visual Arts* (Penguin, Harmondsworth 1970) pp. 340–67.

20. Hedberg p. 57.

21. *PLAC* Vol. III pp. 204–7.

22. *Georgics* II.461–74.

23. *M. Valerio: Bucoliche* ed. Franco Munari (2nd edition, Florence 1970). They were first published by Paul Lehmann in 1946.

24. Munari p. xlviii.

25. *Die Quirinalien des Metellus von Tegernsee* ed. Peter Christian Jacobsen (Mittellateinische Studien u. Texte I, Leiden and Cologne 1965).

26. Servius p. 1; Isidore, *Etymologiae* I.xxix.16 (*PL* Vol. LXXXII cols. 119–20).

27. De vitula elegante, que a rustico promissa voto beato Quirino, sed a domino illius sublata armentis iuncta est, ubi una nocte omne preter eam armentum deperiit. Allegorice Tityrus hic Tegriensis receptor est animalium, que voto deferuntur. Melibeus quidam olim detractor beati Quirini, qui in ultimo egloga paralysi percussus est et curatus inducitur (p. 305).

28. Et melius est, ut simpliciter intellegamus: male enim quidam allegoriam volunt (p. 5, I.5).

29. Refutandae enim sunt allegoriae in bucolico carmine, nisi cum, ut supra diximus, ex aliqua agrorum perditorum necessitate descendunt (p. 33).

30. See Domenico Comparetti, *Vergil in the Middle Ages*, trans. E. F. M. Benecke (2nd edition, 1908/1966) pp. 108–14.

31. See especially St. Gregory's Sermon on the Good Shepherd (*PL* Vol. LXXVI cols. 1127–30) and Prudentius, *Cathemerinon* VIII ll. 33–52 (ed. H. J. Thomson (2 vols., Loeb, 1949–53) Vol. I pp. 70–5).

32. *PLAC* Vol. III pp. 166–80.

33. *The Oxford Book of Medieval Latin Verse* ed. F. J. E. Raby (Oxford 1959) p. 309.

34. R. W. Hunt, 'Verses on the Life of Robert Grosseteste', *Medievalia et Humanistica* N.S. I (1970) pp. 241–51.

35. The Vita Gudiana II, in *Vitae Vergilianae* ed. Jacob Brummer (Leipzig 1912) p. 64: 'Egloga dicitur quasi egaloga, quia ega dicitur capro, logos sermo. Inde egloga dicitur sermo de capris.' For the history of the idea and its effect on later bucolic see

Helen Cooper, 'The Goat and the Eclogue', *Philological Quarterly* LIII (1974) pp. 363–79.

36. Egloga a capris tractum est, quasi diceret egle logos id est caprinus sermo, aut quia de pastoribus agit aut quia feditatem viciorum, quae per hoc animal designatur, reprehendit (ed. Huygens, p. 60 ll. 60–2). Conrad of Hirsau repeats the point almost word for word.

37. In *Anthologia Latina* ed. Alexander Riese, Vol. II (Teubner, Leipzig 1896) no. 893, pp. 334–9.

38. W. Schmid, 'Tityrus Christianus', *Rheinisches Museum für Philologie* XCVI (1953) p. 143.

39. It has some connections with two long passages about oxen in Paulinus' own poems, but these are neither pastoral nor eclogue, though Schmid (and others) argue that they are a part of Christian bucolic (pp. 116–20).

40. Scholars tend to follow either Osternacher, for the ninth century, or Karl Strecker ('Ist Gottschalk der Dichter der Ecloga Theoduli?', *Neues Archiv* XLV (1924) pp. 18–23) for the tenth. As pastoral, the poem would be more in keeping with the eclogues of the ninth century, but the use of rhyme in such a specifically Classical genre would be more characteristic of the later date.

41. George L. Hamilton, 'Theodulus: A Mediaeval Textbook', *Mod. Phil.* VII (1909) p. 174.

42. Primum igitur in hoc opere a docente sensus ponendus est in litera, deinde ipsa litera per allegoriam elucidanda, inde per moralitatem vita legentis instituenda (ed. Huygens, p. 95 ll. 726–8).

43. *PLAC* Vol. IV.1 pp. 169–72.

44. *Arts Poétiques du XIIe et du XIIIe Siècle* ed. Edmond Faral (Paris 1924) p. 226 ll. 136–41.

45. See Lawler's discussion pp. xiii–xv: the work was probably begun in the 1220's and revised later.

46. Pp. 40–1.

47. Faral claims that the connection proves the pastourelle to be descended from the eclogue ('La Pastourelle', *Romania* XLIX (1923) pp. 204–59), but this has never received any support (see W. P. Jones, 'Some recent Studies on the Pastourelle', *Speculum* V (1930) pp. 207–15). John's eclogue is too late to count as evidence for influence from Latin to vernacular; the movement must be in the other direction.

48. *The Stella Maris of John of Garland* ed. Evelyn Faye Wilson (Cambridge, Mass., 1946) p. 127.

49. See Evelyn Faye Wilson, 'Pastoral and Epithalamium in Latin Literature', *Speculum* XXIII (1948) p. 52.

50. Est autem materia uersuum quomodo iuuenis oppressit nimpham, cuius amicus erat Coridon. Per nimpham significatur caro; per iuuenem corruptorem, mundus uel diabolus; per proprium amicum, ratio. Dicit ergo sub persona mundi sic: (*Poetria* p. 24, I.402–5).

51. Philip H. Wicksteed and Edmund G. Gardner, *Dante and Giovanni del Virgilio* (Westminster 1902), texts on pp. 152–72; the description of Giovanni is on p. 124.

52. Ibid. p. 176 ll. 8–9.

53. Et volunt quidam hoc loco allegoriam esse ad Augustum de decem eclogis: quod superfluum est: quae enim necessitas hoc loco allegoriae? (Servius p. 38).

54. Wicksteed pp. 228, 233.

55. Ibid. p. 174 l. 6.

56. *Petrarch's Bucolicum Carmen* ed. and trans. Thomas G. Bergin (1974). For a detailed account of the bucolics of Petrarch and Boccaccio, eclogue by eclogue, see W. Leonard Grant, *Neo-Latin Literature and the Pastoral* (Chapel Hill 1965) pp. 80–110.

57. Petrarch, *Epistolae de Rebus Familiaribus et Variae* ed. Ioseph Fracassetti Vol. III (Florence 1863) pp. 410–11, Epist. Var. XLII: Natura huius generis scriptorum hoc est ut, nisi illo ipso qui edidit exponente, divinari possit sensus eorum forsitan, sed omnino non possit intelligi.

58. Pierre de Nolhac, 'Virgile chez Pétrarque', *Studi Medievali* N.S. V (1932) p. 221.

59. Letter to Fra Martino da Signa (1374?) in Boccaccio, *Opere Latine* p. 216: Theocritus syragusanus poeta, ut ab antiquis accepimus, primus fuit qui greco carmine buccolicum excogitavit stilum, verum nil sensit preter quod cortex ipse verborum demonstrat. Post hunc latine scripsit Vergilius, sed sub cortice nonnullos abscondit sensus, esto non semper voluerit sub nominibus colloquentium aliquid sentiremus. Post hunc autem scripserunt et alii, sed ignobiles, de quibus nil curandum est, excepto inclito preceptore meo Francisco Petrarca, qui stilum preter solitum paululum sublimavit et secundum eglogarum suarum materias continue collocutorum nomina aliquid significantia posuit. Ex his ego Vergilium secutus sum, quapropter non curavi in omnibus colloquentium nominibus sensum abscondere.

60. *Genealogie Deorum Gentilium Libri* ed. Vincenzo Romano (2 vols., Bari 1951) XIV.10: Quis insuper adeo insanus erit, ut putet preclarissimum virum atque Christianissimum, Franciscum Petrarcam...expendisse tot vigilias, tot sacras meditationes, tot horas, dies et annos, quot iure possimus existimare impensos, si Buccolici sui carminis gravitatem, si ornatum, si verborum exquisitum decus pensemus, ut Gallum fingeret Tyrheno calamos exposcentem, aut iurgantes invicem Pamphylum et Mitionem et alios delirantes eque pastores?

61. *De Vita Solitaria* ed. Antonio Altamura (Studi e Testi Umanistici II.1, Naples 1943) I.iii.3 (I.iii.4 in the translation by Jacob Zeitlin).

62. *Il Bucolicum Carmen* ed. Antonio Avena (*Padova in Onore di Francesco Petrarca* I, Padua 1906) p. 220: Ille cristus...semper mandat quod prelati intendant ad cura animarum et frequenter iubet inmergere infirmos parvulos, idest peccatores, in virtutibus; et ipse cristus iubet tondere ipsos peccatores...prohibens lascivos yrcos et repellens a claustris ecclesie.

63. *Buccolicum Carmen* X.46–52 (first section in *Opere Latine*).

64. Letter to Fra Martino, *Opere Latine* p. 217.

65. E.g. sig. Aiii[a] in the 1503 Paris edition (facsimile ed. H. Oskar Sommer, *The Kalender of Shepherdes* Vol. II (1892)).

66. The similarity to drama was noted as early as 1502 by Iodocus Badius Ascensius, the great editor of school texts of the period: see sig. Dviii[b]–Ei[a] of his edition.

67. Benvenuto's commentary, ed. Avena p. 240, 'Ratio nitens que cohercet dolorem.'

68. Their work is described by Grant, pp. 111–15.

CHAPTER II

1. Marie-Thérèse Kaiser-Guyot's *Le Berger en France aux XIVe et XVe Siècles* (Publications de l'Université de Paris X, A 26, Paris 1974), a study taken partly from literary sources, came to my notice only after I had completed this book.

2. *Poésies Complètes du Troubadour Marcabru* ed. J.-M.-L. Dejeanne (Bibliothèque Meridionale 1re série XII, Toulouse 1909) pp. 134–41. Although no examples are extant, it seems likely that the pastourelle was also in existence in northern France by the mid-twelfth century, as Wace appears to draw on the genre: see M. Zink, *La Pastourelle: Poésie et Folklore au Moyen Age* (Paris 1972) p. 9.

3. The first recorded usage is in Thomas Usk's *Testament of Love* (*Chaucerian and Other Pieces* ed. W. W. Skeat (*Complete Works of Geoffrey Chaucer* Vol. VII, Oxford 1897) p. 11 ll. 86–7): 'For me liste, and it me lyketh, of al myne a shepherdesse to be cleped.' Cf. also Chaucer, *Troilus and Criseyde* I.653–4:

> An herdesse
> Which that icleped was Oënone

(*Works* ed. F. N. Robinson (2nd edition, 1957)). For another occurrence from the same period, in Gower, see p. 59 below. There is, however, a song apparently put into the mouth of a shepherdess in Bodleian MS Douce 381 (printed in *Secular Lyrics of the XIVth and XVth Centuries* ed. Rossell Hope Robbins (2nd edition, Oxford 1955) p. xxxviii), though the word is not used. It seems to have been more common for women to help with the sheep north of the Border.

4. 'Trobet vers e pastoretas a la usanza antiga', *Vita* in *Les Poésies de Cercamon* ed. A. Jeanroy (CFMA, Paris 1922) p. 29. He was probably contemporary with Marcabru.

5. There are studies of the *bergerie* elements in the English plays in Millicent Carey, *The Wakefield Group in the Towneley Cycle* (Hesperia 11, Göttingen 1930) and Richard Axton, *European Drama of the Early Middle Ages* (1974) pp. 187–94.

6. There is a useful summary of the history of these ideas in the Middle Ages by Henry Caplan, 'The Four Senses of Scriptural Interpretation', *Speculum* IV (1929) pp. 282–90, reprinted in *Of Eloquence* (1970) pp. 93–104; see especially p. 99.

7. Ed. Paul Lacroix (Paris 1879). The history of the work is discussed on pp. vi, xvi.

8. *Œuvres Poétiques* ed. Maurice Roy (SATF, Paris 1891) Vol. II pp. 223–94 ll. 78 ff.

9. In *Chroniques relatives à l'Histoire de la Belgique* ed. Kervyn de Lettenhove (Brussels 1873) ll. 5772 ff.

10. *Mystère de l'Incarnacion et Nativité de notre Sauveur et Rédempteur Jésus-Christ representé à Rouen en 1474* ed. Pierre Le Verdier (Soc. des Bibliophiles Normands, Rouen 1884–6) Vol. II pp. 76–7, 147–54.

11. *Les Illustrations de Gaule et Singularitez de Troye* I.xxii, in *Œuvres de Jean Lemaire de Belges* ed. J. Stecher (4 vols., Louvain 1882–91) Vol. I pp. 146–51.

12. Ed. J. A. H. Murray (EETS E.S. 17, 1872) pp. 46–62.

13. *The Chester Mystery Cycle* ed. R. M. Lumiansky and David Mills (EETS S.S. 3, 1974) pp. 125–56 ll. 81–2.

14. The *Pastourelles* are section XIV of *Œuvres de Froissart: Poésies* ed. Auguste Scheler (3 vols., Brussels 1870) Vol. II; see nos. I, IV, VII (especially l. 36), XIII.

15. In *Mystères et Moralités du Manuscrit 617 de Chantilly* ed. Gustave Cohen (2nd edition in *Mémoires de l'Académie de Belgique* 2.XII, 1953) ll. 333–40.

16. *Recueil de Motets Français* ed. Gaston Raynaud (2 vols., Paris 1881–3) Vol. I ccxv.

17. *Middle English Metrical Romances* ed. W. H. French and C. B. Hale (New York 1964) pp. 950–85, ll. 587–94.

18. *The Early English Carols* ed. R. L. Greene (2nd ed., Oxford 1977) p. 40 no. 78

19. Arnoul Greban, *Mystère de la Passion* ed. Omer Jodogne (*Mémoires de l'Académie de Belgique* 2.XII, 1965); this edition works from an earlier MS than that by Gaston Paris and Gaston Raynaud. See ll. 4683–714 for the list of equipment, l. 4702 for gloves; for a good example of an illustration, see e.g. Cambridge U.L. MS Add. 4126 f. 49ᵛ (early sixteenth century). The Holkham Bible Picture-Book is B.M. MS Add. 47682 (see Plate I); there is a facsimile with an introduction by W. O. Hassall (1954).

20. *Œuvres Complètes du Roi René* ed. Comte de Quatrebarbes (4 vols., Angers 1845) Vol. II pp. 56, 58. This poem is by Louis de Beauvau.

21. *Two Coventry Corpus Christi Plays* ed. Hardin Craig (2nd edition, EETS E.S. 87, 1957) ll. 317–20.

22. The references are to *Secular Lyrics* p. xl; *Robert Henryson: Poems* ed. Charles Elliott (corrected edition, Oxford 1966) pp. 125–8; C. R. Baskervill, *The Elizabethan Jig* (Chicago 1929) p. 25. On 'Colin' see below, p. 153. The most common 'Jolly –' compound in Middle English is 'Jolly Robin'; Edward assumes the name in *King Edward and the Shepherd*, and Robinson, on its use in *Troilus* V.1174, describes it as 'a common name for a shepherd or rustic', presumably by analogy with French.

23. Froissart, *Pastourelles* VII.35–44.

24. *Hous of Fame* 1223–6; Gavin Douglas, *Aeneid* ed. David F. C. Coldwell (4 vols., STS, Edinburgh 1957–64) Prologue to Book VII ll. 77–8; Spenser, 'February' 35–40 (see p. 156 below).

25. *Compleynt* appended to the *Temple of Glas*, ed. J. Schick (EETS E.S. 60, 1891) p. 64 ll. 417–22.

26. P. 65.

27. B. M. King's MS 24 f. 1ʳ.

28. Reproduced in M. D. Anderson, *Drama and Imagery in English Mediaeval Churches* (Cambridge 1963) pl. 22a.

29. Now in the Victoria and Albert Museum (138–1886).

30. *Chronique de Mathieu d'Escouchy* ed. G. du Fresne de Beaucourt (3 vols., Paris 1863–4) Vol. II pp. 133–4, 142.

31. *The Eclogues of Baptista Mantuanus* ed. W. P. Mustard (Baltimore 1911) I.163–9.

32. *Tottel's Miscellany* ed. H. E. Rollins (revised edition, Cambridge, Mass., 1966) p. 188, and notes Vol. II p. 297. I have repunctuated the passage for clarity.

33. *Ludus Coventriae* ed. K. S. Block (EETS E.S. 120, 1922) p. 69 ll. 185–6. The idea is a vernacular addition: there is nothing to suggest it in the account of the incident in the *Legenda Aurea*.

34. *The Wakefield Pageants in the Towneley Cycle* ed. A. C. Cawley (Manchester 1958); for the song, *Secunda* ll. 183–8; Mak, ll. 195, 476–7; 'Gloria', ll. 656–8 and *Prima* l. 414. See also Nan Cooke Carpenter, 'Music in the *Secunda Pastorum*', *Speculum* XXVI (1951) pp. 696–700.

35. Sung after l. 277, second stanza after l. 331. Other versions are given in Greene, *Carols* pp. 41–2.

36. J. R. H. de Smidt, *Les Noëls et la Tradition Populaire* (Amsterdam 1932) p. 36; and see also pp. 67–8 on the continuation of the *bergerie* tradition in noëls until comparatively recently.

37. *Music in the French Secular Theatre, 1400–1550* (Cambridge, Mass., 1963) p. 46.

38. See Brown pp. 46, 88–9. Though the use of the dialogue rondeau is not limited to the shepherd scenes in the *mystères*, it is characteristic of them. It occurs not only in *bergerie* drama but in poetry too: see the *Pastoralet* ll. 991–8.

39. *Rouen* Vol. II pp. 131, 151–5.

40. *Aucassin et Nicolette* ed. Mario Roques (CFMA, 2nd edition, Paris 1968) XVIII, XX.

41. *Les Dictz de Franc Gontier* in *Recueil de Poésies Françoises des XVe et XVIe Siècles* Vol. X, ed. A. Montaiglon and J. Rothschild (Paris 1875) pp. 198, 200 (the poem is set in parallel with Villon's *Contredictz de Franc Gontier*, a well-deserved parody of the piece). Also in *The Penguin Book of French Verse* Vol. I ed. Brian Woledge (Harmondsworth 1961) pp. 216–8.

42. Ed. Kenneth Varty (1960).

43. Froissart, *Pastourelles* V; there are less exotic lists in III, VII and XIV.

44. René Vol. II pp. 104–51, especially pp. 121–3. On the question of authorship see V. Chichmarev, 'Œuvres attribuées au Roi René', *Romania* LV (1929) pp. 226, 233–4.

45. Ed. Emile Roy in *Le Mystère de la Passion en France du XIVe au XVIe Siècle* Vol I (Dijon 1903) pp. 51–6, esp. ll. 2633 ff., 2820 ff.; see also the discussion on pp. 85*–91*.

46. *Chester* pp. 129–31, *Wakefield* p. 35; and A. C. Cawley, 'The "Grotesque" Feast in the "Prima Pastorum"', *Speculum* XXX (1955) pp. 213–7.

47. See Marie Ungureanu, *Société et Littérature Bourgeoises d'Arras aux XIIe et XIIIe Siècles* (Arras 1955) pp. 165–9.

48. *Romances et Pastourelles Françaises des XIIe et XIIIe Siècles* ed. Karl Bartsch (Leipzig 1870/Darmstadt 1967) II.41; cf. also III.15. The excellent edition by Jean-Claude Rivière, *Pastourelles* (TLF, Geneva 1974–6) was completed too late for me to use here.

49. Ll. 271–322. Strutt writes of nine-men's morris, 'It was certainly much used of shepherds formerly' (*Sports and Pastimes of the People of England* ed. J. C. Cox (1903) p. 256).

50. B.M. Royal MS 2.B.VII f. 4ᵛ, pl. 7 in the facsimile ed. George Warner (1912).

51. Ed. Charles Frederick Ward (University of Iowa Humanistic Studies II.2, 1923) II.cxvii, p. 159.

52. MS Fr. Q.XIV.1 f. 6ᵛ in the Publichnaya Biblioteka im. M. E. Saltykova-Shchedrina, Leningrad. The corresponding text is in René Vol. II p. 111.

53. For carolling see e.g. the frontispiece or Fitzwilliam Museum MS 74 (James' numbering); a shepherdess placing a garland on a shepherd's head, Fitzwilliam MS 64. All these show the Annunciation taking place as a background scene with a separate group of shepherds. The Rohan Book of Hours (early 15c.) shows a shepherdess milking a ewe and a shepherd playing a pipe and dancing, with no figure but the dog paying any attention to the angel annunciant (plate 4 in the edition by Jean Porcher (1959)). Porcher claims that the scene represents the expression of religious joy, but he is perhaps optimistic: artists took a delight in the portrayal of secular *bergerie*, and when they wish to represent the irruption of the divine they will have the shepherds breaking off their pastimes to gaze at the angel. No miniature I have seen makes any attempt to present the two incidents happening successively, that is, the Annunciation in the background and the *same group* of shepherds rejoicing in the foreground.

54. Bartsch III.14; also III.41, II.58, and longer works such as the *Banquet du Bois* (Montaiglon and Rothschild X pp. 206–22).

55. This is W. P. Jones' argument in *The Pastourelle* (Cambridge, Mass., 1931).

56. 'Nou sprinkes the sprai', *English Lyrics of the Thirteenth Century* ed. Carleton Brown (Oxford 1932/65) p. 119; 'As I stod on a day', *Reliquiae Antiquae* ed. Thomas Wright and J. O. Halliwell (1843) Vol. II p. 19; 'Mosti ryden by rybbesdale' and 'In a fryht as I con fere', *The Harley Lyrics* ed. G. L. Brook (3rd edition, Manchester 1964) pp. 37, 39.

57. In John Stevens, *Music and Poetry in the Early Tudor Court* (1961) p. 424. The history of the nursery rhyme is discussed in *The Oxford Dictionary of Nursery Rhymes* ed. Iona and Peter Opie (Oxford 1951) pp. 281–3.

58. *The Works of Sir Thomas Malory* ed. Eugène Vinaver (2nd edition, Oxford 1967) Vol. I p. 101 and note in Vol. III p. 1326. See also *Secular Lyrics* p. xxxviii and no. 29.

59. Ed. G. C. Macaulay (2 vols., EETS E.S. 81–2, 1900–1) Liber Quintus ll. 6102–35. There is one other possible reference to the shepherdess pastourelle in the St. Margaret legend in Trinity College, Cambridge, MS 323: the lord of Antioch finds her watching her sheep and offers her gifts as the would-be seducers conventionally do:

> Ciclatoun ant purpelpal scaltou haue to wede,
> Wid alle þe metes of my lond ful wel I scal þe fede!

The similarity to the pastourelle situation was also exploited by French or Anglo-Norman hagiographers (e.g. in Sloane MS 611). I am indebted to Dr. Karl Reichl for these references.

60. Ed. Barbara N. Craig (University of Kansas Humanistic Studies 31, Lawrence, Kansas, 1954) ll. 1091–1235, 2548–2608, and p. 10.

61. In *Le Théâtre Français avant la Renaissance* ed. Edouard Fournier (2nd edition, Paris 1887) pp. 45–53.

62. *Secular Lyrics* pp. xl, xxxviii.

63. Bartsch II.67, 59.

64. Pastourelle by Serveri de Gerona (1275) in Jean Audiau, *La Pastourelle dans la Poésie Occitaine du Moyen Age* (Paris 1923) p. 104. For the history of the proverb in England see Archer Taylor, 'He that will not when he may; when he will he shall have nay', in *Studies in Old English Literature in Honour of Arthur G. Brodeur* ed. Stanley B. Greenfield (Oregon 1963) pp. 151–61.

65. 'Jois, Amors and Fin' Amors in the Poetry of Jaufre Rudel', *Neuphilologische Mitteilungen* LXXI (1970) p. 277.

66. *Œuvres de Guillaume de Machaut* ed. Ernest Hoepffner Vol. II (SATF, Paris 1911) pp. 159–237; see esp. ll. 1537–78, and l. 1560.

67. Audiau pp. 34–8.

68. *Le Rime* ed. G. Favati (Documenti di Filologia I, Milan 1957) p. 305. Peter Dronke describes the poem as 'perhaps the highest expression of the Arcadian ideal in medieval lyric' (*The Medieval Lyric* (1968) p. 201).

69. *Chansons du XVe Siècle* ed. Gaston Paris (SATF, Paris 1875) p. 51, ll. 15–20. Zink reaches a similar conclusion on the relationship of the shepherdess to nature, by a different route: see especially pp. 95, 102, 118.

70. *Chester* p. 125 l. 3.

71. *Le Bergerie de l'Agneau de France* (1485) ed. H. Lewicka (TLF, Geneva 1961) ll. 65–6.

72. See E. R. Curtius, *European Literature and the Latin Middle Ages*, trans. Willard R. Trask (1953) pp. 183–200.

73. Montaiglon and Rothschild X p. 209.

74. W. G. Thomson, *A History of Tapestry from the Earliest Times to the Present Day* (2nd edition, 1930) pp. 141, 253, 258; further references to shepherd tapestries on pp. 65–6, 72, 93, 119, 181 and 275.

75. *Recollections des Merveilleuses Advenues* ll. 289–96, in *Les Faictz et Dictz de Jean Molinet* ed. Noël Dupire (3 vols., SATF, Paris 1936–9) pp. 284–334. (The poem appears in Molinet's works because he continues where Chastellain left off: see note p. 989.)

76. The poem is printed as an appendix to *Œuvres de Froissart: Chroniques* ed. Kervyn de Lettenhove (Brussels 1872) Vol. XIV pp. 407 ff.; quotation from p. 408.

77. Froissart, *Pastourelles* VIII.23–6.

78. *Chroniques de Jean Molinet* ed. J.-A. Buchon (Paris 1827–8) Vol. III p. 138.

79. *Illustrations* I.xxii, Lemaire Vol. I p. 147.

80. B.N. MS fr. 25467 ff. 1–47ʳ. The play is here given the undistinctive heading *Moralité a cinq personnages*, but the more descriptive title is adopted by e.g. Lewicka in her edition of the *Bergerie de l'Agneau*.

81. *Complaynt* pp. 43–5, 66.

82. *En habes, lector, bucolicorum autores XXXVIII...Farrago quidem eclogarum CLVI.*·. (Basle 1546). The selection was made by Gilbert Cousin of Noseroy, formerly Erasmus' secretary (Grant p. 410).

83. *Vita di Dante* in Boccaccio's *Comento alla Divina Commedia* ed. Domenico Guerri (SI, Bari 1918) Vol. I pp. 7, 103–4.

84. *Œuvres Complètes* ed. Marquis de Queux de Saint-Hilaire (11 vols., SATF, Paris 1878–1903) Vol. III p. 1.

85. Vol. II pp. 203–14.

86. Greban 4683–5.

87. Text in Montaiglon and Rothschild Vol. X pp. 200–4.

88. *Le Curial par Alain Chartier* ed. Ferdinand Heuckenkamp (Halle 1899) gives the French and Latin versions; *De Curialium Miseriis* ed. W. P. Mustard (Baltimore 1928); *The Eclogues of Alexander Barclay* ed. Beatrice White (EETS O.S. 175, 1928), the first three poems.

89. Gavaudan's 'L'autre dia', Audiau pp. 22–5.

90. Bartsch III.17.

91. Bartsch III.23. See also II.55; and in III.2 the process is reversed as the knight instructs a shepherd unhappy in love.

92. *Vita Nuova* IX (ed. Edoardo Sanguineti (Milan 1965) p. 67).

93. Bartsch II.2 l. 50, Audiau V l. 6.

94. Bartsch III.40.

95. Deschamps Vol. III no. 344 ll. 13–14; also no. 354.

96. 20–27 November 1382: see E. Hoepffner, 'La Chronologie des Pastourelles de Froissart', *Mélanges offerts à M. Emile Picot* (Paris 1913) Vol. II p. 34.

97. Ed. Albert Meiller (Bibliothèque Française et Romane 11, Paris 1971) ll. 1396–9.

98. B. M. Sloane MS 2593 f. 33ᵛ. The poem has been printed several times, most recently by R. H. Robbins in *Historical Poems of the XIVth and XVth Centuries* (New York 1959) p. 147, but always inaccurately, especially ll. 11–13. These run in the MS (omitting one word, *wo*, accidentally written twice):

Alle half frendes, wo worth hem ay.
A! Lord, how gos þis word abowte!
Alle trewe frendes wel worth hem ay.

The various editors all bless or curse the wrong people.

99. B.M. MS Royal 16 E XIII, a MS not previously noticed but which must be earlier than either the printed version of 1541 or the version in B.N. MS fonds fr. 12795, dating from after 1536 (f. 28), since it was dedicated and presented to Ann Boleyn. The text is edited from the two printed editions and the B.N. MS by C. A. Mayer, 'Le Sermon du Bon Pasteur: Un Problème d'Attribution', *Bibliothèque d'Humanisme et de Renaissance* XXVII (1965) pp. 290–303. Mayer accepts the attribution of the poem to Papillon given in the French MS, and also dates it in 1539; but the existence of the earlier MS obviously raises a number of problems.

100. In *The Apostolic Fathers* ed. A. Roberts and J. Donaldson (Ante-Nicence Christian Library Vol. I, Edinburgh 1867) pp. 319–435, especially p. 347 ff.

101. Pierre Garnier, publishing at Troyes; see Jehan de Brie p. xvi. For the publishing history of the *Kalender* see Sommer's edition, Vol. I.

102. *Comento* I p. 104, variant; the texts differ particularly widely at this point, developing the metaphor in varying detail – see also Macrì-Leone's edition (Florence 1888) and the translation by Albert S. Cook (Yale Studies in English X, 1901). 'Sono, al mio giudicio, di pastori due maniere: corporali e spirituali. Li corporali similmente sono di due qualità, l'una delle quali sono quegli che, per le selve e per gli prati, le pecore, gli buoi e gli altri armenti pascendo menano, l'altra sono gl'imperadori, i re, i padri delle famiglie, i quali con giustizia e in pace hanno a conservare i popoli loro commessi, e a trovare onde vengano a' tempi opportuni i cibi a' sudditi e a' figliuoli. Le spirituali pastori similmente dire si possono di due maniere: delle quali è l'una quella di coloro che pascono l'anime de viventi di cibo spirituale, cioè della parola di Dio, e questi sono i prelati, i predicatori, e i sacerdoti. . . . l'altra è quella di coloro, li quali in alcuna scienzia ammaestrati prima, poi ammaestrano altrui leggendo o componendo.'

103. *Li Cumpoz Philipe de Thaün* ed. Eduard Mall (Strasbourg 1873) p. 3, ll. 67–70.

104. Barclay, Prologe 45–6; Puttenham, *The Arte of English Poesie* ed. Gladys D. Willcock and Alice Walker (Cambridge 1936) Lib. I.xviii.

105. Molinet, *Faictz* Vol. I, *Arbre* pp. 325–50, *Bergier* pp. 209–24.

106. *Bergerie Nouvelle fort joyeuse et morale de Mieulx que Devant*, in Fournier pp. 54–60. Fournier suggests a date towards the end of the reign of Charles VII (c. 1455–1461); Lewicka, on the basis of one rather insignificant word, suggests 1488 (*Bergerie de l'Agneau* p. 9). The main subject of the play, however, would seem to refer to the 'Ecorcheurs', the 'flayers', freebooting bands of soldiers who got their name from their reputation for pillaging everything down to a man's last garment. The warning trumpet-call mentioned in the play was used to signal the approach of one of these companies just as much as the approach of the English – who are also described as an active threat. Charles introduced measures to control the Ecorcheurs in the 1440's, and a date around then would seem to me most likely.

107. George R. Kernodle, *From Art to Theatre* (Chicago 1944) pp. 65–6, 70–1, 98.

108. Deschamps Vol. II no. 288.

109. *Pierre Gringore's Pageants for the Entry of Mary Tudor into Paris* ed. C. R. Baskervill (Chicago 1934) p. xxiv. The shepherd pageant is on pp. 14–15, pl. VII, from B. M. Cotton MS Vespasian B.II f.15^{r-v}.

110. Kernodle p. 74.

111. E.g. *Mieulx-que-Devant*, and Louis XII's entry into Paris in 1498: see Godefroy, *Le Cérémonial François* (2 vols., Paris 1649) Vol. I p. 241.

112. Molinet, *Chroniques* Vol. IV p. 389: 'et estoit ce dit jeu fondé sur la desertion du pays, lequel revenoit en convalescence, le tout en bregerie.'

113. *Illustrations* I.xxii, Vol. I p. 149: 'Vostre maniere de viure nest autre chose fors le vray exemplaire dun Royaume, et vne espece de regime politique dune chose publique.'

114. *L'Entree du Charles VIII a Rouen en 1485*, facsimile with introduction by Ch. de Robillard de Beaurepaire (Soc. des Bibliophiles Normands, Rouen 1902) p. 7. The pageants were organized by Robert Pinel, who probably also wrote the account.

115. 'La quelle matere fainte sur pastourerie estoit une fiction traictee sur bucoliques comme assemblee de pasteurs faisans conuencion a la bien venue de cedit pasteur' (p. 24).

116. Godefroy Vol. I p. 241.

117. *Mémoires d'Olivier de la Marche* ed. Henri Beaune and J. d'Arbaumont (Soc. de l'Histoire de France, 4 vols., Paris 1883-8) Vol. III p. 135. Cf. also the account of two lions, a hart and an ibex which appeared in the pageants for the wedding of Prince Arthur and Katherine of Aragon in 1501, 'with in evrych of the which IIII bests were II men, oon in the fore parte, and another in the hynde parte', with their legs 'disguysed after the proporcion and kynde of the bests that they were in' (quoted by Sydney Anglo, 'The Evolution of the early Tudor Disguising, Pageant and Masque', *Renaissance Drama* N.S. I (1968) p. 9).

118. *Les Poésies de Martial de Paris, dit d'Auvergne* (2 vols., Paris 1724); see especially Vol. I pp. 69, 78-88.

119. There is a curious, if conventional, verbal parallel between the two: Martial's

> Les Bergiers dansoient,
> Pastoureaulx fleustoient,
> Les oyseaulx chantoient,
> Et Dieu mercioient
> Pour la Paix qui estoit; (I p. 69)

cf. the lines from the *Moralité* quoted above, p. 82. Both the expression and the metre are commonplaces of *bergerie*, but the political context emphasises the similarity – the play looking back to a lost age of peace before the invasions, the poem celebrating its return after the expulsion of the English.

120. Text ed. Stecher Vol. IV pp. 191-206; for a discussion of the pageant qualities of the piece see Hulubei pp. 158-9.

121. See below pp. 111-2.

122. E.g. *Pastoralet* 2960-5, Deschamps Vol. III no. 341; and see below, pp. 88-9.

123. Ed. Christine Martineau-Genieys (Publications Romanes et Françaises CXXI, Geneva 1972). The work was probably written c. 1461-5; it was first printed in 1493, two years after Meschinot's death, and went through some thirty editions before 1539 (pp. cv-vii, lxxix).

124. 'Dixain de la uenue de Iesuchrist, & de Charles le quint Empereur uenu en France, l'an 1539' in his *Chant Natal* (Lyons 1539) sig. diii^b.

125. See Jill Mann, *Chaucer and Medieval Estates Satire* (Cambridge 1973) pp. 56-9, 63-5 and notes for the widespread use of shepherd imagery for the priest in this tradition.

126. *The Minor Poems of John Lydgate* ed. H. N. MacCracken (EETS O.S. 192, 1934) Part II p. 776.

127. 'Les chappeaux des prélatz sont de plus chère chose que n'est le feutre, et, aussi, ne sont-ilz point reploiez ne redoublez par devant. Et peult estre que ce est pource que ilz ne veullent pas reporter aulcun proufit à leur maistre qui les a commis au gouvernement où ilz sont: car les prélatz tondent et prennent voluntiers et retiennent tout le proufit pour eulx-mesmes, comme l'on dit' (pp. 79-80).

128. *The Vision of William concerning Piers the Plowman* ed. Walter W. Skeat (1886/1965) C.X.258-75.

129. Text in Skeat, *Chaucerian* pp. 147-90. On the date see Andrew N. Wawn, 'The Genesis of *The Plowman's Tale*', *Yearbook of English Studies* II (1972) pp. 21-40,

where the early date suggested by Skeat but later challenged in favour of the early sixteenth century is upheld.

130. Ed. F. J. Furnivall, Part I (EETS O.S. 119, 1901) ll. 10881–904; in the original, William of Wadington's *Manuel des Pechiez*, there is only a reference to the 'bon pasteur' and 'ouailles' (ibid. p. 337).

131. Gower, *Confessio* Vol. I ll. 390, 396–401. Cf. also his *Mirour de l'Omme* (*The Complete Works of John Gower* ed. G. C. Macaulay, Vol. I: *The French Works* (Oxford 1899)) ll. 19484–8, 20161–9; and *Vox Clamantis* ed. H. O. Coxe (1850) Lib. III, especially iii.189–96.

132. *The Praier and Complaynte of the Ploweman vnto Christe*, reprinted in *Harleian Miscellany* Vol. VI (1745) pp. 84–106; quotation from p. 103. The work is a Lollard tract which was given a new lease of life by being printed in the Reformation, in 1531.

133. *The Advancement of Learning* (1605; Everyman, 1915/1954) I.vi.7.

134. See Norman Cohn, *The Pursuit of the Millenium* (revised edition, 1970) pp. 94–7, 103–4.

135. Ed. François Guessard and E. de Certain (Collection des documents inédits sur l'Histoire de France, Paris 1862) ll. 7150–1, 7162–3.

136. *Comédie jouée au Mont de Marsan* in *Théâtre Profane* ed. Verdun L. Saulnier (TLF, Paris 1946) pp. 274–323; *Comédie de la Nativité* ed. Pierre Jourda (Paris 1939). See p. 114 below for further discussion of Marguerite's place in the pastoral tradition.

137. Texts in Karl Young, *The Drama of the Medieval Church* (2 vols., Oxford 1933) Vol. II. pp. 14–19, 186–8.

138. Ed. S. Kravtchenko-Dobelmann, *Romania* LXVIII (1944–5) pp. 273–315. The gift is not mentioned in the brief account of the shepherds in the popularized version of the Gospel which may be its source, the *Romanz de Saint Fanuel* (*Revue des Langues Romanes* XIII (27) (1885) ll. 1711–30).

139. *La Nativité et le Geu des Trois Roys* ed. Ruth Whittredge (Bryn Mawr 1944); date on p. 25. Cohen dates the Chantilly *Mystère de la Nativité* c. 1300, but other scholars would place it in the fifteenth century: see Maurice Delbouille, 'De l'Interêt des Nativités Hutoises' in *Mélanges offerts à Gustave Cohen* (Paris 1950) pp. 75–84. The development of *bergerie* in the play would seem to indicate the later date; and the undeveloped versification would be as strange for French in 1300 as one or two centuries later.

140. See Hardin Craig, *English Religious Drama of the Middle Ages* (Oxford 1955) pp. 131, 164, 248, 255.

141. Chantilly *Nativité* l. 108.

142. *Mystère de la Passion* ed. Jules-Marie Richard (Arras 1891).

143. *The Play called Corpus Christi* (Stanford 1966) pp. 151–74.

144. *Hessische Weihnachtspiel* in *Das Drama des Mittelalters* ed. R. Froning, Vol. III (Stuttgart 1892) pp. 904–37, especially p. 917 ff. The play probably dates from the late fifteenth century. As *bergerie* it is closer to English than French: one shepherd has trouble in waking his boy after the angel's speech, and the boy suggests that perhaps he is drunk; later the first shepherd is able to tell his companions the angel's words in Latin. The shepherds leave the stable piping.

145. Reproduced from a Vienna MS in André Mary's translation of the *Roman* (Club des Libraires de France, 1960) facing p. 400. The passage in the *Roman* is lines 20029–33 and 20115 ff. (ed. Ernest Langlois, 5 vols., SATF, Paris 1914–24).

146. *Deutsche Liederdichter des 13. Jahrhunderts* ed. Carl von Kraus (2 vols., Tübingen 1952, 1958) Vol. I 1.V pp. 12–13, and commentary Vol. II pp. 11–12.

147. See also Ernst Guldan, *Eva und Maria* (Graz 1966) p. 163. On the connection of Prudence with self-knowledge, cf. the iconographic representation of Prudentia with a mirror.

148. *Pasteur Evangelique* f. 13ʳ.

149. *Théâtre Profane*, *Comédie sur la Trespas du Roy* ll. 404–6.

150. *PL* Vol. LXXVI col. 1130.

151. Valencia MS 387 (c. 1420) f. 137^r, reproduced in John V. Fleming, *The Roman de la Rose: A Study in Allegory and Iconography* (Princeton 1969) fig. 7.

CHAPTER III

1. See above, p. 65.
2. In *Cantilene e Ballate, Strambotti e Madrigali nei Secoli XIII e XIV* ed. Giosuè Carducci (Pisa 1871) no. CLIX, pp. 214–5.
3. Text ibid. pp. 216–7.
4. In *Sacre Rappresentazioni dei Secoli XIV, XV e XVI* ed. Alessandro d'Ancona (3 vols., Florence 1872) Vol. I pp. 191–210; the shepherd scenes are on pp. 193–8.
5. E.g. Cesare Nappi's *Egloga* ed. Ludovico Frati, 'Un' Egloga Rusticale del 1508', *Giorn. Stor. del. Let. Ital.* XX (1892) pp. 186–204.
6. See e.g. 'Il Contrasto di Tonin e Bighignol' ed. Bruno Cotronei, *Giorn. Stor. del Let. Ital.* XXXVI (1900) pp. 281–324. This is divided into two parts, the first tending towards the idyllic, the second portraying a quarrel and a brawl.
7. Ed. Luciano Banchi (1871; reprinted in *Scelta di Curiosità Letterarie* CXXII, Bologna 1968); 'Fumoso' was the pseudonym of Silvestro Cartaio. The Congrega specialized in rustic plays.
8. In *Parnaso Italiano* Vol. VI: *Lirici Antichi*, ed. Andrea Rubi (Venice 1784); the pastoral section is on pp. 177–84.
9. *Arcadia* in *Opere Volgari* ed. Alfredo Mauro (SI 220, Bari 1961) p. 12 ll. 1–3.
10. It was for long traditional to regard the Melissa whose death is lamented in the final eclogue as the same person as Sincero's lady-love of Prosa VII, so giving the work the illusion of unity. Although some critics still repeat the tradition, the evidence for its truth is very weak, and is not supported by anything in the *Arcadia* itself: see M. Scherillo's edition (Turin 1888) pp. lviii–lxxvi.
11. On the history of the idea of Arcadia see Arthur O. Lovejoy and George Boas, *Primitivism and Related Ideas in Antiquity* (Baltimore 1935), especially pp. 344–8.
12. A very few occasional pieces had been composed in the interim, such as three pastoral epithalamia in the second quarter of the fifteenth century: see Grant p. 294.
13. *Borsias, Bucolicon Liber* ed. Iosephus Fógel and Ladislaus Juhász (Leipzig 1933) pp. 12–20.
14. In *Carmina Illustrium Poetarum Italorum* Vol. VII (Florence 1720) pp. 145–9; Grant gives the date, p. 259.
15. The earliest cycle of this kind was by Geraldini, written in 1484; see Grant pp. 266–73.
16. For their wide diffusion see Mustard's edition pp. 35–40, Grant p. 126. Further commentaries were produced by Filippo Beroaldo (Grant p. 126) and Andreas Vaurentinus; and Badius' was frequently augmented by the notes of Johannis Murmellius.
17. 'Qui in duplo est melior quam Virgilius', quoted by Mustard p. 33.
18. E.g Mantuan VII.127–40.
19. See below p. 132.
20. George Turberville's translation of 1567: *The Eclogues of Mantuan* ed. Douglas Bush (facsimile, New York 1937) p. 22.
21. See Hulubei pp. 86–104, 177–208 for a discussion of these poets and their influence; she comments on their isolation from French writers, p. 205. Alamanni's work does seem to have contributed something to the poem on Loyse, however: see p. 216.
22. François Habert: see Hulubei p. 239.
23. *Marot: Œuvres Lyriques* ed. C. A. Mayer (1964) pp. 321–37; the other eclogues are on pp. 338–59.
24. Mayer pp. 390–8; the attribution is discussed on pp. 56–7.
25. Ballade XI: *Du Jour de Noël*, in *Œuvres Diverses* ed. C. A. Mayer (1966) pp. 157–8.
26. Ed. Félix Gaiffe (Société des Textes Français Modernes, Paris 1910) p. 66.

27. *Chant Natal* sig. diii^b; see above p. 87.

28. Ed. Saulnier pp. 274–323; see above pp. 90–1.

29. *Les Marguerites de la Marguerite des Princesses* ed. Félix Frank (4 vols., Paris 1873) Vol. III, *Fable* (here called *L'Histoire des Satyres...*) pp. 167–200, *Complainte* pp. 62–83, especially 78–83.

30. For an account of their work see Hulubei pp. 224–66. One of the most 'mediaevalist' of these writers was François Habert: see pp. 228–44, 313–5.

31. *Gargantua* ed. Pierre Michel (Paris 1965) XXV, p. 217; see especially the final paragraph.

32. *Art* p. 159.

33. Ed. Feuillerat Vol. III p. 36.

34. The *De Jure regum Anglorum ad regnum Franciae* of Thomas Bekynton, bishop of Bath and Wells, probably written in the 1430's; see Arnold Judd, *The Life of Thomas Bekynton* (Chichester 1961) p. 40. Bekynton was a well-read man who maintained a correspondence with some Italian humanists; just how he got to know Petrarch's eclogues is not known.

35. Albert Feuillerat, *Documents relating to the Office of the Revels in the Time of Queen Elizabeth* (1908) p. 34.

36. *Arcadia*, Feuillerat Vol. I p. 13.

37. Glynne Wickham, *Early English Stages* (2 vols., 2nd edition 1963) Vol. I p. 170.

38. E.g. *Englands Helicon* ed. Hugh MacDonald (Muses' Library, 1949) p. 3 (Edmund Bolton), pp. 174–6 (?Anthony Munday); Drayton, *ISG* IV.142 (*Works* ed. J. W. Hebel (5 vols., Oxford 1961)); Richard Barnfield, *The Shepheards Content, Poems* ed. Montague Summers (1936) p. 29; and many others.

39. *EH* p. 45.

40. In Ravenscroft's *Deuteromelia* (1609), a collection of ballads and folksongs (*English Madrigal Verse 1588–1632* ed. E. H. Fellowes (3rd edition, Oxford 1967) p. 201). It is possible that the song 'Late, lait on evinnyngis' mentioned in the late fifteenth-century Scots poem *Colkelbie Sow* is the same (*The Bannatyne Manuscript* (1568) ed. W. Tod Ritchie (4 vols., STS, Edinburgh 1928–34) Vol. IV pp. 279–308) l. 308.

41. First published in 1600, though probably written earlier; it is printed among doubtful works in *The Complete Works of John Lyly* ed. R. Warwick Bond (Oxford 1902/67) Vol. III pp. 333–87; the song is on p. 358.

42. Greene, *Carols* p. 50, and *Coventry* pp. 31–2.

43. Balliol MS 354. It has been edited twice, by Edward Flügel in *Anglia* XXVI (1903) pp. 94–285, and by Roman Dyboski for the EETS (E.S. 101, 1908 for 1907).

44. *Calendar of State Papers: Venetian*, Vol. IV: 1527–1533, ed. Rawdon Brown (1871) p. 2 (an eyewitness account written just after the event by Gasparo Spinelli, the Venetian Secretary in London); George Cavendish, *The Life and Death of Cardinal Wolsey* ed. Richard S. Sylvester (EETS 243, 1959) p. 25 (the entertainment is not given a date and he might be referring to a different occasion: see also Edward Halle, *The Triumphant Reigne of Kyng Henry VIII* ed. Charles Whibley (1904) Vol. II p. 78).

45. Albert Feuillerat, *Documents relating to the Office of the Revels in the Time of King Edward VI and Queen Mary* (1914) p. 14.

46. 'Pd for mendyng the Shepherde, xx^d' (entry in the Grocers' Wardens' accounts for 1532; *A Calendar of Dramatic Records in the Books of the Livery Companies of London* ed. Jean Robertson and D. J. Gordon (Malone Society Collections Vol. III, Oxford 1954) p. 20).

47. *The Poetical Works of John Skelton* ed. Alexander Dyce (2 vols., 1843) Vol. I pp. 311–60 ll. 76–81, 147–61.

48. Ed. Flügel (*Anglia* XXVI) p. 169.

49. *Garlande of Laurell* ll. 1494–7, Skelton Vol. I p. 420.

50. He describes them as having been written some years earlier and calls them 'egloges of youth' (Prol. 76), but this is taken straight from the prologue to the *Adolescentia*. It is possible, none the less, that the first three eclogues could have been drafted earlier; see White's discussion of the dating, Barclay pp. lvii–lx.

51. Contempsit oraculum regias opes et apparatus, atque Aglaum quendam Arcadem, modici ruris cultorem, qui metas agelli sui cupiditate nunquam excesserat, foelicem esse respondit (p. 23).

52. *Gerusalemme Liberata* ed. L. Bonfigli (SI 130, Bari 1930) Canto VII, especially stanzas 8–11.

53. Conrad 1516–9 (Huygens p. 120), where he compares the allegorical technique of the *Bucolics* with 'proverbiis vulgaribus'.

54. For another striking instance see Barclay's account of the wall-paintings in Ely Cathedral (V.517–24; the idea comes from Mantuan) and Chaucer's descriptions of the 'portreiture that was upon the wal' of the temples in the *House of Fame* and the *Knight's Tale*.

55. *Tottel* 18 pp. 16–18 and *Surrey: Poems* ed. Emrys Jones (Oxford 1964) pp. 12–14. Jones assumes that the lover is also a shepherd (notes on ll. 1–4), but it is clear from the poem that he is of higher rank, presumably a courtier.

56. See above, p. 55.

57. *Tottel* 181 pp. 132–5; for its later history see Vol. II p. 266.

58. *Eglogs, Epytaphes and Sonettes* ed. Frank B. Fieler (facsimile, Gainesville 1968).

59. *Poemata Varii Argumenti* ed. William Dillingham (1678) pp. 185–207. Phineas Fletcher appears to allude to five Latin eclogues written by his father, but these three are all that have survived: see Leicester Bradner, *Musae Anglicanae* (MLA General Series X, 1940) p. 57.

60. Feuillerat, *Documents of Elizabeth* pp. 227–8; 286, 295; 365.

CHAPTER IV

1. Servius p. 5: Dicendo autem 'tenuis avena', stili genus latenter ostendit, quo, ut supra dictum est, in bucolicis utitur.

2. Servius pp. 1–2: Tres enim sunt characteres, humilis, medius, grandiloquus: quos omnes in hoc invenimus poeta. nam in Aeneide grandiloquum habet, in georgicis medium, in bucolicis humilem pro qualitate negotiorum et personarum: nam personae hic rusticae sunt, simplicitate gaudentes, a quibus nihil altum debet requiri.

3. Puttenham III.v.

4. 'Humili voce', Angilbert 73; 'rustica raucisonae...carmina Musae', Modoin I.29, II.121.

5. *Arts* ed. Faral p. 359, ll. 631–2.

6. *Satires, Epistles and Ars Poetica* ed. H. Rushton Fairclough (Loeb ed., 1926) l. 92; Fairclough's translation.

7. V.45–8, p. 86: Sunt tres stili secundum tres status hominum. Pastorali uite conuenit stilus humilis, agricolis mediocris, grauis grauibus personis, que presunt pastoribus et agricolis.

8. E. K.'s 'Generall Argument' to the *SC*; Huygens, *Accessus* p. 27, Bernard p. 60.61, Conrad p. 94.689.

9. See above, p. 12.

10. Barclay I.699.

11. *The Life and Minor Works of George Peele* ed. David H. Horne (New Haven 1952) pp. 224–30.

12. Ed. J. W. Bright and W. P. Mustard in *Mod. Phil.* VII (1910) p. 433 ff.; quotation from 'Author ad librum'.

13. Epistle to Harvey in *SC*.

14. Facsimile ed. August Buck (Lyon 1561; Stuttgart 1964) IV.xx, IV.i.

15. To the Reader of his Pastorals, Drayton Vol. II p. 517.

16. It is so called in the MS, B.M. Add. 34361; facsimile ed. R. C. Alston (Menston 1969).

17. The theory applied to all the arts: cf. Morley's approval of the use of perfect chords in the *villanella*, the musical equivalent of the base pastoral, 'for in this kind they thinke it no fault (as being a kind of keeping decorum) to make a clownish

musicke to a clownish matter' (*Plaine and Easie Introduction to Practicall Musicke*, 1597; Shakespeare Association facsimile 14, ed. E. H. Fellowes (1937) p. 80). A number of Italian *villanelle* make use of parallel fifths to convey the appropriate clownishness (Gustave Rees, *Music in the Renaissance* (1954) pp. 332–4).

18. *Conversations* (Shakespeare Soc., 1842) pp. 2, 4.

19. *M. Valerii Probi in Vergilii Bucolica et Georgica Commentarius* ed. H. Keil (Halle 1848) pp. 4–5. Compare, however, the parody of the opening of the third eclogue current in Rome:

Dic mihi Damoeta, 'cuium pecus', anne Latinum?
non. verum Aegonis nostri, sic rure loquuntur.

(Donatus' Life of Virgil in *Vitae Virgilianae Antiquae* ed. Colin Hardie (Oxford 1966) p. 17.)

20. Ed. H. E. Rollins (Cambridge, Mass., 1931); see especially the eclogue on the death of Sidney, Vol. I p. 36 ff., presumably written in the 1580's; the fragment *Eglogue...concerning Olde Age*, p. 50 ff.; and the *Eclogue: entitled Cuddy* added in the second edition, of 1608, and so presumably written only shortly before that, p. 287 ff.

21. *Epistolae Familiares* X.4.

22. Servius p. 44.

23. Drayton Vol. II p. 517.

24. Eclogue IV.1–2, *Arcadia and Piscatorial Eclogues* ed. Ralph Nash (Detroit 1966) p. 176.

25. Molinet, *Faictz* Vol. III p. 968.

26. *The Poems of Andrew Marvell* ed. Hugh Macdonald (Muses' Library, second edition, 1956) p. 14 l. 23. The poem is a kind of debate on the issues of earthly or heavenly love, mutability or immortality.

27. Puttenham III.v.

28. *Œuvres Complètes* ed. Gustave Cohen (France 1958) p. 918.

29. 'To the Reader', *The Faithful Shepherdess* ed. W. W. Greg in *The Works of Francis Beaumont and John Fletcher* Vol. III (Variorum ed., 1908).

30. Second Sermon on the Lord's Prayer, *Sermons of Bishop Latimer* ed. G. E. Corrie (Parker Society, Cambridge 1844) p. 343.

31. Letter to the earl of Leicester, 1581, in Edward Edwards, *Life of Sir Walter Raleigh* (1868) Vol. II p. 17.

32. Ed. Betty J. Littleton (The Hague 1968); it was first published in 1599 but was almost certainly written in the 1570's (pp. 14, 30–33).

33. Sidney ed. Feuillerat Vol. I p. 13.

34. They are not introduced until the fourth set of eclogues, Vol. IV p. 307.

35. Vol. I 2.xiv and p. 118.

36. Bruce Pattison, 'The Roundelay in the August eclogue of the *Shepheardes Calender*', *Review of English Studies* IX (1933) pp. 54–5.

37. The first part was published in 1586, and the poem grew in the course of the numerous succeeding editions, being completed in 1612. The story of Curan and Argentile is in every recension (Book IV.xx). Curan is the character better known from romance as Havelok.

38. *ISG* (Drayton Vol. I pp. 45–94) VIII.177–90.

39. *The Complete Works of Thomas Lodge* ed. Edmund Gosse (4 vols., Hunterian Club 1883/New York 1963) Vol. III.XI p. 6.

40. *To reuerend Colin: Eclogue I*, p. 19.

41. *Englands Mourning Garment* in *Shakspere Allusion-Books* ed. C. M. Ingleby (Shakspere Soc., 1874) Part I pp. 81–116; quotation on p. 85.

42. *Englands Helicon* p. 115; the poem is Sonnet XV of Richard Barnfield's *Cynthia*.

43. *The Poetical Works of John Milton* ed. Helen Darbishire (Oxford 1955) Vol. II p. 116, st. viii.

44. Mantuan I.2.

45. Lodge Vol. I.IV p. 108.

46. Remy Dupuys, *La tryumphante et solennelle entree faicte sur le nouuel et ioyeux aduenement de...Monsieur Charles...en sa ville de Bruges* (Bruges 1515) sig. Fv^b: Neantmoyns (dient les poetes) et pour son dernier refuge fit residence entre laboureurs, pasteurs, et gens agrestes lesquelz apres tous aultres finablement la contraignirent soy retirer au ciel dont elle estoit premierement descendue. Ainsi doncques est labeur et pastouraige de tous estatz le plus ancien...et outreplus est la vertu plus entiere, moins corruptible.

47. *The Poems of Sir Philip Sidney* ed. W. A. Ringler (Oxford 1962) p. 262.

CHAPTER V

1. The romances of Heliodorus and *Amadis de Gaule* are of greater importance as sources for the plot of the *Arcadia*, but not for the pastoral.

2. Sidney ed. Feuillerat Vol. I p. 285. For convenience I have used this edition for references to both the Old and the New *Arcadia*; the *Old Arcadia* has also been edited by Jean Robertson (Oxford 1973).

3. Vol. I pp. 311, 152. This type of crook is commonly illustrated in mediaeval pictures of shepherds; the hollow-ended crook is sometimes an alternative to the hooked. For the practice of throwing clods at straying sheep see R. Chambers, *A Book of Days* (1863) Vol. I p. 480, and Jehan de Brie p. 77.

4. It was included by the editor of the 1593 edition of the *Arcadia*, but probably against Sidney's intentions; he gives different details of Urania's life in the prose of the *New Arcadia*. The text is in Sidney ed. Ringler pp. 242–56; there is a discussion of the date of composition (probably after the *Old Arcadia* was finished) on p. 494.

5. See above pp. 137–8.

6. Feuillerat Vol. I pp. 7, 27.

7. Spenser, *Teares of the Muses* l. 488.

8. I do not know of any contemporary evidence to suggest otherwise as far as England is concerned; May Queens certainly existed in Scotland, but folk customs were often markedly different north of the Border.

9. The opening words of the piece; the title is editorial. Text in Feuillerat Vol. II pp. 208–17; the ending missing in this version is supplied in Robert Kimbrough and Philip Murphy, 'The Helmingham Hall Manuscript of Sidney's *The Lady of May*', *Renaissance Drama* N.S. I (1968) pp. 118–9. Elizabeth visited Wanstead in the May of 1578 and 1579, but the earlier date is almost certainly correct: see Ringler pp. 361–2 and the discussion of the piece below.

10. Scaliger I.iv, III.xcix.

11. *Maydes Metamorphosis* I, Lyly Vol. III pp. 350–2; Drayton Vol. III pp. 293–300, Sixth Nimphall, where a fisherman makes a third in the debate.

12. Cf. the forester songs from the court of Henry VIII (e.g. Stevens p. 400 (H 35) and p. 408 (H 62)), the 'Come over the woods' theme in French and English pastourelle-type songs (e.g. *Early English Lyrics* ed. Frank Sidgwick and E. K. Chambers (1907/66) no. XXIX; Raynaud, *Motets* Vol. I p. 193; Jones pp. 90–105), and Spenser's identification of forester and rapist in the *Faerie Queene* III.

13. 'Sidney's Experiment in Pastoral: *The Lady of May*', *JWCI* XXVI (1963) pp. 198–203.

14. See Ringler p. 362.

15. E.g. the oak leaves he carved in the Beauchamp Tower in the Tower of London. For another use of the pun see e.g. Hubert's *Grosseteste* l. 35.

16. Ringler p. 361.

17. Eric St. John Brooks, *Sir Christopher Hatton: Queen Elizabeth's Favourite* (1946) p. 95.

18. In *Memoirs of the Life and Times of Sir Christopher Hatton, K.G.* by Sir Harris Nicolas (1847) pp. 68–9.

19. Kimbrough and Murphy pp. 118–9; I have corrected two obvious MS errors.

20. Nicolas p. 69. The reference to his 'too, too many more faults' could possibly be an echo of the 'manie faultes of Therion' of the play, but the phrase is too commonplace to be sure.

21. From the court at Hampton, 18 June, 1578; printed in Brooks p. 170.

22. Ninth Song of *Astrophel and Stella*, ed. Ringler p. 221.

23. Spenser, *Astrophell* ll. 9, 73–8, 31–2.

24. Bryskett's poem also appears in Spenser's *Astrophell*; Davison Vol. I pp. 36–44; Drayton, *ISG* IV.

25. *The Works in Verse and Prose of Nicholas Breton* ed. A. B. Grosart (2 vols., 1879) Vol. I u.121–2.

26. *Colyn Cloute* ll. 53–60, Skelton Vol. I p. 313.

27. *Secunda Pastorum* 436, 449 (he is the First, and apparently the principal, shepherd); *Colkelbie Sow* 267. The Scots form is Celtic in origin; although identical in appearance, the French and English forms are a diminutive of 'Nicholas'. 'Colin and Coll' are used as typical names for servants and horse-boys in *Historical Poems* no. 7, p. 27.

28. The problem of establishing an exact source remains even when an 'original' is known. 'March', for instance, is derived ultimately from Bion's Fourth Idyll, but this was available in both Latin and French versions and Spenser probably did not know the Greek directly; the echo of Moschus in the same poem probably comes by way of Politian. More obscure poets rapidly become impossible to trace through this sort of maze.

29. See the notes in the Variorum edition for discussion of this line. It clearly refers to either *Piers Plowman* or the *Plowman's Tale*, or possibly both; if it does refer to the *Tale* then Spenser must have known it was not written by Chaucer, as he distinguishes it from Tityrus' work.

30. April 99, *Plowman's Tale* 14. 'Swink' and 'sweat' commonly alliterate, but neither the *OED* nor the *MED* recognizes 'forswink' or its participle.

31. Drayton Vol. II p. 518; he actually refers to the *Ship of Fools*, but the context makes it clear that he is thinking of the eclogues, which Cawood had printed at the end of the longer poem. There are also a few echoes of them in his own pastoral.

32. See especially Paul McLane, *Spenser's Shepheardes Calender: A Study in Elizabethan Allegory* (Indiana 1961) and Marien-Sofie Røstvig, 'The *Shepheardes Calender* – A Structural Analysis', *Renaissance and Modern Studies* XIII (1969) pp. 49–75.

33. Ed. Sommer Vol. III p. 19.

34. That it was roughly equivalent to Theocritus' use of Doric was never suggested as a defence in the sixteenth century: Sidney cites Theocritus as well as Virgil and Sannazaro as examples of pastoral poets who did not alter their language. See the discussion in Merritt Y. Hughes, 'Spenser and the Greek Pastoral Triad', *Studies in Philology* XX (1923) pp. 187–90.

35. See Patrick Cullen, *Spenser, Marvell and Renaissance Pastoral* (Cambridge, Mass., 1970) pp. 38–41.

36. See Harold Stein, *Studies in Spenser's Complaints* (U.S.A. 1934) pp. 58–62, 82–6.

37. The thematic similarities to the *Dit de la Pastoure* are so striking as to raise the question of whether Spenser could have read it, although it had never been printed. One MS, now Westminster Abbey 21, was certainly in England in the sixteenth century (see Paul Meyer, *Bulletin de la SATF* I (1875) pp. 28, 36); another, now MS Harley 4431, was in England in the fifteenth and seventeenth centuries but may well have been abroad in between (see Meyer's note in Christine Vol. III pp. xxi–iv). There may of course have been other manuscripts. The only conclusion can be that it is not impossible that Spenser knew it.

38. The point has been made by a number of critics: see in particular Humphrey Tonkin, *Spenser's Courteous Pastoral* (Oxford 1972) pp. 111–31.

39. Bartsch III.44; see above, pp. 64–5. Robin 'flaiole a douce alaine,/car pour Marguerot se paine...'

40. Epistle to Henry Reynolds: 'Of Poets and Poesie', Vol. III pp. 226–7 ll. 29–38.

41. Vol. II p. 517.
42. Vol. IV p. v*.
43. *Sirena* 133–46; *ISG* and *Pa.* III.29–32.
44. *Pa.* VIII.97–100.
45. E.g. *Coriolanus* IV.vi.110–2; *Timon* V.iv.42–4. The references in *2 Henry VI* are to III.i.191–2 (quoted), and see also II.ii.73–4.
46. The consistency of Shakespeare's characterization of Joan is still something of a critical problem; see Leo Kirschbaum, 'The Authorship of "1 Henry VI"', *PMLA* LXVII (1952) pp. 809–22.
47. The phrase is Renato Poggioli's, in his essay on pastoral, 'The Oaten Flute', *Harvard Library Bulletin* XI (1957) pp. 147–84.
48. *EH* pp. 68–9, *Phillidaes Love-call to her Coridon*; cf. Bartsch II.3, 24, 65 etc.
49. *EH* p. 79, by the earl of Oxford.
50. Lodge III.XI, p. 19.
51. *The Spenserian Poets* (1969) p. 148.
52. *Thomas Watson's Latin Amyntas* (1585) ed. Walter F. Staton, Jr, and *Abraham Fraunce's Translation 'The Lamentations of Amyntas'* (1587) ed. Franklin M. Dickey (Renaissance English Text Soc., Chicago 1967) pp. 76–7. 'Lightfoot' is Fraunce's addition; he omits Watson's detail that the tarbox was 'ad latus affixa'.
53. *Tullies Loue* (1589) in *Life and Complete Works of Robert Greene* ed. A. B. Grosart (15 vols., 1881–6/New York 1964) Vol. VII pp. 182–3. The original text reads 'hir dog'.
54. Vol. IX pp. 142–3.
55. *Anatomy of Abuses* ed. F. J. Furnivall (1877–9) p. 149.
56. *Ben Jonson* ed. C. H. Herford, Percy and Evelyn Simpson, Vol. VII (Oxford 1963) pp. 7–49.
57. The poem is on p. 18 of *Daffodils and Primroses* (Part 2d) in Vol. I of Grosart's edition of Breton.
58. See e.g. Drayton, *Muses Elizium* VI; Davison's *Poetical Rhapsody*, *Eglogue concerning Olde Age*, p. 50 ff.; for Sudeley, John Nichols, *The Progresses and Public Processions of Queen Elizabeth* (3 vols., 1823/New York n.d.) Vol. III p. 141.
59. This is from a translation of the first epistle of Watson's *Amintae Gaudia* (1592), sig. Bi^a, by 'I. T. gent.' (1594): see W. W. Greg, 'English Versions of Watson's Latin Poems', *Modern Language Quarterly* VI (1903) p. 129.
60. Eighth Lamentation, *Amyntas* pp. 60–1.
61. *The Poetical Works of William Basse* ed. R. Warwick Bond (1893), Eglogue V p. 215. The MS containing his *Pastorals* is dated 1653, but they were begun much earlier, certainly in the lifetime of the countess of Pembroke (i.e. before 1621).
62. *EH* p. 3, *Theorello, A Sheepheards Edillion* by Edmund Bolton.
63. E.g. Sabie III (the Patriarchs, Paris, Bethlehem shepherds, adopted from Mantuan); *Ecloga: Amor Constans* in Bodleian MS Eng. misc. d.239 f.3^r (Pan, Adonis, Paris, 'godds'); Barnfield, *Cynthia* Sonnet XV (*Poems* p. 63 and *EH* p. 115) (Apollo, Jove, 'and many Gods beside'); etc.
64. *Rosalynde* p. 108; *Olde Damons Pastorall, EH* p. 19; *Phillida and Coridon, EH* p. 23.
65. *Tullies Loue*, Greene Vol. VII p. 184; cf. Adam de la Halle, *Jeu* ll. 5, 172–82.
66. Lyly Vol. III, *Midas* IV.ii.53–4.
67. *The Works of John Day* ed. A. H. Bullen (2 vols., 1881), II.ii.
68. Breton Vol. I.n, Sonet I.
69. *The Shepherd's Hunting*, in *The Poetry of George Wither* ed. Frank Sidgwick (2 vols., 1902) Vol. I pp. 1–79.
70. *Poems of William Browne* ed. Gordon Godwin (Muses' Library, 1894) Vol. II p. 89.
71. In *The Complete Works of Samuel Daniel* ed. A. B. Grosart (1885/New York 1963) Vol. III, III.i.151–5. Warner also makes a shepherd condemn smoking (see below, p. 187); Fairfax, on the other hand, calls it 'Divine Tobacco' in his eighth eclogue (l. 42, ed. W. W. Greg in his *Collected Papers* (Oxford 1966) pp. 29–43).

72. *The Shepheards Oracles* X in Quarles, *Complete Works* ed. A. B. Grosart (Chertsey Worthies' Library, 3 vols., Edinburgh 1880–1) Vol. III p. 231.

73. The details are given on the title page; it was not published until 1634 (Edinburgh).

74. *Eclogue the Fourth* is in Mrs. Elizabeth Cooper's *The Muses' Library* (Vol. I only published, 1738) pp. 364–76; another, unnumbered but headed 'Hermes and Lycaon', is in Bodleian MS Fairfax 40 pp. 647–56 (printed somewhat inaccurately by C. R. Markham in *Miscellanies of the Philobiblon Society* XII (1868–9) sec. 4). For the third, *Ecloga Octava*, see n. 71 above. The opening couplet of the Fifth Eclogue has also been preserved, along with its extensive annotation by Fairfax's son, in the 1789 edition of Camden's *Britannia* (Vol. III p. 50).

75. Cooper p. 363.

76. Gloss to 'March'. The detail comes from Thomas Cooper's *Thesaurus* (1565).

77. *The Poems of Thomas Randolph* ed. G. Thorn-Drury (1929) pp. 101–4. Randolph was born in 1605 and died in 1635; the exact date of composition of this poem is not known.

CHAPTER VI

1. Quoted in Neville Williams, *Elizabeth: Queen of England* (1967) p. 196.

2. *Letters and Papers of Henry VIII* ed. James Gairdner and R. H. Brodie, Vol. XII.I (1890) no. 1212 (p. 557), dated 16 May, 1537.

3. Ibid. no. 1284 (p. 585), dated 26 May.

4. Ibid. Vol. XIV.I (1894) no. 1261 (p. 558).

5. Printed in Malone Society Collections Vol. II (1909) pp. 127–32.

6. Sydney Anglo, 'An Early Tudor Programme for Plays and Demonstrations against the Pope', *JWCI* XX (1957) pp. 176–9; the quotation is on p. 179.

7. *A Sad Warning to all Prophane, Malignant Spirits*...(1642) p. 3.

8. See Anthea Hume, 'Spenser, Puritanism and the "Maye" Eclogue', *RES* N.S. XX (1969), especially pp. 159–62. Paul McLane suggests a concurrent political theme referring to James VI (the Kid) and Aubigny (the Fox), pp. 77–91, 175.

9. *The Marprelate Tracts, 1588, 1589* ed. William Pierce (1911) pp. 226–7, 369–70.

10. *The Works of Thomas Nashe* ed. R. B. McKerrow (ed. F. P. Wilson, Oxford 1958) Vol. I p. 83. For other references see *Martins Months Minde* (1589) sig. E3^b; *A Whip for an Ape* (Lyly Vol. III p. 419 ll. 31–2); in combination with the pastoral metaphors of ecclesiastical satire in *Pappe with an Hatchet* (Lyly Vol. III pp. 408, 411). The whole question of festive abuse in the Marprelate controversy is discussed by C. L. Barber, *Shakespeare's Festive Comedy* (New York 1957) pp. 51–7.

11. In *Ballads from Manuscripts* Vol. I.I, ed. F. J. Furnivall (Ballad Society, 1868) p. 295 ff. There is only one MS, consisting of a single sheet of the poem ending with a catchword, MS Harley 367 f. 150; the whole MS is a collection of miscellaneous papers of John Stowe and others, apparently put together over some fifty years from about 1570 till 1620 and including copies of poems by earlier authors such as Lydgate and Skelton. The MS only takes the *Tale* as far as the Dissolution of the Monasteries, which is why Furnivall includes it in his collection for the reign of Henry VIII. The whole subject, however, suggests the Marprelate era; the first use of the word 'politician' (from the heading) recorded by the *OED* is from 1588 – though the gloss need not be of the same date as the poem; and while there are no direct echoes of the *Shepheardes Calender*, as might be expected in an eclogue of this date, the quality of the poetry and the 'monyment – astonishment' rhyme (105–6) both suggest a date after Spenser.

12. Mantuan VIII.13–14. The idea of the 'loves storye' is also from Mantuan; and in addition the description of the ruined abbeys (101–6) may owe something to Mantuan X.151 and IX.205–11 – though it is more important as poetry in its own right.

13. The immediate source may well be literary, however, from the anti-Catholic satire entitled 'A brefe Dialoge between two prestes servauntis named Watkyn (abbreviated to "Wat:" throughout the text) and Ieffraye', published at Strasbourg in 1528 for circulation in England; it was probably written by William Roy and Jerome Barlowe. The *Dialoge* is the second, and most substantial, part of *Rede me and be nott wrothe* (Arber's English Reprints, 1871). It includes the usual indictments of the clergy for fleecing their flocks (p. 101).

14. Facsimile ed. Josephine Waters Bennett (New York 1941).

15. Nichols Vol. III pp. 134–5.

16. Ed. Feuillerat Vol. II p. 217.

17. B. M. MS Add. 41499A, a MS connected with Sir Henry Lee, ff. 2ʳ–3ᵛ. The piece is impossible to date precisely; the way it speaks of Accession Day as a feast day could suggest an early date, shortly after 1576. E. K. Chambers, in *Sir Henry Lee* (Oxford 1936) p. 270, indicates various *termini* in his discussion of possible contenders for the initials C. H. by which the peasants appear to address the knight.

18. The interpolation is on pp. 101–23 of the edition by Joseph Jacobs (1890). Day's portraits of the shepherds taking part read as if they represent specific people, but final identification is difficult; the most likely is of the third shepherd, Thyrsis, with the young Essex, whose 'more than common inclination to the highest exploits' and 'youthfull desires...to far loftier purposes' were already becoming abundantly clear by this date.

19. Ed. W. C. Hazlitt, *Fugitive Tracts* I.xxix. Hazlitt sums up the piece as a 'somewhat tedious, though exceedingly loyal, lucubration'.

20. Nichols Vol. III p. 140.

21. Ibid. p. 105.

22. Ibid. p. 120.

23. *EH* p. 17.

24. Nashe Vol. III pp. 231–95, especially ll. 132–7, 1843–62.

25. Thomas Watson, *Italian Madrigals Englished* (1590), Fellowes p. 274.

26. Nichols Vol. III p. 109, *EH* p. 44.

27. Fellowes pp. 158–66. There are 'birthday' references in VIII and XI; but for other suggestions see Roy Strong, 'Queen Elizabeth as Oriana', *Studies in the Renaissance* VI (1959) p. 255, and John Buttrey, 'Music for Elizabeth I', *Records and Recording* (April 1970) pp. 15–17. The references to Maying in the collection are of course no indication of the occasion.

28. *Canzonets* (1593), Fellowes p. 135.

29. *EH* pp. 63–6, by 'W. H.', usually identified with William Hunnis; but there is no foundation for the ascription other than the initials, and Hunnis' other extant poems indicate beyond any reasonable doubt that he could not have written these. The name 'Wodenfride' does not occur elsewhere in Elizabethan literature; and that 'Amargana' is 'anagrama' spelled backwards does not help to solve the questions of authorship, context or aim.

30. Peele pp. 265–75.

31. Peele pp. 214–9, stage direction l. 53/4. On the whole subject see Frances A. Yates, 'Queen Elizabeth as Astraea', *JWCI* X (1947) pp. 27–82 (reprinted in her *Astraea* (1975)).

32. Harry Levin assembles a notable collection in *The Myth of the Golden Age in the Renaissance* (1970) pp. 70–1, 112.

33. B. M. MS Royal 12.A.LXVII f. 14ʳ; another poem (f. 13ʳ) compares her care for her flock to Tityrus' concern for his goats.

34. John Lane, *An Elegie vpon the death of the high renowned Princesse*, in *Fugitive Tracts* II.ii. For the use of Elizabeth as Virgo, see e.g. the Sudeley entertainment quoted above (p. 202) and Barnfield's *Cynthia* (*Poems* p. 55).

35. *Poetical Rhapsody* Vol. I pp. 14–17. Rollins ascribes the poem to the Queen's visit to Wilton late in 1599 (Vol. II p. 100).

36. *The Poems of Sir John Davies* ed. Robert Krueger (Oxford 1975) p. 72, no. III.

37. From the wild man's speech at Cowdray, Nichols Vol. III p. 94 (cf. Virgil I.6).

38. *Poetical Rhapsody* Vol. I pp. 25–35.

39. Two works published at this time (the *Triumphs*, 1601, and the *Dialogue in praise of Astraea*, 1602) had both been written earlier.

40. The identification of Dido as Elizabeth was first made by Mary Parmenter, 'Spenser's "Twelve Aeglogues Proportionable to the Twelve Monethes"', *ELH* III (1936) pp. 213–6. Her interpretation is expanded by McLane, pp. 47–60, where he argues that her 'death' is metaphorical and refers to the figurative 'death of England and Elizabeth, a death which seemed, in terms of the Alençon marriage, imminent in the last few months of 1579' (p. 60). This means, however, that the second half of the elegy, on Dido's joy in Heaven, has to be taken ironically – a reading that seems to me poetically impossible.

41. Thomas Dekker, *The Wonderfull Yeare* (Elizabethan and Jacobean Quartos, Edinburgh 1966) pp. 16, 19, 25.

42. Drayton, *Muses Elizium* X.34–5.

43. *Giles and Phineas Fletcher: Poetical Works* ed. Frederick S. Boas (Cambridge 1908–9/1970) Vol. II pp. 1–171, III.30, 32. The poem was probably composed earlier.

44. Wither Vol. I p. 179, ll. 535–8.

45. *Robert Dover and the Cotswold Games: Annalia Dubrensia* ed. Christopher Whitfield (1962).

BIBLIOGRAPHY

The bibliography is classified by language, each being subdivided into primary sources (1) and secondary sources (2) for that language. The languages are in alphabetical order. Cross-references are to the same section unless some other indication is given; some works resist easy classification, but I hope multiple references where necessary will help with location, and I must ask the reader's tolerance for any anomalies. Where more than one edition of a work is cited, the edition used as the standard in the text is listed first; otherwise all entries are alphabetical. The titles or first lines of anonymous poems and lyrics of any significance are included. The place of publication is London unless otherwise stated.

The bibliography does not attempt to be a complete guide to pastoral literature of the period, and especially not to criticism. It is confined to works cited, with the addition of a few major critical works bearing closely on the text.

The arrangement of the bibliography is as follows:

    I. General
    II. English and Scots
    III. French and Provençal
    IV. German
    V. Greek
    VI. Italian
    VII. Latin
    VIII. Spanish

I. General

Richard AXTON. *European Drama of the Early Middle Ages* (1974)

Enrico CARRARA. *La Poesia Pastorale* (Storia dei Generi Letterari Italiani, Milan 1909)

Norman COHN. *The Pursuit of the Millenium* (revised ed., 1970)

Helen COOPER. 'The Goat and the Eclogue', *Philological Quarterly* LIII (1974) pp. 363–79

Peter DRONKE. *The Medieval Lyric* (1968)

William EMPSON. *Some Versions of Pastoral* (1935; Penguin, Harmondsworth 1966)

Mia Irene GERHARDT. *Essai d'Analyse Littéraire de la Pastorale* (Netherlands 1950)

T. P. HARRISON. *The Pastoral Elegy* (Texas 1939/New York 1968)

S. K. HENINGER Jr. 'The Renaissance Perversion of Pastoral', *Journal of the History of Ideas* XXII (1961) pp. 254–61

Jan HUIZINGA. *The Waning of the Middle Ages*, trans. F. Hopman (Penguin, Harmondsworth 1965)

Harry LEVIN. *The Myth of the Golden Age in the Renaissance* (1970)

Arthur O. LOVEJOY and George Boas. *Primitivism and Related Ideas in Antiquity* (Baltimore 1935)

Erwin PANOFSKY. *Meaning in the Visual Arts* (Penguin, Harmondsworth 1970)

Renato POGGIOLI. 'The Oaten Flute', *Harvard Library Bulletin* XI (1957) pp. 147–84

Gustave REESE. *Music in the Middle Ages* (1941)

—— *Music in the Renaissance* (1954)

E. W. TAYLER. *Nature and Art in Renaissance Literature* (1964)

W. G. THOMSON. *A History of Tapestry from the Earliest Times to the Present Day* (2nd ed., 1930)

II. *English and Scots*

1: *Texts*

Sydney ANGLO (ed.). 'An Early Tudor Programme for Plays and other Demonstrations against the Pope', *JWCI* XX (1957) pp. 176–9

ANNALIA Dubrensia   see DOVER

'AS I me lend'   in *HISTORICAL Poems* p. 147

Sir Francis BACON. *The Advancement of Learning* (Everyman, 1915/1954)

BALLADS from Manuscripts, ed. F. J. Furnivall and others (Ballad Society, 1863–73)

The BANNATYNE Manuscript writtin in tyme of Pest 1568, ed. W. Tod Ritchie (STS, 4 vols., Edinburgh 1928–34)

Alexander BARCLAY. *The Eclogues of Alexander Barclay*, ed. Beatrice White (EETS O.S. 175, 1928)

Richard BARNFIELD. *The Poems of Richard Barnfield*, ed. Montague Summers (1936)

William BASSE. *The Poetical Works of William Basse*, ed. R. Warwick Bond (1893)

Nathaniel BAXTER. *Sir Philip Sydneys Ourania* (1606)

Thomas BLENERHASSET. *A Revelation of the True Minerva*, ed. Josephine Waters Bennett (1582; facsimile, New York 1941)

Thomas BRADSHAW. *The Shepherds Starre* (1591)

Richard BRATHWAIT. *Whimzies* (1631)

Nicholas BRETON. *The Works in Verse and Prose of Nicholas Breton*, ed. A. B. Grosart (2 vols., 1879)

Carleton BROWN   see *ENGLISH Lyrics*

William BROWNE. *The Poems of William Browne*, ed. Gordon Godwin (Muses' Library, 2 vols., 1894)

CALENDAR of Dramatic Records   see ROBERTSON

CALENDAR of State Papers (*Venetian*) Vol. IV: 1527–33, ed. Rawdon Brown (1871)

George CAVENDISH. *The Life and Death of Cardinal Wolsey*, ed. Richard S. Sylvester (EETS 243, 1959)

Geoffrey CHAUCER. *The Works of Geoffrey Chaucer*, ed. F. N. Robinson (2nd ed., 1957)

The CHESTER Mystery Cycle, ed. R. M. Lumiansky and David Mills (EETS S.S. 3, 1974)

Henry CHETTLE. *Englands Mourning Garment* in *Shakspere Allusion-Books* Part I, ed. C. M. Ingleby (Shakspere Society, 1874)

CLYOMON and Clamydes, ed. Betty J. Littleton (Studies in English Literature 35, The Hague 1968)

COLKELBIE Sow   in *BANNATYNE* Vol. IV pp. 279–308

The COMPLAYNT of Scotlande, ed. J. A. H. Murray (EETS E.S. 17, 1872)

Mrs. Elizabeth COOPER (ed.). *The Muses' Library* (Vol. I only published, 1738)

Ludus COVENTRIAE   see *LUDUS*

Two COVENTRY Corpus Christi Plays, ed. Hardin Craig (2nd ed., EETS E.S. 87, 1957)

Samuel DANIEL. *The Complete Works of Samuel Daniel*, ed. A. B. Grosart (5 vols., 1885/New York 1963)

Sir John DAVIES. *The Poems of Sir John Davies*, ed. Robert Krueger (Oxford 1975)

Francis DAVISON. *The Poetical Rhapsody*, ed. H. E. Rollins (Cambridge, Mass., 1931)

Angel DAY. *Daphnis and Chloe*, ed. Joseph Jacobs (1890)

John DAY. *The Works of John Day*, ed. A. H. Bullen (2 vols., 1881)

Thomas DEKKER. *The Wonderfull Yeare: 1603* (Elizabethan and Jacobean Quartos, Edinburgh 1966)

DOCUMENTS relating to the Office of the Revels in the Time of King Edward VI and Queen Mary, ed. Albert Feuillerat (1914)

DOCUMENTS relating to the Office of the Revels in the Time of Queen Elizabeth, ed. Albert Feuillerat (1908)

Gavin DOUGLAS. *Virgil's Aeneid*, ed. David F. C. Coldwell (4 vols., STS, Edinburgh 1957–64)

Robert DOVER and the Cotswold Games: Annalia Dubrensia, ed. Christopher Whitfield (1962)

Michael DRAYTON. *The Works of Michael Drayton*, ed. J. W. Hebel (5 vols., Oxford 1961)

EARLY English Carols see R. L. GREENE

EARLY English Lyrics, ed. Frank Sidgwick and E. K. Chambers (1907/1966)

ENGLANDS Helicon, ed. Hugh Macdonald (Muses' Library, 1949)

ENGLISH Lyrics of the Thirteenth Century, ed. Carleton Brown (Oxford 1932/1965)

Edward FAIRFAX. *Daemonologia*, ed. W. Grange (Harrogate 1882/1971)

—— *Eclogue the Fourth*, in COOPER pp. 364–76

—— 'Fairfax's Eighth Eclogue' in *Collected Papers of W. W. Greg*, ed. J. C. Maxwell (Oxford 1966) pp. 29–43

—— *Hermes and Lycaon*, ed. C. R. Markham in *Miscellanies of the Philobiblon Society* XII (1868–9) sec. 4

E. H. FELLOWES (ed.) *English Madrigal Verse 1588–1632* (third ed. revised by F. W. Sternfeld and David Greer, Oxford 1967)

Albert FEUILLERAT see *DOCUMENTS*, SIDNEY

FIVE Pastoral Eclogues see WARTON

Abraham FLEMING. *The Bucoliks of Publius Virgilius Maro* (1575)

John FLETCHER. *The Faithful Shepherdess*, ed. W. W. Greg in *The Works of Francis Beaumont and John Fletcher* Vol. III (Variorum edition, 1908)

Phineas FLETCHER. *Giles and Phineas Fletcher: Poetical Works*, ed. Frederick S. Boas (2 vols., Cambridge 1908–9/1970)

Abraham FRAUNCE. *The Arcadian Rhetorike*, ed. Ethel Seaton (Luttrell Society, Oxford 1950)

—— *The Lamentations of Amyntas* see WATSON (Latin (1))

—— *The Shepherd's Logic*, ed. R. C. Alston (facsimile, Menston 1969)

W. H. FRENCH and C. B. Hale (eds.). *Middle English Metrical Romances* (New York 1964)

FUGITIVE Tracts, ed. W. C. Hazlitt (1875)

John GAY *Poems of John Gay*, ed. J. Underhill (Muses' Library, 1893)

Barnabe GOOGE. *Eglogs, Epytaphes and Sonettes*, ed. Frank B. Fieler (facsimile, Gainesville 1968)

John GOWER. *The English Works of John Gower*, ed. G. C. Macaulay (2 vols., EETS E.S. 81–2, 1900–01)

—— see also French (1), Latin (1)

R. L. GREENE (ed.). *The Early English Carols* (2nd ed., Oxford 1977)

Robert GREENE. *The Life and Complete Works of Robert Greene*, ed. A. B. Grosart (15 vols., 1881–6/New York 1964)

Edward HALLE. *The Triumphant Reigne of Kyng Henry VIII*, ed. Charles Whibley (1904)

The HARLEY Lyrics, ed. G. L. Brook (3rd ed., Manchester 1954)

John HARVEY. *A Discoursive Probleme concerning Prophesies* (1588)

Sir Christopher HATTON see NICOLAS; BROOKS (English (2))

Robert HENRYSON. *Poems*, ed. Charles Elliott (corrected ed., Oxford 1966)

'HEY troly loly lo', in STEVENS pp. 424–5

Richard HILL's Commonplace Book, ed. Edward Flügel, in *Anglia* XXVI (1903) pp. 94–285

HISTORICAL Poems of the XIVth and XVth Centuries, ed. R. H. Robbins (New York 1959)

The HOLKHAM Bible Picture-Book, facsimile ed. W. O. Hassall (1954)

JOLLY Wat, in R. L. GREENE p. 49

Ben JONSON. *Ben Jonson*, ed. C. H. Herford, Percy and Evelyn Simpson (11 vols., corrected ed., Oxford 1963)

—— *Conversations* (Shakespeare Society, 1842)

The KALENDER of Shepherdes, ed. H. Oskar Sommer (3 vols., 1892)

'KEPE well the shepe of cristis folde', in HILL p. 169

Robert KIMBROUGH and Philip Murphy. 'The Helmingham Hall Manuscript of Sidney's "The Lady of May"', *Renaissance Drama* N.S. I (1968) pp. 103–119

KING Edward and the Shepherd, in FRENCH pp. 950–85

Maurice KYFFYN. *The Blessednes of Brytaine*, in *FUGITIVE Tracts* I.xxix

John LANE. *An Elegie vpon the death of…Elizabeth*, in *FUGITIVE Tracts* II.ii

William LANGLAND. *The Vision of William concerning Piers the Plowman*, ed. W. W. Skeat (2 vols., 1886/1965)

Hugh LATIMER. *Sermons of Bishop Latimer*, ed. G. E. Corrie (Parker Society, Cambridge 1844)

LETTERS and Papers of Henry VIII Vol. XII–XIV, ed. James Gairdner and R. H. Brodie (1890–94)

Thomas LODGE. *The Complete Works of Thomas Lodge*, ed. Edmund Gosse (4 vols., Hunterian Club, 1883/New York 1963)

LUDUS Coventriae, or the Plaie called Corpus Christi, ed. K. S. Block (EETS E.S. 120, 1922)

John LYDGATE. *The Minor Poems of John Lydgate*, ed. H. N. MacCracken (EETS O.S. 192, 1922)

—— *The Temple of Glas*, ed. J. Schick (EETS E.S. 60, 1891)

John LYLY. *The Complete Works of John Lyly*, ed. R. Warwick Bond (3 vols., Oxford 1902/1967)

Sir Thomas MALORY. *The Works of Sir Thomas Malory*, ed. Eugène Vinaver (3 vols., 2nd ed., Oxford 1967)

Robert MANNYNG of Brunne. *Handlyng Synne*, ed. F. J. Furnivall (Part I, EETS O.S. 119, 1901)

The MARPRELATE Tracts 1588, 1589, ed. William Pierce (1911)

MARTINS Months Minde (1589)

Andrew MARVELL. *The Poems of Andrew Marvell*, ed. Hugh Macdonald (Muses' Library, 2nd ed., 1956)

The MAYDES Metamorphosis, in LYLY Vol. III pp. 333–87

James MELVILLE. *The Black Bastel* (? Edinburgh 1634)

MIDDLE English Metrical Romances see FRENCH and Hale

John MILTON. *The Poetical Works of John Milton*, ed. Helen Darbishire (2 vols., Oxford 1955)

Sir Richard MORISON see ANGLO

Thomas MORLEY. *A Plaine and Easie Introduction to Practicall Musicke*, ed. E. H. Fellowes (Shakespeare Assoc. facsimile, 1937)

Thomas NASHE. *The Works of Thomas Nashe*, ed. R. B. McKerrow (reprint ed. F. P. Wilson, Oxford 1958)

John NICHOLS. *The Progresses and Public Processions of Queen Elizabeth* (3 vols., 1823/New York n.d.)

Sir Harris NICOLAS. *Memoirs of the Life and Times of Sir Christopher Hatton, K.G.* (1847)

Sir Thomas OVERBURY. *The 'Conceited Newes' of Sir Thomas Overbury and his Friends*, ed. James E. Savage (facsimile of *Sir Thomas Ouerbury his Wife* (1616), Gainesville 1968)

The OXFORD Dictionary of Nursery Rhymes, ed. Iona and Peter Opie (Oxford 1951)

George PEELE. *The Life and Works of George Peele*, ed. Charles Prouty (3 vols.; Vol. I ed. David H. Horne; 1952)

The PLAYE of Robyn Hoode, in *Malone Society Collections* II (1909) pp. 127–32

The PLOWMAN'S Tale, in SKEAT pp. 147–90

The POETICAL Rhapsody see DAVISON

The PRAIER and Complaynte of the Ploweman vnto Christe in *Harleian Miscellany* Vol. VI (1745) pp. 84–106

PUTTENHAM. *The Arte of English Poesie,* ed. Gladys D. Willcock and Alice Walker (Cambridge 1936)

Francis QUARLES. *The Complete Works of Francis Quarles,* ed. A. B. Grosart (3 vols., Edinburgh 1880–1)

QUEEN Mary's Psalter see French (1)

Sir Walter RALEIGH. *The Poems of Sir Walter Ralegh,* ed. Agnes M. C. Latham (Muses' Library, 1951)

Thomas RANDOLPH. *The Poems of Thomas Randolph,* ed. G. Thorn-Drury (1929)

REDE me and be nott wrothe, ed. Edward Arber (English Reprints, 1871)

RELIQUIAE Antiquae, ed. Thomas Wright and J. O. Halliwell (2 vols., 1841–3)

W. A. RINGLER see SIDNEY

R. H. ROBBINS see *HISTORICAL Poems, SECULAR Lyrics*

Jean ROBERTSON and D. J. Gordon (eds.), *A Calendar of Dramatic Records in the Books of the Livery Companies of London* (Malone Society Collections Vol. III, Oxford 1954)

ROBIN Hood see *PLAYE, TALE*

William ROY see *REDE me*

Francis SABIE. *Pans Pipe, Three Pastoral Eclogues,* ed. J. W. Bright and W. P. Mustard in *Mod. Phil.* VII (1910) p. 433 ff.

A SAD Warning to all Prophane, Malignant Spirits… (1642)

SECULAR Lyrics of the XIVth and XVth Centuries, ed. Rossell Hope Robbins (2nd ed., Oxford 1955)

William SHAKESPEARE. *The Works of Shakespeare,* ed. Sir Arthur Quiller-Couch and J. Dover Wilson (39 vols., Cambridge 1921–66)

Sir Philip SIDNEY. *The Old Arcadia,* ed. Jean Robertson (Oxford 1973)

—— *The Poems of Sir Philip Sidney,* ed. W. A. Ringler (Oxford 1962)

—— *The Prose Works of Sir Philip Sidney,* ed. Albert Feuillerat (Cambridge 1912/1965)

—— see KIMBROUGH

W. W. SKEAT (ed.). *Chaucerian and Other Pieces (The Complete Works of Geoffrey Chaucer* Vol. VII, Oxford 1897)

John SKELTON. *The Poetical Works of John Skelton,* ed. Alexander Dyce (2 vols., 1843)

G. Gregory SMITH (ed.). *Elizabethan Critical Essays* (2 vols., Oxford 1904/1967)

Edmund SPENSER. *The Poetical Works of Edmund Spenser,* ed. J. C. Smith and E. de Selincourt (Oxford 1912/1965)

—— *The Shepheardes Calender,* ed. C. H. Herford (1895)

—— *The Works of Edmund Spenser,* ed. E. Greenlaw, C. G. Osgood, F. M. Padelford and R. Heffner (Variorum edition, 10 vols., Baltimore 1932–58)

STATIONERS' Registers. *Records of the Court of the Stationers' Company 1576–1602,* ed. W. W. Greg and E. Boswell (1930)

John STEVENS. *Music and Poetry in the Early Tudor Court* (1961)

Philip STUBBES. *Anatomie of Abuses,* ed. F. J. Furnivall (1877–9)

Earl of SURREY. *Surrey: Poems,* ed. Emrys Jones (Oxford 1964)

A TALE of Robin Hood, in *BALLADS from Manuscripts* Vol. I.1 p. 295 ff.

THEOCRITUS. *Sixe Idillia* (Oxford 1588; 1922)

TOTTEL'S Miscellany, ed. H. E. Rollins (2 vols., revised ed., Cambridge, Mass., 1966)

TOWNELEY Plays see *WAKEFIELD*

The TRIUMPHS of Oriana, in FELLOWES pp. 158–66

George TURBERVILLE. *The Eclogues of Mantuan,* ed. Douglas Bush (facsimile, New York 1937)

TWO Coventry Plays   see *COVENTRY*
Thomas USK.   *The Testament of Love*, in SKEAT p. 1 ff.
The WAKEFIELD Pageants in the Towneley Cycle, ed. A. C. Cawley (Manchester 1958)
William WARNER.   *Albions England*...revised and newly inlarged (1612)
Thomas WARTON.   *Five Pastoral Eclogues*, in *The Works of the English Poets* ed.
   Alexander Chalmers Vol. XVIII (1810) pp. 136–41
Thomas WATSON.   see Latin (1)
William WEBBE.   *A Discourse of English Poetrie*, in SMITH Vol. I pp. 226–302
George WITHER.   *The Poetry of George Wither*, ed. Frank Sidgwick (2 vols., 1902)
The YORK Plays, ed. Lucy Toulmin Smith (Oxford 1885)
Bartholomew YOUNG.   *Yong's Translation of George of Montemayor's Diana*, ed. J. M.
   Kennedy (Oxford 1968)

2: *Secondary material*

M. D. ANDERSON.   *Drama and Imagery in English Mediaeval Churches* (Cambridge
   1963)
Sydney ANGLO.   'The Evolution of the Early Tudor Disguising, Pageant and
   Masque', *Renaissance Drama* N.S. I (1968) pp. 3–44
——— see English (1)
C. L. BARBER.   *Shakespeare's Festive Comedy* (New York 1967)
C. R. BASKERVILL.   *The Elizabethan Jig* (Chicago 1929)
Eric St. John BROOKS.   *Sir Christopher Hatton: Queen Elizabeth's Favourite* (1946)
John BUTTREY.   'Music for Elizabeth I', *Records and Recording* (April 1970) pp.
   15–17
John BUXTON.   *Elizabethan Taste* (corrected ed., New York 1965)
Millicent CAREY.   *The Wakefield Group in the Towneley Cycle* (Hesperia 11, Göttingen
   1930)
Nan Cooke CARPENTER.   'Music in the *Secunda Pastorum*', *Speculum* XXVI (1951)
   pp. 696–700
A. C. CAWLEY.   'The "Grotesque" Feast in the *Prima Pastorum*', *Speculum* XXX
   (1955) pp. 213–7
E. K. CHAMBERS.   *The Elizabethan Stage* (4 vols., Oxford 1923)
——— *The Mediaeval Stage* (2 vols., Oxford 1903)
——— *Sir Henry Lee: An Elizabethan Portrait* (Oxford 1936)
R. CHAMBERS.   *A Book of Days* (2 vols., 1863)
Hardin CRAIG.   *English Religious Drama of the Middle Ages* (Oxford 1955)
Patrick CULLEN.   *Spenser, Marvell and Renaissance Pastoral* (Cambridge, Mass.,
   1970)
Edward EDWARDS.   *Life of Sir Walter Raleigh* (2 vols., 1868)
William EMPSON   see General
W. W. GREG.   'English Versions of Watson's Latin Poems', *Modern Language
   Quarterly* VI (1903) pp. 125–9
——— *Pastoral Poetry and Pastoral Drama* (1906)
Joan GRUNDY.   *The Spenserian Poets* (1969)
Merritt Y. HUGHES.   'Spenser and the Greek Pastoral Triad', *Studies in Philology*
   XX (1923) pp. 184–215
Anthea HUME.   'Spenser, Puritanism and the "Maye" Eclogue', *RES* N.S. XX
   (1969) pp. 155–67
Arnold JUDD   see Latin (2)
Leo KIRSCHBAUM.   'The Authorship of "1 Henry VI"', *PMLA* LXVII (1952)
   pp. 809–22
V. A. KOLVE.   *The Play called Corpus Christi* (Stanford 1966)
Paul E. McLANE.   *Spenser's Shepheardes Calender: A Study in Elizabethan Allegory*
   (Notre Dame 1961)

Jill MANN. *Chaucer and Medieval Estates Satire* (Cambridge 1973)
John NICHOLS   see English (1)
S. K. ORGEL. 'Sidney's Experiment in Pastoral: "The Lady of May"', *JWCI*
   XXVI (1963) pp. 198–203
Mary PARMENTER. 'Spenser's "Twelve Aeglogues Proportionable to the Twelve
   Monethes"', *ELH* III (1936) pp. 190–217
Bruce PATTISON. 'The Roundelay in the August Eclogue of the *Shepheardes
   Calender*', *RES* IX (1933) pp. 54–5
Marien-Sofie RØSTVIG. 'The *Shepheardes Calender* – A Structural Analysis',
   Renaissance and Modern Studies XIII (1969) pp. 49–75
STATIONERS' Registers. *Records of the Court of the Stationers' Company 1576–1602*,
   ed. W. W. Greg and E. Boswell (1930)
Harold STEIN. *Studies in Spenser's Complaints* (U.S.A. 1934)
John STEVENS   see English (1)
Roy STRONG. 'Queen Elizabeth I as Oriana', *Studies in the Renaissance* VI (1959)
   pp. 251–60
Joseph STRUTT. *Sports and Pastimes of the People of England*, ed. J. Charles Cox
   (1903)
Archer TAYLOR. 'He that will not when he may; when he will he shall have
   nay', in *Studies in Old English Literature in Honour of Arthur G. Brodeur*, ed. Stanley
   B. Greenfield (Oregon 1963) pp. 155–61
Humphrey TONKIN. *Spenser's Courteous Pastoral* (Oxford 1972)
Andrew N. WAWN. 'The Genesis of *The Plowman's Tale*', *Yearbook of English
   Studies* II (1972) pp. 21–40
Glynne WICKHAM. *Early English Stages* (2nd ed., 2 vols., 1963)
Neville WILLIAMS. *Elizabeth: Queen of England* (1967)
Frances A. YATES. *Astraea* (1975)
——— 'Queen Elizabeth as Astraea', *JWCI* X (1947) pp. 27–82.

III. *French and Provençal*

1: *Texts*

ADAM de la Halle. *Le Jeu de Robin et Marion* ed. Kenneth Varty (1960)
L'ALLIANCE de Foy et Loyalté, in CHANTILLY pp. 251–9
ALTFRANZÖSISCHE Romanzen und Pastourellen   see BARTSCH
Barthélemy ANEAU. *Chant Natal* (Lyons 1539)
AUCASSIN et Nicolette, ed. Mario Roques (2nd ed., CFMA, Paris 1968)
Jean AUDIAU (ed.). *La Pastourelle dans la Poésie Occitaine du Moyen Age* (Paris 1923)
BANQUET du Bois, in MONTAIGLON pp. 206–22
Karl BARTSCH (ed.). *Romances et Pastourelles Françaises des XIIe et XIIIe Siècles
   (Altfranzösische Romanzen...)* (Leipzig 1870/Darmstadt 1967)
BERGERIE de l'Agneau de France à Cinq Personnages, ed. H. Lewicka (TLF, Geneva
   1961)
BERGERIE Nouvelle fort joyeuse et morale de Mieulx que Devant, in FOURNIER pp.
   54–60
BUCARIUS   see *PASTORALET*
CERCAMON. *Les Poésies de Cercamon*, ed. Alfred Jeanroy (CFMA, Paris 1922)
CHANSONS du XVe Siècle, ed. Gaston Paris (SATF, Paris 1875)
CHANTILLY. *Nativités et Moralités Liégeoises du Moyen Age d'après le MS 617 de
   Chantilly*, ed. Gustave Cohen (2nd ed. in *Mémoires de l'Académie Royale de Belgique*
   2nd series XII, Brussels 1953)
Alain CHARTIER. *Le Curial*, ed. Ferdinand Heuckenkamp (Halle 1899)
CHRISTINE de Pisan. *Œuvres Poétiques de Christine de Pisan*, ed. Maurice Roy
   (SATF, 2 vols., Paris 1886–91)
COMPOST et Kalendrier des Bergers   see *KALENDER of Shepherdes* (English (1))

Eloy D'AMERVAL. *Le Liure de la Deablerie*, ed. Charles Frederick Ward (University of Iowa Humanistic Studies II.2, Iowa 1923)

Eustache DESCHAMPS. *Œuvres Complètes*, ed. Marquis de Queux de Saint-Hilaire (SATF, 11 vols., Paris 1878–1903)

Remy DUPUYS. *La tryumphante et solennelle entree...de Monsieur Charles...en sa ville de Bruges* (Bruges 1515)

ENTRÉE de Charles VIII a Rouen en 1485, facsimile ed. Charles de Robillard de Beaurepaire (Soc. des Bibliophiles Normands, Rouen 1902)

L'ESPOSALIZI de Nostra Dona, ed. S. Kravtchenko-Dobelmann in *Romania* LXVIII (1944–5) pp. 273–315

L'ESTOIRE de Griseldis, ed. Barbara M. Craig (University of Kansas Humanistic Studies 31, Lawrence, Kansas, 1954)

Edouard FOURNIER (ed.). *Le Théâtre Français avant la Renaissance* (2nd ed., Paris 1873)

Jean FROISSART. *Œuvres de Froissart: Poésies*, ed. Auguste Scheler (3 vols., Brussels 1870)

Theodore GODEFROY. *Le Cérémonial François*, ed. Denys Godefroy (2 vols., Paris 1649)

John GOWER. *The Complete Works of John Gower* Vol. I: *The French Works*, ed. G. C. Macaulay (Oxford 1899)

Arnoul GREBAN. *Le Mystère de la Passion*, ed. Omer Jodogne (*Mémoires de l'Académie Royale de Belgique* 2nd series XII, Brussels 1965)

Pierre GRINGORE. *Pierre Gringore's Pageants for the Entry of Mary Tudor into Paris*, ed. C. R. Baskervill (Chicago 1934)

The HOLKHAM Bible Picture-Book see English (1)

L'INCARNACION et Natiuite de nostre saulueur see *MYSTÈRE de l'Incarnacion*

Jean de MEUNG see *ROMAN de la Rose*

JEHAN de Brie. *Le Bon Berger*, ed. Paul Lacroix (Paris 1879)

JOUSTES de Saint-Inglevert, in *Œuvres de Froissart: Chroniques* ed. Kervyn de Lettenhove Vol. XIV (Brussels 1872) p. 407ff.

Olivier de LA MARCHE. *Mémoires de Olivier de La Marche*, ed. Henri Beaune and J. d'Arbaumont (Soc. de l'Histoire de France, Vol. III, Paris 1885)

Jean LEMAIRE de Belges. *Œuvres de Jean Lemaire de Belges*, ed. J. Stecher (4 vols., Louvain 1882–91)

Guillaume de MACHAUT. *Œuvres de Guillaume de Machaut*, ed. Ernest Hoepffner (3 vols., SATF, Paris 1908–21)

MARCABRU. *Poésies Complètes du Troubadour Marcabru*, ed. J.-M.-L. Dejeanne (Bibliothèque Méridionale 1st series XII, Toulouse 1909)

Eustache MARCADÉ. *Mystère de la Passion*, ed. Jules-Marie Richard (Arras 1891)

MARGUERITE de Navarre. *Comédie de la Nativité de Jesus Christ*, ed. Pierre Jourda (Paris 1939)

—— *Les Marguerites de la Marguerite des Princesses*, ed. Félix Frank (4 vols., Paris 1873)

—— *Théâtre Profane*, ed. Verdun L. Saulnier (TLF, Paris 1946)

Clement MAROT. *Œuvres Diverses*, ed. C. A. Mayer (1966)

—— *Œuvres Lyriques*, ed. C. A. Mayer (1964)

MARTIAL de Paris. *Les Poésies de Martial de Paris, dit d'Auvergne* (2 vols., Paris 1724)

MATHIEU d'Escouchy. *Chronique de Mathieu d'Escouchy*, ed. G. du Fresne de Beaucourt (3 vols., Paris 1863–4)

Jean MESCHINOT. *Les Lunettes des Princes*, ed. Christine Martineau-Genieys (Publications Romanes et Françaises CXXI, Geneva 1972)

MESTIER et Marchandise, in FOURNIER pp. 45–53

Jean de MEUNG see *ROMAN de la Rose*

MIEULX-que-Devant, in FOURNIER pp. 54–60

Jean MOLINET. *Chroniques de Jean Molinet*, ed. J.-A. Bouchon (Paris 1827–8)

—— *Les Faictz et Dictz de Jean Molinet*, ed. Noël Dupire (SATF, 3 vols., Paris 1936–9)

A. MONTAIGLON and J. Rothschild (eds.)   *Recueil de Poésies Françoises des XVe et XVIe Siècles* Vol. X (Paris 1875)

MORALITÉ de l'Alliance de Foy et Loyalté, in CHANTILLY pp. 251–9

MYSTÈRE de l'Incarnacion et Nativité de notre Sauveur et Rédempteur Jésus-Christ représenté à Rouen en 1474, ed. Pierre Le Verdier (Soc. des Bibliophiles Normands, 2 vols., Rouen 1884–6)

MYSTÈRE de la Passion, ed. Jules-Marie Richard (Arras 1891)

MYSTÈRE du Siège d'Orléans, ed. François Guessard and E. de Certain (Collection des documents inédits sur l'Histoire de France, Paris 1862)

MYSTÈRES et Moralités   see CHANTILLY

La NATIVITÉ et le Geu des Trois Roys, ed. Ruth Whittredge (Bryn Mawr 1944)

Les NOËLS   see SMIDT

La PASSION de Semur, in ROY Vol. I

Le PASTORALET, in *Chroniques relatives à l'Histoire de la Belgique*, ed. Kervyn de Lettenhove (Brussels 1873)

La PATIENCE de Job, ed. Albert Meiller (Bibliothèque Française et Romane 11, Paris 1971)

The PENGUIN Book of French Verse Vol. I, ed. Brian Woledge (Harmondsworth 1961)

PHILIPPE de Mézières   see *ESTOIRE*

PHILIPPE de Thaün.   *Li Cumpoz Philipe de Thaün*, ed. Eduard Mall (Strasbourg 1873)

PHILIPPE de Vitry.   *Les Dictz de Franc Gontier*, in MONTAIGLON pp. 198–200, PENGUIN pp. 216–8

Robert PINEL   see *ENTRÉE*

QUEEN Mary's Psalter, facsimile ed. George Warner (1912)

François RABELAIS.   *Gargantua*, ed. Pierre Michel (Paris 1965)

RECUEIL de Motets Français des XIIe et XIIIe Siècles, ed. Gaston Raynaud (2 vols., Paris 1881–3)

RECUEIL de Poésies Françoises   see MONTAIGLON

RENÉ of Anjou.   *Œuvres Complètes du Roi René*, ed. Comte de Quatrebarbes (4 vols., Angers 1845)

Le ROMAN de la Rose, ed. Ernest Langlois (SATF, Paris 1924)

ROMANCES et Pastourelles Françaises   see BARTSCH

Pierre de RONSARD.   *Œuvres Complètes*, ed. Gustave Cohen (2 vols., France 1958)

ROUEN Nativité   see *MYSTÈRE de l'Incarnacion*

Emile ROY (ed.).   *Le Mystère de la Passion en France du XIVe au XVIe Siècles* (2 vols., Dijon 1903–4)

STE. GENEVIÈVE   see *NATIVITÉ*

Thomas SEBILLET.   *Art Poétique Françoys*, ed. Félix Gaiffe (Soc. des Textes Français Modernes, Paris 1910)

Passion de SEMUR, in ROY Vol. I

Le SERMON du Bon Pasteur et du Mauvais, ed. C. A. Mayer, 'Le Sermon du Bon Pasteur: Un Problème d'Attribution', *Bibliothèque d'Humanisme et de Renaissance* XXVII (1965) pp. 290–303

SIÈGE d'Orléans   see *MYSTÈRE du Siège*

J. R. H. de SMIDT.   *Les Noëls et la Tradition Populaire* (Amsterdam 1932)

2 : *Secondary material*

Howard Mayer BROWN.   *Music in the French Secular Theatre 1400–1550* (Cambridge, Mass., 1963)

Jacques CHAILLEY.   'La Nature Musicale du *Jeu de Robin et Marion*', in COHEN p. 111 ff.

V. CHICHMAREV.   'Œuvres attribuées au Roi Rene', *Romania* LV (1929) pp. 214–50.

Gustave COHEN. *Mélanges offerts à Gustave Cohen* (Paris 1950)
—— see CHANTILLY, French (1)
Maurice DELBOUILLE. 'De l'Intérêt des Nativités Hutoises de Chantilly et de Lièges', in COHEN pp. 75–84.
Edmond FARAL. 'La Pastourelle', *Romania* XLIX (1923) pp. 204–59
—— see *ARTS*, Latin (1)
John V. FLEMING. *The Roman de la Rose: A Study in Allegory and Iconography* (Princeton 1969)
Grace FRANK. *The Mediaeval French Drama* (Oxford 1954)
Theodore GODEFROY see French (1)
E. HOEPFFNER. 'La Chronologie des "Pastourelles" de Froissart', in *Mélanges offerts à m. Emile Picot* (Paris 1913) Vol. II pp. 27–42
Alice HULUBEI. *L'Églogue en France au XVIe Siècle* (Paris 1938)
W. Powell JONES. *The Pastourelle* (Cambridge, Mass., 1931)
—— 'Some recent Studies on the Pastourelle', *Speculum* V (1930) pp. 207–15
Marie-Thérèse KAISER-GUYOT. *Le Berger en France aux XIVe et XVe Siècles* (Publications de l'Université de Paris X, A 26, Paris 1974)
George R. KERNODLE. *From Art to Theatre* (Chicago 1944)
H. LEWICKA see *BERGERIE de l'Agneau*, French (1)
L. T. TOPSFIELD. '*Jois, Amors* and *Fin' Amors* in the Poetry of Jaufre Rudel', *Neuphilologische Mitteilungen* LXXI (1970) pp. 277–305
Marie UNGUREANU. *Société et Litterature Bourgeoises d'Arras aux XIIe et XIIIe Siècles* (Mémoires de la Commission des Monuments Historiques du Pas-de-Calais Vol. VIII.1, Arras 1955)
M. ZINK. *La Pastourelle: Poésie et Folklore au Moyen Age* (Paris 1972)

IV. *German*

1 : *Texts*

Meister ALEXANDER in *DEUTSCHE Liederdichter* Vol. I section 1
DEUTSCHE Liederdichter des 13. Jahrhunderts ed. Carl von Kraus (2 vols., Tübingen 1952–8)
Das HESSISCHE Weihnachtspiel, in *Das Drama des Mittelalters* ed. R. Froning, Vol. III (Stuttgart 1892)

V. *Greek*

1 : *Texts*

The GREEK Bucolic Poets with translation by J. M. Edmonds (Loeb, 1912/1960)
LONGUS. *Daphnis and Chloe* with translation by George Thornley (Loeb, 1916/1962)
—— see Angel DAY (English (1))
THEOCRITUS in *GREEK Bucolic Poets*
—— see also English (1)

VI. *Italian*

1 : *Texts*

Giovanni BOCCACCIO. *Comedia delle Ninfe Fiorentine (Ameto)*, ed. Antonio Enzo Quaglio (Florence 1963)
—— *Comento alla Divina Commedia*, ed. Domenico Guerri (SI 96, Bari 1918)
—— see also Latin (1)
CANTILENE e Ballate, Strambotti e Madrigali nei Secoli XIII e XIV, ed. Giosuè Carducci (Pisa 1871)

Guido CAVALCANTI. *Le Rime*, ed. G. Favati (Documenti di Filologia I, Milan
    1957)
Giusto de' CONTI. *La Bella Mano* in *Parnaso Italiano* Vol. VI: *Lirici Antichi*, ed.
    Andrea Rubi (Venice 1784)
Il CONSTRASTO di Tonin e Bighignol, ed. Bruno Cotronei, *Giornale Storica della Lette-
    ratura Italiana* XXXVI (1900) pp. 281–324
DANTE. *Vita Nuova*, ed. Edoardo Sanguineti (Milan 1965)
—— see also Latin (1), BOCCACCIO
FUMOSO. *Batecchio* (Scelta di Curiosità Letterarie CXXII, 1871/Bologna 1968)
Giambattista GUARINI. *Il Pastor Fido*, ed. G. Brognoligo (SI 61, Bari 1914)
Cesare NAPPI. 'Un Egloga Rusticale del 1508', ed. Ludovico Frati, *Giorn. Stor.
    del. Lett. Ital.* XX (1892) pp. 186–204
PETRARCH. see Latin (1)
SACRE Rappresentazioni dei Secoli XIV, XV e XVI, ed. Alessandro d'Ancona (3 vols.,
    Florence 1872)
Iacopo SANNAZARO. *Opere Volgari*, ed. Alfredo Mauro (SI 220, Bari 1961)
—— *Arcadia*, ed. M. Scherillo (Biblioteca di Autori Italiani 1, Turin 1888)
—— *Arcadia and Piscatorial Eclogues*, ed. and trans. Ralph Nash (Detroit 1966)
Torquato TASSO. *Aminta*, ed. C. E. J. Griffiths (Manchester 1972)
—— *Gerusalemme Liberata*, ed. L. Bonfigli (SI 130, Bari 1930)

VII. *Latin*

1. *Texts*

AENEAS Silvius Piccolomini. *De Curialium Miseriis*, ed. W. P. Mustard (Baltimore
    1928)
ALCUIN see *CONFLICTUS*
—— *Versus de Cuculo*, in *PLAC* Vol. I p. 270
ANDREAS Capellanus. *De Amore Libri Tres*, ed. E. Trojel (Copenhagen 1892; trans.
    J. J. Parry, *The Art of Courtly Love*, New York 1941)
ANGILBERT. *Ecloga ad Carolum Regem*, in *PLAC* Vol. I pp. 360–3.
ARTS Poétiques du XIIe et du XIIIe Siècle, ed. Edmond Faral (Bibliothèque de l'Ecole
    des Hautes Etudes 238, Paris 1924)
BENVENUTO da Imola. Commentary in PETRARCH, *Bucolicum Carmen*, ed.
    Avena
BERNARD of Utrecht see HUYGENS
Giovanni BOCCACCIO. *Buccolicum Carmen*, in *Opere Latine* p. 1 ff.
—— *Genealogie Deorum Gentilium Libri*, ed. Vincenzo Romano (SI 200–1, Bari 1951)
—— *Opere Latine Minori*, ed. A. F. Massèra (SI 111, Bari 1928)
—— see also Italian (1)
Jacob BRUMMER (ed.). *Vitae Vergilianae* (Teubner, Leipzig 1912)
CALPURNIUS in DUFF p. 218 ff.
Andreas CAPELLANUS see ANDREAS
CARMINA Illustrium Poetarum Italorum (11 vols., Florence 1719–26)
CONFLICTUS Veris et Hiemis in *PLAC* Vol. I pp. 269–70
CONRAD of Hirsau see HUYGENS
DANTE. *Dante and Giovanni del Virgilio* by Philip H. Wicksteed and Edmund G.
    Gardner (Westminster 1902)
—— see also Italian (1)
DONATUS. *Vita Donati*, in *Vitae Vergilianae Antiquae*, ed. Colin Hardie (Oxford
    1966) pp. 5–18
J. Wight and Arnold M. DUFF (eds.). *Minor Latin Poets* (Loeb, 1934)
EN Habes, Lector, Bucolicorum autores XXXVIII…Farrago quidem eclogarum CLVI (Basle
    1546)

Severus Sanctus ENDELECHIUS. *Carmen de Mortibus Boum* in *Anthologia Latina* ed. Alexander Riese, Vol. II (Teubner, Leipzig 1896) no. 893, pp. 334–9

Edmond FARAL   see *ARTS*; also French (2)

Giles FLETCHER.   Eclogues in *POEMATA* pp. 185–207

John of GARLAND   see JOHN of Garland

Antonio GERALDINI.   *Eclogues*, ed. W. P. Mustard (Baltimore 1924)

John GOWER.   *Vox Clamantis*, ed. H. O. Coxe (1850)

—— see also English (1), French (1)

GREGORY.   *Sermon on the Good Shepherd*, in *PL* Vol. LXXVI cols. 1127–30

GROSSETESTE   see HUBERTUS

T. P. HARRISON   see General

HORACE.   *Satires, Epistles and Ars Poetica* ed. H. Rushton Fairclough (Loeb, 1926)

HUBERTUS.   'Verses on the Life of Robert Grosseteste', ed. R. W. Hunt, *Medievalia et Humanistica* N.S. I: In Honour of S. Harrison Thomson (1970) pp. 241–51

R. B. C. HUYGENS (ed.).   *Accessus ad Auctores, Bernard d'Utrecht, Conrad d'Hirsau* (Leiden 1970)

ISIDORE of Seville.   *Etymologiae*, in *PL* Vol. LXXXII cols. 74–728

JOHN of Garland.   *The Parisiana Poetria of John of Garland*, ed. Traugott Lawler (1974)

—— *The Stella Maris of John of Garland*, ed. Evelyn Faye Wilson (Cambridge, Mass., 1946)

MANTUAN.   *The Eclogues of Baptista Mantuanus*, ed. W. P. Mustard (Baltimore 1911)

—— see also TURBERVILLE (English (1))

MARTIUS Valerius   see VALERIUS

METELLUS of Tegernsee.   *Die Quirinalien des Metellus von Tegernsee*, ed. Peter Christian Jacobsen (Mittellateinische Studien und Texte I, Leiden and Cologne 1965)

MINOR Latin Poets   see DUFF

MODOIN.   *Ecloga*, in *PLAC* Vol. I pp. 384–91

NEMESIANUS   in DUFF pp. 456 ff.

The OXFORD Book of Medieval Latin Verse, ed. F. J. E. Raby (Oxford 1959)

PASCHASIUS Radbertus.   *Ecloga Duarum Sanctimonialium*, in *PLAC* Vol. III pp. 45–51

The PASTOR of Hermas   in *The Apostolic Fathers*, ed. A. Roberts and J. Donaldson (Ante-Nicene Christian Library I, Edinburgh 1867) pp. 319–435

Francesco PATRIZI.   *De Christi Natali*, in *CARMINA* Vol. VII pp. 145–9

PATROLOGIA Latina, ed. J. P. Migne (221 vols., Paris 1844–64)

PETRARCH.   *Petrarch's Bucolicum Carmen*, ed. and trans. Thomas G. Bergin (1974)

—— *Il Bucolicum Carmen*, ed. Antonio Avena (Padova in Onore di Francesco Petrarca Vol. I, Padua 1906 for 1904)

—— *Bucolica Carmina*, ed. Iodocus Badius Ascensius (Paris 1502)

—— *De Vita Solitaria*, ed. Antonio Altamura (Studi e Testi Umanistici II.1, Naples 1943)

—— *Epistolae de Rebus Familiaribus et Variae*, ed. Ioseph Fracassetti (3 vols., Florence 1859–63)

PICCOLOMINI   see AENEAS Silvius

POEMATA Varii Argumenti, ed. William Dillingham (1678)

POETAE Latini Aevi Carolini, ed. E. Dümmler and others (Monumenta Germaniae Historica, 4 vols., Berlin 1881–1923)

Marcus Valerius PROBUS.   *M. Valerii Probi in Vergilii Bucolica et Georgica Commentarius*, ed. H. Keil (Halle 1848)

PRUDENTIUS.   *Prudentius*, ed. H. J. Thomson (2 vols., Loeb, 1949–53)

Paschasius RADBERTUS   see PASCHASIUS

RADBOD.   *Egloga de Virtutibus Beati Lebuini*, in *PLAC* Vol. IV.1 pp. 169–72

Peter RAMUS.   *P. Virgilii Maronis Bucolica, P. Rami...exposita* (2nd ed., Paris 1558)

Iacopo SANNAZARO.   *Piscatorial Eclogues*   see Italian (1)

J.-C. SCALIGER. *Poetices Libri Septem*, facsimile ed. August Buck (Lyons 1561/ Stuttgart 1964)

SEDULIUS Scotus. *Carmina* in *PLAC* Vol. III pp. 151–237

SERVIUS. *In Vergilii Bucolica et Georgica Commentarii*, ed. George Thilo (Leipzig 1887)

Tito STROZZI. *Borsias, Bucolicon Liber*, ed. Iosephus Fógel and Ladislaus Juhász (Leipzig 1933)

THEODULUS. *Theoduli Eclogam*, ed. Joannes Osternacher (Urfahr-Linz 1902)

Martius VALERIUS. *M. Valerio: Bucoliche*, ed. Franco Munari (2nd ed., Florence 1970)

VIRGIL. *Eclogues, Georgics, Aeneid I-VI*, ed. H. Rushton Fairclough (Loeb, revised ed. 1935)

—— *Eclogues*, ed. Robert Coleman (Cambridge 1977).

—— commentaries: see PROBUS, RAMUS, SERVIUS

—— translations: see FLEMING and DOUGLAS (English (1))

—— lives: see BRUMMER, DONATUS

WARNERIUS Basiliensis. *Synodicus*, ed. Johann Huemer, *Rom. Forsch.* III (1887) pp. 315–30

Thomas WATSON. *Thomas Watson's Latin 'Amyntas' (1585)*, ed. Walter F. Staton, Jr., and *Abraham Fraunce's 'The Lamentations of Amyntas' (1587)*, ed. Franklin M. Dickey (Renaissance English Text Society, Chicago 1967)

—— *Amintae Gaudia* (1592)

—— see also GREG, 'English Versions' (English (2))

WICKSTEED   see DANTE

Karl YOUNG. *The Drama of the Medieval Church* (2 vols., Oxford 1933)

2: *Secondary material*

Leicester BRADNER. *Musae Anglicanae* (Modern Languages Association of America General Series X, 1940)

Henry CAPLAN. *Of Eloquence* (1970)

Luigi CASTAGNA. *I Bucolici Latini Minori* (Letterature d'Oltralpe e d'Oltreoceano 5, Florence 1976)

Domenico COMPARETTI. *Vergil in the Middle Ages*, trans. E. F. M. Benecke (2nd ed., 1908/1966)

Helen COOPER   see General

E. R. CURTIUS. *European Literature and the Latin Middle Ages*, trans. Willard R. Trask (1953)

W. Leonard GRANT. *Neo-Latin Literature and the Pastoral* (Chapel Hill 1965)

George L. HAMILTON. 'Theodulus: A Mediaeval Textbook', *Mod. Phil.* VII (1909) p. 169 ff.

J. H. HANFORD. 'Classical Eclogue and Mediaeval Debate', *Romanic Review* II (1911) pp. 16–31, 129–43

Betty Nye HEDBERG. 'The "Bucolics" and the Mediaeval Poetic Debate', *Trans. of the American Philological Assoc.* LXXV (1944) pp. 47–67

Arnold JUDD. *The Life of Thomas Bekynton* (Chichester 1961)

Arthur O. LOVEJOY   see General

Max MANITIUS. *Geschichte der Lateinischen Literatur des Mittelalters* (Handbuch der Klassischen Altertumswissenschaft, 3 vols., Munich 1911–31)

Pierre de NOLHAC. 'Virgile chez Pétrarque', *Studi Medievali* N.S. V (1932) pp. 217–25

F. J. E. RABY. *A History of Secular Latin Poetry in the Middle Ages* (2nd ed., Oxford 1957)

Wolfgang SCHMID. 'Tityrus Christianus', *Rheinisches Museum für Philologie* XCVI (1953) pp. 101–65

Karl STRECKER. 'Ist Gottschalk der Dichter der *Ecloga Theoduli?*', *Neues Archiv* XLV (1924) pp. 18–23

H. WALTHER. *Das Streitgedicht in der Lateinischen Literatur des Mittelalters* (Quellen und Untersuchungen zur lateinischen Philologie des Mittelalters V:2, Munich 1920)

P. H. WICKSTEED   see DANTE (Latin (1))

Gordon WILLIAMS. *Tradition and Originality in Roman Poetry* (Oxford 1968)

E. Faye WILSON. 'Pastoral and Epithalamium in Latin Literature', *Speculum* XXIII (1948) pp. 35–57

VIII. *Spanish*

1: *Texts*

GARCILASO de la Vega. *Garcilaso de la Vega y sus Comentaristas*, ed. Antonio Gallego Morell (Biblioteca Románica Hispánica IV.7, 2nd ed., Madrid 1972)

Jorge de MONTEMAYOR. *Los Siete Libros de la 'Diana'*, ed. E. Moreno Báez (Real Acad. Española Bibl. selecta 2.xviii, Madrid 1955)

——   see also YOUNG (English (1))

INDEX

Abel, 57, 71, 90, 120, 139, 159
Accession Day, 197, 200–1, 204, 206; tilts, 146, 200–1
Adam de la Halle, *Jeu de Robin et Marion*, 32, 48, 55, 56, 57, 59, 91, 181, 183, 202
Aeneas Silvius Piccolomini (Pope Pius II), 73, 107, 118, 119–21
Alamanni, Luigi, 111
Alan of Lille, 43, 169
Alcuin, 9, 13, 14. *See also* Conflictus Veris et Hiemis
Alexander, Meister, 94
allegory, 6, 24–5, 49–50, 105, 124, 132, 183–4, 187; in *bergerie*, 79–90, 98–9; in early mediaeval eclogues, 16, 17, 22–3, 26, 28–9, 34; in Barclay, 122; in Mantuan, 109–10; in Molinet, 134; in Petrarch and his imitators, 36–8, 45–6, 81; in Sannazaro, 104; in Spenser, 154–5, 157, 163; in Virgil, 3, 5, 28–9, 34, 109
Amadis de Gaule, 229 n. 1
Andreas Capellanus, 62
Andrelini, Publio Fausto, 111
Aneau, Barthélemy, 87, 90, 114
Angilbert, 9, 13, 128
Annunciation to the Shepherds, 91–2, 98, 163, 167, 182, 196; eclogues, 4, 107, 191; in art, 53, 55, 57, 220 n. 53; 'Pax in terra', 84, 90, 178
Apollo, 20, 21–2, 55, 71, 110, 120, 123, 127, 130, 182, 202, 205
Arcadia, 7, 70, 104, 106, 146, 173, 191, 207. *See also* Sannazaro; Sidney
Arcadian pastoral, 101, *105–7*; in England, 58, 123, 126
art: as evil, 142–3, 163; and nature, 7, 71, 105, 126, 131, 135–6, 141; quotations, 134, 151
artes poeticae, 26, 30, 80, 128
artistic representations, 51, 52–3, 54–5, 57, 68, 94, 96, 114, 116, 136, 140, 220 n. 53; Byzantine, 16, 25, 95
'As I gan wandre', *see* 'Kepe well the shepe'
'As I me lend', 76–7, 118, 221–2 n. 98
Ascensius, Iodocus Badius, *see* Badius
Astraea, 4, 10, 23, *39, 104, 141, 161; identified with Elizabeth I, 205–6, 207, 209, 210; identified with the Virgin, 31, 205
Aucassin et Nicolette, 56, 59, 65–6
Augustine, St., 4
Augustus (Octavian), 3, 9, 20, 206

Bacon, Francis, 90
baculus, 30, 53. *See also* crook
Badius, Iodocus (Ascensius), 108, 217 n. 66
Banquet du Bois, 67, 68, 71, 73, 76
Barclay, Alexander, 52, 72, 73, 80–1, 108, 109, *118–23*, 124, 125, 129–30, 133, 153, 158, 162, 181, 195
Barnfield, Richard, 178, 184, 231 n. 63
Basse, William, 182, 185
Baxter, Nathaniel, 184–5, 187
beast-fables, 3, 84, 122, 146, 161–2, 168, 188, 195–6
Belmisseri, Paolo, 111
Benediktbeuern Christmas play, 91
Benvenuto da Imola, 36, 38, 41
bergerie: definition, 48
    conventions, 50–9, 93, 135; contrasted with Arcadian pastoral, 105–7
    eternal, 95, 97, 99; idyllic, 49, 56, 62, 63, 66–8, 197, 207
    in English Renaissance, 115–6, 118, 120, 123, 145, 147–8, 158, 163–4, 170, 172, 177, 180–8; in French Renaissance, 111–5; in Germany, 93, 94; in Italy, 100–2, 104
    See also mediaeval pastoral
Bergerie de l'Agneau de France, 84, 85
bergerie moralisée, 48, 49, 51, 75, 76, 80, 85, 102, 170, 171, 198
Bernard of Utrecht, 14, 26
Bethlehem shepherds, 38, 71, 110, 120, 182
Bible, 6, 28, 48, 80, 91, 128, 186; Biblical shepherd distinguished from Classical, 25–6; Apocalypse, 190; Isaiah, 12, 16; Psalm XXIII, 95, 205; Song of Songs, 190
Biblical exegesis, 29, 49, 98
Black Death, 39, 41, 43
Blenerhasset, Thomas, 198, 199, 206
Boccaccio, Giovanni, 5, 13, 14, 17, 19, 20, 29, *36–40*, 41, *42–3*, 45, 46, 59, 103, 108, 119, 131, 153, 160, 196; *Ameto*, 14, 102, 103; on Dante, 35, 72, 79; *Genealogia Deorum*, 37; *Olympia*, 42–3, 169
Bodel, Jean, 75, 82
Bolton, Edmund, 182, 184, 196, 202–3
Bradshaw, Thomas, 187
Brathwaite, Richard, 193
Breton, Nicholas, 73, 140, 178–9, 181, 183
Bromyard, John, 87
Brooke, Christopher, 169, 185
Brown, Howard Mayer, 56